D1527283

White Gloves, Black Nation

GENDER AND AMERICAN CULTURE

Mary Kelley, *editor*

Editorial Advisory Board
Jane Sherron De Hart
John D'Emilio
Linda K. Kerber
Annelise Orleck
Janice Radway
Robert Reid-Pharr
Noliwe Rooks
Barbara Sicherman

Emerita Board Members
Nancy F. Cott
Cathy N. Davidson
Thadious M. Davis
Sara Evans
Wendy Martin
Nell Irvin Painter

The Gender and American Culture series, guided by feminist perspectives, examines the social construction and influence of gender and sexuality within the full range of American cultures. Books in the series explore the intersection of gender (both female and male) with such markers of difference as race, class, and region. The series presents outstanding scholarship from all areas of American studies—including history, literature, religion, folklore, ethnography, and the visual arts—that investigates in a thoroughly contextualized and lively fashion the ways in which gender works with and against these markers. In so doing, the series seeks to reveal how these complex interactions have shaped American life.

A complete list of books published in Gender and American Culture is available at https://uncpress.org/series/gender-and-american-culture.

GRACE SANDERS JOHNSON

White Gloves, Black Nation
Women, Citizenship, and Political Wayfaring in Haiti

The University of North Carolina Press *Chapel Hill*

This book was published with the assistance of the Z. Smith Reynolds Fund of the University of North Carolina Press.

© 2023 The University of North Carolina Press
All rights reserved
Set in Arno Pro by Westchester Publishing Services
Manufactured in the United States of America

Library of Congress Cataloging-in-Publication Data
Names: Sanders Johnson, Grace, author.
Title: White gloves, Black nation : women, citizenship, and
    political wayfaring in Haiti / Grace Sanders Johnson.
Other titles: Gender & American culture.
Description: Chapel Hill : The University of North Carolina Press, [2023] |
    Series: Gender and American culture | Includes bibliographical references and index.
Identifiers: LCCN 2022037859 | ISBN 9781469673677 (cloth : alk. paper) |
    ISBN 9781469673684 (paperback : alk. paper) | ISBN 9781469673691 (ebook)
Subjects: LCSH: Women—Political activity—Haiti—History—20th century. |
    Social classes—Haiti—History—20th century. | Haiti—Politics and
    government—1934–1971. | Haiti—History—1934–1986.
Classification: LCC HQ1236.5.H2 S36 2023 | DDC 305.42097294/0904—dc23/eng/20220818
LC record available at https://lccn.loc.gov/2022037859

Cover illustration: Silhouettes of two women walking through Port-au-Prince. Courtesy of the Suzanne Comhaire-Sylvain Collection, Department of Special Collections, Stanford University Libraries.

For Daphne and for the women who make
regular appearances in my dreams

Contents

Illustrations

White Gloves, Black Nation

Introduction

On August 9, 1946, a *femme du peuple* (woman of the people) walked into the Legislative Palace in Port-au-Prince, Haiti.[1] She entered the building as members of the National Constitutional Assembly deliberated women's voting rights. She pressed through the crowd of politicians and curious onlookers, making her way toward a section reserved for women. There, the elite and middle-class members of Haiti's first women's rights organization, the Ligue Féminine d'Action Sociale (LFAS), were seated, listening to assembly representatives' impassioned debate. Although partitioned away from the rest of the assembly audience, these women saw the moment as a political renaissance.

The 1946 constitutional assembly was the third assembly free of foreign intervention since the end of the US occupation (1915–34). During the occupation, the US government dissolved the national assembly, took over the national banking system, and rewrote Haiti's historic 1805 Constitution that prohibited slavery and declared the nation's people Black and sovereign from French colonial rule.[2] The end of US military rule saw the emergence of new political parties, organizations, and cultural and intellectual institutions, including a literature and journalism boom. As historian Matthew Smith has argued, the twenty-year postoccupation period was Haiti's "greatest moment of political promise."[3] Most notably, Haiti experienced a revolution. Eight months before the 1946 assembly, a group of young students—claiming to continue the fight for sovereignty started in the nineteenth century and influenced by the postoccupation and World War II milieu of Marxist philosophy, socialist politics, and cultural nationalism in the twentieth century—coordinated a series of political protests against the US-supported Haitian president Élie Lescot. The public uprisings, dubbed the "Revolution of 1946," lasted for a week and culminated in the military overthrow of Lescot. At the August 1946 assembly, national representatives gathered to restore the terms of the nation's governance and have a special vote for the next president. Ultimately, they elected Dumarsais Estimé.

Although ousted president Lescot had privately supported LFAS calls for women's rights, the nine months leading up to the assembly birthed many new genuine and strategic political alliances for women activists. In this context, the group of formally educated teachers and financially affluent women who came together in 1935 to establish a women's "movement for social improvement" and to advocate for "Haitian women of all social classes" also spilled into the streets of Port-au-Prince in early January 1946 as they and their students called for new representation in the state.[4] After a decade of petitioning the government for equal citizenship rights, including the right to purchase property, hold their own professional wages, and vote in all local and national elections, these women presumed that the political energy drawn to the assembly proclaiming the rights of the people would also see the merit of gender inclusion.

It is possible that the unnamed woman was charged by the same expectancy and zeal for inclusion as the LFAS members when she reached and requested entry into the section reserved for women's rights hopefuls. But before she could cross the threshold, a member of the Garde d'Haïti (Haitian military police) turned her away. As the woman was forcibly removed from the area, "members of the L.F.A.S. protested [her removal] and were backed up by the crowd," but the woman was escorted out of the palace.[5] Noting the commotion, Assemblyman Castel Démesmin, a *noiriste* (Black power nationalist), assessed her ejection as a political forecasting, "a sign [that] women of the people will always be rejected by these women."[6] He further appealed to his fellow representatives to cast their ballots against women's suffrage: "I ask you to vote against this proposition because only these scheming women will stand to benefit from the right. Save the revolution by first saving the country from women."[7] According to the assemblyman, *these* women—members of the LFAS—were calculating political opportunists who spurned their own and jeopardized the nation's sovereignty.

The unnamed woman's ejection from a moment of constitutional debate provided fodder for the ongoing anti-suffrage discussions that pitted the LFAS leadership's social privileges against their authenticity as critics of gender inequality.[8] According to opponents and supporters, women like the leadership of the LFAS—teachers, doctors, anthropologists, attorneys, novelists, poets, office administrators, and social scientists—had drastically different life experiences from those of the unnamed woman. Beyond the assembly walls, the woman would have likely worked for, or around, the women represented by the LFAS leadership, rather than with them. These differences, according to critics, inhibited LFAS leaders from representing all women. Assemblyman Démesmin further conjectured, "Who will benefit from these rights? The women of the countryside, or rather these spoiled women who have everything in their hand: money and power?"[9]

The assertion that LFAS women would accrue more social and material wealth that would further rotten their social position was not unique. It was a frequent and often substantiated critique of women's movements in the early twentieth century. Particularly in the Americas, early women's movements often had limited cross-class analysis and embedded anti-Black practices.[10] Although the Black and *mûlatre* (mixed-race or light-skinned Black people) membership of the LFAS was more class-diverse than the leadership, including a small percentage of urban working-class and peasant women, the assemblyman's statement communicated a particular lacuna between the urban elite, merchant, and professional classes and the rural peasant, urban working, and poor classes. Even though the unnamed woman was stopped by the military police and verbally defended by members of the LFAS, her ejection from a moment of constitutional debate echoed the LFAS women's perceived political and physical distance from the majority of Haitian women. That day, LFAS women were literally positioned differently to Haitian citizenship than the *femme du peuple*, and thus LFAS women's ability to advocate on women's behalf was questioned.

The scene of separation also opened the debate for criticism about the philosophies espoused by the LFAS and turned into a referendum on feminism. The promise of women's suffrage legislation was eclipsed by representatives debating women's political sincerity, intellectual capacity, national loyalty, and self-control as voting citizens. At one point Assemblyman Emile St. Lôt, a *noiriste* and president of the leftist coalition Front Révolutionnaire Haïtien (FRH), called the women "bad mothers" and "dictator[s]."[11] The debate during the assembly, similar to the suffrage debates around the globe in the early twentieth century, revealed the misogyny embedded in the discourse of modern republican citizenship.[12] While some critics questioned women's capacity, others simply could not conceptualize a national governing body that included women. One op-ed respondent sarcastically questioned, "Would women now be members of the military?"

Women had, in fact, served in the nineteenth-century revolutionary army and fought as *cacos* (Haitian guerilla army members) in the wars against the US occupation, but the perplexities of women's participation in governance and working together across class, color, and cultural difference also left some women befuddled. During one of the earliest LFAS lectures on Haitian feminism, LFAS members argued that elite women needed to work with urban working and peasant women to improve women's position in the country. In response to this suggestion, one woman attendee wrote that the proposition was incendiary and that the presenter should have "kept her gloves on," implying that she was acting out of class character to suggest that elite women would share social space or touch women of another class: "[Even] if you talk to your cook, put on your gloves."[13] With these prejudices, quandaries, and concerns circulating, *féminisme* bounced off the hallowed walls of the assembly as a political slur and crescendoed with a chorus of boos that followed the removal of the *femme du peuple*. Shortly after the unnamed woman's ejection, the members of the LFAS voluntarily left the assembly, followed by taunting boos and a military escort. By the end of the assembly, there were no women represented.

The national newspaper *Le Nouvelliste* covered the assembly debate and reported that the members of the Ligue Féminine were assaulted.[14] No media outlet mentioned the unnamed woman's dismissal. However, several days after the assembly, the LFAS membership narrated the events in the booklet *La femme haïtienne repond aux attaques formulées contre elle à L'Assemblée Constituante* (*The Haitian Woman Responds to the Attacks Levied against Her at the Constitutional Assembly*). The document included political essays penned by LFAS members who attended the assembly, including President Madeleine Sylvain-Bouchereau, Vice President Alice Garoute, novelist Cléante Desgraves Valcin, journalist Yvonne Hakim Rimpel, and educator Marie-Thérèse Poitevien. With the booklet, the women responded "to those who insult us" and to one another about the meanings of "*Le Féminisme.*" The women had been practicing this textual reflexivity for over a decade. In late 1935 the LFAS founded the bimonthly newspaper *La Voix des Femmes* (Women's Voice), in which they presented their research about women in Haiti, interrogated women's political role throughout the world, and theorized and fictionalized the experiences of Haitian women. The essays in the booklet, which are discussed in chapter 3, were theoretically sophisticated and strategically pointed.

The unnamed woman's ejection appears in the last essay of the booklet. Crafted in a chronicler format, it is a play-by-play of the constitutional assembly dialogue. In accordance with this form, the LFAS authors make no reference to assemblymen who do not speak, specify the social or political makeup of the audience, or provide any clarity on the cartography of the space. However, several lines before the last section of dialogue, the authors insert a parenthetical note:

(*Une femme du peuple veut entrer dans la tribune réservée aux femmes, le gendarme l'en empêche, les membres de la L.F.A.S. protestent soutenues par la foule, l'orateur veut dénaturer l'incident.*)[15]

(A woman of the people wanted entry into the area reserved for women, the gendarme barred her from the space, the LFAS members protested and were supported by the crowd, the speaker wanted to distort the incident.)

The unnamed woman's entry breaks the chronicler form.[16] She was not supposed to appear. She was not accounted for in the other records of the day. But with the parenthetical reference, LFAS women at once signaled their political practice of improvisation, disrupted the historical erasure of another woman, refused their own invisibility, and attuned the reader to their power of narration by writing their marginal positions in the assembly into the text. Powerfully, when the *femme du peuple* enters the script, she brings all the other "marginal" actors with her.[17] It is only in the context of the unnamed woman's effort to enter the women's section that we learn that our chroniclers are partitioned away from the action, not only as audience members, non-assemblymen, or omnipresent observers but also as women.[18]

The note impresses upon the reader that the assembly was talking about LFAS members and their access to citizenship, but not with them or other women. In this parenthetical break, the women bear witness to the intersections and technologies of gendered and historical power.[19] In so doing, they also narrated their missed opportunity to include the unnamed woman in "women's" space. The reference to the *femme du peuple* appears only a few dialogue exchanges before the end of the script. With no formal conclusion, the booklet evidences the women's early exits from the assembly. The script abruptly ends and the unnamed woman's presence and absence linger unsettled.

White Gloves, Black Nation rests in the tensions and resonances of this historical and archival moment. It attends to the disquiet between elite and middle-class women's claims to the state on behalf of Haitian women and their attempts, miscalculations, restrictions, successes, desires, and at times unwillingness to share space as they "worked to uplift and redress the conditions of all women."[20] The book documents these women's history of organizing and political theory, while considering organizers' refashioning of Haitian politics for their own purposes through archival practice, public and private displays of self-reflexivity, and an organizational focus on national and international gender equality. To tell this story, I use the bountiful, yet largely ignored, textual archive of women's rights politics, including manifestos, essays, speeches, and research reports. This book narrates and uses this record to account for the women's movement in the history of post–US occupation

Haitian politics. It also attends to the small adjustments, like the LFAS author's parenthetical notation, that open up the semilegibility of these women's practice and alternative possibilities of engaging the concept and utility of women's politics in Haiti. I offer that these women's most profound articulations are found in the subtext of the spectacle (manifestos, marches, and martyrdom) of political performance. In this way, the book traces parenthetical notes, mentions of melancholy, undeveloped photos, and addendums to letters to account for these women's political praxis.

White Gloves, Black Nation moves away from the tempting debate about the spectrum of representation that is articulated in the assemblyman's comments in 1946 and echoed throughout scholarly and popular histories as a query of political efficacy. Instead, the book turns to practice and what could be accounted for, achieved, learned from, built upon, or avoided with our attention to these politically performative moments.[21] That is, I am less concerned with the moral assessment of whether elite and middle-class women *can* represent themselves and other women but rather with *how* they represented and worked with women (or did not do so) within the multilayered spectrum of political and social locations in Haiti. Whereas other scholars have used LFAS women's work and class status—signaled through education, wealth, religion, color, travel, comportment, and clothing—as a reason to question these women's politics, I offer that their class performance is a place to dwell and study the intersections of gender, race, class, and culture that often overdetermine political rhetoric and historical articulations of politics in Haiti. This attention to political practice and performance is not an erasure of these women's privilege or exclusionary practices. As this book shows, these women were culpable in fortifying the very inequalities they sought to undo; but attending to these women's lives and work from the sole perspective of radical efficacy flattens the theoretical, practical, and historical complexity of their work, ideas, and ultimate outcomes.

In attention to the practice and subtext within these women's political lives, this book is also a pointed engagement with historical accountability. Here, accountability is rendered in both attending to the bias grain of archival production and interrogating the power therein, as well as naming and asking critical questions of these women's liberatory project and witnessing the beauty and messiness of their work.[22] This formulation was developed in my navigation of the spectacular, subtle, and oral history archive. That is, in the more than forty oral histories I collected for this project, the work of the LFAS was repeatedly summed up by this response given by a Haitian community activist and great-niece of an LFAS member: "Oh, those women who got dressed up to have tea. Yes, they won the right the vote."[23] This response, and others like it, revealed a simultaneous recognition of political significance and disavowal of the LFAS's political praxis. On the rare occasion when their comportment was not mentioned, LFAS women were characterized as conservative grandmothers of a more radical, late twentieth-century women's movement. Between the oral and traditional historical records, LFAS women's work has been routinely oversimplified as both perfunctory and pioneering. On either end of this spectrum, these women's work and feminist history have not "fit" in the polemic history and historiography of radical or conservative post–US occupation Haitian politics. Given the historical disorientation and silence of early twentieth-century women's activism, I ask: How do we historically locate an opulent, foreign-educated, self-interested, burgeoning professionalized class of women who understood themselves as the descendants of 1804 Haitian revolutionaries, *used* and studied women, and boldly called themselves feminists?

White Gloves, Black Nation answers this question with an invitation to sit in the moments of almost connection—the space between the members of the LFAS and the *femme du peuple* just as their experiences of womanhood almost touch, but not quite. This practice of archival dwelling makes room for the quandary that LFAS women (for whom many specific names and personal histories are shared in this book) accounted for the woman in the assembly hall, but that she is still unnamed, or named only by her social position. Thus, dwelling is not an invitation to pathologize difference or romanticize women's "unity" through sameness or sisterhood, making women, and by extension the nation, strong. Rather it is an invitation to hold difference and complexity, however uncomfortably, in the same frame. And to see what can be learned from the method, analysis, and feeling in this holding.

This book, then, is a methodological invitation to think with women's intersecting differences in the historical archive, and it is a record of how these women's theories of feminism germinated from their reflections on difference. While this might seem obvious, the overwhelming body of scholarship about women in Haiti rehearses separation. Most essays, research projects, and books focus on peasant women, elite women, market women, or middle-class women. These works are responding to the undeniable and often stark differences in women's social standing and daily reality, but they also often obfuscate the dialectical ways in which these women's lives reinforce one another's. The infrequency of material that holds different women in the same historical, sociological, literary, and theoretical frame then can unintentionally reinforce ideas of oddity that suggest gender relations in Haiti are indecipherable or impenetrable or that they cannot be instructive for understanding global meanings of race, nation, and belonging. These scholarly categorizations also underscore the limitations of the archival capture, language, and cataloging practices that silo women's lives.

Attending to the difference in the historical record points to the nuance of mid-twentieth-century politics and contextualizes the radical promise and the extreme violence against women, not only as practices of individuals but also as parts of extensive interpersonal and systemic webs of local, national, and international power. From this gathering place, we are reminded that even within a shared class, Haitian women experience and experienced gender differently. In the early and mid-twentieth century, these differences shifted from minute to hour, roadway to threshold, and name to unknown name. The history of early twentieth-century feminists' practice shows that they recognized and experimented with naming that could account for the differences and intersections between and among women. They experimented with new words, created new physical spaces to bring women together, and even created and published alternative academic social categories to hold the abundance of nuance among women. For these reasons, *White Gloves, Black Nation* follows the historical reappearance and often silencing of women like the unnamed woman, the LFAS's political doctrine to represent all women, and women's political practice to think about the archive, national belonging, and the possibilities of modern Haitian politics.

As evidenced in the assemblyman's comments, a politics that would draw women close or within the same rhetorical frame provoked the anxieties of certain Haitian politicians in the postoccupation period. Thus, I also ask: Why does the assemblyman invoke "the revolution" in this moment? What is the relationship between these women (the *femme du peuple* and LFAS women) and the revolution? Is he referring to the 1946 student revolution that occurred months prior, or to the emancipation and independence revolution a century and a half before? What does it mean if he is referring to both? And how are these gloved and tea-sipping women in the twentieth century a threat to the revolution of the early nineteenth or mid-twentieth century? In both the early nineteenth century and mid-twentieth century, women were uniquely woven into the radical discourse of revolution (as compatriots and enemies) and partitioned away from the articulation of radical practice. The palimpsestic quality and historical ambiguity of the assemblyman's comments offer an alternative configuration for considering Haitian politics. What could happen if we observed women *du peuple* / "of the nation" / "of the people" and women who were what I call state-adjacent or aspirational within the same frame over time?

How could this attention to gendered proximity and difference inform meanings of citizenship, Blackness, and belonging? How would that attending upend the hardened frame of revolutionary ideation and political possibilities that were (pre)formulated in postoccupation politics? I offer that these women's sartorial presence, archival practice, and intellectual work unhinged Haitian politics from the exceptional tropes and social factions of revolutionary nationalism and as a result threatened the conceptual foundations and afterlives of "the revolution" as a rhetorical and institutionalized tool used to uphold interpersonal, political, and state power in the postoccupation period.

White Gloves, Black Nation, then, provides a history of Haitian women's political organizing in the early twentieth century through a microhistorical interrogation of the women's political practice. The book also engages the turn in Caribbean scholarship to trouble Haitian exceptionalism, Caribbean sovereignty, and radical politics that focus on liberal formulations of "the human" and "rights." Instead, this history focuses on the local and transnational narratives of the everyday and the minutiae of a movement to account for the asymmetry, irony, and moments of possibility within these women's political practice.[24] While scholars in anthropology, cultural studies, sociology, and literary studies have challenged Haitian exceptionalism, this book makes an important historical contribution to this discourse by offering evidence that early in the twentieth century women activists were already suggesting that an exceptional articulation of Haiti was worrisome. Following these women's work, the book echoes the critique that narratives of exceptionalism foreclose the ability to observe Haiti as a site of everyday negotiations of race, class, and nation in the Caribbean and the African diaspora.

Finally, *White Gloves, Black Nation* examines the contradictions in these women's thought, practice, performance, and re-performance as both an entry point to historicize modern Haiti and as a political orientation that I call *political wayfaring.* I show that while the movement for suffrage and women's rights is an important legacy of these women's work, their evolving research practices and archival curation reveal their political impulse. Wayfaring, the act of going from one place to another or traveling, privileges and historically locates these women's political process. Here, they navigated philosophical contradictions, engaged in self-reflection, insisted on self-promotion, and experimented with different methods of intellectual and political practice. This was a deeply introspective, aspirational, and affective intellectual journey. In this process, women organizers intentionally and deliberately moved through the radical milieu of the early and mid-twentieth century. They picked up what worked, put down what did not serve them, and traveled a meandering road toward gender equality that they found would help them navigate political, national, and personal belonging as well as produce long-lasting intergenerational outcomes.

Madeleine Sylvain-Bouchereau nodded toward aspects of this political practice in an issue of *La Voix des Femmes* one year into the movement: "In our keynote speeches, our newspaper, our articles, we have never ceased to proclaim that, while recognizing the principle of equality of the sexes, we are not currently demanding its immediate application in Haiti."[25] While the women did not propose any sudden change to society in the early years of the movement, they were moving swiftly in the direction of their evolving vision of citizenship—speeding up in some moments, slowing down in others, and on occasion going backward and retracing their movements.[26] In this regard, answering the question of how to locate these women offers no clear navigational pings. In both the archival record and the historical narration, the women's orientation moves. These shifts were political, spatial, and temporal. Politically, the women's wayfaring was complicated by what Caribbean feminist critic Lizabeth Paravisini-Gerbert argues are the fairly *local* ways Caribbean women's *movements*, rather than *a* feminism, hold space for multiple "feminisms that often clash with each other as women of different classes and races strive to achieve sometimes contradictory goals."[27]

White Gloves, Black Nation shows that Haitian women's practices of feminism were varied, even within movements. This book also considers some of these political clashes as moments of crossing, where women's differences intersected and the feeling of a high-impact hit came from women's unwillingness or inability to account for their relationships to power at these intersections. Attending to these crossings, this history of LFAS women's work also highlights the relationship between women's labor and physical movements within and between urban, rural, national, and international spaces. The book does this by amplifying women's archival record of their travel and the routes that connect and create overlap between women's lives.

The historical record of these women's movements, body of work, and evolution of thought and practice echoes Caribbean transnational feminist M. Jacqui Alexander's generous reminder that the "oppositional consciousness is a process rather than a given before the fact of the political practice."[28] This attention to process provides a template to query these women's pace as a part of the practice. While these activists' insistence on a "not immediate" pace might be perplexing or even suggest political passivity, their record revealed that their slowed public-facing political performance was not an indication of the urgency in their thought and praxis. Moreover, as political wayfarers, these women hurried to pick up pebbles of Marxism and slowly brushed by branches of Black nationalism. They stopped to rest under the trees of Christian conservativism, but they also decided that the shade was not expansive enough for their vision. The women used local and international concepts like feminism as road maps to orient themselves, but they routinely walked just off the road of these feminist politics to account for their shifting modalities of movement. In their wayfaring, the women released their political journey from a site-specific location (radical, feminist, communist, Pan-Africanist, and so on) or destination (full suffrage, women's rights, and so on) and attuned us to how they moved through and practiced their politics in a season of heightened radicality.

The early women's movement was sustained and evolved over the political landscape of seven Haitian presidents, who represented the spectrum of political leadership, including foreign-supported, conservative elites, Black middle-class pragmatists, military juntas, and Black nationalists. The movement's survival could communicate pragmatism that made the women's gender politics nonthreatening to any of the political waves of the period. In the dynamic context of the early and mid-twentieth century, however, in which intellectuals, activists, and politicians across the political spectrum were jailed, exiled, and killed for their political beliefs, political survival suggests an agility that merits historical attention. *White Gloves, Black Nation* follows the history of this half-century of changes in state actors. However, the book is also thinking with Michel-Rolph Trouillot's assertion that "Haitian and foreign observers alike have tended to inflate the role of politics in shaping the course of the country's history. They often see the stages of historical evolution in terms of changes of regime, to a degree that masks underlying continuities."[29]

One of these continuities is the Haitian women's movement. These women's organizing practice also revealed that other continuities included the recycling and recrafting of physical, psychological, and sexual violence against women. An additional continuity included women's navigation of physical and political space. Not only was the organizing and intellectual practice of this movement formulated beyond the politics of the state, but this praxis, which reveals continuities despite state changes, was also not always linear or marked by incremental progress. The most obvious example of this is the surge in sexual violence against women after women won suffrage rights and voted for the first time. The 1946 assembly, which the book opens on and returns to in chapter 3, captures the web of bold and subtle queues about women's political journey that anchor this book. By retracing the movements of the unnamed woman and the LFAS, the next section accounts for the historical context of women's political history in the post-occupation period.

A Radical Milieu

The unnamed woman walked into the crosshairs of a volatile political moment. Following the exile of President Lescot in January 1946, the political climate was charged with urgency and frustration about political representation. Although no weapons were drawn inside the August 1946 assembly, a political battle was anticipated. Participants came armed with the rhetoric of their respective beliefs, and they were willing to strategically fire at anyone who did not advance their cause. In particular, leftist organizers critiqued the leadership of elite *mûlatre* presidents since the end of the US occupation who did not, in either their class status or color, represent the nation's Black majority. Compounding the debates over the extended reach of the elite and merchant-class-controlled state, national insecurities were heightened because of post–US occupation rural-to-urban migration, shifting interwar and post–World War II global markets that exacerbated economic disparities, and a rise in anticolonial Black nationalism.

The leftist activists and politicians who came to the 1946 assembly had varying ideas about the country's future, but all were determined to overthrow any semblance of the old regime. Among these groups were *noiristes*, communists, labor organizers, and socialists. Assemblyman Démesmin, who announced the unnamed woman's removal, identified as a noiriste—a political position that supported Black representation in national governance and policy in favor of the nation's Black majority. While this political orientation was not antithetical to women's rights, the LFAS had garnered the support of several leftist politicians who were not aligned with the political practice of the leading noiristes. Specifically, the vocally pro–women's rights assemblymen were members or sympathizers with the Parti Communiste Haïtien (PCH) and the Parti Socialiste Populair (PSP), including PSP president Max Hudicourt.

In the immediate aftermath of the 1946 revolution, noiristes and Marxists groups, including the PCH, came together under the leftist umbrella organization the Front Révolutionnaire Haïtien (FRH). The FRH had a mixed membership of noiristes and Marxist groups, but it was primarily led by noiristes, with Emile Saint-Lôt serving as president.[30] However, by June the PCH became disillusioned with the noiriste leadership's focus on color over class differences, and it temporarily aligned with the PSP.[31] The PCH and the PSP both had a mix of Black and *mûlatre* members, but the PSP had a larger lighter-skinned membership and was uniquely focused on issues of class over race, making it a political opponent of noiristes. When the PCH chose to collaborate with the PSP in mid-1946, Matthew Smith states that "the noiriste assault on the PSP was harsh and personal."[32]

At the assembly on August 9, these personal attacks were levied against the LFAS women. Women's rights debates were a stage for politicians to pronounce their concerns for the nation along color and class lines.[33] Despite the cultural and class dynamism of the moment, including the growth and expansion of a Black middle class, politicians and activists explained the conflicts of the nation through inter-class (elite minority/peasant majority) and color (Black/*mûlatre*) divisions. Radical movements accentuated these differences in their political rhetoric to legitimize their claims on state power.[34] By the last months of 1946, the noiriste call for Black middle-class representatives for the Black poor majority had assumed strategic, if not philosophical, primacy in national politics.

The anti–women's rights assemblymen could not effectively argue that the mixed Black and *milat* contingency of LFAS women was anti-Black, but Saint-Lôt and his supporters did socially and aesthetically locate the women apart from Blackness. The geographic distance announced in Saint-Lôt's statements between the "women of the countryside" and the "spoiled women" of the urban centers communicated a sociospatial difference between women. This difference was not a political fabrication. Rather, as Trouillot has captured in his analysis of class, color, and culture in modern Haiti, these differences located women within the guerrilla warfare between the state (the urban, educated, multirace, mostly *milat*, and resource wealthy) and the nation (the rural and urban working-class Black majority).[35] In Trouillot's formulation, governance and rights were the priority of the state that protected the Black nation from foreign intervention and negotiated international trade, while culture and production were the purview of the nation that worked the land, traveled between rural and urban areas, and embodied the African ancestry of the colonial-era revolutionaries. Naming women based on their spatial orientation, then, articulated different social and political ideologies and claims to citizenship.

In this equation, the unnamed woman was of the nation. She likely lived or spent the majority of her week working in the capital city Port-au-Prince, but her social location was from the countryside, or *moun andeyò* (people from the outside). She was outside the urban political center. At the same time, the *du peuple* qualifier to *femme* connotes that she also represented *pèp la*/the people/ the Black nation, and so her removal from the assembly was met with an uproar that paralleled the 1946 protesters.[36] In comparison, the LFAS women were within the urban center, but they were state adjacent, as they could not yet represent the state, but were affiliated through education and familial networks to men who had representation and power in the state. The juxtaposition of the *femme du peuple* being completely outside the state, while the LFAS leadership were state adjacent, meant that, as suggested in the assemblymen's questions, women's rights—a liberal claim for representation through the government—were elite and middle-class women's domain. This distance between the state and nation was then dramatically reinforced with the physical partitions and separations of and between women at the assembly hall.[37]

The optics of the incident did not support the feminism that the LFAS women championed, nor did it locate them as they conceived of themselves. Throughout the 1930s, '40s, and '50s, members of the LFAS developed an organizational practice that drew women together across difference through intellectual pursuit and an interrogation of the material realities of women's place within the state and nation. The women never explicitly aligned themselves with any political party, but over the postoccupation period they celebrated and even echoed philosophies from every political sector, including communism, Marxism, and *noirisme* (chapter 2). However, the primary focus of the early women's movement was studying, cataloguing, and sharing women's lives and needs. As founding member and LFAS vice president Alice Garoute articulated early in the movement, "The conquest of our rights is only part of our program. Even if our brothers never elevate us to the rank of citizens of Haiti, we will continue our work of compassion and solidarity towards the women of the people and the peasants."[38]

The women understood the state and nation divide not as a spatial, class, or cultural divide, but as a gender divide. Although they "want[ed] the so-called stronger sex (or rather the State) to give the means to expand their knowledge" and power, LFAS women situated their social and political position outside the state, in the nation, alongside the majority of women.[39] With this perspective, LFAS leadership acknowledged and sought to shrink the gap between women's adversely disproportionate different life experiences, because, according to Sylvain-Bouchereau, "we believe that it is not enough to form a female elite capable of competing with the male elite, but that it is above all important to raise the intellectual level of the woman of the people who constitute the majority of the female population, outside of which no reform can be sustainable."[40]

This LFAS philosophy tethered women's different class and social positions together, even as they understood that women could subject other women to marginal citizenship. In an essay titled "Life in the Countryside," LFAS member Marie-Louise Barou wrote, "I don't have the impression that morally, the house mistresses are concerned with what their workers think, suffer, or enjoy." When further discussing urban domestic workers, she concluded, "[They] may be the least privileged class of the feminine proletariat."[41] Barou's classification of urban working-class women (like the unnamed woman in the assembly) announced an awareness of a spectrum of gender experience in Haiti. At the same time, the mistresses could have been members or friends of the LFAS members. Her reference to the mistresses' concern for other women, however, mirrored a political ethos of the LFAS in which the women used their political practice to transform ways of woman-to-woman engagement that would in turn offer new visions of and opportunities for women. Beyond the state, the LFAS proclaimed that women needed to know and be accountable for one another's material needs and emotional desires.

Here, LFAS leaders also articulated the feminine as a specific class—a laboring class.[42] Women shared both the work of physically reproducing laborers and citizens and the devaluation of their labor as mothers, agricultural and domestic workers, intellectuals, and urban professionals. As *La Voix des Femmes*'s editor-in-chief Jeanne Perez outlined it, "We no longer want to resign ourselves to being nothing but reproduction machines and servants of the lord and master."[43] Haitian women's rights organizers wanted women's material contributions to the country to be recognized and honored: "Haitian women have an equal, if not greater, share than that of men in the production of agricultural wealth. She has an equal—if not greater—part than that of men in the work of national education, the most important of all human tasks; why should she have a diminished position when it comes to discussing and deciding on issues that concern the moral and economic future of Haiti, which belongs to Haitian women as much as Haitian men?"[44] Women's production of agricultural wealth was a reference to the women peasants, market women, and *madan sara* (women commerce specialists) who cultivated, transported, and marketed the nation's food across the nation. Additionally, women's contribution to education included the informal and formal education women offered young people.

While LFAS women drew peasant women's work into their frame of gendered labor oppression, the LFAS leadership was also a part of a new professionalized intellectual group of women who were teachers and researchers. Earning but not allowed to hold their own wages, elite and middle-class women were thinking about their labor in new ways. The framing of their bodies as machines, their attention to the proletariat, and the outstanding colonial-era Napoleonic Code that deemed women minors and thus not legally able to hold their own wages was a social-material reality amplified by the 1940s urban Marxist and labor movements in Port-au-Prince. For LFAS members, their rhetoric regarding their alienated labor was fortified by their decade of activism through their night schools for women and education-housing facilities for working-class girls and women. Both initiatives, which lasted into the 1960s, were designed to educate the non-land-owning rural peasant and urban working classes, and expand the urban middle classes in an effort to build sustainable social change for women. As I discuss further in chapter 2, this work also attempted to disrupt the knot of economic and state power that was centralized in Port-au-Prince and that upheld a state-versus-nation dichotomy that undermined women's political desires. It is no wonder, then, why the LFAS received the support of Marxist assemblymen; but their observations about women's labor also sheds light on the unnamed woman's bold movements toward the woman's section.

The unnamed woman did not wander into the assembly hall; her intention to join women was clear. Perhaps she was a member of the LFAS, or a student at their night schools, or a participant in the Foyer Ouvrier, the LFAS women's community center in Port-au-Prince. She may also have been inspired by the activity outside the assembly and felt emboldened to walk in. While the LFAS women documented what happened inside the assembly, outside the assembly the public proclamations for governmental change were ablaze. Most notably, Black labor organizer Daniel Fignolé, leader of the Mouvement Ouvrier Paysan (MOP), had galvanized his legion of urban working-class supporters emphatically named the *rouleau compresseur* (the "steamroller") to form a street protest outside the assembly and "roll over" any opposition to workers' rights in the forthcoming constitution and presidency.

The MOP openly supported women's rights, had a section for women in its *Chantiers* newspaper, and made demands on the state through its women's department, Bureau d'Action Féminine, founded in 1948 and led by Carmen Jean-François Fignolé. It is possible, then, that the unnamed woman rolled into the assembly with the support and assuredness of these other leftist groups behind her. Madeleine Sylvain-Bouchereau later recalled (as I will discuss in chapters 2 and 3) that there were many groups of women interested in women's social and cultural improvement in 1946 from leftist organizations to Christian right organizations. Although the LFAS was the only organization to not be party affiliated and to have an explicit feminist practice that included a social, political, and economic agenda, each group played a role in the movement for women's rights.[45] The unnamed woman could have belonged to or moved with any of these women's groups.

The support and opposition of women's rights organizers were often strategically used by politicians to meet other projected agendas, but the *femme du peuple* was incorporated as a part of, focus of, or the subject of concern for each of these collectives. Here again, the women's archive reveals nuance. It is in the LFAS's narration of their protest against the unnamed woman's removal that we also learn of the LFAS women's temporary alliance with the crowd. As narrated by the LFAS, the majority of the assembly attendees shared disapproval of the dismissal of the *femme du peuple*. This is the same crowd that booed the LFAS's presence. Yet as the women archived and bore witness to the fleeting alliances in the midst of deeply dichotomous politics, they also recorded the recurring truth of women's mid-twentieth-century political complexity. Women were hailed in the political theater as multiple factions objected to the treatment and condition of the unnamed woman and women like her, but they also put forth little subsequent action to change or include her participation. As Haitian feminist Sabine Lamour cautions, the entry of affluent women into the labor market after the US occupation often "signifies a misleading form of transcendence of the internal cleavages of race and class" among women. Lamour argues that even if "the frameworks of access to the labor force of women from the wealthy and poor classes reconfigured themselves, internal divisions evoking gender, class, and race were reinforced" and "the logic of coloniality" for women across classes remained.[46] Thus, akin to a Greek chorus, the crowd, written in via Haitian women's archival practice, expresses the political, social, and even moral complexity of the dramatic political moment—on a stage where revolution was invoked, change was demanded, and women were valorized and vilified but ultimately escorted away from the business and history of the state.

Women's Citizenship and the Afterlives of Revolution

In 1935 Madeleine Sylvain-Bouchereau along with Alice Garoute, Thérèse Hudicourt, Fernande Bellegarde, Olga Gordon, Marie Corvington, Alice Téligny Mathon, Esther Dartigue, Maud Turian, and Georgette Justin formed the Ligue Féminine d'Action Sociale. The women openly challenged and questioned gender inequality in politics and used suffrage as a primary target for the nation to achieve its revolutionary promise. After two decades of petitioning, marching, and writing about, and to, members of the national government, the 1950 Constitutional Congress amended Article 8 of Haiti's constitution, granting women age twenty-one and older the right to vote in local and national elections. Haitian women first voted in a national election in 1957.

A cursory study of the women's movement, rights, and feminism in Haiti will offer as examples the Ligue Féminine d'Action Sociale and the 1950 suffrage win. The LFAS's legislative achievement was the product of political organizing by a burgeoning class of professionalized women who maintained that the democratic promise of the first Black republic in the Western Hemisphere was unfulfilled. For these women, the Black Jacobins who avenged a new world of independence and freedom at the end of the eighteenth century and into the nineteenth century had ignited the slow burn of an Atlantic slave system but were negligent in their exclusion of women from full citizenship rights.[47] At the beginning of the nineteenth century the architects of the Haitian Constitution had already accomplished the unthinkable by merging a decolonial movement with Black freedom and humanity.[48] Untangling a people's modern existence from cargo and capital into (human) beings, the authors seized the common winds of freedom and liberation in the Atlantic world and turned a modern tide.[49] The struggle, the national constitution, and the body of literature produced by Haitian authors in the early nineteenth century added political and ontological value to African people by making Blackness the condition of and synonymous with republican citizenship and humanity in Haiti.[50]

In the profundity of 1804, the founders tucked women into the condition of citizenship.[51] Women were explicitly addressed or referentially hailed in the 1805 constitution three times. One time was in Article 10: "Fathers and mothers are not permitted to disinherit their children." Another was in Article 13, by way of Article 12, which pronounced, "No white man of whatever nation he may be, shall put his foot on this territory with the title of master or proprietor, neither shall he in the future acquire any property therein." This pronouncement was accompanied by Article 13: "The preceding article [12] cannot in the smallest degree affect white women who have been naturalized Haytians by Government, nor does it extend to children already born, or that may be born of the said women."[52] Finally, and more referentially, was the pronouncement in Article 22, "Of Governance," that stated, "The State will appropriate a fixed annual allowance to her Majesty the Empress [Marie-

Claire Heureuse Félicité], which she will continue to enjoy even after the decease of the Emperor." Within these articles, women were constitutionally crafted as mothers, wives, and white.

In less explicit ways, women were further removed from citizenship through prohibitions communicated in Article 9: "No person is worth being a Haitian who is not a good father, a good son, a good husband, and especially a good soldier." As not father, son, husband, or enlisted soldier, women's claims to Haitian citizenship had no place.[53] African-descended women's value as citizens was as reproducers of children for whom "the chief magistrate is the father" and whose "exception of color" was "ceased" with the proclamation within the same Article 14 that "the Haytians shall hence forward be known only by the generic appellation of Blacks." The bold stroke of Blackness onto the citizenry espoused racial unity and political strength that informed subsequent radical movements and cemented the historical stature of the first Black nation in the Western Hemisphere and redacted non-white Haitian women.

As an international document of revolutionary standing, the Haitian Constitution still echoed the colonialism that oriented the Atlantic world and that was deeply enmeshed with gendered and sexual violence, oppression, and exclusion.[54] In particular, the authors of the constitution articulated a militarism and ownership over women's bodies and land that continued colonial logics throughout modern Haitian history.[55] Women's marginalization in the formative moments of the country foretold the limits of revolutionary promises anchored in liberal individualism.

Still, LFAS women invoked women's role in the revolution to claim inheritance to state representation, regularly referencing Marie-Jeanne Lamartinière and Marie-Claire Heureuse Félicité Bonheur, respectively one of the few named women who fought in the Revolutionary Army and the wife of independent Haiti's first leader, Jean-Jacques Dessalines. The women also cautioned against revolutionary romanticism. As LFAS president Madeleine Sylvain-Bouchereau delineated in 1946, "women are slaves," "have no rights," and cannot serve as soldiers—military service being a constitutional means to claim citizenship. In Sylvain-Bouchereau's assessment, the triumph of the Haitian revolution—emancipation and sovereignty—was tempered by women's prohibition from social and civil rights and the continuation of the eighteenth-century French Napoleonic Code that deemed women legal minors in the twentieth century.[56] Sylvain-Bouchereau's assertion of political bondage was a grave assessment of the philosophies of emancipation and independence articulated in the revolutionary republic. In her formulation, enslavement and noncitizenship were pillars of Haitian women's modern national belonging.

From this standpoint, early twentieth-century women's rights organizers identified themselves as modern abolitionists. Here the pace of their wayfaring picked up as their demands addressed the century-and-a-half-long delay in their emancipation. The women's assessment interrogated not only their place but also, as a result of their placement, the system itself. Thus when told by women's rights skeptics and multiple presidential administrations to wait until women were educated and prepared to participate in governance, they responded, "If we had waited until the slaves were educated, or for enlightened men to decree the abolition of slavery, I believe that we would still have slaves because it is the regime itself which prevented the development of their personality. Likewise, if we want to wait for Haitian women to be intellectually equal to men before giving them the means to ever achieve this equality, we will not achieve any result."[57]

The patronizing response from state leaders for women to wait for rights was not the same as the women's deliberate (not) immediate political pace. Instead it was a disorienting and perplexing forced temporal disjuncture.[58] Resonating with Black theorists throughout the twentieth century who critiqued the dispossession of Black people waiting for freedom, rights, and protections, the women charged the regime itself—the Haitian state—with failing the promise of radical liberation.[59] According to LFAS members, many freed Black men adopted the role of oppressor: "[In] 1804, the slaves of yesterday became masters. They understood the meaning of the word 'liberty.' [But] equality had a vague significance to them, and fraternity seems to be devoid of sense to them."[60] LFAS women challenged the presumption of a shared revolutionary experience. While leftist organizers often claimed to continue the work of the 1804 revolution through the political advancements of the 1946 revolution, women troubled these historic and fraternal connections by questioning the revered characterization of the self-sacrificing male citizen. As LFAS member and first Haitian woman novelist Cléante Desgraves Valcin noted, "It takes a certain heroism to abolish oneself of the privileges from which one benefits," but she conjectured that true national heroes do this work. As certain men upheld colonial laws that maintained gendered labor exclusion, refusing to "loosen the strap that the Napoleon Code represents for [women]," Valcin asserted, "We cannot claim that all of our men are heroes."[61]

Valcin's discursive swiping of revolutionary capes challenged twentieth-century radicals' claims on a revolutionary past and modern Haitian leadership.[62] LFAS women still rhetorically connected themselves to revolutionary heroism. For them, women were "the symbol of Haitian patriotism: the women who were imprisoned, shot, drowned, hanged, martyred next to their brothers for the ideal of liberty, and the conquest of the homeland."[63] Although presented as equal physical sacrifice to that of men, women's bodily injury in the national liberation project was not equal or materially acknowledged, prompting women's rights activists to query the relationship between women's corporeal sacrifice and sovereignty.[64] Here, the interrogation of the regime itself laid bare the "scripts of violence" against women as an integral component of the nation's formulation.[65] The women wondered if their capacity to "shape the souls" of revolutionaries despite being "mistreated and fondled by [their] master[s]" earned them citizenship.[66] The women pointed to the stories in Haitian cultural memory that sacrificed women for the liberties of the nation, echoing Haitian feminist scholar Régine Michelle Jean-Charles's argument "that rape plays a role alongside other forms of violence in the creation of nation and national identity, and that women's bodies are understood to be territories of colonial conquest."[67]

The terms upon which women could claim revolutionary citizenship were often dire. For this reason, revolution was referential for women activists. It was a placeholder for the promise and their deep love for the nation. As a result, LFAS women were at times ambivalent about national revolutionary rhetoric, but they also used it and desired to be included in it. As Caribbean theorist Sylvia Wynter might argue, they were navigating two conflicting premises: "On the one hand the egalitarian premise of the one man/woman vote at the level of the political, while on the other, the premise of inequality, of dominance and subordination based on the ascriptions of race and wealth at the levels of the social and the economic structures. Premises that [she argues] still underlie our present order of knowledge."[68] This ordering of knowledge, I offer, accounts for these women's historical dislocation, narrows the frame of Haitian politics, and forecloses the ability to read political projects in Haiti beyond failure or success, rather than attending to the process of that practice.

In this way, *White Gloves, Black Nation* considers the relation between the performance of politics and citizenship in Haiti, since, as Haitian literary theorist Kaiama Glover writes, "the commitment to radical social revolution in Haiti is part of the very fabric of the nation."[69] This form of politics is the progeny of the Haitian Revolution, but it was reared over the long nineteenth and early twentieth centuries as the threat of foreign invasion, exclusion from global markets, and an ever-evolving cultural nationalism recalled 1804. It is a radicalism forged in exceptional tropes of the martyred revolutionary heroes fighting against colonialism and racism, sacrificing themselves in the name of the people.[70] In the wake of the US occupation, this radical politics proliferated, and it further developed meaning as political actors navigated their access to local, state, and global power.[71] In this way, inclusion in and the practices and performances of radical politics, not rights, were the greatest measures of citizenship.[72]

Glover critiques this preoccupation with radical politics and the exclusion of women's work during the mid-twentieth century. She provocatively offers the title "disorderly feminine" to account for the nonaligment, nonparticipation, and "distinctly narcissistic bent" of Haitian women's political practice in the twentieth century that "unsettles the fantasy of selflessness that so often and so unhelpfully subtends the narratives of (nationalist) revolutionary actors in Haiti." Probing the possibilities of Haitian women's political legibility, she also excludes LFAS women from this definition. She argues that disorderly women like mid-twentieth-century Haitian author Marie Vieux Chauvet were "arguably more radically minded than the reformist Ligue" and that "the world Chauvet presents" in her work could not "be legislated into decency."[73] These women had different approaches to political life. However, the terms of the LFAS's exclusion from the possibilities of this alternative practice of politics remain informed by the rubric of radicality. The measure of the LFAS's political practice is prefigured through their presumed emphasis on rights that forecloses any interpretation of political thought or practice beyond the liberal frame that they critiqued, refused, and were often constrained by.

This constraint is felt in scholarship and popular histories where LFAS members are cast as the conservative bourgeoisie foremothers of more radical feminist groups in the late twentieth century.[74] In her analysis, Haitian feminist sociologist Carolle Charles states that early feminist activists were elite intellectuals who "represented the interests of middle-class women" and who "suffered from [their] narrow class perspectives."[75] "For the Ligue," Charles writes, "female suffrage was important because it also opened the door to public office, facilitating social mobility for a privileged minority."[76] Literary scholar Myriam Chancy takes issue with Charles's narrow definition of the LFAS's work and proposes arguing that, "Faced with finding solutions to poverty, illiteracy, limited education, inaccessible careers, voting rights, and protection under the law, Haitian feminists could not afford to be narrow in their vision."[77] Chancy maintains that Charles's characterization contributes to divisive images of Haitian women along class and color lines and submits that "what is essential to the proper evaluation of Haitian feminism on the global scale is to recognize that the category of 'oppressed' is not a static one."[78] While Chancy's argument that categories of oppression are not static is important and well taken, her jump to transnational universality of Black women's oppression also evades the accountability that Charles's assessment points toward. But taken together, both Charles's and Chancy's work presents a nonutopic feminist frame that can hold the complexity of these women's work informed by local, national, regional, and global markets, politics, and movements. This frame also uniquely challenges the supposed teleology and performance of Haitian political work, one in which all roads do not end in victory, and all victories are not measured by a revolutionary relation to the state.

LFAS women were certainly focused on rights, but this focus was not singular or nonreflexive. Observing LFAS women's organizing as a suffrage movement alone falls flat within the prototypes of politics in Haiti and within the proposed possibilities of women's activism in the nation. In *White Gloves, Black Nation* I do not attempt to identify a new category in which to place these women, their encounters, and their practices. Creating a new category would suggest that these women's process of intellectual and political engagement was unique rather than specific to the times. Rather, I look at the work to see how their practice and movements probed the contours of the frames that do exist. This book argues that the efforts and accomplishments of the LFAS should be read with attention to these women's shifting power as authors and actors, and acted upon in the history of early and mid-twentieth-century Haitian politics.

In her legal history of Haiti, Mirlande Manigat offers other coordinates for reading the LFAS women's wayfaring in the context of twentieth-century politics: "With the passage of time, that sifts feelings and reactions, it is difficult to measure the impact of the creation of the Ligue and the characteristics of the context in which it was formed. Other feminists or women's movements have since taken place in the country, more radical if not more operational, and have relegated the pioneer of the women's movement to a place where it sometimes remains embalmed, and praised—certainly for drawing the path of women's politics—but otherwise criticized for failing to follow the radical strategy."[79] Manigat locates the measure of the LFAS's politics at the intersection of memory and history. By her assessment, if we can abide in a measure of time, early twentieth-century Haitian feminism's place can be felt. Through this method of assessment, the historical record of women's lives can be approached beyond liberal valuations of success or failure, or authentic and inauthentic, but through an analytic frame that can hold and account for the ongoing meaning of moments like these women's almost connect at the assembly hall. This method marks the stakes for caring for a political present that holds the past, present, and future accountable. *White Gloves, Black Nation* traces the historical record of this (almost) feeling, where something between women could have opened, but instead remained closed.

Calibrating political meaning at history and memory, this book holds these almost moments ajar to revisit familiar archives and rehearsed histories. In this way, Manigat's words at the end of the quotation regarding the failure to "follow the radical strategy" incite an interrogation of the various ways to not only engage Haitian women's political practice in the early twentieth century but also interrogate the impermanence of the radical historical frame. For example, almost two years before the 1946 assembly the Martinican poet and activist Aimé Césaire famously pronounced that Haiti was the "place where négritude first stood up."[80] Inspired by the work of Haitian Pan-Africanist Anténor Firmin and *indigéniste* Jean Price-Mars, Césaire's proclamation of *négritude*'s maturation and rise referenced the 1804 Haitian Revolution. He made his statement shortly after he and his wife, Suzanne Césaire, visited Haiti for a monthlong lecture series for the Haitian Congrès de la Connaissance (International Congress of Philosophy) in 1944. In advance of Césaire's arrival in Haiti, Jeanne Sylvain, LFAS member and coeditor of *La Voix des Femmes*, wrote to her siblings that the "Martinican poet (or Guadeloupean?)" was coming that September.[81] By October she and other members of the LFAS had attended the lectures, and as Sylvain mentioned in two sentences of a family letter, "Aimé Césaire, the young Martinican sent from Free France" who was there to talk about radical practices in French prose, "speaks literature so marvelously." She continued, "I learned that there were more Haitian philosophers than I knew."[82] Her passing announcements reflect a unique exchange between Black Caribbean thinkers in the 1940s that historian Annette Joseph-Gabriel eloquently depicts in her study of French Caribbean women thinkers like Suzanne Césaire at the center of "Caribbean cultural citizenship."[83] Sylvain's commendation and zeal for considering new intellectual histories of Haiti resonate with Joseph-Gabriel's assertion that the "Césaire effect" that followed the 1944 lectures in Haiti inspired surrealist thinking and a jolt to the post–US occupation political awakening in Haiti that was ultimately reflected in the 1946 revolution.

Sylvain's letters also reveal that radical politics, even those that influenced other global movements, were not preformulated, overdetermining, or even philosophically solidified. Here, I intentionally quote Sylvain's announcement months before Césaire's arrival in which she is uncertain of Césaire's nationality. I cite this not to suggest Sylvain did not know who Césaire was—in fact Sylvain and her sisters studied and worked extensively with Césaire's contemporary, Jean Price-Mars, and would have been familiar with Césaire's work—but rather to account for the subtlety of and possibility in uncertainty, not knowing, forgetfulness, and ambivalence in the midst of historically dynamic political and rhetorical shifts in national, regional, and diasporic thinking. This uncertainty paired with her assuredness and enthusiasm about learning new Haitian philosophers months later echoes the rapidly evolving context of political thought as well as a consideration that while *négritude*, and by extension the Black radical tradition, stood up in Haiti in the nineteenth century, in the mid-twentieth century Haitians were also navigating these histories and meanings for themselves.

The historical navigability of mid-twentieth-century political practice and the historiography of it returned me to the responses about the LFAS: "Oh, those women who got dressed up to have tea. Yes, they won the right to vote."[84] At the time, I was open to a nuanced reading of the period in which clothing and tea could (and did) provide valuable points of inquiry, but paired with responses about women's enfranchisement, the clothing commentary read as a subtle devaluation of the LFAS's political acumen. Adorning their work in malaise and flippant disregard, the comments casually placed these women outside the history of relevant (read as radical politics) of the early twentieth century. And in the early twenty-first century, when I conducted these interviews, they allowed organizers to illustrate grassroots approaches that put them in close proximity to the people, while methodologically and historically separating themselves from the conservative feminist foremothers and leaders of the LFAS in the early twentieth century. However, as I returned again and again to the comments, I saw an invitation. Between the "oh" and the "yes," the statement left a space to consider the political productivity of contradiction. These comments and the women in *White Gloves, Black Nation* were repeatedly gesturing toward a means for repair, and a need to complicate narratives of Haitian politics. By celebrating and tempering the work of early Haitian feminists, respondents were offering a reckoning with the parameters of the radical—feminist or otherwise.

In this way the affective space between history and memory manifested between "oh" and "yes," is urgent. I conducted many of these interviews in the years before and in the tender moments after the 2010 earthquake in Haiti. As I listened to similar comments and sentiments reverberate in the pre- and post- moments of the earth shaking, I was struck by how steady and consistent the resonances of the "oh" and "yes" were across this tectonic shift in time. How does one account for the historian's fetish for change over time when this discourse stayed? In a series of essays just before and after the earthquake, feminist scholar and anthropologist Gina Athena Ulysse called for new narratives of Haiti "or at least other narratives, for the old ones no longer suffice."[85] During the first days of 2010, "new" and "other," like "oh" and "yes," felt urgent. The pace of history, the significance of its production, and its utility quickened.

Where I had been focused on *new* stories, I was also drawn to *other* stories as I listened to women recount their experiences of political life alongside so much loss. Ulysse's call was urgent because leaders of the Haitian women's movement and many, many women transitioned from the land of the living to that of the dead during the 2010 earthquake and immediately after. The call was urgent because narratives of exceptionalism—resilient, poor, pitiful, supernatural, weak, strong—that circulated during that period were old and, drawing from Trouillot, odd narratives that failed to communicate or intentionally erased ordinary, human narratives of Haiti.[86] The circulation of nonhuman depictions of Haiti are, and have historically been, a place where Haiti and Haitians experience brutal consequences that are often enacted on women's bodies.[87] As a result, the urgency for other narratives is translated in this text through a reverence for those who lost their lives while trying to navigate the contours of citizenship through feminism because the well-versed narratives of Haitian politics risked a stagnant curiosity about women's political practice.

Haitian women activists in the twenty-first century contend with many of the same conditions that early twentieth-century Haitian women activists managed: a disproportionate wealth gap, marginal recognition by the state (even while given a space in it, like the Ministry of Women), foreign invasion (US and UN), unequal and predatory global markets (the petroleum crisis), sexual violence, and the meaning of and access to education as well as medical and mental health services. In this way the text offers additional ways to read familiar stories of Haitian politics, not only of class, culture, and color difference but also of in-betweenness, repair, and failure in places where victory was claimed, and victory where we imagined loss, and loss where there was loss.

Women and the Archive

Where scholars differ on the political significance and quality of the early women's movement politics, there is little disagreement about these women as thinkers and intellectuals. Haitian feminists researched, collected, catalogued, and curated the lives of women in the early twentieth century. Yet their record as theorists and co-collaborators, with many of the most well-known thinkers of the time, is largely unstudied.[88] The leadership of the LFAS alone included the first woman lettered attorney, first woman anthropologist, first woman gynecologist, and first woman social worker. These women implemented and manipulated the philosophies and methods of their respective disciplines in their politics. In the 1930s and '40s this scholarship was created with and particularly influenced by Haitian *indigénisme*. The cultural nationalist and research practice developed by intellectual and statesman Jean Price-Mars petitioned Haitian theorists and politicians to privilege Haiti's African ethnic ancestry as a primary site for understanding and planning the nation's government, philosophies, and society. As Chantalle Verna's compelling history of Price-Mars's multipronged political project emphasizes, the praxis of *indigénisme* necessitated close proximity—*rapprochement culturel*—ethnographic study, and any contexts that drew different African people near one another was a particular preoccupation of this thought.[89]

In 1917 Price-Mars gave a lecture to a group of elite women titled "Women of Tomorrow." In the speech he argued that despite their differences poor and elite women were ultimately bound by their shared African ancestry.[90] In the 1930s Price-Mars's intellectual peers included members of the LFAS who incorporated the challenge to suture the cleavage between women of different classes and culture. In particular, *indigénisme* was professionalized through the Institut d'Ethnologie in the 1940s and fused into the research practices of many early twentieth-century intellectuals like LFAS member Suzanne Comhaire-Sylvain, whose most frequent subject of study was women and girls in the rural peasant class and the urban poor, individuals like the unnamed woman.

This engagement was complicated. At once, members of the LFAS were collecting data and publishing research about women and the conditions of their lives that few scholars had done or have done since. These women were also documenting their proximity to other women for personal, professional, and political reasons. It is, then, worth considering if and how these women were engaging the practice of research differently than their peers. How did Haitian women study one another? Was there a practice formulated between women? As evidenced in the small trace of the *femme du peuple*, some women did document women differently. Yet while it is important to name these women's act of placing themselves and other women in the historical record, it is also necessary to do the work that these women wrestled with, which is to name their power in this process. This book attends to, "the articulation," as

Lamour offers, "of [the] complex hierarchy among [Haitian] women themselves, according to the color of their skin, their nationalities, and their class status and positionalities" that are in their archive.[91]

LFAS women engaged with the archive as researchers within a frame of study that was set between subject and object, observer and observed. They, like their colleagues and foreign scholars, contributed to the material study and documentation of Haitian peasant, poor, and working-class women.[92] These women's archival practice was historically met with a turn in anthropological study where Haitian and Caribbean lives and livelihood became the axis upon which studies of otherness, ethnicity, and cultural retentions revolved.[93] As scholars like Price-Mars and Jacques Roumain founded the Institut d'Ethnologie and led the field of anthropology in Haiti, they provided the tours, resources, and connections, often coordinated by women, that allowed scholars like Zora Neale Hurston, Katherine Dunham, Lavinia Williams, Melville Herskovits, Alfred Métraux, and others to do their work and develop theories of humanity and Blackness that traveled the world. From this work, generations of scholars, including members of the LFAS produced academic scholarship, conducted independent research, journaled, fictionalized, satirized, highlighted, ignored, and employed women. Between their public presentations, newspapers, short fiction, research notes, personal letter writing, and family scrapbooking, early Haitian feminists' work reveals different conditions of archival production.

These women were informed by disciplinary practices, but they also collected, catalogued, and narrated differently. What was the meaning of these women's work to different groups of women? If we take Caribbean historian Marisa Fuentes's charge to not only see power in historical narratives but also name and actively work against the "bias grain" in the archive and narrate through that power, we see that the respective paucity and abundance of information about different women shows how different and similar these women's lives were, naming both the possibilities and limitations of their political practice in the early and mid-twentieth century.[94]

Despite the disproportionate documentation of women in general, we have to reconcile the differences in the scattered and partial archive of elite and middle-class women, and the many pages of information about peasant and working-class women. Said another way, elite and middle-class women's archive was certainly destroyed and scattered over time (see the conclusion of this book), but the content of the archive also reveals another example of Trouillot's argument that silences in archives are a reflection of inequalities experienced in the past.[95] In this case, elite and middle-class women were not exposed to the exceptional curiosity and surveillance of research in the same way that peasant, poor, and working-class women were conscripted into (and refused) these studies and political agendas. Where silences in the archives of Black women are often created by colonizers, foreigners, or "men," these silences were in some cases co-constructed between women.

Building on Fuentes's invitation, *White Gloves, Black Nation* considers what it means when Haitian feminist women share and contribute to the limited archive of other Haitian women.[96] Here, archives are limited not only in the relative amount of information they contain, as they are pieced together, but also in how that information represents and creates a limited image of Haitian women. Again, reminded of the unnamed woman, these historical flashes both reveal the spectrum of Haitian women's lives and refract a contradiction in the promise of their politics.

Attending to these women's national belonging beyond the state and rights and through their archival practice is to name their archiving as an articulation of women's citizenship. These women's respective and overlapping archival locations account for their historical existence, but they also catalogue their varied embodied experiences of womanhood and how they were positioned in relation to gender, race, and class in Haiti. The archival practice of these women not only locates them sociohistorically but also reinforces what Mimi Sheller offers, that "citizenship can be understood as a set of intertwined practices and collective repertoires for defining, legitimating, and exercising the rights of some bodies against others: who can occupy public space, who can speak in public, who can bear arms, who can vote? Who does the state have an obligation to protect, and who is empowered to judge, punish, and imprison others?"[97] And who was empowered to archive the moment? Women's citizenship belonging, then, can be sited through their archival capacity, allowances, and methods. These capacities, of course, are not always traceable in traditional archives. Black women's archival record reminds us that these histories are often stored in the inside seams of dresses, tucked in treasured books, marked by knotted cords, braided into hair, or sewn into a family quilt.[98]

Still, these archival practices communicate a social and historical location, even when women are archiving as a refusal of that location. We will not know how the unnamed woman, upon whom the LFAS's parenthetical reference hinged, would have narrated that moment. In this way *White Gloves, Black Nation* thinks with the "feminist" archive as anthropologist Deborah Thomas suggests, as a process in which "archiving thus becomes less the development of a list of bounded traits, practices, and statistical indicators that make us who we are and more an articulation of processes that both constrain and open up the range of futures that are possible at any given moment, both within and beyond the space of the nation-state" and the traditional arche-types of political citizenship.[99]

This vision and utility of archiving are communicated throughout Haitian women's history at home and abroad. Like the many Black internationalist women of the early twentieth century, Haitian women shared photos, doc-uments, and stories nationally and internationally.[100] They also choreo-graphed, staged, and performed their versions of history across the country and diaspora. As a transnational practice, Haitian women saved materials in the diaspora, and other women documented the nation for those who were away. Haitian women captured images, words, sounds, and feelings for the next generation of political wayfarers who might request direction. From the is-sues of *La Voix des Femmes* that were shipped to women in the United States, France, and the Belgian Congo, to dozens of self-published feminist essays from across the century stored in worn file cabinets and under-the-bed librar-ies, to the memories that were patiently stowed away in community centers across the diaspora, Haitian women have located one another and preserved each other's presence.[101] This book is indebted to this archival practice. In this practice, women often expressed care for the revolutionary promise of the nation while envisioning the utility of the material remnants of the revo-lution for alternative futures (see "A Pilgrimage"). From informal advice col-umns, to full-scale research projects, Haitian women's archival practice made space for their belonging, charted women's desires, and offered a curriculum for "a future real conditional" in which, as Tina Campt explains, their practice was "an attachment to a belief in what should be true."[102]

In consideration of these processes and possible futures for women's lives, LFAS women's record looked something like love. Although she never par-ticipated in the organization's leadership, writer Marie Vieux-Chauvet was one of the foremost thinkers of the twentieth century and a contemporary of the women who founded the LFAS. While Kaiama Glover reminds us that Vieux-Chauvet was politically nonaligned, Vieux-Chauvet's body of work suggests that she was preoccupied with the complexity of women's political subjectiv-ity in the early twentieth century.[103] In particular, through her best-known protagonist, Claire Clamont, in her trilogy *Love, Anger, Madness*, Chauvet of-fers us a bold calibration of women's history, politics, and love. Claire is a forty-year-old virgin who lusts after her sister's husband, hides from her friend's pain, uses tourist postcards as pornography, oversees her father's dwindling properties, speaks cruelly to and yet wants the affection of her servant Augustine, and kills the dictator's representative. Through the labyrinth of Claire's deepest thoughts and actions, Vieux-Chauvet's work gives us room to interrogate love as caring and calculated, deep and shallow, defined and messy, public and private, national and foreign, conservative and experimental, long-lasting and quickened, consistent and mostly inconsistent, evolving, negotiated, playful, erotic, aware of our actions and more often painfully aware of our inaction.

This love is voluminous.[104] It is sometimes unproductive, excessively adorned, and self-interested. It is a love in which, as LFAS leader Jeanne Perez noted, women "perhaps can have a personality other than the one that we have so often swallowed."[105] This love holds space for the political and historical processes of women who dress up for tea as a political theory and practice of being in the world that these women worked and wrestled their greatest visions for themselves from.

This love is not a romance. And if read as Carolle Charles has earnestly reminded, this love should not be romanticized. For thinking alone, Charles offers, cannot "violate the norms and constraints imposed by [class and color] hierarchies."[106] This love, then, does not excuse abuse, rather it names, probes, and ultimately dismantles its power. It is toward the intersection of affect, intellectualism, and action in which this book charts the path of LFAS women's work beyond the political scripts but rather in the direction of the slow clearing of new roads to address oppressive systems. Vieux-Chauvet was not explicitly writing about the leaders of the LFAS, but her work helps to narrate the scene that was set by these women's archives and moves along the frequency of thought posed by historian Colin Dayan, who asks, "What does the ethnographic precision of Haitian novelists say about the constraints of what is generally called 'history'?" *White Gloves, Black Nation*, then, considers the multiple mediums through which women articulated their lives not only as expressions of class, culture, and color distinction but also as their own negotiation and recasting of these stratifications and as a collective articulation of Haitian modernity.

These women prioritized their desire, encouraging one another to seek joy and bask in intellectual wit while also moving in the direction of their collective belonging. Here, it might be useful to return to the 1946 assembly moment. In LFAS vice president Alice Garoute's response to an assemblyman's assertion that elite and middle-class women's rights activists were "full of manure,"[107] Garoute replied, "Manure is fertilizer of the greatest order."[108] "Mud," referring to the man, "dirties everything it touches."[109] Garoute's retort exemplifies the ways in which LFAS women activists repeatedly negotiated their own culpability, reoriented the political discourse to account for their belonging, and played with the conceptual shortcomings of radical actors' thought.

These women produced a record that made space for them to be both the protagonists and antagonists of their own philosophical creations.

Naming and Terminology

Garoute's distinction between mud and manure is a reminder of the particularities of language, translation, strategic vocabulary, and naming. The terminology in reference to gender, race, color, class, and cultural dynamics in Haiti requires careful navigation.[110] Taking this into consideration throughout the book, I use the words and spellings that are particular to the time period that I am discussing.[111] The most complicated terminologies for the purposes of this project are those that account for race, color, and class, particularly Blackness. Michel-Rolph Trouillot explains that since the Haitian Revolution and independence from French colonization in 1804, "the nation has always conceived of itself as a 'black' community."[112] Throughout *White Gloves, Black Nation* most actors use this understanding of Blackness to describe a shared African ancestry between Haitians and other African-descended people.[113] However, given the intellectual and political dynamism around race, racism, and research on Blackness in the mid-twentieth century, these affiliations are not assumed.

I attempt to indicate when Blackness is used in politics but not always adopted as a salient social rallying point. In particular I make note of individuals' use, sometimes in the same sentence, of *noir* and *nègre*. This history covers the chronological shift in the Black Francophone world when the term "noir," used until the late 1920s to connote color and African descendancy, was nuanced by African-descended people's increased use of the sociopolitical term *nègre*, often articulating a shared African ancestral and political meaning as "Black."[114] As a result, familiar terms like "Black," "white," and *mûlatre* are situated within the historical context.

Additionally, color is defined by a series of epidermic and somatic factors that include comportment, skin tone, family lineage, hair color, language, and economic resources. For example, within this formulation there are several classifications for light-skinned Black individuals, including *griffe* (mixed race person or person with a copper tone), *brun* (brown or tan), and *clair* (light brown or olive tone), among others. For this reason, I follow the example of historians such as Kate Ramsey and Matthew Smith in my application of the terms *milat* and "Black."[115] As Smith explains, the use of the Kreyòl term *milat* "is a more encompassing definition of someone who is both light-skinned and of a certain social class" and culture.[116] Similarly, "Black" refers not only to skin tone but also to social and political position. As a result of intersecting and overlapping national and international histories of colonization, slavery, and postcolonial globalization, "Black" has material and symbolic meaning. Charles argues that, "Blackness in Haiti is also a conceptualization of class interest in the language of race. It is a racial symbol whose meaning hides class conflict . . . it is racial capital."[117] At times Blackness was even based on philosophy, affinity, or sentiment. For example, one interviewee recalled her first trip to the Institute d'Ethnologie and "a certain Jacques [Roumain] was there. And although we would say that he was *mûlatre*, he seemed black (*noir*)."[118] The salience of impression or the sensation of having a particular quality of Blackness was significant to women activists in their politics and in how their work was understood historically.

For these reasons, LFAS women thought a lot about naming and terminology. As this book reveals, names and naming had the capacity to widen the gaps between women or draw them closer. For example, as shown in chapter 3, Suzanne Comhaire-Sylvain was so vexed by what she perceived were the inaccuracies of Haitian class definitions in academic scholarship (largely produced in the United States) that she developed a new class-categorizing system to account for class and cultural variation in Haiti. Names and naming are also significant in this book because women were often misnamed, called out of their names, or not named in the historical record. Throughout the text I use names to establish familiarity and historical significance. For example, in most of the book women are mentioned by their full names and then subsequently referred to by their last names. While this is a traditional academic nonfiction form, it is also a reminder that in some cases throughout the book women are only identified by their last names because they are only named in the archive through their relationship to husbands or fathers. In other cases, there are women who only have a first name because of the absence of legally recognized relationships to these same men or institutions.

As a result, the story follows the names as they appear in that historical moment. This means, for example, until 1936–37 when Madeleine Sylvain-Bouchereau gets married to Max Bouchereau, she appears in the book as Madeleine Sylvain. And in chapter 1 when the narrative is focused on girls and in the "dwelling spaces" (discussed below), I use the women's first names. Of course, there are many more women whose names are not recorded. Haitian historian Yveline Alexis has with great honor and respect set an example of how to name the unnamed Haitian women in the archive.[119] In this book, I narrate the women as they are presented in the text or oral narratives. As historical redress or archival rendering, none of these names simply appear.

The historical labor of seeking, cross-referencing, and still not finding Black women's names in the twentieth century while adopting archival techniques of scholars who study enslaved African women in the seventeenth, eighteenth, and nineteenth centuries is indicative of the matrixes of erasure regarding Haitian women's lives.

Book Structure

Thus, while wrestling with how to name women at different moments of archival visibility, *White Gloves, Black Nation* sets a scene for the memory of these women, their political practice and thought. To this end, the book is organized by moments of women recording and reconciling their politics through archival and reflexive practices. Each chapter moves between LFAS women's published and unpublished writing about their practice (mostly written in the late 1930s and '40s) and the historical record of these moments. Each chapter takes the women's theories of the historical moment as a launching point. Led by the women's political wayfaring, the book is set outside of the US occupation in the 1930s and '40s but spans the period of the US occupation through the mid-1950s.[120] For this reason, especially between chapters 3 and 4, the book is not organized in exact chronological order, but rather moves about the political season of the 1940s, when the women's national and international experiences and political contexts bounced off one another across the decade.

While accounting for the mutilated, silenced, and colonized qualities of the archive, I approach these women and their words as trusted historical interlocutors.[121] I trust them as narrators and theorists of their own stories that I interweave with oral histories, newspapers, and other archival material.[122] Chapter 1 begins during the US occupation, when many of the leaders of the women's movement were children or young adults. The women in this chapter represent various sectors of Haitian society, yet their narratives are drawn together by Sylvain-Bouchereau's assertion of Haitian feminist genealogy that "the Haitian woman was literally transformed" during the US occupation. Using oral histories, writings of Haitian politicians, US military records, newspapers from the US Black press, and US congressional reports, the chapter traces that literal transformation and demonstrates how differently classed women were drawn toward and stood in for one another in both anti-Black and antioccupation political actions, and in everyday moments of change as a result of the occupation. I argue that the mutilation of Haitian women's flesh during the occupation marked the nation's nonsovereignty, relocated women outside of Haitian citizenship, and propelled a postoccupation feminist politics focused on physical safety, social inclusion, and state rights.[123] The conditions of the archive make it difficult to ascertain what women felt (that is, their emotions) during the occupation, but Sylvain-Bouchereau's "literally" being in conjunction with the occupied archive that turned these women into nonhuman, flesh, helps to historicize a tactile feeling of the occupation. To do this, I stabilize the backdrop of these women's lives through the unstable archive of US occupation mapping and infrastructural reporting.[124]

Chapter 2 begins at the end of the occupation and discusses the early organizational structure, workshops, and research projects of the LFAS. The chapter is told through the lives and research of the Sylvain sisters: Madeleine, Suzanne, Jeanne, and Yvonne. The Sylvain sisters used the LFAS as a platform for their respective intellectual interests. They encouraged the production of interdisciplinary feminist scholarship through the study of urban and rural working-class women and girls. Using the LFAS's monthly periodical *La Voix des Femmes* alongside several urban journals such as *Le Matin, Le Nouvelliste, La Semeuse, Haïti-Journal*, and *La Phalange*, the chapter examines the philosophical and political intersections with other postoccupation movements. It also follows public debates about feminism, family, and citizenship aesthetics through the LFAS's attention to women's ownership of their labor, creativity, and leisure time. Chapter 3 starts in 1944 and returns to the 1946 revolutionary moment. The chapter considers LFAS women's assertion of social and political enslavement—"the woman is a slave"—and puts it alongside their political platform concerning parental rights and the condition of the Haitian family structure, particularly the practice of *plasaj* (a Haitian common-law marriage that can include multiple sexual and romantic partnerships and that usually incorporates a shared financial arrangement). The chapter observes how legislation around women's rights was used to control women's domestic and public movements, including rural-to-urban migration.

Chapter 4 examines how the local and national debates in chapter 3 took on unique meanings in the women's international travel and politics. National women's organizations were not the only participants to play a role in the journey toward women's rights. The unnamed woman at the 1946 assembly may have invited herself to the women's space based on perceived and real political affiliation or alliances, but the LFAS women made some strategic invitations in advance of the assembly. The leaders of the LFAS held memberships and affiliations in multiple international women's movements, including the Women's International League for Peace and Freedom, Pan-American

Women's Congresses, the United Nations Council on Women, and the International Council of Women of Darker Races. LFAS women leveraged these organizational and interpersonal relationships for their national initiatives and used the international climate to coax national leaders to their side. For example, days before the August 9 assembly, attorney Sadie Tanner Mossell Alexander, the first Black woman to receive a PhD in economics in the United States and member of the National Association of Colored Women (NACW), wrote a letter to NACW president Mary McLeod Bethune reminding her that Madeleine Sylvain-Bouchereau, with whom she was familiar through Sylvian-Bouchereau's studies in the United States, requested a letter of support from the NACW. Bethune wrote the letter and later reminded the soon-to-be president Dumarsais Estimé of her support for the LFAS throughout his presidency.

Over the postoccupation period, Haitian women's movement leaders collaborated with Black American women like Bethune and Eslanda Robeson; cheered on Ethiopian women's efforts against the Italians; sought out alliances with white French, German, and US women; shared strategies with Puerto Rican mayor Felisa Rincón de Gautier and Argentinian first lady Eva Perón; sought advice from Indian women's rights activist Lakshmi N. Menon; and ultimately conceptualized themselves as members of both the "Latin" American and African diasporic worlds. This multilingual and multisited orientation to their work meant that LFAS women's political engagements extended beyond interlocuters governed by Haiti's colonial past, including France and the Francophone world, and intersected with women who were similarly navigating multiple overlapping diasporas. LFAS women's political journey intersects with the history of Black women's internationalism in the early and mid-twentieth century. Like Black women throughout the Caribbean, Europe, Africa, and North America, these Black women leveraged their education and resources for their national work and extended that work into a shared sphere of African diasporic politics.

However, the LFAS women's domestic performance and focus on intellectual development and labor meant that in the first two decades of organizing, their public attention to race and color was less pronounced. Women's travel, study, struggle, connection, and disconnection with women and men throughout the African diaspora offered these women opportunities to experiment with their race politics. This global formulation, from the early moments of organizing under US foreign rule to Suzanne Comhaire-Sylvain's research in colonized Belgian Congo, revealed the ways in which women sought to understand the conditions of citizenship for women in Haiti while being outside the nation. The chapter considers how LFAS members used public performances and theater to authenticate their citizenship and draw themselves physically closer to ideas of Blackness in international presentations in Germany, Buenos Aires, and the southern United States. Here, I consider how Haitian women's international politics and transnational experiences of race and class informed their understanding and strategic use of race in national contexts. The discussion of the idea of Blackness and Haitian identity in the diaspora in chapter 4 is continued in chapter 5 with the history of the women's participation in the 1956–57 Haitian election season. In the political milieu of Black nationalist rhetoric and the women's own evolution in thinking about race, the chapter shows how LFAS women strategically communicated political unity among women by declaring a shared *nègre* identity. With a national platform that articulated the intersection of race, class, and gender, Haitian women's politics turned and collided into the rise and presidency of François Duvalier (1957–71).

In addition to traditional chapters, *White Gloves, Black Nation* is also told through three dwelling spaces. Akin to a wayfarer's daydream, these breaks stand to hold important affective and sentient space for locating these women's political practice and lives. "A Bridge," "A Pilgrimage," and "A Feeling" echo M. Jacqui Alexander's charge to "chart the failures of anticolonial nationalism and decolonization movements to take seriously the psychic and pedagogical aspects of decolonization" and "the conscious and ongoing reproduction of the terms of one's existence while taking responsibility for this process."[125] In *White Gloves, Black Nation* these psychic aspects happen within the larger national and global context of radical politics, Black internationalism, and anticolonialism, but they also happen interpersonally and internally between and within women. These nonchapters map political locations that often go historically unmarked, like grief, whimsical curiosity, and insecurity, as a reminder of the multiple registers of history and the pace of a wayfaring political practice.

White Gloves, Black Nation ends with an invitation to interrogate the multiple ways to encounter Haitian women's political history. Haitian feminists in the early twentieth century shared leadership, practiced a regional and national politics, and gestured toward the peasant majority, but they were not singularly preoccupied with them. Their leadership was not romantic, their philosophies were complicated, and their practice was evolving. They were often unable to see beyond their privileged class-cultural lens on the world, and they were aware of this blindness even if they were sometimes unable to grasp the depths and contours of the darkness. However, their collective body

Alice Garoute (front center, dark dress) and schoolteachers, including Lydia Jeanty, passing through the crowd and the Garde d'Haiti [*sic*] Headquarters during the 1946 Revolution, January 11, 1946. "Haitian Revolution photographed by Byron Coroneos, January 7–11, 1946," Manuscripts, Archives and Rare Books Division, Schomburg Center for Research in Black Culture Archives, The New York Public Library.

of work, including research notes, personal letters, speeches, and prose, reveals that wrestling with differences was central to these women's intellectual study and political formulation even when it was less apparent in their practice.[126] In their work these women invited deep reflexivity that named, if only parenthetically, the overlapping systems of class, color, and culture that operated between Haitian and African-descended women.

White Gloves, Black Nation submits that early twentieth-century Haitian feminists' work troubled the conceptual foundations and afterlives of "the revolution" as an uncomplicated rhetorical and institutionalized touch-point for freedom. This framing benefits from Michel-Rolph Trouillot's charge to question and, when possible, resist the exceptional representations, theories, and histories of Haiti. It is important to state, then, that Haiti is no exception. Feminists, feminism, and those attached to these personal and political subjectivities have failed to meet the possibilities of their visions, and have historically, simultaneously harmed and helped women with whom they claimed collectivity but who did not always claim them. In particular, women of African descent have had fraught and often painful relationships with feminisms that cannot and refuse to see their experiences as intimate, intersectional, local, and global.[127]

Building on Caribbean feminist scholarship that invites constant wrestling with postcolonial politics, this book is attuned to how women in the early and mid-twentieth century ultimately used feminism as a portal to engage or disengage with the conditions of modern citizenship and sovereignty.[128] It presents a story of women's political practice at the gritty margins—the generative space of multiple contacts and possibilities—of women's curation, participation, production, and consumption of the archive.[129] It uses this space and practice to understand the promise of women's life experiences both individually and collectively in the early twentieth century.

CHAPTER ONE

Rites of Passage

In the meantime, one morning the American Marines arrived on our shores, taking control of the police station, the Customs House, the Public Works and the Sanitation Department. They dismissed some and appointed others . . . and little by little we got used to the khaki uniforms worn by the Americans and our policemen. . . . Right away I faced countless difficulties, I was only nineteen years old.
—Marie Vieux Chauvet, *Amour, colère, et folie* (1968)

We see that the Haitian woman was literally transformed.
—Madeleine Sylvain-Bouchereau, *Haiti et ses femmes* (1957)

A theory in the flesh means one where the physical realities of our lives—our skin color, the land or concrete we grew up on, our sexual longings—all fuse to create a politic born out of necessity.
—Cherríe Moraga, *This Bridge Called My Back* (1983)

Ghislaine saw boiled lobsters washed up on the shores of her hometown of Jérémie when she was eight years old. They had been there for close to a decade and a half, but she had not noticed. When they arrived in 1915, they were pink and raw. Years after their coastal invasion, the Caribbean sea and sun had baked them to a scaly burnt red. Ghislaine and her sister, Henrietta, rarely interacted with them, but when the girls passed them in the streets they laughed among themselves, as Ghislaine still did eighty-two years later, mouth covered and body leaned in to embrace her jest.[1]

She was a girl then, and the "boiled lobsters" were the US Marines, military personnel, businesspeople, and families who made an official invasion of Haiti in the middle of 1915. They had been circling the ports and establishing business connections with the Haitian merchant elite for the first decade of the century before the invasion. Had Ghislaine spent more time with her favorite Aunt Claira (her father's sister), who ran a small import-export business, maybe she would have seen them more often. Maybe she would have noticed that her aunt and her employees hurried their pace around 4:45 P.M., as "natives" were not allowed on the docks after 5:00 P.M. But she didn't start trailing behind Aunt Claira and playing on the bows of cargo ships until she was nine, ten, or eleven years old, and then, she fondly remembered, once accompanying Aunt Claira on a date with a US Marine. Her aunt told her it was a game. Aunt Claira played with men and never married because she did not want any man to have access to her money. If he took her money, she would lose her freedom, and so might Ghislaine, since Aunt Claira's income supplemented her brother's (Ghislaine's father) income. It was all fun and all quite serious.

It was on the port that Auntie Claira "ran," on July 28, 1915, that US president Woodrow Wilson ordered the officers to leave their ships already docked in Port-au-Prince and forcefully invade the capital. The Wilson administration characterized the military occupation as the Caribbean frontier of World War I. According to the administration, Haiti's proximity to the United States and the presence of some 250 German merchants in the country made the nation a potential breeding ground for anti-Allied forces. Additionally, the assassination of Haitian president Vilbrun Guillaume Sam on July 27, 1915, was, for Wilson, the final example of Haiti's weak state structure. The concern for Allied interests and political stability in the region was coupled with the longstanding US paternalistic and racist belief that Haitians were incapable of governing their own nation.[2] To show Haitians how to govern and stabilize state operations, Wilson and his supporters initiated the military occupation with plans to strengthen Haiti's political and physical infrastructure through government restructuring, foreign investment banking, and the construction of schools, roads, and railways.[3]

Born in 1918, the same year that Wilson dissolved the Haitian national assembly and rewrote the constitution, Ghislaine was among the many young people known as the "occupation generation," who grew up under foreign rule in Haiti. As far as she could remember, the lobsters' presence was "not that pronounced" in Jérémie, on the southwest side of the country, and they did not bother her, but they consumed the energy of the adults around her. Her maternal grandparents were particularly unnerved by them. Ghislaine's Grandmère Alice told and retold the stories of their family's decisions to resist the occupation. Grandmère's favorite story was one that showcased her influence on the men around her. As she told it to Ghislaine, several months before the crustaceans arrived, Grandmère Alice sent a letter to her childhood comrade Louis Borno, minister of foreign affairs and justice and future president (1922–30). After sharing the recent events of her life, she strongly encouraged Borno to consider nominating her husband, Auguste Garoute, "a man of valor and good integrity," for the Tribunal de Cassation, the supreme or final court of appeal in Haiti.[4] Before the end of Borno's term as minister of foreign affairs and justice in February 1915, Auguste was appointed as a judge on the highest court in the country. Within months of his appointment,

Grandpère Auguste was petitioned to sign the Haitian-American treaty of September 16, 1915, that would diplomatically allow the lobsters' arrival. Grandpère Auguste and "Monsieur Cabeche" were the only two representatives who refused to sign the protectorate.[5] The men were outnumbered in their dissent, and the United States was granted governmental and military authority over Haiti.

The Garoute family celebrated Grandpère Auguste's refusal. Ghislaine sat quietly nearby while Grandmère Alice shared the story with her friends as she offered them tea, read books, put on small plays, and discussed how to remove the foreigners. These women would later lead a series of antioccupation protests planned out in Grandmère Alice's salon, and by the end of the occupation, in 1935, Alice Garoute and some of her guests would found the Ligue Féminine d'Action Sociale (LFAS). But at the time, the clanking of teacups and saucers at her grandmother's gatherings became a natural accompaniment to the strange beings' clamoring. Ghislaine's account of her grandmother, and the "mother" of the Haitian feminist movement, Alice Garoute, backchanneling her grandfather's political position and "voting" against the US protectorate and occupation is an example of the tactics Haitian women used to influence the nation's governance long before an official women's movement was established. Her account also uniquely captures the perspective of the young girls who would mature into young adults and lead the women's movement. This chapter focuses on the experience and transformation of the lives of young girls under the US occupation and how they and the women around them were drawn into political organizing.

In 1941, seven years after the official withdrawal of the US military from Haiti, one of those girls, Madeleine Sylvain-Bouchereau, the first president of the women's rights organization LFAS, took stock of the passage and pacing of time for women under the occupation. Sylvain-Bouchereau was ten years old when the US military arrived in Haiti. She was born into a "distinguished family in the famous Black Republic" on July 5, 1905. Her mother and father, Eugénie and Georges Sylvain, were leaders of the antioccupation organization Union Patriotique (UP).[6] Along with her sisters, Suzanne, Yvonne, and Jeanne, Madeleine witnessed her mother and her mother's friends, like Grandmère Alice, fundraise to support the antioccupation movement and study the history of the nation. In 1941 she was doing her own studying at Bryn Mawr College School of Social Work outside Philadelphia (United States).[7] There, she took the time away from her responsibilities as LFAS president to reflect on the social status of women and the history of women's political organizing in Haiti.

Sylvain-Bouchereau's time in Philadelphia was celebrated by the major US African American media outlets, including the *Chicago Tribune* and the *Pittsburgh Courier*, which reported on the "Haitian girl" who scored a "meritorious victory" for all Haitian women when she earned her fellowship.[8] In her late thirties with a law degree from the University of Haiti (1933), Sylvain-Bouchereau was not a girl, but she was using the opportunity to write about the political maturation of Haitian women that mirrored her own growing up during the early twentieth century. Her work, which was later published as *Haiti et ses femmes* (1951), spanned the precolonial era of Ayiti, through the colonial period of Saint Domingue, into the revolution, and ended in the 1950s. In the "brief and incomplete" tome of 250 pages, Sylvain-Bouchereau compiled surveys, ethnographic studies, and histories from throughout the half-island, most frequently citing her sisters' research. She also documented the history of the LFAS. Among the details about organizational achievements and setbacks, philosophical differences, and political shortcomings, she also identifies the US occupation as a catalyst for the Haitian women's movement.

In the wake of the occupation, in which women were targeted for physical and sexual violence and used as political negotiating tools, Sylvain-Bouchereau accounted for the transformative experiences of life during the occupation. Documenting the ways women took advantage of financial and social opportunities and organized in clandestine and public ways against and for the US presence, Sylvain-Bouchereau concludes, "In analyzing these facts, we see that the Haitian woman was literally transformed. [She] evolved, more educated, often economically independent, accepting her social responsibilities. . . . Women could not fail to realize the inferior situation that was imposed on them in their nation, [and] aspire to the freedom granted to [their] overseas sisters."[9] In Sylvain-Bouchereau's assessment, women attained postoccupation resources and political consciousness, and she maintained that before the foreign invasion, "Feminism was unknown in Haiti. Although women played a considerable role in Haiti, they never thought to come together around a collective action for the revindication of their rights."[10] In pairing the experience of occupation with political, economic, and physical awakening, Sylvain-Bouchereau casts a wide net to account for Haitian women's transformational experience during and after the US occupation. She also established a political chronology echoed in Haitian women's history that marks the immediate postoccupation period as a "renaissance for Haitian women" and the LFAS as the manifestation of that rebirth.[11]

While education, financial freedoms, and renewed engagement in state politics were outcomes of the occupation for some women, other women were grieved, and harmed in physical, emotional, and socioeconomic ways by the occupation, which did not afford an evident postoccupation renaissance. As LFAS member and future vice president, Maud Desvarieux, later communicated in her essay, "Lived Pedagogy," about the history of women's political organizing, even for those who did experience a political revitalization, "the American occupation of 1915–1934 was a demoralizing agent."[12] Considering the differing and interrelated experiences and resonances of the occupation, Sylvain-Bouchereau's emphasis on women's shared experience of change during the period warrants consideration.

As young girls born into and growing up under occupation, these women were physically and cognitively transforming, maturing, and developing new senses of being. The stories that women told, retold, and historicized during and after the occupation reflect both coming-of-age tales and adolescent expressions of desire, dissent, and experimentation.[13] Read as both political history and autobiographical synthesis, Sylvain-Bouchereau's emphasis on women being *littéralement transformée* invites a focus on the process of women's transformation. Her use of *littéralement* points toward a totalizing physiological and material shift for Haitian women—in body, in flesh, in relationship to one another, and to the material and ametaphysicality of their world—a rite of passage. Focusing on the quotidian transformation, rather than the presumed shared experiences as women, this chapter traces the occupation as an accumulation, an altering of being in relation to the state. It attends to the archival record of women's physical transformations to account for the physical and psychological duress of the occupation for some women, and also account for the ways in which women educated, trained, and supported one another through a season of maturation. Tracing women's different occupation experiences through the military records of infrastructural development, I draw an image of what the occupation felt like (tactile, by touch) and how these feelings (the accumulation of tactile engagement with the occupation) rendered literal change.

The seemingly static and formulaic construction reports from the US military's work on over 500 miles of roads, bridges, and railways in Haiti offer one record of women's subtle and cumulative experiences of occupation.[14] In the process of building, reconstructing, and monitoring these thoroughfares, the occupation administration not only produced an abundant archive of the invaded landscape, but they also recorded other outcomes. In the side notes and mundane descriptions of their work, their casual references reveal women altered and were altered by the occupation. The banality of documentation threatens to flatten the recurring reports of women's raised, punctured, lacerated, and dismembered flesh at the hands of occupation personnel's vile intent and frequent recklessness. In what Marisa Fuentes has identified as a "mutilated historicity," Haitian women overwhelmingly "appear in the archive disfigured and violated" leaving us with a "degraded" historicization of the occupation in which "flesh injuries are the remains with which we must construct their history."[15]

Lingering at the intersection of women's injury and the record of occupation landscape there is also evidence of women suturing the multiple shifts in personal and physical environment into new and particular articulations of themselves and the nation. In his discussion of Haiti's sovereignty during the US occupation, Haitian geographer and poet Georges Anglade argues that understanding the impact of the occupation involves the consideration of how capitalist development at the beginning of the twentieth century necessitates "a new configuration of natural space" in political, philosophical, and historical understandings of the nation.[16] In this chapter I locate this new configuration alongside women's physical and political transformation and reconfiguration. In so doing, I show how young women used transient encounters in the variable occupation landscape as a means to clarify assumptions about their identity, experiment with social boundaries, refuse claims on them, and test the perceived normalization of the occupation's power that would translate into a postoccupation politics.

Occupation Generation

Like many children who grew up during the US occupation, Ghislaine Charlier made sense of what she was seeing, hearing, and experiencing within her logic. Ghislaine saw the foreigners more often in Port-au-Prince, where she regularly traveled and attended school. Although they were not physically present in her schools, she observed a connection between the boiled lobsters and her foreign white teachers, who were "color and class prejudiced, even to children."[17] Ghislaine was reared in a wealthy family of antioccupation organizers, and by the time she noticed the military presence, her description reflected an overexposure to the sun mirrored by the extended stay of an occupation that had lasted over a decade and would continue for another. She was not alone in her assessment of the sunburned occupiers' skin resemblance to cooked crustaceans. Other young people who grew up during the US occupation also made this observation. Novelist Marie Vieux Chauvet, who was born in 1916 and wrote her first piece of fiction when she was twelve, used the terminology "boiled lobster" to describe the appearance of the American invaders. In her 1961 trilogy, the phrasing appears in the mouth of her nineteen-year-old protagonist Claire, who remarks, "It's my birthday today, and we are literally being cooked alive, and M. Long [the US American] looks like a boiled lobster."[18]

For some children it was the foreigners' skin; for others it was their funny speech patterns, their lack of manners, or seemingly basic misunderstanding of social inclusions and exceptions that made the occupiers' presence curious. Ghislaine, for example, was clear that social stratification and color prejudice existed in Haiti prior to the occupation, "that the petite bourgeoisie were envious of the bourgeoisie, and that they were accused of rejecting *les noirs*." A light brown–skinned girl, she did not feel this way about class envy or *les noirs*, but she knew that Jérémie, the city of poets and historic homes, was also known "even in colonial time as a centre of the most bitter racial and colour prejudice."[19] Even Grandmère Alice had to climb her way into social acceptance in the city. Still, Ghislaine found it odd that adults would include children in this practice.

Children from the period recount memories of oddity and familiarity with the foreign military presence in Haiti. Flag-raising ceremonies at school and learning American quips and practicing them with peers were a part of digesting the random sounds, sights, and rumors of a nation under siege. For example, the vivid adolescent memory of activist Jean Dominique is captured in his writings and those of his daughter J. J. Dominique, who recounts that her grandfather forbade her father to pledge allegiance to the stars and stripes that flew over his school in Port-au-Prince.[20] Or the horrifying account of author Edwidge Danticat's uncle, who, upon walking down the street as a child, saw some marines playing what he thought was soccer. The game was familiar, suggesting that the foreigners might not be the monsters his parents had described them to be. Only as he got closer did he realize that the strange-shaped ball they were kicking was a man's head.[21]

Stories like these suggest that the occupation presence invaded children's experiences and imaginary in subtle and spectacular ways. From the earliest days of the occupation, a casual walk down the street like the ones Ghislaine and her sister took could quickly become life altering for children and adults alike. On the morning of August 26, 1915, one month after the foreign marines arrived, Caroline Dagille sent the "age 17 or 19"-year-old Ludowick Jeudi to run her morning errands near the corner of Rue du Pont and Rue Oswald Durand in Cap-Haïtien. That same morning Louie Joseph, "a Haitian negro," was in the military's regional headquarters, which was housed in the railroad station on Rue du Pont. Joseph was accused of stealing a woman's cow. When the woman arrived to make her report, Joseph saw his accuser and ran. Running west, Joseph was halfway across the bridge when Corporal Fred Parsons drew his gun and shot twice in Joseph's direction. The street was busy, but "after the first shot was fired the street was practically cleared of people only for a few children that were on the west side of the bridge and they ducked." Joseph stopped and surrendered.[22]

Ludowick, who had just turned onto Rue du Pont, also stopped. "[Ludowick] was hit, and he turned and ran along the Rue Oswald Durand until he dropped at the point where his body was found." When Dagille found Ludowick, the young man was sitting "in a chair against a building on the Rue Oswald Durand, about 200 yards from the Rue du Point," his cooling flesh slowly matching the temperature of the wall behind him interrupted by the warmth of Dagille's touch. Ludowick's parents lived in the country and had entrusted Dagille with his safety, but as the autopsy report revealed, the bullet's trajectory left little chance for survival.[23] From the witness statements, US military officials concluded that "death probably occurred about 8:30 A.M.," yet according to the military reports, "None of the natives present could state the time definitely."[24]

Between walking down the street and falling to the ground, into a chair, or onto one another, away from severe injury or death, children surely lost track of time. Seconds slowed to minutes, hours, and days, and the morning likely passed in a flash as young people crouched down, calves shaking from the combination of mortal fear and the quickened muscular contractions of squatting too fast and too long as overzealous bullets flew. As these children were forced into maturity, their time was calculated by the random death of a peer whose proximity—a small bridge width away—both hastened and retarded the days' lapse. In these ways, the occupation was disorienting for many children and adults. For a disproportionate number of young Haitians and their loved ones, the occupation was measured by the accumulation of subtle grips, brushes, grabs, and gentle holds alongside abrupt violence. As Dagille determined what to do with the lifeless body of the young man who had been released, now twice, into her care, other children "hid in the folds of [their] mother's skirt."[25]

The furrow of the occupation in the lives of young Haitians in the early twentieth century was pleated along physical, emotional, psychological, and spatial lines. As a geopolitical event, the occupation was an experiment in US imperialism and paternalistic regional practices, as well as an accelerant to the Haitian military state.[26] After President Vilbrun Guillaume Sam's death and the US invasion in 1915, Phillippe Dartiguenave was named president.

Dartiguenave served in the executive position, overseen by the US military, for some of the most violent years of the occupation. But by 1922, Dartiguenave was frustrated with his weakened presidential position and expressed his disapproval of the US government moving Haitian money to US banks. Recognizing his growing dissent, the US government ousted Dartiguenave and appointed Louis Borno president of Haiti alongside US major general John H. Russell as high commissioner. The Borno and Russell government oversaw, ignored, and denied the violence of the occupation with both men as uneven but overextended arms of US presidents Warren G. Harding (1921–23) and then Calvin Coolidge (1923–29).

This foreign governance was also, as historian Raphael Dalleo has asserted, "an aberration in the teleology of revolutionary sovereignty" in Haiti and throughout the region in which new ways of imagining, being, and relating to the nation and one's fellow citizens emerged.[27] As a nineteen-year-long event, the occupation was painfully and other times ambiguously woven into the quotidian experience of Haitian life. As communicated in Marie Vieux Chauvet's depiction of the occupation, "*In the meantime*, one morning the American Marines arrived on our shores, taking control of the police station, the Customs House, the Public Works and the Sanitation Department. They dismissed some and appointed others . . . *and little by little* we got used to the khaki uniforms worn by the Americans and our policemen." The interim period of "in the meantime" coupled with the slow familiarity and then immediacy of her following statement, "*Right away* I faced countless difficulties. I was only nineteen years old," relays a complex pacing of time that was testified to and witnessed by young people and caretakers throughout various occupation records.[28]

Maturing and Moving through the Occupation Landscape

When the children dropped to the ground, and Ludowick lost his life, and Dagille went searching for him, "a corporal who was measuring the road asked [a private], 'who [is] shooting?'"[29] As an unwieldy experiment of US empire making, the first five years of the occupation were notoriously violent. Much of the violence was directly related to the construction of and surveillance over Haiti's transportation routes and infrastructure.[30] The roads and railways charted by the US military were used to penetrate the nation for easier transport of goods and military arms and to monitor dissent toward the foreign occupiers. This development was systematized. Across the nation, US military corporals measured, mapped, and reported on the conditions of the roads every ten days. In this process they reported on the living conditions of Haitians throughout the nation and casually accounted for their invasion of the space. As one report describing an area in St. Marc read, "Native houses scattered along the way could billet from 2 to 8 men apiece. There are no good camp sites due to the low and wooded nature of the ground."[31]

In reams of reports, the US military mapped the topography of the nation alongside its observations of potential opposition: "All sections quiet," "No bandit activities," or plans for their own attacks, "The nature of the country surrounding the two miles of river bed would make ambushing very easy."[32] The unpredictable events of the US occupation occurred alongside the highly calculated and mundane practice of measuring, building, and surveying Haitian land and citizens. In the occupation archives the detailed descriptions of Haitian topography as it related to military construction projects and combat with citizens are underscored by the vivid record of "necessary" and "unavoidable" deaths, autopsies, and court testimonies related to these roads. In the records of violent incidents and of transportation construction and surveillance, women's lives, care, work, and transformation were captured.

The scenarios for women's encounter with the project of occupation happened in various ways. Much of the violence on roads in the first three years, however, was related to the forced labor of the corvée system. Under this system, individuals accused of a crime or those who failed to pay their property taxes or for vending licenses could be forced to work on government construction projects without compensation, bringing harsh labor, long work hours, injury, and even death. The corvée system was a modern Haitian law that recalled the French colonial and immediate postrevolutionary period.[33] The French used the law as an additive to the system of chattel enslavement to build the infrastructure of Saint-Domingue, and Haiti's third head of state, Emperor Henry Christophe, used the system to build the roads that facilitated the construction of the Citadelle and the defense of the new nation against French postcolonial incursion.

Under the leadership of US Navy officer Major Smedley Butler, the US military revived the corvée system to expand its presence throughout the nation. For the US military and champions of the occupation, the rapid construction and reconstruction of roads and railways in the first decade of the occupation were celebrated.[34] However, the expansive infrastructural growth was not favorably reviewed by all. One critic surmised that the corvée system was a military chain gang designed to reinstitute slavery on the island. Indeed, in responding to praise regarding the rapid road construction, Major Butler wrote to future US president Franklin D. Roosevelt, then assistant secretary of the US Navy, "It would not do to ask too many questions about how we do this work."[35] There was no transparency about the corvée system, and conscription was indiscriminate. There is little evidence of women working in the corvée system, but there were no laws that prevented women from being forced into this labor. As a result, women and men altered their behaviors, travel routes, and interpersonal plans in response to the threat of this punishment. People went out of their way to avoid the streets, walking long distances "in the strange light of the undergrowth" in the mountains and across unoccupied roads to move through the country.[36]

The brutality and surveillance that accompanied the corvée system heightened many Haitian frustrations and discontent with the US presence in Haiti and encouraged others to swell the ranks of antioccupation movements, including the political and military-focused *cacos* and the more diplomatically oriented Union Patriotique. The *cacos* had existed in various forms since Haitian independence and fought on behalf of causes and government leadership that maintained the nation's sovereignty, often referring to their decades of differently aligned combat as fighting for the "revolution."[37] Within the first four years of the US occupation, *caco* soldiers and loyalists numbered around 5,000, and as one *caco* soldier wrote in July 1919, the "public opinion [was] more and more with the revolution."[38] Under the leadership of Charlemagne Péralte and Benoît Batraville, the tactical organization was drawn from combat strategies used by Jean-Jacques Dessalines in the early nineteenth century, and units were active throughout the country with a focus on the central and northern regions of the nation. The armed combat between *cacos* and the US Marines and corvée work conditions led to over 2,250 Haitian deaths in the first decade of the occupation. Many of these deaths were in armed combat, but others were at the hands of overzealous, predatory, and careless acts of the US Marines. For young people growing up, deaths like Ludowick's reminded children that their safety could be compromised without reason or notice.

While some people bypassed major roads to avoid conscription into the corvée system, women remained disproportionately visible on the roads. As market vendors, caregivers, landowners, business proprietors, and domestic servants who had to travel to conduct the business of their homes and of other women's homes, not only were women in the street, but they were also captured as a part of the occupation landscape.[39] Images from military official records and from marines' personal archives routinely capture the landscape with, for example, "a typical country woman riding a burro."[40] In this case, even young people, like those on the bridge or Ghislaine, were familiar with women being fused into the aesthetic of occupied space.

Women's presence on public roads was common and often unquestioned. Some men used this familiarity for their own protection. In a confidential military report of "political activity" near Cap-Haïtien, an imprisoned *caco* leader revealed that another higher-ranking soldier, General Theophil, had just completed a full tour of the north, visiting almost every town for recruitment of *caco* soldiers. The informant shared that "Theophil was disguised in dress of a market woman, [and] usually travelled with a buro [*sic*]."[41] Theophil was not alone in this practice. According to the interrogation report, "The prisoner further stated that he had seen General Petit Severe who told him that he had in possess—seven buro [*sic*] loads of rifles, which are now near Cape Haitien [*sic*], and had been brought across the border, with plenty of ammunition, and more was coming. He said Petit Severe was a fugitive from justice in Cape Haïtien [*sic*], but that he, Petit Severe, came in and out of town as he pleased, always disguised as a market woman."[42] In this case, the gender performance facilitated a *caco* attack on US military officers. The frequency with which observers recall seeing women and the apparent ease with which *caco* members transported weapons and conducted national and international (Dominican Republic) recruitment could communicate a banal image of women in the streets.

However, regular visibility on roads functioned as an advantage and a disadvantage to girls and women during the US occupation. While guerrilla fighters used women's presence in the streets as strategy, young girls and women still had to move strategically in public. Young girls and women traveled in groups to ensure safety. As a different *caco* informant revealed, in some cases, as of the wife of *caco* leader Benoît, it was everyday protocol for women to stay together: "Mme. Benoit goes very often to Mirebalais, Lascaobas, and Port au Prince to buy supplies. As a rule there are a number of other market women with her. . . . She rides a big Bay colored mule, and always carries a revolver underneath her dress."[43] Forced to reconcile the volatility of occupation life and the targeted threats to her kin, Mme. Benoit also used the well-worn images of women in transit to camouflage her technologies of defense.

Yet even when they took precautions, women could not always avoid unprovoked confrontation. At dusk on September 1, 1919, Eleanor Charles and her mother, Elizabeth Saint-Bernard, walked home from an extended day of vending and shopping at the Gonaïves *marché*. Carrying their extra produce, the teenager and her mother traveled the six-mile stretch of road between the market and their home in Petite Rivière des Bayonnais.[44] As they made their way toward "the iron bridge on the St. Marc road," Private Edward Paul Pietszak drove up next to them and instructed the mother and daughter to get into his car. Eleanor and her mother immediately ran in the opposite direction. But Private Pietszak caught Eleanor. She dropped the day's produce. She testified that he "dragged her into the bushes" that lined the street. Her dress and skin were torn. After Pietszak raped Eleanor, he placed one gourde into her "bruise[d] and lacerat[ed]" hand.[45] The currency exchange allowed Pietszak to maintain that the sexual assault was a paid transaction.[46]

Eleanor's dress was mended or thrown away, and her broken flesh likely healed, but as evidenced in Saint-Bernard's petition to the courts for "one hundred gourdes damage on the grounds that the girl has lost her reputation and it will be difficult for her to get work to do," the women's lives were altered.[47] Even if paid, the financial compensation could not restore her daughter's reputation, body, or psyche to a preattack condition. Eleanor and Saint-Bernard represented the most vulnerable citizens of the military occupation.[48] Their lives necessitated a regular presence in the streets. As market women, farmers, servants, schoolgirls, and traveling family, these women's livelihood placed them in direct view of US Marines' public surveillance. In their journeys to, from, and during work, these women traversed roads of the country, where they were exposed and least protected against the unwanted solicitation of foreign and Haitian men.[49]

Young girls and women's safety had been tenuous before the occupation. But under the occupation, this public vulnerability reiterated differences between women and their social status, gender divisions, and the quotidian manifestations of an occupied state. While some middle-class women worked as secretaries or schoolteachers, for many wealthy families physical labor outside the home, and the frequent presence in the street that this necessitated was prohibited for girls and women. For these families movement in the street marked women's exposure to compromised sexual morality. Most elite women were given a Catholic education and were taught social etiquette, sexual conservatism, and public piety.[50] Elite girls and women were discouraged from public labor that would expose them to the unsupervised solicitation of men, or worse, allow space for them to indulgence in their own sexual desires. Most simply, women's different relationships to public space were communicated in the experiences of walking to work or from the market, walking leisurely or to school, or being barred from moving in public space all together. At all social levels, however, control of and violence against women was not met with accountability by those enacting the harm in physical, legal, and discursive ways, but instead women were met with blame, shame, and further vulnerability regarding their movements.

The introduction of more military vehicles and soldiers driving them put women at even greater risk. Eleanor and Elizabeth were running from a man in a military-issued vehicle in order to avoid being taken into it, but military personnel's reckless driving and an increase in military vehicles on the modified roads also threatened women's physical safety. During the 1921 US Senate hearings regarding the occupation, African American orator and visitor to Haiti James Weldon Johnson testified to his skepticism regarding the benefits of the new roads:

> In fact, in some instances, the road is a drawback to the Haitian farmer. I went over the road and I saw an automobile frighten a market woman. She was on one mule, and she had a horse loaded down with all her produce going to market, and her child was on another one, and the horse got frightened and ran and scattered all her produce from one end of the road to the other. . . . When these automobiles come along, these poor people scramble up the sides of the mountains, or down the declivities, trying to get out of the way. . . . I do not think [the road] is worth quite that much to the Haitian farmer who is trying to get his produce to town.[51]

While Johnson may have overstated the inefficiency of the newly constructed roads, his account of the market woman's experience transporting her produce and her children is instructive. In transit, women and children's livelihoods and lives could be quickly destabilized.

The occasional automobile accident was a probable consequence of the increasingly transient world of the twentieth century. Yet the collision between occupied and occupiers often provided subtle revelations about the conditions and meaning of the occupation for Haitian woman. In particular the record of accidents on the roads offers an image of the bodily injury that altered women's physical reality during the occupation. On Tuesday, September 5, 1917, Adirenng Senatus from Jacmel testified that "between 9:30 and 10 o'clock I tried to cross the street near the open market [in Port-au-Prince]. I was carrying a basket of fruit and a package. I stepped from behind a sprinkler wagon when something struck me. I do not remember anything after that until I reached the hospital." When she woke up, Adirenng had "a laceration on [her] left leg just above the knee externally, about six inches long," "a deep laceration of [the] lower left leg internally about twelve inches in length. Numerous contusions of left foot, and a contusion under the right eye." Adirenng's body was violently altered. She had been hit by a Quartermasters mortar truck driven by Private Sterling R. Hold, USMC. Private Hold testified that he did not see Adirenng and that he was driving "carefully and slowly" at the moment of the crash, and Adirenng stated that she had no reason to believe that Private Hold hit her on purpose. Hold further testified, "This accident was unavoidable and was not due to any carelessness on [his] part," and the court agreed.[52] As a singular incident, Adirenng's accident seems unfortunate, but in the context of other accidents on the road her injury and ultimate death expose US officials' beliefs about Haitians' capacity to render their own bodies and move, as well as Haitian women's rejection of those beliefs.

Several reports from automobile or horse accidents on the road provide evidence that US officials generally endorsed the idea that Haitians did not know how to move. In a case several months after Adirenng's, a pedestrian named Joseph Jean was hit with "a glancing blow" by the shoulder of Captain Mayer's horse.[53] During the incident inquiry the leading investigator asked several military witnesses questions including, "Can you state whether the natives of Port-au-Prince as a whole seem to be careless of their persons while on the streets as pedestrians, or do they show the same care that is shown by people in the States?" Furthering the leading questions, the investigator continued, "Considering the fact that you were present when the accident occurred do you believe that the man was knocked down through his own carelessness or through the carelessness of Captain Mayer?" The witnesses respectively replied, "Through the man's own carelessness" and "his lack of judgment by not stepping back behind the cart." The inquiry concluded that the "accident was wholly unavoidable," and more, that Port-au-Princians were predisposed to personal endangerment and negligible concern for their own bodies.[54] In Adirenng's case, the court even presented medical records to insinuate that she was mentally unwell.

Although articulated as "unavoidable," road accidents were not banal incidents of happenstance. Rather, these moments were maddening and violent referendums on Haitian bodies and ways of being. On the night of May 9, 1922, Estrea Jean Gilles, a nineteen-year-old market woman, was hit by a car driven by US first lieutenant John A. Tebbs as she walked along L Street in Cap-Haïtien. Gilles suffered serious injuries, "at the left ankle joint, the ligaments of which had been ruptured and the lower end of the tibia had been thrust through the skin at the inner side of the joint. The fibula was fractured in the lower third. In addition to the wound through which the tibia protruded there were a few slight abrasions about each knee, right shoulder, right arm and right little finger, contusion right side of the back."[55] She was literally transformed. She was also hospitalized, and a court of inquiry proceeding was initiated to determine Lieutenant Tebbs's culpability in the accident. During witness testimony, Colonel George Van Ordan, the first military official on the scene, testified that Tebbs must have been driving at a reasonable speed and shown an effort to stop his car before hitting Gilles, because if the Haitian bystanders believed he was driving recklessly, the accident would have provoked an immediate outcry from people in the street.

Van Ordan's assessment suggests the street was a site of public dissent, a place where Haitians and US military officials alike were familiar with the collective display of acceptance and refusal of the occupation.[56] His account also repeats the discourse of irrationality as he recounted, "I have several times come near to striking pedestrians due to their erratic movements." As Van Ordan failed to follow Haitians' movements, it is also possible that the absence of a public outcry following Gilles's maiming did not necessarily mean the absence of dissent. Objection to the occupation was not limited to organized, or even spontaneous, protests. In a more quotidian way, women used transient encounters as a means to establish their public character beyond the dehumanizing discourses circulated by occupation officials. For example, in the hospital after the car accident, Gilles gave a statement regarding the crash. She explained that she had been suffering from a toothache on the day of the accident and was self-medicating by rinsing her mouth with *tafia*, a local alcohol. She did not know how the crash occurred but concluded, "I don't drink." Gilles seemed less concerned with attributing blame for her injuries—a broken and later amputated left leg—and more concerned with documenting that intoxication was neither her intent nor her habit. Perhaps because Gilles knew that witnesses smelled alcohol on her at the scene of the accident and presumed that this could be used, as it was, to tarnish her character and corroborate stereotypes of Haitian women, Gilles's declaration was an active defense against an alteration of her character.

Estrea, like Eleanor, Elizabeth, and Adirenng, was grasping at self-representation. At nineteen years old, she was likely aware of the sometimes crippling social stratification in early twentieth-century Haiti.[57] As a market woman, her desire to establish her character was not necessarily geared to elite sensibilities, nor did her values necessarily reflect status aspiration.[58] As Carolle Charles argues, working-class and poor Haitian women historically defined for themselves meanings of respectability and uses of their bodies.[59] Conceivably, Estrea was defending her character so that she could remain a trusted saleswoman in the very streets where she was hit.[60] Estrea's collision with the occupation highlights both the symbolic and literal ways that women were transformed by the occupation. As US occupiers considered such collisions "unavoidable," or the result of Haitian women's being "careless," they thus turned Haitian women's disfigured flesh and bones into oddities while sanctioning the bodily injury and ultimate death of Adirenng, Estrea, and others.[61] The way women and men used and engaged with the occupied space—walking or simply being in it—justified their extinction. Accidents did happen, but the condition of these accidents—nineteen years of foreign occupation and the discourse that Haitians were predisposed to and culpable for their own injury and deaths—exemplified the everyday amplification of anti-Haitian violence and nonsovereignty during the occupation.[62]

Altered Awareness and Women's Occupation Knowledge

The testimonies of Caroline, Eleanor, Estrea, and Adirenng are among the few archival traces in the already small record of women's voices under the occupation. These women's voices are encountered through formal statements about assaults to them or their loved ones. In the context of the unceremonious harm recounted by US military officials who claimed these young women's carelessness and predisposition to negligible concern for their own bodies, these women account for their thoughtfulness about themselves and their loved ones. Caroline's seeking after the child in her care, Elizabeth's demand for reparations, Estrea's toothache and self-care with *tafia* all communicate this much. This self-care, however, was often not legible to occupying forces and did not always protect women from the carelessness of military officials and their families. Still their statements cite women's awareness and strategic engagement with the subtle and often harmful ways in which US military officials attacked Haitian women's subjectivity. Entering the archive at the "moment of their disappearance," Estrea and Adirenng's testimonies were recorded in hospitals days before their deaths.[63] Given the gravity of their injuries, it is most certain that these women had a sense of fatality. Thus, these statements were an urgent accounting in the midst of the gradual accumulation of occupation changes.

Yet women's quickened articulation of life coupled with the insistence of their "unavoidable" deaths on occupied roads also reveals women's extensive and expanding knowledge of themselves and deep familiarity with the changing contours of the occupation landscape. On July 15, 1919, Marie Louise wrote a letter to her brother-in-arms, the *caco* leader and strategist Charlemagne Péralte. She enthusiastically reported to Péralte that his tactics of armed resistance against the US military were weakening the American soldiers' morale in Port-au-Prince and that his popularity was growing nationally and internationally. Nevertheless, she concluded with a warning: "I also tell you that the occupation has built a bridge at Arcahaie. There is a trap there with a car—warn your men."[64] Signed "Your affectionate sister," Maria Louise's letter was one of many correspondences written and transported by women who supported either the "Haitian revolutionaries" or the "Yankees" during the US occupation. Marie Louise's proximity to Péralte makes her words unique as an intimate moment within antioccupation guerrilla warfare. Equally noteworthy is Marie Louise's documentation of the infrastructural developments of the nation. She knew that the same bridge that would be counted in the tally of improvements brought to Haiti by the US occupation also threatened her loved one and his comrades.

Marie Louise's concern for her kin along with her knowledge regarding the military's construction efforts reflects another unique intersection between Haitian women's lives and their use of and treatment in public space during the occupation. Women in Haiti capitalized on the nation's altered transportation landscape and the disruption of public space to manage their economic, social, and political lives during the period. Women's opinions of the occupation often rested with opportunities to exercise citizenship in ways that corresponded with larger philosophies and goals for their lives. In this regard, Marie Louise was a fellow revolutionary driven by her beliefs to risk her safety, to do what was "necessary for the victory of the revolution." She also confronted the precarity of the occupation by engaging risks on her terms, later leveraging the value of her home so she could help defer the travel expenses of a sympathetic "Englishman" who would spread the word of the revolution throughout Europe.[65]

While many of the conflicts of the occupation were framed within support or rejection of the US occupation, in her work on Haitian and US relations, historian Chantalle Verna has demonstrated that feelings were complicated beyond pro- or antioccupation.[66] This ambivalence about sides is evident among young women whose support or refusal of the occupation was less about a relationship to the militarized and occupied state and more toward the assault and insult to ways of being, often revealing the fallacies of both the pro- and antioccupation positions. For example, early in the day on April 12, 1919, four young women—Louise Ismael, Marilia Lindor, Claircia Delva, and Claircilia Telisma—were arrested by a Haitian gendarme member, Bernadel, and "charged with obstructing traffic and peddling goods on the streets without a license" in Petit Goâve. Some hours later the women were released from the court without paying a fine or with a license. But before sundown, "on the same day the above mentioned women were arrested again on the same charge." The US military official reporting the merchant infractions concluded, "As a matter of fact, the peddlers know that they can escape punishments, [so] it is very difficult for the gendarmerie to maintain order and keep peddlers off the streets." While the four women's actions frustrated the commanding official, the report regarding the four women was not for their arrest. Rather, Louise, Marilia, Claircia, and Claircilia's knowledge, repeated offenses, and subsequent release from military custody and fines were used as evidence to bring charges of negligence against gendarme Bernadel. According to the US military court, Bernadel was being punished because he "simply sent [the four women] to the Bureau Communal to pay for a license, failing to impose punishment." Although Bernadel arrested and escorted the women to court twice, he was charged with negligence because, as his commander explained, "it was necessary to impose a small fine and have the offenders pay for a license, or impose some other punishment in order that other peddlers should obey the law and city regulations." Based on the available evidence, a greater tax should have been levied against the women, or they should have been "imposed" with physical assault.

Bernadel's subsequent punishment as a result of the women's infraction reveals the complexities of gender, social status, and the occupation's authority over the streets they were constructing and surveilling. The women's return to the street and Bernadel's restraint from physical punishment suggest that when possible, women also refused to be transformed by the paraphernalia of militarized authority during the occupation. The gendarmerie most frequently enacted the day-to-day will of the occupation forces by collecting vending taxes, settling public disputes, attending to accidents, and making arrests. As noted in the introduction, it was the gendarmerie who physically separated the *femme du peuple* from the LFAS women in the assembly hall. The US military created the gendarmerie as a national military and policing arm during the first days of the occupation. As many scholars have written, the gendarmerie was largely composed of Haitian nationals who were trained with the explicit agenda to fight against the citizenry and impose foreign laws on behalf of the United States.[67] In addition to the roads and women's transformation, the gendarmerie was arguably one of the most long-lasting legacies of the occupation period. Members of the gendarmerie were recruited from all sectors of Haitian society, but the majority of the enlisted were working-class and peasant men. In the gendarmerie, they were given a small wage, housing in barracks, and classes in literacy and artillery.

For their service on the wartime side of the US military, their relationship to and claims on the nation were tenuous. Haitians with varying degrees of support or rejection of the occupation were deeply conflicted about the gendarmerie's roll in the occupation. For example, the leaders of the *caco* movement made their understanding of the gendarmerie clear. In a public letter from 1920, they wrote of the gendarmes, "It is to be stated that the majority of Haitiens [*sic*] who belong to the Gendarmerie are men which are not conscientious, in one simple word they are (worthless) and of worthless doings, if they were really conscientious they would never fight against us."[68] Repeatedly referred to as "bad Haitiens" by the *cacos*, the gendarme soldiers' value and relationship to nation was measured through their political awareness. Interestingly, though, the members of the gendarmerie were also the men that *caco* leaders sought to recruit into their army. When General Theophil and Petit Severe were making their way about the country in women's clothing, they were going to gendarmerie camps to recruit disillusioned soldiers. At the end of his tour, Petit Severe had allegedly recruited "practically all the gendarmes in the north" who "were prepared to join the cause, and that the plan would be to attack the small gendarmerie station, enlist such gendarmes as would follow, and then proceed to the larger towns where white officers are stationed."[69]

The *cacos* chastised and recruited the gendarmes, while the US military sought to control the gendarmes, but their most frequent interlocutors were women on the streets. Just as Marie Louise's intelligence provided strategic support for the *cacos*, women's knowledge of the road also made them critical informants for the occupation's military intelligence. In the same *caco* statement that deemed the gendarme worthless, the *caco* leaders issued a warning: "the Haitian guides who are always ready to show the American officers the roads . . . will be killed." Frequently, these guides were women, and they knew the threat of retribution was real. Claire Saint-Lot, a vendor from Bellanger (Arcahaie), expressed this sentiment in a December 1921 report. She "heard from the mouth of the named Silenciaux, Charles Boco, Charleaus Glaude, Augustin, [and] Malette that they [a *caco* unit] were going to make a revolution and that they would not permit the whites to remain more than two months . . . and that having surprised the conversation, she [was] so closely watched by these brigands that she cannot even visit her plantations for fear of being assassinated."[70] Being watched closely and fearing that she would experience the fate the *cacos* threated to the guides did not stop Saint-Lot from divulging the *caco* soldiers' plans to the US military through a gendarme.

Until the mid-1920s, most gendarme units patrolled communities in which they had become familiar. For example, in the case of Claire Saint-Lot, she "made her report to the said gendarme [Merveus Denna] who [was] her son in law." Even when gendarme officers were not in a familiar city, the frequency with which they saw women on the streets and monitored their routines for security and bureaucratic purposes meant they grew to know them. Moreover, while officers were a political point of contention, some women used the gendarme to defend themselves against petty theft and domestic disputes. Additionally, in the four young women's case, it is possible that Bernadel knew these women and did not see them as a threat to the equilibrium of taxed peddlers. Or perhaps he needed one or all of these women for military intelligence. Women's presence and familiarity in the streets made them particularly powerful in their ability to barter information for their own needs and their understanding of the boundaries of occupation control.

The threat of women's "knowing"—a consciousness that women performed by being in, witnessing, supporting, and ignoring regulations on public space—revealed the fragility of the militarized (pro- and anti-) occupation state. Both gendarmes and *cacos* realized the advantages of women's familiarity with the nation's thoroughfares, and women negotiated this power in subtle ways. Bernadel's commanding officer, then, was most frustrated that the women knew ("[they] know that they can escape punishment") and tested the occupation's authority.[71] The women's audacity to return to the street revealed the US military's porous bureaucratic and military controls over the nation, and these women's keen awareness of the limits of occupation power. Similarly, Claire Saint-Lot used her knowledge to compromise antioccupation agendas. In both contexts, these women's knowledge and actions were threatened with public physical violence. The US military officer's emphasis on setting an example with the women only further established that women were both the targets and witnesses of regularized corporeal harm throughout occupation life.

When the women returned to the street, they also mocked the militarization of the state that presumed control over their labor, movement, and decision making. These women then were not measuring their citizenship based on ideals of nationalism or loyalty, but were claiming their relationship to the nation through their deep understanding of the nation's physical and economic landscape. Their refusal to remain confined unsettled multiple levels of bureaucracy within the occupation system and frustrated fragile balances of power that Haitians and US military officials were trying to navigate. It is worth considering, then, that the regular refusal by women—not just armed *cacos*, disengaged gendarmes, or antioccupation activists—was a part of the acceleration, wild frustration, and violent outburst that soldiers were enacting in the first decade of the occupation. Historian Yveline Alexis has shown that Haitian women "brandished silence and feigned ignorance" even when US military officials threated them with death. Women's refusal to share information to support the occupation efforts "unleashed [the] anger" of officials and accelerated attacks on Haitians.[72] Women's refusals also fundamentally shifted how foreign marines engaged, and created new systems of bureaucracy and surveillance to curtail these moments. Beyond infrastructural development, Alexis shows how modern technology like radio and aircraft were deployed to compromise everyday exchanges between Haitians.[73] The inertia that these women's responses created added to national and international initiatives against the occupation that eventually made it untenable.

Women's knowledge was a threat to the occupation, and the occupiers responded to this threat with a culture of surveillance. The military reports on road construction show that surveillance was embedded in the infrastructural development. US military officials explicitly denied the connection between road construction and military penetration into the country. As one high-ranking officer testified, "The corvée system was employed during the American occupation for the purpose of building roads. The sole objects of these roads were not military, although they undoubtedly had a great military value."[74] Yet the military reports repeatedly address insurgent whereabouts, community sentiment toward the occupation, and capacity to recruit occupation enthusiasts.[75]

While the evidence of encounters in the occupation landscape suggests that working-class, peasant, and urban and rural poor women had greater exposure to the intersecting dynamics of infrastructural change and bodily harm, surveillance was ubiquitous. As a young person, Ghislaine remembers an atmosphere of surveillance that was captured in the archives and in literature about the period.[76] In the story that she recited about her grandfather's vote against the US protectorate over Haiti, she repeated that her grandfather and "Monsieur Cabeche" were the lone resistors. In the 1920s, US military records of "rebel activity" reveal that this same political comrade was being closely monitored. The report categorized him as "Robert Cabeche, a member of a family know [*sic*] to be contrary to the Occupation and Gendarmerie." Surveillance of the Cabeche family and families close to Ghislaine reveal that they were also monitored on the street. In particular, wives and children were perceived as possible transporters for antioccupation literature and paraphernalia.

The US occupiers monitored information circulation because during the first decade of the occupation their reputation for brutality was spreading. Yet the reality of violence and impending harm toward Haitians was repeatedly denied by occupation officials. The 1920 US Senate inquiry into the occupation captures this disavowal. By the early 1920s the US military claimed victory in the "*cacos* wars." In large part these victories were measured through the capture, killing, and public display of the naked body of *caco* leader and intellectual Charlemagne Péralte in 1919.

The rumors of continued indiscriminate violence led to several US Senate investigations. During the 1920 investigation, Admiral H. S. Knapp, who served in Haiti and did a "thorough study of the conditions there," was asked several questions. When asked, "Is it true that some 3,000 Haitian men, women, and children have been shot by American troops since the occupation of Haiti in 1915?" Knapp replied, "It is very possible that 3,000 Haitian men in all have been killed. These operations were necessary to restore order and respect for human life and property that were endangered by the Haitians themselves, especially in the northeastern part of Haiti, which has been the stronghold of Haitian bandits called 'Cacos'."[77] As Knapp accounted for the "necessary" deaths, he reminded his interviewer that "it was unavoidable that many casualties should occur." He then concluded, "As far as women and children are concerned, the answer to this question is, No. There may possibly have been cases of women being shot during action when these women were in the company of bandit bands; but such cases, if any occurred, were accidents incident to the campaign and were not the result of an intent and were in spite of every desire of the American troops engaged. I have heard of no case whatever [*sic*] where children have been killed even under the circumstances spoken of above."[78] Women were shot during "action" against the *cacos*, but not solely as collateral damage. Military records reflect that soldiers saw women close to the *cacos* as an equal threat and intentionally brutalized and killed them. And yet, less proximity to *cacos* did not diminish women's endangerment. Most strikingly, according to Admiral Knapp's conclusions, the physical harm and deaths of Estrea Jean Gilles, Eleanor Charles, and Adirenng Senatus were simultaneously inevitable and impossible. Women's and young girls' injuries and deaths did not exist in the Senate testimonies. Even as military officials recorded these women's often fatal physical injuries, officials were unwilling to publicly account for this harm.

The simultaneous vivid documentation of injury and silence of this injury communicates Haitian women's disposability under the occupation. In particular, where the incidents happened (on the street) and how they were documented (within the "miscellaneous" happenings of "necessary" infrastructural adjustments) echo Caribbean feminist scholar Donette Francis's assertion that postcolonial Caribbean spaces—"like ships, cane fields, taxicabs, photographic studios, and behind hibiscus bushes . . . can also function as clandestine sites, they become abject spaces hidden from public view. As a result, when females tell stories of abuse in such spaces, they are often met with disbelief resulting from the event's unverifiability."[79] Thus during the occupation, these women were both actively accounted for and—through the misnaming as careless, disobedient, drunken women (who were girls) and girls (who were women)—erased.

Growing Refusal

The lives and thoughts of Estrea, Adirenng, Eleanor Charles, Elizabeth Saint-Bernard, Louise Ismael, Marilia Lindor, Claircia Delva, and Claircilia Telisma were not acknowledged or they were distorted by the US military reporting, but antioccupation supporters, including Marie Louise, the Garoute family, the Sylvains, and many others were sharing and spreading girls' and women's stories across the region. On May 15, 1920, nine months after the attack on Eleanor and almost five years into the US occupation of Haiti, the headline of the African American newspaper the *Chicago Defender* read, "U.S. Troops Attack Haitian Girls." The article projected a story of rape and murder of Haitian girls and women into the African American consciousness. Reverend S. E. Churchstone-Lord, an African American pastor of the African Methodist Episcopal Church in Port-au-Prince, reported the alleged attack to the paper: "White soldiers of the American army are sending a reign of terror throughout the republic and attempting to beat the Haitians into submission. The most serious charge . . . against the white soldiers is that on one night nine little Haitian girls, ranging in ages from 8 to 12 died as a result of being criminally assaulted. The further charge is made that members of the native constabulary are compelled by the white officers to procure native women for use of the whites as concubines."[80] According to the report, when girls escaped death or sexual assault, some were still forced into sexual servitude that was brokered by Haitian members of the gendarmarie at the behest of white US soldiers. In his communique, Reverend Churchstone-Lord further revealed "that the Haitian people preferred Colored United States troops in the event the American government continued to maintain protectorate over the republic. They declared that the white troops are too arrogant and are known for their disrespect for the native Haitians, especially women and girls."[81]

Reverend Churchstone-Lord's report in the *Chicago Defender* exposed a structure of brutal rape, assault, and murder of Haitian girls and women by white US military and occupation authorities to the United States. Although few incidents were investigated by the US military or the Haitian Gendarmerie during the occupation, Haitians disclosed the assaults on Haitian women through word of mouth, newspapers, journals, public letters, and, when possible, courts-martial. It is through these means that Reverend Churchstone-Lord received knowledge of the Haitian girls' deaths and revealed the story to the *Chicago Defender*.

While African Americans were present in Haiti in various capacities as clergy and emigrants to the country and reported on the conditions of the occupation to their respective circles and presses, Haitian antioccupation groups used foreign periodicals as a way to circumvent the highly censored press in Haiti. In particular, vocal proponents of the urban *desoccupation* movements such as Auguste Garoute and intellectuals including Jean Price-Mars, Perçeval Thoby, and Georges Sylvain advocated for Haitian sovereignty and defended the nation's capability of self-governance via the nationalist organizations Union Patriotique (UP) and Union Nationaliste. Through public forums and print media such as the *Courrier Haitien, Le Nouvelliste, Haiti Intégrale, La Patrie*, and *Le Matin*, these men voiced their discontent and warned their country about the dangers of the occupation to the Haitian polity.[82] Although the UP and the *cacos* never had an official alliance, they were symbolically bound by their shared contempt for the occupation and concern for, as one *cacos* general put it, the "ladies and young girls" who were "condemned" and "left to die of wounded pride."[83]

The limited presence of women in the archive suggests that beyond the protection that the *cacos*, UP, or other antioccupation movements presumed they could provide for women, most women were navigating the conditions of their livelihood on their own terms. Part of this navigation was with how they engaged the documentation of their stories. As seen above, many women were conscripted into a relationship with the state that resulted in their witness testimonies appearing in occupation archival records. In other cases, women took the opportunity to share their accumulated experiences of violence with other women.

Toward the end of 1920, following the attack on Eleanor Charles and the summer attack on the nine Haitian girls, the Union Patriotique began plans to send a delegation to Washington, D.C., to present their concerns over US Marines' misconduct and propose a strategy for ending the occupation. Fundraising became a central component of the UP's operational efforts and a necessary variable for the antioccupation organization's ultimate success. Women activists bore the responsibility for securing the organization's financial security and future.[84] The UP women's first order of business was to secure money for the commission to Washington, D.C. Eugénie Malbranche-Sylvain was at the helm of this women's collective effort. Malbranche-Sylvain, like her husband Georges Sylvain, was well versed in antioccupation politics. As one of the "wives, daughters and sisters" of the UP, she "was keen to contribute [her] personal efforts in this work of national liberation."[85] In Port-au-Prince, Malbranche-Sylvain garnered the support of her friends Alice Garoute and Thérèse Hudicourt, who combined their resources to establish an urban antioccupation women's collective and mined the streets of Port-au-Prince for donations.[86]

On the inaugural day of fundraising in November 1920, a reported two hundred Haitian women took to the streets of Port-au-Prince.[87] The names of the hundreds of women who traversed the urban center that day are unknown. It is likely, however, that Malbranche-Sylvain's fundraising compatriots were other vocal antioccupation women activists including Régina Carrié Thoby (Mme. Perçeval Thoby).[88] Among Malbranche-Sylvain's companions her teenage daughters, Madeleine and Jeanne, were also likely nearby—perhaps holding their mother's collection bucket or simply walking in her shadow chatting about their teenage lives, absorbing the intricacies of mass mobilization. If the future women's activists did not accompany their mother, they surely heard of the day's success.[89] US military surveillance reports suggested that the majority of the marchers were children. Most of the reports used the presence of children to invalidate the event, and some reports claimed that the children's presence was a political ploy by the UP to get sympathizers.[90] Some children may have joined the crowd to engage in the general festivities of the marches, but these children were also witnessing and living under the precarious conditions of the occupation and chose to protest the foreign presence.

The women knocked on doors and walked the streets, collecting funds from passersby. At the end of the first day, the women collected $100 US dollars.[91] In the five months between October 1920 and February 1921, Haitian women led the fundraising initiative to subsidize the Union Patriotique's delegation to the United States. The campaign spread throughout the country to all sixty-one committees of the UP. Women were the predominant fundraisers and administrative managers in these various chapters. As financial keepers of the 1921 trip to the United States, women were instructed to spend two to three days a week soliciting funds from families in their respective neighborhoods.[92] The UP women spent weeks in the homes of families across the country. It was in these intimate encounters to fund the *desoccupation* movement

that women shared and collected the stories of the atrocities of the occupation. During these visits women of the UP heard how women had been changed
by the occupation, documented women's experiences, and later transmitted
these narratives to the organization's membership and to unaffiliated women
and men throughout the country and the region. From this reservoir of knowledge, the women synthesized the narratives and situated them at the center
of the 1921 UP's delegation report. The stories were also reported in US newspapers, and several years later they were printed in the book *Occupied Haiti*
after Haitian women requested a woman-led investigative commission.[93]

Malbranche-Sylvain and Garoute helped catalog the stories of a generation of young people growing up under the occupation.[94] In a bold rebuttal to
the conclusions presented at the US Senate hearings that Haitian girls and
women were not touched, harmed, or killed by the US occupation, the list of
grievances that women collected about other women's experiences revealed
otherwise. This record included stories of girls and women being burned and
buried alive, hung, and shot. Some of the women were named: Hergénée,
Athélia and Cloraine Etienne, Mme. Bregarde, Dorléan Joseph, Mme. Rosier,
Madame Garnier, Madame Lumenesse Madame Eucharice Cadichon, Madam
Prévoit. And others were accounted for through their relationship to other
injured women, as mothers, sisters, daughters, and caretakers for pregnant
women. The evidence of violence toward women was extensive and offered a
grave record of the physical and emotional mutilation of Haitian girls and
women as both direct and indirect targets of occupation violence.[95] Often
harmed or executed at the breached boundaries between the occupied public
space and their homes, the coordinates of women's transformation bisected
families and flesh.

Haitian women witnessed, remembered, recalled, and recorded each
other's lives and transformation.[96] In February 1921, during the first weeks of
the Warren Harding administration, the UP delegation, which included
future Haitian president Sténio Vincent and Haitian representative to Washington Perçeval Thoby, departed Haiti with the stories that these women collected. The men arrived in Washington during a season of political positioning
and readjustment. In the months preceding their arrival, then senator Harding repeatedly discussed Haiti and used the US occupation as an example of
President Woodrow Wilson's chaotic and unorganized foreign policy. With
the hint of US Marines' misconduct circulating in the air of US public and
political opinion, Harding capitalized on the rumors of naval abuse during
the 1920 US presidential elections, accusing the Wilson administration of
"the rape of Haiti."[97] The savvy campaign strategy for Harding, however,

adversely affected the initiatives of the UP months later. By the time the UP collected the money to send a delegation to Washington and testify to the US military's abuses toward Haitians, the election season had passed and Senator Harding was then president-elect Harding.[98] The conditions in Haiti were less useful to the president-elect.

The timing of the Union Patriotique's arrival in the United States was inopportune and compromised some of the imagined goals of the diplomatic trip. While Harding and other US government officials declined the Union Patriotique's requests for formal conversations, Vincent and Thoby met with the leaders of the National Association for the Advancement of Colored People (NAACP), who had questioned the occupation from the beginning.[99] NAACP president W. E. B. Du Bois, Secretary James Weldon Johnson, and Treasurer Addie Hunton met with the UP delegation. The relationship between the UP and the NAACP had blossomed over the prior two years. In 1920, while the United States wavered on sending a commission to investigate the occupation, the NAACP sent Johnson to Haiti for a two-month fact-finding mission.[100] In a series of articles in the *Nation*, Johnson reported that US Marines were "violently steeped in color prejudice" and that they raped and assaulted women so frequently that it was not viewed as a crime. According to Johnson, these violations against Haitian women (and men) resembled early twentieth-century anti-Black violence in the United States.[101]

The growing awareness and concern for the violence enacted on Haitian girls was also the primary concern for Black women across the region who witnessed similar technologies of violence used by colonial and postcolonial militarization against women of the "darker races" globally. By 1920, Mary Church Terrell, president of the National Association of Colored Women (NACW), and Margaret Washington also expressed concern and an organizational pivot to address concerns of anti-Black violence in the United States and the Caribbean. In August 1922 a small group of women including Theodora Holly, African American activist, Haitian resident, and French language editor for the United Negro Improvement Association (UNIA)'s newspaper the *Negro World*; Mme. Charles Dubé, a Haitian teacher and philanthropist; Mary Church Terrell; Margaret Washington; Addie Hunton; and Mary McLeod Bethune, NAACP member and future president of the National Council of Negro Women, founded the International Council of Women of the Darker Races (ICWDR). The primary focus of the organization's inaugural year was "Haitian women and children."[102] Holly spearheaded most of the investigation into the conditions of Haitian women and children. Holly was the daughter of emigrationist Bishop James Theodore Holly. Her parents were pioneers in the emigrationist movement and moved to Haiti to escape the racial prejudice of the United States. Fluent in English and French, Holly was invested in communicating the life and experiences of Haitian girls to Black people in the region.[103]

The ICWDR began "study clubs" in which members of the organization would invite fellow members and nonmembers to read texts by African-descended people throughout the world, ultimately strengthening the darker races through familiarity of self and one another. This self-study was a central component to developing the Black women's intellectual tradition. For example, several years later in 1930s Paris, the Nardal Sisters, Jane and Paulette Nardal, hosted a *cercle d'amis* (circle of friends), where they also established women's spaces to consider the future of African-descended people in the modern world.[104] The ICWDR created an alternative curriculum with research projects that centered Black women. This body of work also included public lectures to which Theodora Holly was the most sought-after speaker. She talked to young girls and women about the history of Haitian women and culture in both the United States and Haiti. In addition to Holly's public lectures, the women collected newspapers and photographs of Haitian and US African American women. In a letter to Margaret Washington, Holly illustrated the significance of this print media exchange, explaining that she had given a lecture to a girls' club in Port-au-Prince and showed the young women Washington's picture as an example of an "inspirational" Black woman.[105]

This was also a project of repair. The transnational networks refigured the Black girls and women beyond vulnerability and physical injury. Through the effort to heal Black women's corporeal and discursive collective experiences, Haitian and US African American women helped to shape the meaning of Black international politics of the period. The ICWDR invested a large portion of their resources into investigative trips. One of the most important of these trips was Addie Hunton's 1926 trip to Haiti. When Hunton arrived, Eugénie Malbranche-Sylvain and Thérèse Hudicourt escorted her around Port-au-Prince. The trip resulted in the 180-page publication mentioned above that included statistics, interviews with Haitian women, and opinions independent of the occupying forces. As communicated in the full title of the report, *Occupied Haiti: Being the Report of a Committee of Six Disinterested Americans Representing Organizations Exclusively American, Who, Having Personally Studied Conditions in Haiti in 1926, Favor the Restoration of the Independence of the Negro Republic*, the team concluded that the US military should leave Haiti immediately.

Although the military did not leave at that moment, the trip was one of a flurry of national and international antioccupation collaborations. These organizations, such as the multinational membership of the Joseph School, focused on the experience and education of young children under the occupation. Haitian women, such as Madame Charles Dubé from the ICWDR, Rosina Jean-Joseph, a teacher of business, and Madame Dantès Bellegarde, wife of diplomat to France and philanthropist Dantès Bellegarde, led this educational movement. These "most prominent Haitian women who [had] done commendable work for the amelioration of the sort of their more unfortunate sisters" decided to establish the L'Oeuvre des Femmes Haitiennes pour L'Organization du Travail. These women included Mme. Etienne Mathon, former president of La Zelatrice, a woman's organization in Port-au-Prince and future co-founder of the Ligue Feminine d'Action Sociale; Mme. Servincent, former director of the Primary School; Mme. Clement Pethel, former president of Femina, a social and charitable work organization; Mme. Louis Guillaume, president of the Association of Older Students of St. Rose de Lima; Mme. Tancrede Auguste, former first lady and president of La Creche, an institution for unrecognized and abandoned children; Mlle. Annais Boucherau, independent social worker in Port-au-Prince; Mme. Justin Madieu, primary school founder; Mlle. Henrietta Valen, principal of the Night School for Adults; and Mlle. Henriette Bianby, social worker and primary school principal.[106]

The surge in women-led organizations focused on girls was a response to the impact and injury of the occupation on young women. Between its inaugural meeting on March 2, 1926, and September of that same year, L'Oeuvre des Femmes Haitiennes opened the Jean Joseph Industrial School and gained the support of wealthy and politically influential Haitians and US Black Americans, including Mme. Dantès Bellegarde, Mme. François Dalencour, Mme. Pascal Elie, Eugenie Jean Joseph, Mary McLeod Bethune (president of the National Federation of Colored Women's Clubs), Eva T. Bowles (secretary for Colored Work of National Board YMCA), and Layle Lane (socialist activist, teacher, and treasurer of L'Oeuvre des Femmes Haitiennes). "The school was founded "by a group of Haitians to develop Native Industries and afford a practical education for the Masses."[107] The founders were primarily concerned with industrial education for young people. In a fundraising letter to Theodore Roosevelt, Harriet Gibbs Marshall, African American educator and pianist, thanked the former US president for his financial support of L'Oeuvre des Femmes and the Jean Joseph School, but she emphasized,

"There are many gentleman members in this organization but we deem it wise to have women officers to awaken them to civic obligations and activity."[108]

Through the economic strategy to balance the nation's import-dependence with production and export of local good and crafts, the women mobilized a self-help and uplift ethos.[109] L'Oeuvre des Femmes specifically sought to mold girls and women into good housekeepers and wives, producing "beautiful children in the streets."[110] The uplift agenda lacked a critical analysis of gender roles and power, but these late-occupation alliances established important connections between Haitian activists and African American women that would be drawn out over the decades of the twentieth century. When Addie Hunton returned from her trip, she optimistically reported that "high officials" were taking notice and that her "quiet propaganda in behalf of Haiti" may result in change.[111] Hunton's propaganda to impact the US perception of the occupation was far from quiet. In 1926 alone, she gave addresses about Haiti at the California State Convention of the National Association of Colored Women, National Federation of Colored Women's Clubs, the NAACP Chicago Convention, the National Association of Colored Women in Oakland, California, and the Pan African Conference the following year in New York. Hunton's work alongside Malbranche-Sylvain and Hudicourt's participation in the Women's International League for Peace and Freedom meant that the Haitian women's stories were being shared across the region.[112]

Yet, in the meantime, Haitian girls' lives continued to be altered by the actions of occupation personnel. Several months after Hunton's trip, Perceval Thoby wrote a letter to W. E. B. Du Bois stuffed with clippings from the Haitian newspapers *l'Essor* and *Le Courrier Haitien* reporting on the rape of an unnamed eleven-year-old girl. In his letter, Thoby implored the editor of the African American newspaper *The Crisis* to publish the news that "the american [*sic*] Occupation is trying to hide the facts." Thoby knew that there was risk in sharing the information, as he revealed in the letter that the editor of *l'Essor*, Luc Dorsainvil, had been dismissed from his position as head of the passport service in the Department of the Interior as a punishment for sharing the details of the attack. But Thoby also knew the facts were "perfectly true," and he wanted to honor the reality that in the "numerous cases of rapes by marines . . . the families, either by shame or fear of reprisals, have always avoided to make complaint or publish the facts in the papers."[113] Of course, many women had reported this violence, but Thoby also assumed there were many more unaccounted for.

Thoby also understood the power of the press. Although the US government monitored and punished authors and publishers, antioccupation organizing and nationalist appeals by Haitians accelerated in Haitian newspapers, journals, and literature in the late 1920s. For example, in October 1924 US military intelligence reports show that this type of information spread was a threat to the occupation. The report identified that a "political group in the United States, consisting of Weldon Johnson . . . and others of the Garvey group, had sent instructions to the anti-occupation group of Port-au-Prince (Sylvain, Hudicourt, Cauvin, and others), to commence an active propaganda throughout Haiti that the Occupation was to be withdrawn very shortly." In addition to hinting toward a political alliance between the NAACP, the UNIA, and the UP (referenced as the "Black Party") regarding transnational antioccupation organizing, "The rumor of the immediate withdrawal has spread to all parts of Haiti" and led to public demonstrations throughout the country.[114] Thoby, and perhaps Theodora Holly, who would have been central to translating these earlier correspondences, used similar press platforms to spread information and "embarrass the Administration" (US president Calvin Coolidge) about attacks on women. Interestingly, and despite the evidence of international networks between Black women in the region, the US agents presumed that the threatening alliances between the NAACP, the UNIA, and the UP were between and led by the men of these organizations and not the women. As addressed below this would be an embarrassing oversight in the coming years.

In addition to using the popular press to pressure the occupation's end, Haitians also used publishing to influence national thought. In 1927 Malbranche-Sylvain's son, Normil Sylvain; Thérèse Hudicourt's nephew, Max Hudicourt; Theodora Holly's brother, Arthur Holly; and several writers and intellectuals including Emile Roumer, Jacques Roumain, Jean Price-Mars, J. C. Dorsainvil, and young Ghislaine's future husband, Étienne Charlier, founded the journal *La Revue Indigène*. Through the journal the authors celebrated the African ancestry of the Haitian people and denounced French culture and thinking as the foundation of Haitian thought. Their collective works and pronouncement of an indigenous African-based Haitian episteme were further framed by Price-Mars's 1928 publication *Ainsi parla l'oncle* (So Spoke the Uncle), in which Price-Mars articulated a cultural nationalism that centered the life experiences of the Haitian peasant majority, including scholarly attention to agricultural practices and Vodou. This intellectual surge in Haitian nationalism and information circulation was further amplified through the 1929 student strikes at the US industrial education school in Damien, the mounting frustration by opposition and US occupying forces with Borno's puppet presidency, and most notably the women's protests during the 1930 Forbes Commission's visit to Haiti.

In March 1929, the newly elected US president Herbert Hoover inherited the growing discontent regarding the occupation, and by the end of the year he had to address, if not question, the military's denial and silencing of reports from Haiti. In 1930 Hoover approved a commission to investigate the occupation, led by W. Cameron Forbes. The five-person committee of white men did not anticipate the demonstration they received.[115] A decade after Régina Carrié Thoby, with Malbranche-Sylvain and other UP women, fundraised for antioccupation missions for her husband and Sténio Vincent, she, along with Justinien Ricot, and Thérèse Vieux-Clesca, took to the streets again on March 1, 1930. This time their peaceful protest gained national and international attention as they led the largest independent opposition protest during the occupation.

In advance of the Forbes Commission's arrival, US high commissioner Russell denied Perceval Thoby and leaders of the UP a permit for the march. But the decision was overturned by Forbes when Régina Carrié Thoby proposed a peaceful parade of women without men. On March 1, following a prayer and mass at the l'Eglise du Sacré-Coeur, some 10,000 women (various numbers were reported) marched in the streets with "banners raised" in protest of the occupation. As agreed upon based on the permit, men did not attend the protest, and according to international newspaper coverage Mme. Thoby "came out on the steps and warned the crowd that it was exclusively a women's manifestation."[116] Walking down Champ-de-Mars, the "somber crowd of women and girls circle[d] the statue of the Emperor [Henry Christophe]." And "on their knees, two children place[d] a wreath of flowers at the foot of the Liberator [Jean-Jacques Dessalines]." For those (men) observing from afar, "La Dessalines disappeared under the shadows of the crowd. . . . His daughters surround[ed] him and their sweet voices s[a]ng the national anthem."[117]

As the crowd of women spontaneously grew, it may have looked like a serendipitous gathering, but Mme. Thoby had orchestrated the demonstration for days while getting government permission. As she explained in multiple newspaper interviews, when the date for the demonstration was scheduled for the first of March, Commissioner Russell suggested the day was ill advised because it was also the date for Carnival. But as Mme. Thoby recounted in *Le Nouvelliste*, "I responded to him, that one does not contradict the other . . . *et voila*, with a little effort and a lot of will, we were able to bring together what I ardently hope will continue to save our dear Haiti."[118]

In sharing the events in the newspaper, Mme. Thoby—"one of the admirable organizers of [the] women's manifestation in favor of the Liberation of

Haiti"—made it clear that she managed the demonstration but that she was also managing the public's knowledge and popular opinion about the event's inner workings. In the interview, readers learned that Mme. Thoby used the scheduled Carnival street crowds for her own exposition. In her recount of the negotiations with Commissioner Russell over the previously planned Carnival date, she revealed, "So [Russell] concluded that he could do nothing about [the date] and that [the date] came directly from the Government." Printed with an extended dash separating Russell's reported speech from Mme. Thoby's inner thoughts, the interview continued on the newspaper page, "But I could not help but smile to myself and say to him with a bit of irony: The Government . . . you just have to say it to yourself and it will be accepted immediately."[119] As Thoby understood it, Russell was the government, so she questioned Russell's suggestion that there were additional bureaucratic channels. By disclosing Russell's deflection of responsibility to "the Government" of which he had previously claimed to be the leader, Thoby laughed at and poked holes in the coherence of occupation logic and authority. Sharing her inner thoughts and the seemingly arbitrary, yet knowingly violent, chain of command to which Russell ascribed, Mme. Thoby staged her own calypsonian critique of the occupation government.

Perhaps anticipating that the readership would enjoy this subtle refusal, Mme. Thoby craftily inserted her critique and publicly offered a hint of doubt around Russell's and by extension the US military's capacity to govern. *Le Nouvelliste* aptly concluded in bold letters above the interview, "The total abstention from the Carnival and the colossal demonstration of ten thousand women and young girls, yesterday, constitute the most convincing testimony that the Commission could collect and the most concrete testimony of a sacred union of all the social classes for the liberation of Haiti."

These girls and women turned the political tide. Alice Garoute and, by then, twelve-year-old Ghislaine were in the crowd and among the wave of refusal.[120] At the end of the commission it was clear that a US military withdrawal was afoot, starting with the replacement of Grandma Alice's childhood peer, President Louis Borno, with interim president Eugene Roy. The *desoccupation* of Haiti started with an intended complete withdrawal of US military forces by 1936. Roy's presidency was a six-month transitional position until the legislature voted for the new president. On November 18, 1930, Haitian nationalist and antioccupation leader Sténio Vincent became the new president. A decade prior, antioccupation women had walked the streets of Port-au-Prince to fundraise for Vincent's travel to the United States. With Vincent as president, the women assumed they would have an ally and friend who understood and would support their growing political acumen. However, because of Vincent's preoccupation with maintaining his own political power and repression of any political agenda that threatened his moderate agenda, the women failed to gain his full support. As a result, the early years of Haitian women's postoccupation organizing involved a keen navigation of shifting political philosophies, methods, and relationships.

IT IS IMPOSSIBLE TO CONCEIVE THE COMPLEXITY of emotions that women and their families felt in the early days of military invasion, but fear, concern, confusion, and frustration were likely among them. Children who were the age of Eleanor Charles or Alice Garoute's oldest grandchildren at the time of the invasion have told the most revealing accounts of the day-to-day shift in society during the US occupation. Together, young people folded the experience of the occupation into other parts of their lives. For many, the occupation was like other variables of young life that incited caution and calculated curiosity. Haitian literary scholar Nadève Ménard argues that "occupied novels"—texts curated during the occupation—reveal insight into the psychological condition of those living through and growing up under occupation.[121] What these texts, oral histories, and archival records show is that by conscription, necessity, or preservation, young people absorbed the occupation into their experiences of growing up.

Some children experienced the temporal and spatial difference between before and after the occupation, and other children born into the occupation, like Ghislaine Charlier, had never known another Haiti. And yet, her characterization of the US Marines was an observation and attention to a presence that was deeply familiar and vividly out of place. In her summation, the occupation was necessary for mention in order to orient the observer, but omnipresent in a way that incited perfunctory acknowledgment. Similarly, Marie Vieux Chauvet's protagonist Claire mentions the US occupation in passing as she describes another moment regarding her childhood friendships. In Claire's internal dialogue the occupation occurred and proliferated alongside the other events of her young adult life, including the death of her father, romantic love interests, and the occasional heat wave.

Like Vieux Chauvet's Claire, Ghislaine held an unceremonious place for the occupiers in her memory of early childhood. "In the meantime" she was a girl like many girls shadowing the women in her life. Some women's ambivalence toward the occupation was a privilege of social and economic class, while others' ambivalence was a quotidian disavowal of militarized governance. Women were transformed by the occupation, and they transformed the occupation in different ways. Different women were also drawn toward and stood in for one another in both anti-Black and antioccupation political actions. As women navigated their rights to traverse the changing physical and political infrastructure of the occupation, mobility and movement met at the moment of maturation.

Taken together, the stories of Ghislaine, Eleanor, Estrea, Caroline, Adirenng, Claire, Louise Ismael, Marilia Lindor, Claircia Delva, Claircilia Telisma, Marie Louise, Vieux Chauvet, and Madeleine communicate a literal transformation of the young women under occupation that is akin to Francis's articulation of Caribbean girls' and women's postcolonial lives as "antiromance" in which they connect "pivotal scenes of subjection to subject formation." Francis explains that being "surveilled through legal and cultural discourses," girls' and women's historical experience "exposes the folly of believing that somehow the national, the diasporic, or the intimate sphere are privileged spaces for reconciliation of otherwise impossible differences." Yet rather than letting these stories "be gloss[ed] over for their cumulative effect," Caribbean women writers use "sustained self-examination" to think of the many moments, like those of the occupation, "rather than a moment of tragedy, exhaustion, or nightmare [. Theirs] is a moment of hyperconscious awareness that makes use of past failures to build usable futures."[122]

This awareness was a critical component of Haitian women's political wayfaring. It was reflected in women's use of knowledge gathered during the occupation as well as in Sylvain-Bouchereau's assertion of transformation. As girls and young women walked the streets of Haiti, kicking up the same unsettled dirt, marching in the same altered streets, and recounting their stories to one another and occupation officials, they were drawn close to and apart from each other while being simultaneously transformed. Located at the intersection of girls' and women's different forms of transformation and accounting for the tactile experience of occupation, Haitian women's postoccupation politics emerged and reflected a new configuration of national belonging through, around, and beyond the state.

A Bridge

The terrible political news that reached us that evening by way of a few passengers off the British boat prevented my parents from punishing what they called my insubordination. It was July 27, 1915, a dreadful date that would forever destroy my father's political ambitions, ruin his good health and lead him straight to his grave.

—Marie Vieux-Chauvet, *Amour, colére, folie* (1968)

[There is] hidden labor involved in the production of Black women's history. . . . There is a psychological and sometimes physical cost associated [with] producing monographs dedicated to [Black] pain. The labors of writing about haunted and hunted subjects . . . is producing a body of scholarship dedicated to grieving publicly.

—Jessica Millward (2016)

My mother has given birth to more women than me, and perhaps in her death she will breed even more.

—Edwidge Danticat, *The Art of Death* (2017)

On August 3, 1925, in an open-air caravan flanked on either side by their brothers and mother, Jeanne, Yvonne, Madeleine, and Suzanne Sylvain processed next to their father's body. Georges Sylvain died on the morning of August 2, and by the next day's sunrise over a thousand people lined the streets of Port-au-Prince to mourn the "Apostle of Liberty" who "sacrificed his life for the liberation of his country."[1] Sylvain did not transition in physical combat or as a victim of wanton violence executed by US military forces. Rather, he died with family by his side at his home on Rue Christophe. Born in Puerto Plata, Dominican Republic, in 1866, Sylvain migrated to Haiti at a young age and later studied and transcribed one of the earliest and most famous books of Haitian Kreyòl folktales, *Cric? Crac! Fables de la Fontaine*. This text celebrated Haiti's language and culture and accounted for the theory and art of the Haitian narrative form. Sylvain's care with *Cric? Crac!* endeared him to the Haitian people and reflected his sentient attention to the nation he and his family called home. As exhibited in the 1999 reproduction of the book, the editors of the feminist press FOKAL invited the readers "to reflect on this work and to taste all the flavor of Georges Sylvain's words."[2] A poet, an attorney, and a politician (founder of the Union Patriotique), Sylvain used juridical and lyrical mediums to experiment with the possibilities, philosophies, and practices of Haitian citizenship.

Moving through the center of occupied Port-au-Prince, the Sylvain sisters' loss was met by the new day's breeze that whispered through the crowd of "heartbroken" mourners and rustled the black flags that were displayed in front of "almost all the houses on Rue des Fronts-Forts, Rue Bonnie Foi, and Grand Rue."[3] In comparison to the spectacular deaths of Charlemagne Péralte or the silenced dismemberment and death of Estrea Jean Gilles, Georges Sylvain's death was ordinary. Yet, the outpouring of mourning and reverence for his life was extraordinary. On the day of the leader's burial, shopkeepers unanimously decided to close their stores, so they and their employees could participate in the funeral services.[4] Condolences were sent to the Sylvain family from throughout the Caribbean and the Americas. As one newspaper reported, "It is not the mourning of a few thousand; the [entire] nation is mourning." "From the balconies of the rich to the courtyards of the poorest of the poor," Sylvain's death drew "the youth, craftsmen, [and] the upper bourgeoisie [,] putting side by side the most dazzling luxury and the most sordid rags. Without attention to the conditions of society they paid homage to this victim of patriotic duty."[5]

In a temporary blurring of class-cultural difference, multiple Haitian media and US military surveillance reports documented that the funeral procession was one of the greatest public displays of national unity the country had ever seen. "To pay tribute to the fallen leader in the middle of a battle for the liberation of his compatriots," Le Nouvelliste reported that when Sylvain's body passed, "the mass of peasants who filled the upper market fell to their knees spontaneously."[6] And La Poste reported that "when the body of Georges Sylvain appeared in front of the market at the Cathedral, all the market women, buyers and vendors present, as if from an order, knelt down . . . and nothing but sobbing was heard."[7] These reverent touches to the ground were a different kind of accumulation. This was an amassing of collective care alongside loss. In 1925 few could imagine that the occupation would continue for another decade, but the droves of people who flooded the streets of Port-au-Prince shared a sentiment that Sylvain had hastened the end of the occupation if not remained a constant thorn in the foreign military's side. In the public discourse his writing and political leadership were translated as weaponry against the occupation. And his death was articulated as a casualty of war. Not all death under the occupation could be accounted for in the ledgers of combat loss. As expressed in the epigraph above from the fictional character Claire whose family was disoriented by the US Navy and whose father died suddenly from the news of the foreign occupiers' arrival, many Haitians framed ordinary death within the milieu of nonsovereignty. Thus, Georges Sylvain's body may not have been counted among the official fatalities of the occupation, but his death and the outpouring of grief served as proxy for the many losses and rituals of death that transpired and were denied in his decade-long fight against the US occupation.

Sylvain's death also marked a transition for antioccupation organizing. As signaled in his posthumously compiled and published book *Dix années de lutte*, during the first decade of the occupation Haitians produced an expansive and nuanced repertoire of organizing between *caco* fighting, UP urban activism, and daily acts of refusal. Moreover, Sylvain's death coincided with a shift in the US military's application of occupation law. After the 1920 and 1921 Senate commissions and inquiry trips to Haiti, the US government instructed the US occupying forces to temper and more extensively record their actions. This adjustment in the military approach to the occupation produced several new outcomes. First, the increase in documentation led to an expanded record of everyday activities in Haiti, simultaneously leaving traces of different women's lives. Second, increased and expanded systems of surveillance allowed the US military to infiltrate and weaken the *caco* operations at multiple levels, leading to the deaths of key leaders, less frequent battles, and a decline in combat deaths.

Yet Haitian newspapers and US military records show that the Haitian death toll and injury as a result of confrontation with occupation officials continued to rise, resulting in a simultaneous frustration from Haitians who tired of the careless ways in which their people lost their lives after 1925 until the 1929 occupation riots. For example, on the same day that Georges Sylvain's funeral services were taking place, US occupation intelligence teams reported that "US automobile 1819" hit two unnamed Haitians who "sustained contusions on the face and left leg, the other received minor scratches only."[8] The case was pending until one of the victims, unidentified by the military, was released from the hospital. *Le Nouvelliste* revealed the victim was "a child [who] was run over and brought to the hospital." The article insisted that "automobile accidents are becoming too frequent and measures need to be taken."[9] The decrease in spectacular forms of combat violence drew more attention and organizing to the everyday ways in which the occupation continued to impact Haitian's lives. For many people lining the streets of Port-au-Prince on August 3, Sylvain's funeral events were an accounting for the cumulative losses of the occupation that often could not be accounted for by combat reports, or were silenced by denial.[10]

Sylvain Family, 1921. Standing: Henry, Yvonne, Jeanne, Suzanne, Madeleine, Normil, Pierre. Seated: Georges and Eugene Sylvain. Courtesy of the Suzanne Comhaire-Sylvain Collection, Department of Special Collections, Stanford University Libraries.

Within days of Sylvain's death, leaders of the UP put out ads to collect images, speeches, and thoughts from the day of the funeral and from any of the poet's prior speeches or writings. When *Dix années de lutte* was published, it was a critical document of collective public mourning. It was a reconciliation of the relationship between the ordinary deaths and the extraordinary conditions of occupation through scholarly production.

The simultaneous outpouring of grief, care, tales of grandeur, and efforts to account for and record life that took place during the funeral ceremonies was the very expression that had captured Sylvain's eldest daughter, Suzanne, since she was a little girl. A sickly child whose illnesses brought her close to her own mortality, Suzanne was comforted by folklores that her caregiver Amise told her while nursing her back to health. Enchanted by these stories, the young Suzanne voluntarily attended the end-of-life ceremonies—wakes, funerals, and burials—of those she knew and did not know to hear loved ones narrate the life of the deceased.[11] She was particularly drawn to the provocative performance of the wake, the pre-funeral ritual of sitting with or dancing around the body of the deceased while family, friends, and elders told stories over the dead. According to her family, these rituals soothed Suzanne's physical ailing and charged her curiosity.[12] It is likely that much of that same tranquility and anticipatory energy pulsed through the crowd on August 3. Stories likely circulated, and there was probably even, for some brief moments, laughter. Suzanne's familiarity with the rituals of death and burial may have provided some comfort. Still, Suzanne's pleasure in dwelling with the sounds and sites of celebrating the dead did not guard her from falling into a period of deep sorrow following her father's death, beginning a "long eight years" in which her eldest brother, Normil Sylvain, and mother also died.[13]

The familial loss and its attendant meanings hovered over Suzanne's and her sisters' thinking and organizing work. Madeleine, who had just returned home from her studies in Jamaica at the Immaculate Conception Academy before her father died, took on new responsibility for her three younger siblings.[14] And shortly after her parents' deaths, Suzanne left Haiti to study abroad. When she returned to Haiti for an extended period, she revisited the death space through her research in Kenscoff, which, in 1937, she characterized as a "dead city."[15] Fifteen miles outside the rapidly growing Port-au-Prince, Kenscoff had a population of approximately 7,500, with houses spaced throughout a sea of "pine and eucalyptus trees," atop steep mountains that were "also covered with about one hundred gravestones" at the town's entrance.[16] Suzanne traveled to Kenscoff to study the rituals of the dead. Like the mourners at her father's burial a decade earlier, her detailed sketching of grave sites and memorials, which I discuss further in chapter 4, suggests that she got close to the material record of people's mourning. She knelt on the ground. She touched the earth and the stone. And she sketched women's graves. In her later scholarship about funerals in Kenscoff, Suzanne wrote extensively about mourning. She explained that in the village there are two kinds of mourning: *grand deuil* and *petit deuil*. Petit mourning begins the day of the funeral, and for the immediate family this period lasts six months. She also explained that ten years after the death of a mother or father, the children initiate a service to begin the grand mourning, which lasts an additional two years for the mother and eighteen months for the father. At the end of the period, the bereaved hold a ceremony or mass for the peaceful rest of the deceased spirit, and sing a *libera*—a song of release and freedom for the spirit—over the tomb.[17]

Suzanne arrived in Kenscoff a decade and two years—*grand deuil*—after her parents' death. During this time she wrote four sequential essays in the Ligue

Féminine d'Action Sociale's bimonthly journal *La Voix des Femmes*.[18] She wrote about an unexpected reunion with a young woman from Kenscoff whom she remembered from her childhood who sold food near her home; she wrote of the continuities between the Kreyòl language and African languages (a subject close to her father's interests); she listed a series of jokes that included women and their relationship to family; and she retold a folktale about mother-daughter connections and women's unrequited desires for one another.[19] In her research and writing that moved between storytelling, playfulness, and wonder, she crafted a conceptual wake. In her four submissions to *La Voix des Femmes* she released her final processes of mourning onto a public platform and produced a *libera* for her father, mother, and elder brother. Suzanne's research and relationship to organizational politics coincided with her processes of mourning. Similar to the impetus for the creation of *Dix années de lutte*, the Sylvain sisters navigated their personal and collective loss in the final years and immediate aftermath of the occupation in their publishing record and political practice.

In her reflections on the urgency of creating during familial loss, Edwidge Danticat attends to writing as a navigational tool to make sense of losses as well as to create new visions for and versions of Haitian women.[20] Suzanne's choices and rapidity of her articles in *La Voix des Femmes* during her fieldwork reveal the primacy of a similar affective pull of mourning in women's political practice and performance in the first years of formal organizing. Taken together, Madeleine Sylvain-Bouchereau's literal transformation and Suzanne's preoccupation with death space offer a reorientation for the rebirth of women's politics after the US occupation that is informed by exclusions from the state but propelled by navigations of collective loss, longing, and creative mourning. The Sylvains' grief alongside the nation's mourning in 1925 draws historical attention to this renaissance. That is, the death space—not only the transition from this world to another (in this context Guinea) but the happenings around this transition (the processions, the possessions, the wake, the ordering of bodies in cemeteries, the mourning)—harbored new meanings under military occupation. Dying and death during and after occupation were written into the political landscape and generated subtle adjustments in these women's political frame throughout the early and mid-twentieth century.

Suzanne and her sisters took the example of their parents' intellectual and political organizing as well as their grief for them into their work as they processed the end of the occupation and the beginning of "Haiti's Second Independence." In the occupation period, women made claims on individual self-determination and collective belonging through the witnessing, refusal, and documenting of their experiences. As the girls and elders of the *desoccu-pation* period started a postoccupation women's movement, they turned toward studying women's experience as a path for organizing across difference. This public mourning was intertwined with their earnest interest in new political possibilities that started with learning about the women with whom they encountered or shared experiences under the occupation—the same women who knelt and cried as the Sylvain sisters and their father passed by.

CHAPTER TWO

Publishing Rights
Women's Writing and Research Practices

In 1937 Madeleine Sylvain spent her semester vacation from Bryn Mawr School of Social Work with friends in Montreal. When she completed her final projects for the term, she made her way to the Thirtieth Street Station in Philadelphia and boarded a train bound for Quebec. There, she met up with Philippe Cantave, a longtime family friend and the Haitian ambassador to Canada. In the biting Canadian cold, Cantave escorted Sylvain around town as she visited tourist sights and made several public speeches.[1]

The Canadian press was enthusiastic to meet with and interview Sylvain when she arrived. *La Presse*, the leading newspaper in Montreal, followed her throughout her weeklong stay in the city. During this time, a reporter asked her, as the editor of *La Voix des Femmes*, about the condition of Haitian women. She responded, "Haitian women do not have any rights. The law treats us as if we are children, criminals, or insane."[2] Madeleine's bleak assessment of women's rights under the law was fundamentally accurate. In the interwar period, Haitian women's citizenship was dictated by civil codes drawn from the French Napoleonic Code. Under these laws, women in the twentieth century were considered minors. Married women in particular were not allowed to hold their own wages, purchase property, or move within or outside of the country without spousal permission. Socially, women were criminalized for their decisions in their familial and sexual partnerships. Either through their parenting choices, decisions to separate from or divorce their husbands, or through *plasaj* (nonlegal marriage or common-law marriage with the possibility of multiple partnerships), women were targeted by local and national political leaders as evidence of national weakness and immorality.[3]

Sylvain's transparency and open criticism of her country's social order may have appeared unpatriotic and even criminal to some of her critics at home. In 1937, Sténio Vincent, former antioccupation organizer and Haitian president, was not receptive to critique. In the early 1930s he imprisoned and threatened exile to Haitians who made comments like Sylvain's. The headline that accompanied her interview, "In Haiti, Women Have No Rights," would have frustrated the president who was already dealing with criticism for his mild response to the October massacre of hundreds of Haitians on the Haitian-Dominican border. Preoccupied with foreign alliances and public perceptions of his leadership, Vincent would not have welcomed additional international critique.[4] However, Sylvain saw herself as an unofficial diplomat of the nation that was emerging from the occupying governance of the United States.[5] In her public presentations, she boasted about Haiti's revolution and independence in 1804 and highlighted folklore as one of the many gems of the country. Her trip to Montreal, while recreational, was also an extension of the international work that her mother and father carried out during their antioccupation organizing. In the postoccupation period, Sylvain and her compatriots continued to garner support for their women's movement throughout the Caribbean, Latin America, and North America. These women pledged that Haitian women's reality and "voice must be heard and listened to."[6] So they spoke frankly.

This chapter looks at the ways members of the Ligue Féminine d'Action Sociale (LFAS) used publicity, authorship, and research as mutually informing technologies to experiment with ideas of citizenship, womanhood, and differences between women in Haiti and abroad in the five years immediately following the US occupation. As discussed in chapter 1, Haitian women had transformative experiences under the US occupation, and for some, this transformation spawned a new sense of social consciousness regarding women's position in the country articulated through political organizing. As fundraisers, activists, and members of antioccupation movements, women like Madeleine Sylvain, Alice Garoute, and Thérèse Hudicourt had also accumulated a record of leadership. This experience was cultivated alongside and on behalf of other antioccupation activists and nationalists like Sténio Vincent. Having had close political and personal ties with Vincent, these women anticipated that the transition toward *desoccupation* and the new legal doctrines therein would reflect an appreciation for women's active participation in earning the nation's sovereignty.[7] They did not.

Over the course of the 1930s, there were two constitutional conventions and countless opportunities to change women's legal status. The conventions resulted in no movement or negative results for women's rights. In June 1935, one year after the full military withdrawal of US soldiers, Vincent announced a constitutional referendum that extended his presidential term and allowed him to succeed himself. This constitutional change gave Vincent undemocratic power over the nation but left women's constitutional status unchanged. The continuity between the transition period from occupied to nonoccupied nation was evidence that the end of the occupation would not necessarily translate into the end of political or social gender inequality. As a result, women

GETS FELLOWSHIP

Madeleine Sylvain standing for photo captioned "Gets Fellowship," *Chicago Defender*, October 2, 1937. Sylvain won a fellowship to study at Bryn Mawr College. Courtesy of the Suzanne Comhaire-Sylvain Collection, Department of Special Collections, Stanford University Libraries.

remained interested in legislated changes to their rights, but they also acknowledged a need for a more circuitous route. They used some of the techniques
that they developed during the occupation organizing to communicate their
relationship to the nation and move through the windy and often bumpy road
of the 1930s and Vincent years. In particular, this chapter shows how women
used the organization Ligue Feminine d'Action Sociale, scholarship, workshops,
community programming, and feminist rhetoric to experiment with the possibilities of citizenship for Haitians in the early twentieth century.

When Sylvain made her comments to the Canadian press in 1937, the LFAS
was only in its second year of social service and political activism, and in her
assessment, their "progress [was] still hardly perceptible."[8] Yet over the following two decades, Sylvain and her friends and allies worked to articulate a
politics to "solve the problems nearest [to] their hearts as mothers and apos-
tles of a broader life."[9] From the outset, the founders of the LFAS knew their
mission to study and advocate for women's political rights was prodigious.
Sylvain admitted several years into their work that "this program may seem
ambitious, but the members of the League have faith in the potential of Haitian women, believing that they can work together in a friendly spirit, sustained by their devotion to their ideal."[10]

The LFAS membership's faith abided in women. They believed in and
committed to women's intelligence, labor, and practice of friendship. Months
after Sylvain's statement of infancy, criminality, and madness as characteristics
of women's lives in Haiti, the LFAS leadership still optimistically maintained,
"Our fight is not a *chimère*." Their goals were neither monstrous philosophies
set to destroy and disorient the nation nor a mirage of the women's well-
educated imaginations. Yet this chapter also considers how the public image,
scholarship, and articulated goals of the movement were crafted and sometimes
tempered by women's sense of efficacy and ambivalence toward organizing
work as a means to change their experiences of national belonging. If these
women's claims on citizenship were well-crafted fantasy at best and well-
informed desires at worst, what did the performance and practice of these
imaginings and study reveal about the possibilities and limits of politics in
Haiti? And how could their thinking and practice approximate the most elu-
sive component of their work: the goal to articulate a politics for all women?

Early Women's Rights Organizing

During the two decades of establishing their own intellectual communities
through fundraising and reading groups in the occupation period, Alice Ga-

route and Thérèse Hudicourt studied the history of political organizing in Haiti. Through popular history and storytelling, they discussed Catherine Flon, Défilée, and the daughters of a revolution that introduced the modern world to Black freedom. Yet history seemed to be repeating itself. Just as women in the precolonial and colonial periods had become symbols of liberation for the nation, after the demonstrations in the 1930s they also remained mythical foremothers with no concrete rights in the independent nation. The national history suggested that gender equality would not come without action from a united front with clear demands for the Haitian government transitioning out from foreign rule.

This history also suggested that a movement needed clear leadership. Alice Garoute was an obvious choice. She was socially respected and politically savvy, and through her antioccupation organizing, she skillfully led a generation of women into activism. Born Alice Thézan in 1874 into a *milat* (light-skinned upperclass), "petit bourgeoisie" family in Cap-Haïtien, Garoute was older than many of the women she sought to recruit to the movement. For the younger women, Garoute offered a wealth of organizing knowledge and legacy. Her mother, who was rumored to carry a revolver in her corsage, participated in late eighteenth-century operations led by Jean-Pierre Boyer-Balezais to overthrow the Lysius Salomon government (1879–88). Garoute's family was exiled to Jamaica for several years, and when they returned, Garoute was a teenager committed to studying the history of her country. By the end of the US occupation, Garoute was also committed to training and supporting younger women's leadership. Although she was known for her sharp tongue, she was also charismatic. She told folktales about the past and often professed to know the future through her selectively shared card-reading practice.[11]

In the new cohort of activists, Garoute certainly saw a bright future for Eugénie Malbranche-Sylvain's four daughters: Madeleine Sylvain (-Bouchereau), Suzanne Comhaire-Sylvain, Yvonne Sylvain, and Jeanne Sylvain. The four had emerged from their parents' political shadow to become intellectuals and activists.[12] In particular, Madeleine—the young girl who was a teenager when her mother canvassed the streets of Port-au-Prince in the 1920s—entered law school one month after the Sacre l'Coeur women's march and completed her studies in law at the University of Haiti the year before the 1932 Constitutional Convention. Her legal insight and family legacy of activism also made her the ideal face of the women's movement. In anticipation of the nation's full independence in 1934, Sylvain and Garoute joined their collective expertise and worked for two years discussing their respective visions for a women's political organization.

Almost immediately, a potential opening for women's rights was presented in the form of the 1932 Constitutional Convention. As the nation emerged from US authority, the convention was under the occupation regime, but it was overseen by elected president Vincent and the elected assembly members, who included Pierre Hudicourt, Jean Price-Mars, Denis St. Aude, and Dumersais Estimé. However, as soon as the opportunity seemed to open, it was just as quickly shut. The assembly members left Article 8 of the 1932 Constitution unchanged: male citizens age twenty-one years or older were the only citizens eligible to vote in national or regional elections.[13] As legal scholar Mirlande Manigat has explained, "the preoccupation of the moment concerned the most immediate equality of powers and of obtaining *desoccupation*," so women's rights were, according to the assembly, not a pressing issue. In response, the women actively waited.

Throughout the occupation, educated and affluent Haitian women established relationships with Caribbean and African American women, including women in the simultaneously US-occupied Dominican Republic.[14] For Garoute and Sylvain, the women's movement in the Dominican Republic initially seemed like an example and possible regional partnership for women's political organizing. Through the end of 1933 and early 1934, the proximity of the two nations suggested some possibility of Haitian and Dominican women's collective organizing, but according to archival records and public history, the relationship that did ensue in the winter months of 1934 was fleeting.[15] A number of reasons may explain the short-lived collaboration. First, both Haiti and the Dominican Republic were occupied by the United States at the turn of the century (1915–34 and 1916–24, respectively), but the occupation ended in the Dominican Republic almost a decade before it ended in Haiti. This time provided elite, mostly white identified, Dominican women the opportunity to develop a concrete feminist discourse outside the occupied state.[16] Second, the discourse on feminism that elite Dominican women developed in the 1930s was quickly intertwined with the anti-Haitian and anti-Black Dominican *Hispanidad* espoused by General Rafael Trujillo (1930–61).[17] Third, and somewhat related, women on both sides of the island fed upon rumors and myths negatively stereotyping women in both countries, limiting the possibility of cordial alliances and continuing a long-standing hostility between Haiti and the Dominican Republic since the early nineteenth century.[18]

Despite this context, oral history among Haitian feminists and their families consistently maintains that when Garoute and Sylvain drafted their plans for the first Haitian women's political organization, an unnamed woman from the Dominican Republic's feminist movement contributed to their conversations.[19] In this account, Garoute and Sylvain invited the woman to share her experience in the Dominican women's movement, and after sharing her thoughts, she encouraged her hosts to start a similar organization in Haiti. In the first months of 1934, Garoute and Sylvain formalized the plans for a new organization called La Ligue Féminine d'Action Sociale (LFAS).

The LFAS had a rough start. In February, Sylvain invited a select group of women to discuss the organization. After several meetings, she and the group developed an organizational philosophy, an operational structure, and a political platform. The overarching philosophy of the collective was to seek the "improvement of Haitian women's economic, intellectual, social and political conditions."[20] By March, the structure of the organization took shape with the election of an eight-member executive committee. The remaining membership, which was estimated at nearly one hundred within the first three weeks, was divided into six subcommittees.[21] The executive committee and subcommittees then developed a platform that included the physical, intellectual, and moral improvement of Haitian women's condition in order to improve their awareness of their social obligations; the protection of children, women, and the elderly and the improvement of domestic life; and the fight for civil and political equality.[22] At the end of March, the organization had a governing body and clear goals, but it was missing government authorization.

When the LFAS leadership submitted the petition for authorization, the women likely suspected it would be a few days before the government approved the organization. They were particularly confident because many members of the LFAS were well acquainted with the transitioning Vincent administration. Garoute and Sylvain lived and socialized in the same powerful circles as Vincent. Garoute and her family were even known to host the Vincent family, the president and his sister Résia Vincent, at their Jérémie home.[23]

As a result of his work in antioccupation Haitian and US politics, Vincent was elected president four years before the occupation's end and appeared to be an ideal choice for the president given his nationalist views and founding membership in the Union Patriotique. As historian Matthew Smith has shown, Vincent's nationalist sentiments had wide appeal early in his presidency.[24] However, as the physical oppression from the US Marines subsided, Vincent became paranoid that he would lose the political popularity as the nation's savior from US imperialism.[25] He also lost political and military power once the US government departed. Although Vincent was an old family friend and a comrade to LFAS members in the nationalist movement, as the US Marines were leaving, the president became suspicious of former allies. In the absence of foreign military support, Vincent used his executive power to monitor and repress organizations, unions, and social and religious gatherings.[26]

Vincent was particularly anxious about the younger generation of nationalist activists who were turning away from the philosophies of nationalism espoused in the 1920s, and toward a radical Marxist philosophy of governance for the country.[27] LFAS founders' friends and family were among these newly minted Marxists, including Thérèse Hudicourt's nephew and attorney, Max Hudicourt, and noted writer and poet Jacques Roumain. In the years after Hudicourt and Roumain helped found *La Revue Indigène* in 1927, their cofounder and Madeleine Sylvain's brother, Normil Sylvain, died (1929).[28] But the ideas of the indigenous literary movement that celebrated African ancestry and encouraged an intellectual renaissance that studied Haitian culture, religion, and language were very much alive.

Although the indigenous movement (*indigénisme*) was powerful in discourse by 1933, its proponents had not developed any politically oriented action.[29] Thus Hudicourt, Roumain, and others turned toward other philosophies. Through their study of Marxism, communism, and radical leftist thought, the young intellectuals began to promote a political agenda that focused less on color and culture and more on the economic disparity within the country. They wanted to rebuild the nation by reviving the civil and economic productivity of the nation's masses. President Vincent, however, saw Marxist activism as a threat to his liberal nationalism. In order to ensure his executive control, Vincent initiated violent campaigns of surveillance and imprisonment against Marxists and their sympathizers. Under this repression, Roumain and Hudicourt were arrested in 1932 and imprisoned in 1933 for spreading communist propaganda and planning an attack on the US occupying government.[30]

The end of Roumain's and Hudicourt's three-month incarceration coincided with Sylvain, Garoute, and Thérèse Hudicourt's petition for organizational authorization. Vincent certainly recognized the names on the petition and likely reflected on the founders' familial and social affiliations. Perhaps he even remembered his visits to the Garoute home and the collection of books and newspapers that included Marxist material.[31] Or perhaps he was more concerned by Madeleine Sylvain's presence as a young intellectual in the orbit of other twenty-year-old thinkers like Hudicourt and Roumain who all lived and socialized in the same circles. Whatever his musings—perhaps the mention of a women's labor department or improvements to women's roles in domestic and family life—the petition flagged the brewing of more radical intentions, and Vincent's government rejected the petition. Denied authorization, the initial formulation of the LFAS dissolved in April 1934.[32]

In her account of the first attempt to start the LFAS, Sylvain identifies two reasons for the organization's false start. First, she maintained that the Vincent government "took offense" to the aggressive agenda of the organization. According to Sylvain, Vincent and his administration were particularly offended by some of the detailed goals of the organization, specifically citing "the construction and development of public secondary schools for girls, economic independence for married women, equal salary for equal work, women's suffrage, freedom to establish a women's labor department, and a prohibition on brothels."[33]

Second, she explained that political and experiential differences among members created divisions within the organizations.[34] In her assessment, Sylvain characterized the two factions that emerged within the organization. On one side, she explained, there was a majority of "timid and conservative" women who did not want to be on the wrong side of the government. On the other side, there was a small group of "enthusiastic and dedicated" women who were relentless warriors in the cause for women's rights but were unable to develop a political platform that would have wide national appeal.[35] These distinctions located women beyond their class status into a patriotic location of willingness and commitment. For those "timid and conservative" women the cause of women's rights was admirable, but the threat to their safety and that of their families was a legitimate concern. Women were not exempt from arrest, and the men in their families were not exempt from political or legal action in response to women's actions.[36] In this way, Vincent's taking offense to the organization's platform combined with his administrative turn to violent repression was a deterrent.

Sylvain made no overt connection between the repression of leftist thought by the Vincent administration and the rejection of the LFAS's first petition for authorization. However, in her account of the approximate one hundred members of the first installation of the LFAS, she mentions only one member by name, Mme. Pierre Hudicourt.[37] Sylvain explains that Thérèse Hudicourt was instrumental in developing the organization, and as a result of her experience in social work and familiarity with national politics, she was elected president of the LFAS.[38] Hudicourt's presidency, however, may have put the young organization at risk.[39] Although the founding members of the LFAS never established an official alliance with any political party or movement, the familial connection between Hudicourt and her Marxist nephew, and to a lesser degree her husband, had the potential to trouble the Vincent government.

Despite the initial setback, the "enthusiastic and dedicated" women immediately went back to work. On May 10, 1934, Sylvain along with Alice Garoute, Thérèse Hudicourt, Fernande Bellegarde, Olga Gordon, Marie Corvington, Alice Téligny Mathon, Esther Dartigue, Maud Turian, and Georgette Justin led a group of women teachers, attorneys, doctors, journalists, and social workers to develop a more palatable agenda for government authorities and founded a new LFAS. The organization carried the same name, but it had a revised platform that was structured around the mission to address issues of poverty, hygiene, childcare, and the moral, physical, and intellectual conditions of women in all social classes. The Vincent government was satisfied with the LFAS's modified initiatives and granted the organization legal authorization with "little difficulty."[40] Although much of the mission of the first version of the LFAS was incorporated into the second formation, the public face of the organization was oriented toward social service. Sylvain later wrote, "The founders thought that feminism, more than a movement of political liberation, was above all a movement for social improvement, and it's this feminism that the women inaugurated."[41] Thus, from the outset the women untethered the movement from a strict focus on political rights within state governance, and prioritized changes in the social structures of the nation. In this regard, the founders surmised that a public-facing mission of altruism would appease the government and appeal to a larger audience of women and men.[42]

After they established their mission, the LFAS leadership's first priority was to expand the membership and strategically situate themselves within the national political discourse in order to advance their social agenda. To draw support, they sought to disseminate a message of multiclass women's activism and unified Haitian womanhood. It was a simple concept in theory, but the leadership makeup of the LFAS suggested that the organization was at least a social club for elite women and at most a philanthropic organization with little understanding of the experiences of the majority of women in the nation. The leadership's educational and career credentials marked them as members of an elite class. Sylvain, the new president of the organization, was an attorney. Garoute, the vice president, was an intellectual and the wife of a high court justice. Thérèse Hudicourt, former president and treasurer, was a social worker from a prominent family. Fernande Bellegarde, the secretary general, was the daughter of the former French ambassador and future US ambassador Dantès Bellegarde. Sylvain's sisters, Yvonne, Jeanne, and Suzanne, were all prominent members of the organization, and were also respectively the first female doctor, certified social worker, and anthropologist in the country. And the list went on.[43]

The founders of the LFAS were pioneers in the professional history of Haitian women, but their educational and intellectual advances represented a small fraction of Haitian women or society writ large in the early twentieth century. Yet as historian Chantalle Verna suggests, given the economic surge, global networks, and steady rise of the educated population in the immediate postoccupation period, this group of women was part of "a more ordinary professional class," whose "privileged status was less a function of the wealth they accumulated or prominent positions they held than tied to knowledge, skills, or contacts they acquired."[44] At the same time, in 1934 the public perception of the women's class and cultural competence was central to their organizational success. Specifically, in postoccupation Haiti, political organizing was increasingly articulated through class and color rhetorical divisions. For example, the growing contingency of leftist activists argued that the fundamental problems of the nation were based on class rather than color.

While Marxist leaders like Roumain acknowledged color prejudice and conflict, they saw political ideology based on color divisions as a veil, masking the real issue of unbalanced wealth distribution in the country.[45] This standpoint differed from that of a group of young intellectuals known as the Griots, who studied the work of Arthur Holly and Jean Price-Mars and believed that color prejudice was the central problem of the nation. This group included Louis Diaquoi, Lorimer Denis, and François Duvalier. They came together at the end of the 1920s and at the moment of establishing their own journal *Les Griots* in 1938, its members imagined themselves as a continuation of the project of *La Revue Indigène*.[46] By the 1940s, however, these men expanded the ideological concepts of *indigénisme* into an explicitly antiliberal and Black nationalist rhetoric, known as *noirisme*.[47] In addition to celebrating African-descended beliefs and traditions such as Vodou, folklore, and dance, *noiristes* further argued that darker-skinned people had an "ancestral heredity" that was from the African-descended founding fathers of the nation, and as a result, they (*noir* Haitians) were more authentic nationals and the rightful leaders of the country.[48] While politically provocative, in the early 1930s, as Matthew Smith has shown, *noiriste* discourse "did not assume a precise articulation until the mid-1940s."[49]

Like *noiristes* and Marxists in the 1930s, LFAS women were similarly roving through the possibilities of their own political articulation. Although the full political impact of these political ideologies on national politics was not yet clear in the early 1930s, as the LFAS worked through its inaugural year, the divisions articulated by these groups had significant impact on the women's political approach. The majority of the organization's membership was Black with color and class diversity, but the leaders' social prestige made them appear *milat*, a reminder of the exclusionary social practices of people in their economic and professional status that could deter many women from participation. As a result, the women repeatedly articulated that the LFAS was for "Haitian women of all social classes."[50] The women also situated the organization as a research unit that would collect information about women that would be useful for national service projects and intellectual research. Seven years earlier than the Institut d'Ethnologie which was established to study Haitian culture, the LFAS positioned their organization as an institution to study women.

Workshopping Feminist Theories

In June 1934, the LFAS leadership showcased the organization to win the "favorable public opinion" of the nation.[51] The women imagined their disfavor by some as a public relations issue, one that could be amended by being more visible, and by doing and sharing research that would demonstrate the relevance of their sentiments. To this end, from June 13 to July 14, the LFAS sponsored its first major event in a four-week lecture series on Haitian feminism. These workshops, which would turn into regular sessions for the organization, were designed to bring social and cultural awareness to the nation and promote discussion on current events. Moreover, through the workshops, LFAS leaders sought to address the most pressing philosophical debates of the nation and then "take them out of the domain of the abstract" into action. The gatherings were advertised as a "democratic" space where participants were free to discuss their vision of representative governing and illustrate their competence as engaged citizens through concrete plans for the nation's future.[52] As a group, the workshop attendees determined whether or not an issue deserved further intellectual attention or political action.

At an entry fee of 2.50 *gourdes*, guests were encouraged to join members of the LFAS and their distinguished lecturers each Wednesday at the Port-au-Prince Union Club, where the month's topics were feminism and women's education, Haitian women in history, the modern organization of education, and feminism in France.[53] The workshop topics previewed the organization's evolving identity, but the topics alone did not draw participants to the sessions. The distinguished lecturers heightened the workshops' appeal. The workshop speakers were Jean Price-Mars, the "architect of *indigénisme*"; Dantès Bellegarde, foreign diplomat and minister of public instruction; and Maurice

Dartigue, director of rural education (1931–41). In 1934 there were few men who were as publicly known as Price-Mars, Bellegarde, and to a lesser extent, Dartigue. The presentations were not recorded, but the men's public record and prior positioning in intellectual debates suggest that the lectures were animated and likely controversial. In particular, Price-Mars and Bellegarde had developed a reputation as sparring partners.

Price-Mars was famous for his critique of Haitians' "collective Bovaryism."[54] Price-Mars charged the Haitian elite with escapist daydreaming in which they pined after and imagined themselves as extensions of France rather than acknowledging and celebrating, where appropriate, the contexts and conditions of their country. In 1917 Price-Mars gave a lecture to a group of elite women titled "Women of Tomorrow." The lecture, which became an iconic representation of Price-Mars's forward thinking and brutal honesty, reflected his interest in women's rights as a component of his philosophic commitment to *indigénisme*. In his studies of rural culture and society, peasant women's lives captured his attention and led him to critically analyze the intersections between class, gender, culture, and color in Haiti.[55] Parsing Haitian women into two categories of peasant and elite, Price-Mars argued that despite their differences, poor and elite women were ultimately bound by their shared African ancestry. However, he went on to advise elite women that they were further removed from this ancestry but that through relationships with peasant women they could mend this divide and reclaim a more authentic Haitian womanhood. He delineated that peasant women's bodies and work "still in the primitivity of African traditions" were the interlocutors and "witnesses" to their pure African past.[56]

As ancestral sisters, Price-Mars also asserted that peasant and elite women were also connected in their role as women in a patriarchal society. Price-Mars asserted that Haitian women were Haitian men's "tools."[57] That is, peasant women were literally tools of agricultural and market labor, while pious, expensively dressed, elite women were ornaments for elite men's construction of their social identity, respectability, and masculine reputation. Price-Mars named a gendered objectification that was not unlike the characterization of a slave—evacuated of any significance beyond use for capitalist or patriarchal gain. To restore their personhood and defeat patriarchy, Price-Mars implored the women to stop "sucking the marrow of Christian traditions" that were leaving women with "intellectual poverty."[58] He encouraged them to be "impregnated in their brains" with cultural and civic education to help Haiti move prosperously into the twentieth century.[59] Price-Mars's endorsement of intellectual conception in place of immaculate conception, which he argued kept young Haitian women consumed with social appearances rather than personal development, was a direct challenge to the elite conservative and Catholic education that many of the women received.

At the LFAS workshop, Price-Mars facilitated the discussion "Haitian Women in History."[60] If he presented any portion of his previous lectures, his words would have had significant impact on the workshop audience and organizers. His participation likely served two roles for the budding organization. First, Price-Mars's presence reflected LFAS leaders' willingness to openly critique class, cultural, and color privilege. In particular, Price-Mars advanced Black African descendancy as a legacy of the nation. Yet the celebration of African ancestry did not necessarily equal the absence of color prejudice. As Michel-Rolph Trouillot, Matthew Smith, Kate Ramsey, and others have pointed out, elite and middle-class Haitians often celebrated culture without challenging prejudices toward the history and people who practiced the culture every day. However, in order to be released from the collective Bovarysm, elite and middle-class women had to not only study or celebrate peasant culture but incorporate the forms of thinking into their own work and lives. He invited an epistimic shift in affluent and educated women's thinking.

In Price-Mars's formulation, rural women embodied a cultural authenticity that LFAS women had to respect and include in their feminist practice in order to develop a unified women's movement. As a result, any national women's movement had to seriously include and celebrate a platform of cross-class, cross-cultural, and rural-urban organizing. Yet Price-Mars's assertion toward women hinged on simplifications and essentializing of women and Blackness. In Price-Mars's formulation, peasant women's bodies and cultural capital were to be offered up for elite and middle-class women's entry into the land of origins. This violence would be enacted by women, onto women.

At the same time, Price-Mars's vision did the important work of addressing the commonality and intersection of women's lives not only as African descended but also as Black women. His attention to Haitian women's intimate relationships with men identified these women's shared oppression in a patriarchal society. In his assertion that women reject their objectification through the pursuit of critical education, Price-Mars identified scholastic achievement as the means by which women could overcome domestic mistreatment, the trappings of consumerism, and limited civic involvement.[61] This formulation not only unified Haitian women as leaders in domestic spaces but also could have validated the LFAS leadership's educational and professional achievements.

Paradoxically, Price-Mars provided women with a response to patriarchy, but he was less demanding of Haitian men. Price-Mars, unfortunately, missed the opportunity to incorporate men in his critique of women as property, capital, and possession.[62] For example, when addressing accountability within monogamous marriages between men and women, Price-Mars explained men's multiple partnerships within marriage as a cultural trait of African ancestry, without addressing the contractual agreement or the power dynamics within marriages that left many married women subject to the decision-making processes of their husbands. However, in 1934 the continued absence of a critical engagement with men's sexuality in the patriarchal society would unify women to push for legal reforms to family laws. As addressed in chapter 3, women sought financial control of their professional earnings and became intellectual experts on intimate partnership formations throughout the country, ultimately defending women's engagement in plasaj relationships from government regulation.

Anchored in a celebration of African ancestry and the importance of women's education, Price Mars's lecture was complemented by professor Maurice Dartigue's lecture on modern organization of education. At the time of the summer workshops, Dartigue had recently finished his studies in education at the Teacher's College at Columbia University in New York.[63] When he returned to Haiti, he continued to work as an educator and developed a reputation as an expert in rural and industrial education. During the summer break, Dartigue's wife and LFAS founding member Esther Dartigue likely invited her husband to share his thoughts with the organization.[64]

As she later wrote of her husband's legacy, Esther admired Maurice's insight toward Haitian education, which supported elementary teaching in Kreyòl, establishing a core curriculum around Haitian, Latin American, and North American culture, and replacing French textbooks with English books. However, Esther was frustrated by the elite's slow response to her family's call for improvement in rural education. In particular, she supported her husband's advocacy of industrial education for Haiti's uneducated population.[65]

Some members of the audience may have been slow to receive these suggestions. Historian Millery Polyné's work shows that at the end of the occupation and into the early postoccupation period, many wealthy and educated Haitians were concerned that industrial education would turn the nation into a country of semiskilled laborers instead of a country of researchers and liberally educated thinkers.[66] Like Price-Mars, Dartigue also believed in mending the gap between peasant and elite women through education. It was, as Dartigue saw it, necessary to educate the peasant class in order to create an informed citizenry and improve the national economy.

Dartigue and Price-Mars both presented education as a gender equalizer. Through education, women would maximize their contribution to the nation, and as a result, they would earn political rights based on their credentials as thinking, productive citizens. Certainly, the injustice in this equation was that national belonging was governed by liberal distortions of reason as a measure of valuable citizenship for the ultimate purpose of capitalist labor extraction, and further that men were not held to the same standard of citizenship. However, in the 1930s the concept that women of any class could be formally educated and considered intellectual experts in a field of study was a profound proposition.[67]

Price-Mars's and Dartigue's political and professional sentiments were on the extreme and moderate end, respectively, of the political spectrum compared with those of the final workshop speaker, Dantès Bellegarde. By the 1930s, Bellegarde's list of accomplishments and accolades was extensive. He had served as Haitian ambassador to both France and the United States, spoken at the second Pan-African Congress, helped lead the anti–US occupation movement, written two books on Haitian history and culture, and befriended some of the leading thinkers and activists of the early twentieth century, including African Americans W. E. B. Du Bois and Rayford Logan, and his countryman and fellow workshop speaker Price-Mars.[68] Bellegarde, however, was far more conservative in his philosophies of Haiti than his friend and intellectual sparring partner Price-Mars. Bellegarde recognized the power of African-descended people uniting for civil rights throughout the world, but he was cautious of *indigénisme*. He believed in Western liberal thought and ultimately desired that Haiti and Black people in the region integrate into Western society as equals in the dominant white-Anglo culture.[69] Dantès's concept of feminism in women's education corresponded with his more conservative beliefs. From this standpoint, Bellegarde and Price-Mars were publicly characterized as ideological foes.[70]

The philosophical discord between Bellegarde and Price-Mars was, perhaps, the impetus for their invitation. Bellegarde's daughter and LFAS secretary general Fernande Bellegarde was aware of the differences in political thought between her father and the other workshop speakers. But the rivalry between the thinkers had the potential to draw large crowds to the LFAS event.[71] Apart from inciting ideological banter, historian Patrick Bellegarde-Smith explains that the iconic debates between Bellegarde and Price-Mars throughout the twentieth century were an outgrowth of larger questions of Haiti's modern history, which were "Who are we?" and "What does it mean to be Haitian in the modern world?"[72] Haitian feminists were grappling with these same questions. To this end, the perspectives of Price-Mars, Bellegarde, and Dartigue on Haitian feminism provided varying perspectives to a group of women who claimed to represent half of a nation in a moment of modern identity reformation.

The end of the monthlong series coincided with the official end of the US military occupation on August 1, 1934. At the end of the workshops, the common theme across the presentations was research and education. As outlined in their goals for the events, the participants were left with the decision on how they would act. However, if education was the avenue to equal citizenship, the paths to citizenship among women were not the same or equally accessible. Although Price-Mars's and Dartigue's projections for Haiti's future included culturally enriched education, in the 1930s European-inspired and Catholic-infused education, as supported by Bellegarde, was the most respected and desired education by many Haitian women across all classes.[73] Industrial education could harness the physical labor that many peasant and working-class women were already putting into their plots of land or market businesses. Yet industrial education was based on the premise that there were students for this education. Elite women were not among this applicant pool. Similar to the debates on industrial education for African Americans in the United States, the emphasis on women's physical labor had the potential to reify gendered class divisions by further demarcating the labor pool into semi-skilled trade and professional workers.[74] Within Dartigue's plan, the LFAS could justify an uplift and philanthropic approach to political practice, but how, they debated, could this approach be developed in an inclusive feminist framework?

The ideas espoused during the LFAS workshops encouraged Haitian women to consider how they would craft their politics and further insert their gendered analysis into cultural debates of the time. The philosophical standpoints regarding Haitian national identity, social practice, and economic productivity articulated at the inaugural workshop series were also the same lines that were drawn in national politics of the 1930s and '40s. Thus, in the first year of educational events, the other LFAS lecturers included André Liautaud, Frédéric Kébreau, Dantès Bellegarde, Pierre Sylvain, Hermann Corvington, Raymond Doret, Robert Théard, Marc Marval, Etienne Charlier, Esther Dartigue, Alice Garoute, and Madeleine Sylvain. Garoute and Sylvain's choice of speakers was an intuitive acknowledgment that they would have to contend with varying intellectual and political philosophies for the duration of the LFAS's existence and their political lives. Yet the workshops also illustrated that women could frame the parameters of these debates to benefit their political agendas. As the architect of this forum, the LFAS established a regular home for public dialogue.[75]

The LFAS attempted to bring all political perspectives into debate. Sylvain expressed that the purpose of the LFAS gatherings was to talk and shift notions of women's national belonging with calculated measure: "We do not intend to enact laws or make plans that would undermine the power of the nation or exceeds both our possibilities and our aspirations. We only wish to collaborate in social progress by bringing our loyal and nonaligned assistance to the Government."[76] Sylvain articulated a nonpartisan, reformist agenda that discursively ensured men were not dwarfed by women's political capacity. In this framing, the political success and longevity of the organization and their fight for women's rights hinged on their ability to address, maneuver, and sometimes ignore the issues likely raised at the first workshop series. LFAS women articulated feminism as a political gesture that could be adopted by any political group rather than a hardened, and possibly threatening, political movement. Over the following decade this wayfaring often left the organization and the concepts of feminism that they espoused under attack from multiple sides, politically aligned and not. As these concepts were funneled through their political practice, LFAS members turned to education, publication, and publicity. How could elite women be reeducated to the experiences of poor, peasant, and working-class women? How could "all" women be incorporated in the national structure of education? The journey of attending to these goals would be traversed over the following decade through written media and social work.

La Voix des Femmes

After the summer workshop series, the LFAS's organizational focus was women's education. Under the umbrella of education, the members included scholastic, civic, social, and sexual education. The organization's rigorous programming schedule in areas throughout and around Port-au-Prince reveals the significance of this focus. In October, the women established a night school for women's illiteracy training in Saint-Antoine, continuing the work of their initial version of the LFAS, where they established a night school in Saint-Anne. By November 1934, the LFAS counted one hundred students between the two schools. Madeleine Sylvain also started a Girl Scout troop, implemented a practice of conducting regular social surveys regarding women's role in society, established research committees like the "Legislation" committee to study Haitian women's position under the law, and established regular visits to women residents in orphanages, mental health asylums, and the penitentiary. The women fundraised through dinners, artistic showcases, and private contributions to fund these initial efforts.

Sylvain expressed concern early on that hiring new teachers for the night schools could strain their limited resources, but some initiatives, like the LFAS educational courses for women and children in prison, were supported by Résia Vincent, President Vincent's sister, and "she had received the necessary high approvals" to use government funding for the program. The pace of the women's work was noted not only by the president's sister but also by women's enthusiasm to join the organization. As Fernande Bellegarde, LFAS secretary general, wrote in her report in November 1935, the effort to establish an additional LFAS chapter in Port-de-Paix was an "eloquent testament" to the work of the organization.[77]

The busied pace of the LFAS's first several years ultimately had one purpose. As Sylvain explained, "We Haitian feminists, we ask above all for the ability to educate ourselves through the creation of high schools for young girls, the increase in the number of our primary schools for young girls, [and] the revision of the programs of women's education in order to make them more applicable to our needs."[78] As trained professionals, the LFAS leaders modeled the benefits of scholastic education. The LFAS routinely applauded their leaders for their academic achievements and encouraged them to multiply their academic pursuits.[79] In this respect, LFAS president Madeleine Sylvain and her three sisters, commonly known as the Sylvain sisters, were a perfect example.[80]

Sylvain began her work with women and children at the age of twenty-two when she founded the social support agency Pupilles des Saint-Antoine. The center provided basic needs for women and their children such as clothing and food. Madeleine enrolled in law school in 1930 and earned her degree in 1933.[81] As Sylvain practiced law and led the LFAS, her sister Yvonne became an obstetrician-gynecologist. She was the first woman admitted and graduated from the Haitian School of Medicine in 1940. As a specialist in venereal disease, she had many patients who suffered during the rise in syphilis cases in the first half of the twentieth century.[82] In the 1920s and '30s, her experience was tested as she negotiated the devastating effects of the nationwide yaws epidemic.[83] Moreover, as the demographic landscape of the country changed with rural to urban migration following the US occupation, Yvonne's work was affected by the poor sanitation conditions of overcrowded urban neighborhoods that facilitated the spread of bacterial and parasitic diseases such as tuberculosis and malaria. These diseases routinely led to prenatal death and infant sickness and mortality. Working at the epicenter of women's urban healthcare, Yvonne became concerned about women's living conditions as a public health crisis.[84]

Similarly, Jeanne's experiences as a social worker gave her exposure to women's domestic conditions across social classes. In letters to her sisters, Jeanne frequently wrote of her exhaustion given the overwhelming number of clients in need of her services.[85] While Madeleine's, Yvonne's, and Jeanne's careers provided an understanding of law, medicine, and social work, Suzanne's work wove together all of these aspects of Haitian life. When Suzanne left Haiti after her parents' death in 1925 and 1931, she studied at the Sorbonne in Paris and worked as a research assistant at London University. As an anthropologist, Suzanne spent weeks, months, and years studying African retentions in Haitian culture and language. She became noted for her comparative work on West African coastal languages and Haitian Kreyòl.[86] Her scholarly focus was linguistics and storytelling in Haitian and West African languages, but her time in the Haitian countryside among the majority peasant population gave her insight into the multiple articulations of Haitian culture, practices of marriage, and women's public and private work.[87]

With this education and cultural exposure, the sisters represented multilayered professional expertise that had cross-class relevance for their feminist agenda. Unlike her father's campaign for national sovereignty, however, Madeleine's concern for women's rights was slow to gain the attention or concern of the nation. Among those who were aware, the movement was not understood or supported because some questioned feminism as a foreign import from Europe or North America. Even for those who agreed with the premise of equal rights, many did not see the reality. As one critic explained, "Equality of the sexes is a *chimère*. It will never become a reality."[88] To combat the discourse of impossibility, the LFAS used written media to help the nation better understand their political concepts. To do this, the Sylvain sisters and other members of the LFAS documented their experiences, showcased their work, and disseminated their thoughts and scholastic achievements through the LFAS newspaper, *La Voix des Femmes*. Established during a popular surge in print media, it was the first of its kind in Haiti.[89] Women had never operated and published a newspaper with an explicit mission to address women's political and intellectual lives. From the first publication issued in October 1935, the newspaper was essential to the LFAS's growth as it expanded its organizational reach and established women, and members of the LFAS in particular, as creative researchers and rigorous intellectuals.

By February 1936, *La Voix des Femmes* contributors had a firm editorial foot-ing and strong handle on periodical prose and contemporary national events. The content of *La Voix des Femmes* ranged from editorials on politics to arti-cles about international affairs. As it was a monthly publication, a small number of its pages were concerned with advertisements and social activities, but the majority of the periodical included historical and sociological essays about women. Additionally, the ethnographic research printed in the newspaper provided unprecedented documentation of women of all classes.[90] Jacques Roumain and Jean Price-Mars had written books and essays on the condition of peasant life; however, no periodical shared peasant women's daily lives with the nation. The newspaper exposed the country to the multiple life ex-periences of Haitian women and emphasized women's shared experiences by joining their stories on the printed page.

The newspaper was also a space for women to engage in critical self-reflection and social analysis, while producing and publishing original research on Haitian women that grounded their feminist theories. The editors, Alice Garoute, Madeleine Sylvain, Jeanne Perez, and Cléante Desgraves Valcin, characterized *La Voix des Femmes* as the microphone for the oppressed: "*La Voix des Femmes* will denounce injustices and abuses and will unite all Hai-tians in a common love for the country."[91] They situated themselves as social justice brokers, as Madeleine explained: "*La Voix des Femmes* wants to be the link between all Haitians who do not know enough [about women]. [*La Voix des Femmes*] will try to connect with all women throughout the world, free or oppressed, to work for women's emancipation."[92]

The newspaper had full circulation in the major cities of each region and in cities where there were LFAS chapters, including Les Cayes, Cap-Haïtien, Saint-Marc, Port-de-Paix, and Jacmel.[93] In these areas it is most likely that the core readership consisted of elite and middle-class women. The newspaper was also circulated in North America, through subscription, LFAS members carrying is-sues of the paper with them, or having issues mailed to them when they traveled. For example, Bryn Mawr College held a subscription to *La Voix des Femmes* even before Madeleine Sylvain became a student and alumna. Through *La Voix des Femmes* the LFAS members situated themselves as key voices in the press corps of Haiti and the "intellectual family" of Latin America.[94] They were not just *women* journalists. They were critical thinkers on topics that concerned them and the nation. Among the readers, the journal was celebrated for its scholarly rigor and style, and during the Paris Exposition in 1937 the writers of *La Voix des Femmes* were awarded a journalism prize for excellence in reporting.[95]

Haitian postmarked copy of *La Voix des Femmes* labeled for Madeleine Sylvain-Bouchereau at Fisk University, Nashville, Tennessee, September 1947. Sylvain-Bouchereau spent one academic year teaching French at Fisk. Her visiting professorship was a part of the regular intellectual exchange between Haitian intellectuals and historically Black colleges in the United States. The LFAS distributed the newspaper via subscription and used the international travel of its membership to expand its distribution. Courtesy of the Suzanne Comhaire-Sylvain Collection, Department of Special Collections, Stanford University Libraries.

The editors used the newspaper to maintain the atmosphere of intellectual debate established in their workshops. As a result, *La Voix des Femmes* had a section in each issue devoted to guest respondents' answers to the question, *Pour ou contre le féminisme?* ("For or Against Feminism?"). The newspaper also included republished essays and speeches from thinkers throughout the region, including writers from Colombia, Cuba, and Peru.

Revolutionary Rhetoric and Diasporic Discourse

In the early years of the newspaper, the women explained feminism, by rerouting the history of women's politics and their organizational practice through a patriotic national landscape. Drawing on the affective markers of the 1804 Haitian Revolution, the LFAS set the stage to naturalize the idea of feminism in the way that revolution was normalized in political discourse. In an essay titled "Would you be a feminist in Cap Haïtien?," referring to the role of the North as the home of revolutionary thinkers such as Henry Christophe and Baron de Vastey, editor Jeanne Perez used the organization's recruitment to locate feminism and their work in the memory of the nineteenth-century revolution. With an organizational agenda to spread their message beyond Port-au-Prince, Perez wrote, "Cap is an important part of the country from the intellectual point of view. . . . Why wouldn't we be feminists in Cap Haïtien? Who is the one who will proudly boast of being anti-feminist, if he understands that feminism only claims the material and moral improvement of women?" Combining nostalgia for the intellectual and revolutionary history of the former capital city, Perez attached antifeminism to anti-intellectualism and antirevolutionary sentiments. In her exclamation, Perez joined the cause of revolution with that of feminism. Thus she further explained to the readership, "Feminism is not a scarecrow for knowledgeable people"; instead, it was a call to arms as she concluded, "Vive la Cité du Grand Roi, et Vive le feminisme!"[96]

Perez's merger of feminism with a revolutionary past was a common practice in postoccupation politics. Her call on the "Grand Roi," Henry Christophe, drew her readership into a postrevolutionary world. This was a world where the epicenter of nineteenth-century revolution remained a site to cultivate the future they sought in the present. In the first years of organizing, LFAS members used revolutionary rhetoric to establish legitimacy of their claims and the inevitability of their equal citizenship. As Perez wrote, "One might want to stifle [the woman] in order to force her to underestimate herself and to believe herself only good at slavery to the male spirit, [but] her native virtues will wake up like a sleeping giant and make the minor the more dedicated and brave citizen."[97] According to Perez, there was an impulse within women to be free. Like enslaved Africans of the colonial era, these women contemplated, imagined, and rehearsed their freedom beyond their condition.

Perez's comments also pointed toward an intentional psychoanalytic and emotional shackling of women that was used to fortify the "male spirit." This asymmetric engagement with the condition of gender experience had a spiritual quality that had to be exorcized from women and men. For Perez, then, this was not just a war of words; it was a battle of principalities. She argued that even women's memory, as an extension of themselves and self-knowledge, was threatened by those who try to "plunge their memory into the sea of forgetfulness so that future generations are not able to have pride in" and remember the "beautiful example[s] of courage, firmness, goodness, and patriotism" exemplified by women who fought in the revolution, such as Marie Claire Heureuse and Marie-Jeanne Lamartinière.

Perez identified historical silencing at the site of memory and retrospective significance.[98] The asphyxiation of women's historical memory was an assault on their practice of learning and capacity to transmit knowledge to the next generation. The threat on women's memory also established a stronger collective desire to chart and account for women's history and presence. As editor-in-chief of *La Voix des Femmes*, Perez ensured that the periodical was a space to account for, store, and craft the historical memory of women in the nation. As a result, for the first three years, women from the nineteenth-century Haitian revolution were invoked in nearly every issue of *La Voix des Femmes*. In statements like the one below from August 1936, Perez called upon the memory of these women:

> And can we lose the memory of this brave Haitian woman: Henriette Saint-Marc? Stoic and serene, she was led to death between two soldier's hedges, preceded by her coffin. And this Port-au-Princienne was hanged on charges of having supplied powder to insurgents in the Arcahaie Mountains. . . . Who can deny the existence of Sanite Belair who, going to torture with her husband . . . refusing, with a very manly pride to allow herself to be blindfolded, she was shot with her husband like two heroes! . . . Will we forget Madame Chevalier who, too, at the time of being executed with her husband cried that it was "a glory to die for the Fatherland." . . . We will also remember Madame Pageot who saved Dessalines from ambush, on October 17, 1803, at Petite-Riviere. . . . I could go on . . . but do not forget the anonymous women who took their active part in this war from which our Haiti emerged.[99]

The litany of revolutionary remembrance was a political libation, sprinkling the first pages of *La Voix des Femmes*. Through this written ritual, Perez ensured that women's history remained in the present with an expectation that future generations would remember. Perez and others recognized that they were not in the throes of a bloody battleground, but they did call upon the courage of these women as reminders that they could, like their foremothers, stay in the field of war for women's rights. Moreover, they were proud and willing to sacrifice their time, energy, and resources to move toward their ideas of belonging in the nation.

LFAS women claimed and defended the memory of Haitian women, and they connected this memory with other contemporary African-descended women of the period. In the second issue of *La Voix des Femmes* in November 1935, the members of the LFAS aligned themselves with Ethiopian women. The Ethiopian wars against the Italian invasion started the same month as the first issue of *La Voix des Femmes* (October 1935). In their documentation of Ethiopian women's rumored military participation, LFAS women observed their work as a parallel movement for sovereignty: "After an Ethiopian officer

Notre Rédacteur en Chef
Madame Jeanne Perez
Collaboratrice au Temps-Revue
Où elle a donné des articles d'une veine pay-
sanne pleine d'une fine sensiblité.

Jeanne Perez was editor-in-chief of *La Voix des Femmes* until 1938. She founded her own newspaper, *La Semeuse*, in 1938 and served as a contributing writer to the Haitian papers *Temps-Revue*, *Croisade*, and *Relève*, November 1935. Bryn Mawr College Libraries, Special Collections.

claimed that: 'Even women will be on the battlefield to help their men,' a rumor spread that many Ethiopian women have enlisted for the army. They would go to the front, after their training as volunteers. 'LFAS,' in the name of all Haitian women, sends its sympathies to the valiant Ethiopian women who remind us of our Marie-Jeanne at Crête à Pierrot."[100]

In 1802 Marie-Jeanne Lamartinière, alongside her husband Louis Daure Lamartinière and revolutionary leader Jean-Jacques Dessalines, defeated Charles Leclerc's French colonial army of over 2,000 soldiers at Crête à Pierrot in the Artibonite Valley. Dressed in military apparel as she wielded a rifle in one hand and a machete in the other, Marie-Jeanne served as a nurse and a soldier. Suturing the anticolonial battles of women in Haiti and Ethiopia, LFAS women stretched time and Haiti's revolutionary example across the Atlantic Ocean and into Africa. This was the LFAS's first organizational connection with Ethiopia, but throughout the late nineteenth and early twentieth centuries, Haitian and Black internationalist leaders drew parallels between Ethiopia and Haiti. For example, Madeleine Sylvain's uncle Benito Sylvain, who was aide-de-camp (personal assistant) to Ethiopian emperor Menelik II, was a cofounder of the 1900 Pan-African Conference in which the three "free" Black nations of Ethiopia, Haiti, and Liberia were the focus.

The women also documented and celebrated the successes of African-descended women on the western side of the Atlantic. In the same issue, the women announced events in the United States sponsored by the National Association of Colored Women (NACW) and wished the African American women's organization well. Through publishing and connecting Black women's global experiences, the LFAS modeled practices shared by other Black internationalist women.[101] This practice mapped the overlapping geographies of Black women's political work and resonated with later twentieth-century Haitian feminists who, as Desirée Rochat argues, engaged in a "Black diasporic archiving praxis." This praxis involved "collective records interpretation" through "community memory." Similarly, LFAS women sought to translate and transfer a revolutionary history that not only remembered women but was "an explicit community building" practice that would certify twentieth-century women's inheritance to citizenship.[102]

The LFAS's support of Ethiopia also serves as an example of how the women picked up issues and thinking along their political journey that aligned them with various Haitian radical groups in the 1930s. In the August 1936 issue where Perez invoked women revolutionary ancestors, the newspaper ended with the recurring section, "Facts, Gleanings, Echoes." In this issue *La Voix des Femmes* editors shared praise for François Duvalier and Denis Lorimer's "beautiful and strong essay" published in the *Revue de la Société d'Histoire et de Géographie d'Haiti* titled "La civilsation haïtienne: Notre mentalité est-elle africane ou gallo-latine?" In the essay, the two cofounders of the Griots queried Haitian historical allegiances to French thought and history, asking, "Why teach the history of France to Black youth whose ancestors were separated from their land a few hundred years ago and that [now] have a history of their own in this country? What interest is it for these young minds [to learn] the adventures of Clovis or Charlemagne, Joan of Arc or the Sun King when they have Louverture, Dessalines, Christophe and so many others?"[103]

Just months before, Madeleine Sylvain had posed a similar line of questioning in her essay "Let's Be Proud to Be Haitian," in which she blamed a national "inferiority complex" on an unhealthy preoccupation with France: "As soon as the child is old enough to understand, the hope of a trip abroad dangles in his eyes. France becomes the fabulous country of his dreams. Everything comes together to fill him with disdain for his native land. At school all his textbooks are French, on each page the child develops the love for France and the regret of being born Haitian. . . . Yet what people can boast of having a better past than ours!"[104] As both the Griots and Sylvain celebrated Haitian history over French history, they also both couched that pride in a contemporary alliance with other people of African descent. In both regards, the groups openly supported Ethiopians, and as the LFAS reported in July 1936, "[Haitians] cannot remain indifferent to the unjust oppression which threatens an African people."[105] Interestingly, the July statement was made in a report after an LFAS lecture from socialist and future PSP leader Étienne Charlier. In the lecture, Charlier urged the audience to remain informed about the conflict in Ethiopia and to support Ethiopians.

In a decade's time it would be difficult to find members of the Griots and socialist organizers on the same political page, but in the mid-1930s multiple Haitian political groups found common ground in their concern for anticolonial movements. The LFAS, the Griots, and socialists also had their respective skepticism about Vincent's occupation transition government. Vincent's previous sympathies for anticolonial organizing and nuanced understanding of Haitian sovereignty were overshadowed by his efforts to maintain state power. Most significant for the LFAS was Vincent's unscheduled call for a constitutional referendum in June 1935 in which he dissolved the legislature and gave himself unchecked undemocratic executive power. The philosophies of gender inclusion, government restructuring, and recalibration of wealth gaps that the respective leftist groups supported did not match the goals of Vincent's evolving dictatorship.

Here, Ethiopia and anticolonialism were not the only areas where the LFAS and the Griots' thinking drew from the same source. In the 1930s every *La Voix des Femmes* newspaper began with an epigraph that used a quote by Turkish leader Mustapha Kemal Ataturk that read, "A people who are divided into two categories of individuals, each living their own lives, men on the one hand, women on the other, will always be a weak people. We must arrive at a collaboration between both sexes for the good of the country." The recurring quotation framed women's full citizenship as an essential element of national survival. The quote was also evidence that LFAS women were not alone in this thinking. Kemal Atatürk was the great "modernizer" of Turkey who pronounced a nationalism of continued revolutions that would transfer state power to all citizens, including women. Kemal Atatürk's popularism that incorporated redistribution of power and national identity as a primary rubric for organizing the nation was celebrated by the Griots.

The Griots translated this thinking to Haiti by privileging a social and biological authentic Haitian identity that was Black (*noir*). They also adopted a popularist leadership model in which the Black middle class would lead the popular Black majority into a new governing era. While the Griots and the LFAS shared appreciation for the Turkish leader's ideas, the groups' respective application of these philosophies varied significantly. In particular, in the 1940s the Griots' interest in Atatürk's philosophies were absorbed into their *noiriste* politics. LFAS members supported many of the foundational tenets of *noirisme*, especially the celebration of Haitian African ancestry, but by the mid-1940s the political performances of both *noirisme* and feminism placed these groups on different ends of the political spectrum. Still, at a philosophical level both groups maintained a commitment to defending and connecting people of African descent globally.

Thus, throughout the Ethiopian-Italian war (October 1935–May 1936), LFAS women cheered their fellow women patriots on and connected their political practice to similar decisions made by Ethiopian women. For example, when it was announced that Haile Selassie's daughter "left with her Ethiopian sisters, under the linen cap, to bring her maternal care to the wounded and dying," the *La Voix des Femmes* celebrated the Ethiopian princess and connected her service as a wartime nurse to their own efforts to build up Haitian women's education in nursing. The LFAS established nurses as warriors on the front lines of national health care and as a professional medium to close the economic gap between women. Several months after the announcement of the princess nurse, Perez ran a three-page essay titled "Our Nurses," in which she argued, "The woman: slave, artist, worker, or queen, is drawn toward a patient by an unexplainable impulse. At that moment, she no longer thinks of anything but snatching the suffering person from the evil [of sickness]. The woman is therefore born a nurse as she was born a mother."[106]

The divinity placed on nursing was a characterization of nationalist care. At the same time, Perez's emphasis on the instinctual quality of this care signaled a recurring quandary for LFAS women who struggled with how to locate themselves in relation to self-sacrificing motherhood. Historian Darlene Clark Hine's work shows that the meanings of nursing for Black women throughout the region in the early twentieth century were complicated because "nursing did not pose a threat to gender structure." In particular, "the image of the black nurse as a self-sacrificing, dutiful, warm, caring mother figure," was familiar and also confining to feminist activists.[107] However, as discussed in chapter 3, LFAS women often used the mother category less as an inevitable roll for women but rather, in the absence of alternative language, as a name to communicate their care for other women and the nation. Perez went on to write, "What a marvelous channeling of her maternal instincts: to devote herself to those who are suffering . . . these battalions [of nurses], so full of humanity, who wear the little white hat and white uniform like a badge of honor."[108]

In their white armor, Haitian nurses, like the Ethiopian princess, were soldiers for the well-being of the nation. Yet the LFAS's praise and support of Haitian nurses extended beyond galvanizing rhetoric. As Perez explained in her essay, the LFAS's support of nursing was important to the organization's goal to elevate women's formal education and establish a professional class of women. Perez also identified nursing as a particular area of distinction between women's US occupation and postoccupation experiences. The Nursing School of Haiti was founded in 1918, and in collaboration with the Catholic Church, the US military oversaw its operations. According to Perez, Haitian women's enrollment remained low during the occupation despite the US emphasis on public health and health care as one of the intended governmental outcomes. However, in the postoccupation period, "understanding the invaluable benefit of the work and finding a salaried employment adequate to their capacity, Haitian women came to take their place in the honorable battalion of nurses in great numbers."[109] Perez writes that after Haitians took over the school in 1930, enrollment immediately increased.

In 1936 the school counted 321 students, 158 graduates, and 18 promotions. The majority of these nurses were from working-class and poor families. The salaries earned and the continuing education required for nursing meant that these women were growing the professional class and helping the LFAS to realize the vision of closing the wealth gap between women. As Perez noted, the expectation was that women would also share both their education and income with their communities.

The connection between African-descended women's nursing and care for the nation across space and history was an essential component of the women's practice both internationally and nationally. The references were not just points of comparison. Rather, they placed these women in a legion of women like them who were expanding throughout their own countries for their nation's sustained independence. In this vein, LFAS women took several literal roads throughout the nation to extend their political reach. These journeys were vividly captured in *La Voix des Femmes*. In the first two years of organizing, the LFAS celebrated its expansion into cities outside of Port-au-Prince. As

Dr. Yvonne Sylvain in medical office with young girl. Dr. Sylvain opened the first shelter and health center for mothers and children at the Centre d'Hygiène de la Saline. Courtesy of the Suzanne Comhaire-Sylvain Collection, Department of Special Collections, Stanford University Libraries.

an urban-based organization, the LFAS was unique in postoccupation politics in that it not only had national messaging (as other political movements did) but also had active chapters throughout the nation. Within months of its formal founding, the women established organizational chapters in Port-de-Paix and Saint-Marc. When recounting the success in establishing the Saint-Marc chapter, executive secretary Bellegarde wrote that September 15, 1935, was "one of the dates that we must mark as a milestone in the history of our organization."[110] On that day a group of LFAS leaders rose early in the morning and traveled in two cars to meet the new members of the LFAS in Saint-Marc. Novelist and attendee Cléante Desgraves Valcin recounted the journey:

> On the brown and very stony road, the two steel beasts, sweating, blowing, but not deterred, are often stoned by an unknown teasing spirit. But, led by the skillful hands of two young friends of the League, MM. Sylvain and Moïse, they roll, roll on without stopping and here we are very quickly in Arcahaie where we park for a few minutes. Then we leave. Oh!

the sea—the sea that I love so much—plays hide and seek with us. We sometimes meet her for five, ten, fifteen minutes. She is on the same path.

As stones from the road kicked up against the cars and the sea accompanied them north, the journey to their new members was, for Valcin, as noteworthy as the destination. The sights, sounds, and stops along the way located them on a path of skillful leadership and excitement for the landscape of their organization and nation. In the mythically characterized journey of beasts, gods, and a personified sea, Valcin showcased the odyssey of organizing work in the 1930s. With the distinction of being the first Haitian woman novelist, Valcin produced a body of work in which she captured the nation, but she and other members used *La Voix des Femmes* to explicitly narrate their evolving relationships with one another and their collective feminist ideas.[111] The women's documentation of their travels throughout the country was a record of personal reflections and evidence of the LFAS's political breadth. As Madeleine Sylvain referenced in her speech "Notre Conception du Féminisme," at the annual LFAS conference on June 7, 1936, "I address a special thank you to the members of our subsidiaries who wanted to travel, to leave their homes, [and] their jobs to prove their commitment to the ideal that unites us. Can we say at this moment that the Haitian woman is satisfied with her condition, that she does not wish to evolve, when representatives of several cities of the Republic were not afraid to face the fatigue of a long and painful travel for the sole purpose of showing solidarity, to support their sisters?"[112]

Responding to those who questioned LFAS women's political practice or sincerity, Sylvain's attention to women's gravitation toward one another suggested that even if critics could not make sense of their politics, they could track and account for women's desire in their efforts to draw closer to one another. Of course, the narration of laborious intranational travel was also an opportunity to account for the hours and miles that many women in trade traveled on foot or by donkey every day, carrying the nation's sustenance and economy.

LFAS women recognized the effort that women put forth for one another and the country. The September 1935 trip to Saint-Marc was evidence of this recognition. The Port-au-Prince LFAS contingency, including Cléante Valcin, Jeanne Perez, Madeleine Sylvain, Jeanne Sylvain, Fernande Bellegarde, Lyla Poitevien, and Madames Price-Czaikoski and A. Laroche, was greeted by the Saint-Marc leadership. The coordinating committee included Carmen Marcelin (vice president), Myrta Lanier, (secretary general), Marie Aline Adé (assistant secretary), Dina Jumelle (treasurer), Vida D'Meza (assistant treasurer),

Marie Coliman, Marie Nahoum, Beatrice Verna, and D. Alexis.[113] The women gathered over the course of the day with "close to 100 people" (women and men) in attendance. They listened to speeches by various LFAS members including Madeleine Sylvain, whose "warm, sympathetic, persuasive speech overc[ame] apathy and hesitation" from those cautious of the women's politics. Valcin attested "that before leaving the room, [Sylvain] won a lot of hearts for the feminist cause."[114]

If attendees were not moved by the speeches in favor of feminism, they were likely enticed by the Saint-Marc committee's hospitality. Beatrice Verna; her husband, Clément Verna; and her cohost Madame D. Alexis presented their guests with a revolutionary feminist menu that included "Helena Wood ham, Mary Winsor cucumber, Claire Heureuse fish, Adélina salad, and Marie-Jeanne coffee."[115] The menu's fusion of food with the names of US suffragists and Haitian revolutionary women was an aesthetic and strategic display. Earlier in the year, the US suffragists Wood and Winsor, best known for their women's rights protests for which they were both arrested, visited Haiti and the LFAS women. The women were sent by Boris Stevens, the Inter-American Commission for Women president, to show support for the Haitian ratification of the Treaty on Women's Nationality that was signed by Haitian ambassadors at the 1933 conference in Montevideo. LFAS women's alliances with regional women's movements is discussed further in chapter 4, but during the 1935 celebration in Saint-Marc the LFAS women characterized themselves as women's liberators. Paired with the legacies of Haitian warriors, Marie-Jeanne, and queens Claire Heureuse and Adélina Soulouque (empress consort and wife of Faustin I), the reception garnished the LFAS's growth in national zeal and concluded in a spontaneous collective singing of "La Dessalinienne" at the end of the night.

In the first years of organizing, the revolutionary references in the *La Voix des Femmes* essays established a familiar context among the readership. Sometimes, however, the rhetorical choices made divisions even more apparent. In one essay in 1937, Alice Garoute wrote, "Our moral misery is as painful as the greatest material suffering, and we turn our gaze to the one who can, by a gesture or a word, raise us to the rank of free citizens of our country." While the statement was meant to appeal to male senators who were voting on a constitutional amendment to liberate women's wages, the framing universalized the material conditions of Haitian women. Most women's extreme material dispossession was more extreme than any "moral misery," and LFAS leaders sometimes struggled to recognize their own privileges as they sought to identify and fight against gender oppression. Additionally, while the patriotic rhetoric was used as a tool of unifying propaganda, Perez also tempered the nostalgia, reminding women, "We must always look straight ahead, and only occasionally turn our thinking to the past to draw comfort from the memory of the great forefathers and mothers." To this end, the LFAS used the newspaper as a forward-focused compass.

Research and (Self-)Reporting

Although the editors were well known to the elite and ordinary professional class of the urban centers, in the first years of the LFAS, their national popularity was less established. The women used the newspaper as a marketing tool to craft their own celebrity. Until *La Voix des Femmes*, monthly images of Haitian women engaged in intellectual or political action did not exist. Rather, the primary images of women presented to the nation were through newspaper advertisements with images of white women and men from France and the United States.[116] Through the newspaper, the LFAS constructed alternative public images of Haitian women and beauty. Their public personas were shaped through imaging in their writings and through photography. For example, the newspaper routinely displayed images of Sylvain, Garoute, and other leaders in authoritative positions, dressed in professional clothing or draped in academic regalia.[117] The women were not beautiful because of cosmetic appeal, but rather because of their scholastic and professional accomplishments. The LFAS leadership also presented the image of Haitian woman's citizenship as universally attainable through education and civic engagement. Although visual images often rehearsed the visual of class difference and drew attention to national disparities in wealth, in their prose and short stories, LFAS members used the pages of *La Voix des Femmes* to experiment with alternative representations of women and their experiences as mothers, daughters, lovers, and leaders.

In particular, *La Voix des Femmes* used scholarship and study to draw different women together. When coupled with *La Voix des Femmes*, anthropologist Suzanne Comhaire-Sylvain's methodologies and conclusions regarding family, memory, and history became representative of and instructive for feminist scholarship in the first half-decade of the movement. In April 1937, after Comhaire-Sylvain returned to Haiti from studying in Europe, an ad in *La Voix des Femmes* read, "She is our one distinguished and eminent doctor of letters (Ph.D.) who, in her thesis, illustrates the brilliant intellectual capacity of men and women. . . . LFAS expresses the hope that Mme. Suzanne Comhaire-Sylvain becomes the pivot point around which Haitian feminism will definitely evolve."[118] The LFAS picked up her example and hinged its political practice to Comhaire-Sylvain's scholarship. In particular, Comhaire-Sylvain's study of peasant life and culture became an area of study that could potentially draw women of different classes closer to one another. Thus, in the nascent years of the women's movement, she wrote four articles about rural life, folklore, and death in Kenscoff, Haiti, in February and March 1938 that were published in *La Voix des Femmes*. The essays became an early prototype for Haitian feminist theories.

Comhaire-Sylvain wrote and published while still conducting research. Her first publication, "Vocabulaire des croyances paysannes," was a glossary of words used by the rural peasant population. Printed in dictionary-style columns, the essay compared Haitian Kreyòl words to similar words and meanings from the Dahomey in Africa.[119] After a brief introduction to the four-page spread, Comhaire-Sylvain begins with "ABOBO"—the expression of agreement, affirmation, and invocation heard during Vodou dances and ceremonies. She explains that when saying "ABOBO," "certain individuals tap their mouth with two fingers at the same time." She then matches the Haitian "ABOBO" with the Dahomean expression "BOBOBO," "a noise that one makes when tapping an open mouth with two fingers." Drawing linguistic parallels between Haiti and Dahomey, she engages her readers in a lesson about Haiti's African past, revealing the continuity of linguistic technologies and meanings between the cultures.[120] For the community of women's rights activists, intellectuals, and feminist theorists reading Comhaire-Sylvain's work, her attention not only to the script and diction but also to the performance of the words was instructive. Their feminist study and political practice had to account for and connect women at multiple registers of being and knowledge, reorienting women to one another through a shared grammar of gestures.

Comhaire-Sylvain's work established an early archive of the embodied elements of Haitian language that had not been attended to. This approach was recognized by feminist leaders, but other theorists in the fields of anthropology and sociology recognized Comhaire-Sylvain's methods as well. Several months after Comhaire-Sylvain published in *La Voix des Femmes*, African American scholar Carter G. Woodson reviewed her other published work, *Le Créole Haïtien, Morphologie et Syntaxe* (1936) and *Les Contes Haïtiens, Part I &II* (1937) alongside anthropologist Melville Herskovits's *Life in a Haitian Valley* (1937). Woodson questioned the quality of Herskovits's research, arguing that his "first excursion" in Haiti could not "justify his . . . speaking like one having authority."[121] But he marvels that "working in the same field in which Dr. Herskovits has chosen to labor, has recently appeared Madame Suzanne Comhaire-Sylvain." Counting Comhaire-Sylvain among "the most intellectual people of

Haiti," Woodson was particularly taken with what he identified as her unique documentation choices: "She then shows the method in which they [folktales and Kreyòl language] are recited by the people themselves, how they are extended or widely known among the Haitian people and the means by which they have reached other parts."[122]

The method that Woodson references was the tapping of two fingers on the mouth, the eyebrow raises, or the postures that served as points of connectivity across status. These were the same intersections where the LFAS hoped women might meet. Comhaire-Sylvain's work became the foundations for a formalized written Kreyòl in the late twentieth century, but in the 1930s her work, method, and choice of publication on a feminist platform offered a literal dictionary and grammar book for communication between women.

Comhaire-Sylvain's index offered a fragile space for exchange and connectivity that highlighted gendered experiences of culture, class, and labor between Haitian women. This space was articulated in Comhaire-Sylvain's second publication in *La Voix des Femmes*, "Adelsia." The short story essay was a contribution to the recurring section in *La Voix des Femmes* titled "Notre Paysanne." Harkening back to Price-Mars's invitation in *Ainsi parla l'Oncle* (So Spoke the Uncle) to seriously engage an *indigéniste* narrative practice that centered and "integrate[d] the popular Haitian thought into the discipline of traditional ethnography," Comhaire-Sylvain's journal submission documented women's thought and charted her ethnographic practice. In the essay, she tells the story of a young girl named Adelsia who guides her through the intricate physical and social landscape of Kenscoff. As the story evolves, Comhaire-Sylvain reveals that she knows Adelsia from childhood. As a young girl, Adelsia accompanied her grandmother on her journeys from Kenscoff to Port-au-Prince to sell their produce. Comhaire-Sylvain recalled that the grandmother-granddaughter pair sold peaches and artichokes. The two women were over a decade apart in age, but they remembered each other.

When the women met again as adults, Adelsia was a business woman, mother, and locally celebrated dancer.[123] Adelsia guided Comhaire-Sylvain through her days and ultimately to the Kenscoff cemeteries. Comhaire-Sylvain's detailed notes, hand-drawn maps, and sketches of tombs in her research notebooks suggest she spent significant time in the cemeteries. The pages of measurements, names, and notes connecting the cemetery plots with members of the community also suggest that Adelsia and Comhaire-Sylvain had to abide in one another's presence for extended periods of time. Comhaire-Sylvain's notes do not indicate hourly intervals, but her narration in *La Voix des Femmes* fills in some of the space between the women. In the published text, Comhaire-Sylvain shared bits of the women's conversation about money, marriage, children, and death. Accounting for the business acuity and thought that emerge from women's vending throughout the region, Comhaire-Sylvain informs the reader that Adelsia never attended school, but "her mental calculations are remarkable."

As Comhaire-Sylvain argued in her later publications, she does not mention Adelsia's facility with calculations as mere accolades, but as an invitation to think about how women count, both as valuable members of the nation and considering their systems of measuring (i.e., varying-sized pots, touch, and smell among venders and market women) and their value as members in the society. In the pages of *La Voix des Femmes* Comhaire-Sylvain argued that women and their metric systems mattered. Through her attention to multiple ways of knowing, created and perfected by women, she encouraged women to draw closer to one another through mutual awareness and "integrat[ing]" this thinking into their definitions of Haitian womanhood. Beyond a representation of Haitian women's different life experiences, Comhaire-Sylvain's work offered instruction on how to think and do Haitian feminism. The feminist project was the triangulation between research, method, and archive. The story, then, was not just to *show* Adelsia's life, but to *see* Adelsia and Comhaire-Sylvain together, navigating, reconciling, and sharing on the feminist pages.

Comhaire-Sylvain recorded the ways women studied, challenged, and corrected one another, as well as the gaps in the process of translating their lives to one another. This is most evident in her retelling of the women's conversations about marriage. Adelsia was in a plasaj union—a common-law relationship that may or may not have involved multiple partners. As Comhaire-Sylvian praised Adelsia's business skills and parenting ethos, she questioned Adelsia's role as a second wife to her husband. She expressed regret that Adelsia would never hold the title "Madame," stating that "she will one day be 'Manzè Adelsia,' 'Sor Adelsia,' and even 'Grann Adelsia' but she will not carry the title 'Madame.'"[124] Plasaj was a fetishized area of inquiry in early twentieth-century ethnographic studies and foreign reporting that often used the unions as examples of the nation's nonmodernity. However, in her published and unpublished writing about the practice, Comhaire-Sylvain consistently wrote that plasaj was a "relatively stable union."[125]

Within the context of the feminist newspaper, Comhaire-Sylvain's early reservations regarding legal and monogamous marriage reflected an early and ongoing discord in feminist discourse. On the one hand, legal marriage provided an avenue for social mobility that blurred class, cultural, and color divi-

Two women in Marbial. Comhaire-Sylvain was a member of the United Nations Educational, Scientific and Cultural Organization (UNESCO) research project with her mentor and colleague Alfred Métraux in the Marbial Valley of Haiti from 1948 to 1950. Jeanne Sylvain also worked on the project. Photo by Alfred Metraux, © musée du quai Branly–Jacques Chirac, Dist. RMN–Grand Palais / Art Resource, New York.

sions.[126] On the other hand, legal marriage placed women's financial and citizenship rights within the hands of guardian men and the state. Although Comhaire-Sylvain studied plasaj and other members of the LFAS critically engaged the meanings of plasaj in their prose, by the beginning of World War II, the LFAS publicly supported legislation that encouraged legal marriage (discussed further in chapter 4).[127]

When Adelsia and Comhaire-Sylvain discussed plasaj, Adelsia expressed that she wanted to be called "Madame." Her desire for the title was less about prestige and more about her desire to spend more time with her husband, concluding that being in a legal marriage would help establish the priority of her place in her union. She also explained that even if marriage were discussed in her union, it would first be proposed to "Maria," her husband's first wife. For this reason, Adelsia clarified, she would not request marriage or the name "Madame" because "Maria was her friend." Here, Comhaire-Sylvain documents women's care for one another and expands the archive of plasaj beyond monogamy and polygamy, to the practices of friendship.

The partnership that Adelsia honored was her relationship with Maria. Where ethnographers and anthropologists, including Comhaire-Sylvain, accounted for the economic and sexual arrangements within plasaj partnerships, Comhaire-Sylvain also documented the affinity between kin women. Adelsia appeared in Comhaire-Sylvain's other academic publications regarding peasant life, but this version of Adelsia was specifically told in the *La Voix des Femmes* essay. Adelsia's words encouraged the readership to think of multiple partnerships beyond morality and possession and through relations of care. It catalogued how women could be together. This frame also tempered Comhaire-Sylvain's preoccupation with respectability and expanded the limited archive that Comhaire-Sylvain was prepared to put Adelsia in.

Yet again, in the area of women's financial freedom and death, Comhaire-Sylvain documented her own miscalculations regarding Adelsia's life. In particular, she ruminated on the material assets and the distribution of wealth and status. For over half of the bio-narrative, Comhaire-Sylvain calculates Adelsia's assets and relationships as she discusses the precariousness of family, social status, and property ownership for women upon their death or death of a family member. These concerns mirrored one of the LFAS's first legislative initiatives. In the 1940s the women's organization made its first legislative campaign about women's rights to hold their wages and property within marriage. Comhaire-Sylvain understood and documented that the moments during and directly after death were also periods of power brokering, where traditional gender hierarchies could yield to the supernatural and sacred. Comhaire-Sylvain framed her retelling of Adelsia's life through death and its impact on love, relationship to land, ancestry, and relationship to other women.

In her closing statements Comhaire-Sylvain acknowledged her preoccupation with Adelsia's material assets and attention to death when she concludes, "But she [Adelsia] is young and so she is not thinking about death."[128] Adelsia was, in fact, reflexive about death and assets, but not in the ways that they resonated with Comhaire-Sylvain. Adelsia's concern with financial resources upon death were less about material loss, and more about preparation. Comhaire-Sylvain's text reflects this dissonance when she explains that "more than marriage, women were saving money to celebrate and memorialize their family." The value in material assets for Adelsia was in her capacity to be prepared for the inevitable. Yet for Comhaire-Sylvain's audience, her narration of Adelsia's life also drew a fragile connection between women, placing them in the material and discursively shared spaces of social and corporeal life and death.

While Adelsia would not receive author credit, Comhaire-Sylvain's choices in documentation and reflexivity within the text reveal the formulations of a particular women-centered ethnographic practice. Comhaire-Sylvain was accountable to the multiple registers of translation and was frequently publicly reflective when she got it wrong. Comhaire-Sylvain documented differently than her peers, and *La Voix des Femmes* intentionally archived and engaged with the research. Editors and contributors to *La Voix des Femmes* regularly used the platform to share their perspective on popular ideas by inserting jokes, short comedies, and folklore highlighting the daily misogyny in their most common exchanges. Here, *La Voix des Femmes* editors used Comhaire-Sylvain's translation work to mark the terrain of gender discrimination, and allow their readers to participate in a type of reflexive play. In her third *La Voix des Femmes* essay in 1938, "La Femme dans le proverbe créole," Comhaire-Sylvain took a sarcastic tone to provide a litany of proverbs that discuss women. From "Actions are for men, conversation is for women," to "He who has a daughter has a son-in-law," Comhaire-Sylvain did the simultaneous intellectual work of documenting, transcribing, and translating Kreyòl as she also satirically commented on the profundity and irony of the proverbs. Her tone was light, but she gestured toward the contradictions in overessentializing the liberatory possibilities of Haitian culture. With little prose accompanying the two pages of proverbs, the list of phrases that would ring familiar to Haitian ears was also evidence of the limitations of *indigéniste* thinking—a return to African cultural traditions— without a gendered analysis. This was not a rejection of *indigénisme*, but rather a charge to the philosophies that informed her work and the work of the LFAS.

Without attention to women, the nation's most compelling ideals, like revolution and freedom, could be evacuated of their radical potential. Comhaire-Sylvain illustrated that intellectual and cultural traditions and the proverbs that carried them were entangled in the deep dispossession of women as self-determining beings. In particular, she identified the ways in which the woman's body ("Heavy women have virtue"), value ("Girls are poor merchandise"), and relationships ("Not all mothers are mothers") were used to mark the boundaries of belonging and citizenship. This unacknowledged disconnect between social discourse and the quotidian assaults on women's character further annunciated the need and demand for members of the LFAS to wrestle with their feminist project.

The longest of Comhaire-Sylvain's four essays provides a window into the tensions of developing a political practice that accounted for women's difference and shared experiences. In the March 1938 issue of *La Voix des Femmes*, subscribers were introduced to the folktale "Adelmonde." Adelmonde is the story of a mother and daughter who have a profound love for one another. Comhaire-Sylvain recorded that each time the mother and daughter saw each other, "joy danced in their black eyes." In the story, Adelmonde's beauty, laughter, and loving spirit capture the attention of the Queen of the Water, who kidnaps Adelmonde, makes her one of her many daughters, and threatens Adelmonde and her mother with death if they attempt to reunite. Adelmonde and her mother wept and longed for each other for many days. Adelmonde ultimately devises and enacts a plan of escape and is reunited with her mother, but as the narrator within the folktale recounts, before she was able to congratulate the mother and daughter on their reunion, she was distracted by a mysterious touch and when she turned back to the women, they were gone. The folktale ends with an inquiry: "Have you seen Adelmonde? Did she return to the water? If you see her, please come fast and tell me."[129] At the end of the folktale Adelmonde and her mother's reunion results in their mutual disappearance.

Comhaire-Sylvain's retelling of the story on the feminist platform served as an interlocutor and transmitter of narratives and folklore centering Haitian women. Of the many folktales Comhaire-Sylvain could have translated, she chose a narrative in which the cast of characters were women who negotiated relationships complicated by deep love, desire, sister-motherhood, and meanings of separation and loss. In her story choice we might first consider that Comhaire-Sylvain bears witness to her own loss—mourning and searching for her own mother (parents) at the intersection of death and women's intellectual recovery and practice. In addition to a reflection on personal loss, this narration leaves room for reading this story as an introspective moment for Haitian feminists. Could, for example, *La Voix des Femmes* readers have identified with the Queen of the Water—truly desiring a relationship with Adelmonde, but at the expense of ignoring the a relationships and cultural frameworks in which she existed? Did the story resonate with organizers of the early women's movement who continually butted against the incongruences between their aspirations and theories of feminism alongside the diversity of women's life experiences? Or could it have been an unforeseen foreshadowing of a moment nearly a decade later when women attempting to unite in the 1946 assembly would be evacuated before they could come together?

As the "pivot" point for Haitian women's nascent formulations of feminism and political praxis, the examples that Comhaire-Sylvain published in *La Voix des Femmes* located women. In both the Adelsia and Adelmonde essays, men are absent. Comhaire-Sylvain even remarked that although she spent a lot of time with Adelsia, she "never saw Adelsia's husband." Women were their own pivot point. Even within institutions and structures constricted by patriarchy, women centered their care, framed theories of belonging, made decisions, wrote, maintained relationships, and got out of relationships for one another.

Comhaire-Sylvain reflected this in her method, recording, and decision to publish in *La Voix des Femmes*. She documented her process of changing consciousness and invited women affiliated with the LFAS to consider their own practice. The *La Voix des Femmes* pages, then, documented a process of changing consciousness that exemplified a Black feminist ethnography as a Black feminist archival practice.[130] Comhaire-Sylvain's work in the pages of *La Voix des Femmes* was different not only because women were doing this work, which they were, but because of the type of methods and recalibrations of practices, social boundaries, and even naming that was informed by women's individual and collective experiences. They were theorizing the contexts of their lives at the moments of everyday exchange. Thus, they were seeing women and differences among them on the page at the intersections that built women's theories, research, and political practice.

Returning to Adelsia and Comhaire-Sylvain's shared space on the *La Voix des Femmes* pages, Comhaire-Sylvain recorded their initial knowledge of each other in the space of transit and in the exchange of gourdes for peaches or artichokes at a doorway or street stand. At this location, their lives quickly yet respectfully graze one another or almost touch, but not quite. In remembering one another they recognized this transient space as a site of inquiry. Women in these spaces blurred the lines between rural and the urban. Women met regularly at foyers and backdoors, brushing by one another in kitchens, during the transfer of children, and at sacred services of all kinds. Women's mobility were sites of exchange that shuttled culture and ideas between the porous boundaries of difference. As a result, the LFAS agenda to study women turned the organizational interests to urban centers, namely, Port-au-Prince.

City Routes and Rural Intersections

The project of studying women in urban space was an opportunity to conduct research that recognized Haitian women's mobility not just physically but culturally. While much of Comhaire-Sylvain's research was focused on rural folklore, the physical distance between women in the rural and urban centers incited the LFAS women to focus their research on the more proximal relationships between urban women of different classes. To this end, the LFAS conducted investigative projects and held "study sessions" in Port-au-Prince.[131] The study sessions were designed for in-depth research on topics related to Haitian women. In November 1939, the first two "problems" submitted to the group for review were Haitian women's legal status and recreation and leisure time.[132]

In 1939 Comhaire-Sylvain conducted a yearlong study in Port-au-Prince interviewing over 1,000 urban working-class girls between the ages of nine and sixteen years old about how they spent their leisure time. Her study was grounded in the assumption that leisure-time activities had the potential to corrupt a girl's social respectability, and as a result, this unaccounted-for time needed observation.[133] Comhaire-Sylvain found that many of the girls she interviewed were servants in elite homes and as a result, spent over ninety-eight hours a week working. A small percentage of these girls were enrolled in school full time, but the large majority were part-time students, and of those many missed school frequently. Comhaire-Sylvain found that working-class young girls in the urban center, having work, school, and responsibilities at home, had little time for leisure activities. When they did take time to play, they often did the same things that middle-class and elite girls did: talk with friends, dance, and play games. She asserted, "Rich or poor, our young girls of Port-au-Prince are highly social."[134]

The contours of their social lives were different. In particular, the education variation between girls presented different opportunities to differently educated girls. According to Comhaire-Sylvain, variation in education could be made more consistent across class difference by providing an alternative place for children to get scholastic education if they missed school. For this she suggested that the LFAS open a weekend library.[135] Although she supported scholastic education, she also suggested, "However if we want to raise the intellectual and moral level of the Haitian woman it is not enough to improve the level of studies, we must also introduce a little understanding of art in children's leisure time." Qualifying her statement, she explained, "*Introduction* is not the appropriate word; it exists at an embryonic state in the love of singing, of storytelling, and of dance, which are admittedly very well developed."[136] However, at an embryonic level, art could go awry.

From Comhaire-Sylvain's observations, girls' artistic energy needed to be cultivated in adult-supervised social gatherings where young people saw theatrical productions, art exhibits, and educational films. She further instructed her LFAS sisters and readership that they—the scholastically educated women of the nation—must teach the less-educated class and "show them what constitutes beauty."[137] Comhaire-Sylvain proposed that young women's education in aesthetics begin with leisure activities that focused on their physical health. In response to this suggestion, coeditor of *La Voix des Femmes* Cléante Valcin provided a list of ideal sports for women. Each sport, including volleyball, cycling, and swimming, emphasized strengthening girls physically and mentally. Valcin's description of these activities included length of play as well as physical or mental ailments that could be cured by the activities.[138] Comhaire-Sylvain explained, "We should definitely consider placing our young girls in all sorts of sports organizations to improve the beauty and vigor of the race."[139] Fitness as a response to girls' leisure time was an explicit concern for what young women were doing with their bodies and how that behavior represented women within a familial, community, and national context. Although Valcin and Comhaire-Sylvain discussed athletics at length, their interest with sports was less about athleticism and more about influencing young girls' behaviors. According to the LFAS, a fitness campaign would keep young girls occupied and away from sexual exploration and sex work.[140] The study of leisure time was, in fact, a way to address elite women's concern for young girls' comportment, their public behavior, and sometimes, their efficient labor.

In their celebration of education and Haitian women's diversity, the LFAS adopted the philosophy that knowledge and intellect had an aesthetic currency. The ability to discern beauty would result in the capacity to change the standard and quality of life. In this way, the LFAS sought to cultivate women's critical perspectives. To do this, the LFAS founded two libraries in Port-au-Prince and Port-de-Paix and organized night courses in history, home economics, and Haitian culture through the various LFAS chapters throughout the country, including Miragoâne and Jacmel.[141] The curriculum was vast, including grammar, foreign language, and writing classes, but the core courses were in childcare and home management with an average class size of fifty students.[142] In 1943, the LFAS also opened a women's community center called the Foyer Ouvrier. The center offered classes in childcare, language, and cooking. The center also provided space for another library and extracurricular activities such as folkloric singing, dance, and sports.[143] In her 1943 end-of-the-year report, Madeleine Sylvain-Bouchereau announced, "The Foyer Ouvrier is in full formation and is already visited by more than 460 workers. It is a continuous creation which adapts to all needs and which realizes collaboration and understanding between the different classes."[144]

The emphasis on cross-class education through the Foyer was developed alongside the harsh pronouncements of class division. Two years prior to the 1939 study, Valcin penned an essay about domestic workers that foreshadowed LFAS women's ongoing challenge to balance self-reflexivity in their political practice. Valcin recounted what she argued was the fate of some young women who leave "their plot of land where promising vegetables grow . . . to come here [Port-au-Prince] in the pursuit of an impossible happiness." "Like a bar of soap," her "dreams melt and die within one to two weeks." Valcin continued, "Tired of doing all the work alone, you employ her, but only to realize that you have recruited a student. . . . You find the courage to educate her, she adapts herself to her work more or less, and you reap some kind of satisfaction. But one morning, 'vlan!' [gone!] your student announces that she is returning to her home, and will get you a replacement." She concluded, "Your student-servant leaves, often never to come back, abandoning her job to a 'friend' as incompetent as she used to be." With this, Valcin suggested that the LFAS women should establish training schools for house servants: "Those who are unfit to become servants, due to being uneducated or rogue, would remain home to nurture the generous soul of the Haitian land, and multiply its produce."[145]

Valcin's words harbored uncritical projections with an uncomfortable historical truth that women activists were not always willing or able to see other women. Her rapid switch between the patronizing and patriotic conclusions reflected a recurring dissonance between the LFAS leadership's articulated desire for an inclusive politics and their journey toward this particular consciousness.

In the crevasses of Valcin's words, however, she also narrates Haitian women's multiple and interlocking relationships to labor. Tired of doing all the work alone, Valcin accounts for women's unpaid, underpaid, and exploited domestic and nondomestic labor that economically and socially supported men's political, economic, and social power, but left women to seek their own freedoms by confining other women's freedoms. The unrecognized labor power of elite Haitian women was transferred to a double abuse of women's labor through the employment of domestic workers at significantly lower wages than the value of their labor to work for women like the LFAS leadership. Within the coming decade, fellow Black woman internationalist and Trinidadian Communist Claudia Jones would identify this as superexploitation, but on the pages of *La Voix des Femmes* the article revealed women activists' evolving navigation of power and interest in cross-class collaboration.[146]

Locating women at the intersections of labor, capitalism, and migration, Valcin also captures working-class women's refusal. A woman's decision to flee uneven economic contexts, despite deep familiarity with her woman employer or family, also documented varying desires, meanings of freedom, and the limitations of a political practice that presumed Haitian women shared the same concerns. The domestic worker's disappearance was a reminder that LFAS women could organize publicly and privately but that they were not in charge of the terms of women's engagement. Moreover, the description of the woman's decision to change employment as "rogue" also revealed women activists' potential part in policing and containing certain Haitian women.

Additionally, the suggestion that these young women would easily reintegrate back into the lives on the "generous soul" of the Haitian land also flattened the often complicated and diverse experiences of rural life for women. This essentializing dismissal of young women who did not satisfy elite and middle-class women's service desires into the amorphous realm of the Haitian countryside was a recurring response of some elite Black women throughout the diaspora concerned with Black girls' urban migration and women's proper performance in public space.[147] Yet what Valcin and few in the urban centers knew was that the countryside, particularly the farthest inland, was not a bastion of green pastures. Instead, women and men were crossing the border into the Dominican Republic to live and work in the neighboring country for little pay, but with a hope similar to that of the girls migrating to Haiti's urban centers, that the alternative location would offer new opportunities for economic and social advancement.

Weeks after Valcin's essay, Dominican Republic president Rafael Trujillo cast Haitian women out of his country, through a violent campaign of anti-Haitianism that placed the Dominican national financial crisis on the shoulders of Haitians working the western estate lands of the country. In two weeks' time during October 1937, Trujillo ordered the deportation and execution of an estimated 20,000 Haitians. In the multiple archival sources used to create a full catalogue of *La Voix des Femmes*, the months between September 1937 and early 1938 are missing. Although LFAS president Madeleine Sylvain was in Philadelphia at the time, Suzanne Comhaire-Sylvain's collection of other newspapers specifically during the months of October and November suggests that the women heard about the massacre and followed the events closely. Haitian president Vincent was less transparent and publicly responsive about his knowledge of the massacre, giving opposition fighters more evidence of his compromised allegiance to the Haitian people.

Unlike Vincent, LFAS members were constantly reflecting on their culpability within the ever-changing political and social systems of the country. For example, Valcin, Alice Garoute, and Madeleine Sylvain would later liken working-class women's labor exploitation and access to political power and education to enslavement, making Valcin's narrative of a domestic worker's escape even more revealing within the body of the women's journalistic archive. Thus, in the contexts of the massacre of Haitians, grave economic inequality, and women's marginal political position in national governance, LFAS members assessed the first five years of organizing and expressed frustration with the outcomes of their work. In the October–November issue of *La Voix des Femmes* in 1940, Madeleine announced that the LFAS would "withdraw their forces." She emphasized that the leaders had not "let themselves be dazzled or dismantled" by the work they had done in the first five years of organizing, but that in order to truly develop "a vast action including a considerable number of women of all classes and all trades working under the leadership of autonomous committees," the women needed to reassess their approach.

Articulating the desire for a broader political reach, Sylvain-Bouchereau further explained that the LFAS leadership was closing ranks: "For the moment, it is a question of uniting a conscious group, free from lukewarm or doubtful elements," who by "studying can prepare and train executives on the necessary philosophies of the major questions which concern the future of the country."[148] This semihorizontal leadership structure ran in the face of institutional and state governing practices in Haiti. Instead, what Sylvain-Bouchereau described sounded like the Haitian rural agricultural practices of a *kombit*, in which crops are grown, rotated, and shared through the labor of a committed community network so that everyone can be nourished. Far from a romanticized vision of political solidarities, Sylvain-Bouchereau recognized that their desired impact would require multiple seasons of hard and concentrated work.

THE FIRST DECADE of LFAS women's political organizing came to a close alongside the final two years of World War II. In her final essays of 1943, Madeleine Sylvain-Bouchereau oriented her thoughts about the history, promise, and shortcomings of women's activism in the tone of a wartime report. "At the dawn of 1944 we all come together under this flag of the fight against evil, against ignorance, against illness, against misery and against injustice and thanks to the persevering collaboration of all of those who dedicate themselves, we will restore society to better foundations."[149] Her call for a unified restorative movement that would remake the foundations of the nation, and possibly the region and world, was a hopeful recasting of a complicated ten years of experimenting with various trajectories of women's activism. Madeleine was in a war of her own. She could not have predicted but possibly felt how her tactics and that of her organization would have to be more coordinated to defend herself and the LFAS's practice against the deep political battle lines drawn over the course of the decade. Thus, perhaps frustratingly, Madeleine's assessment of the LFAS's work from several years before remained relevant. Speaking on behalf of the organization, she wrote, "[We] recognize that the ideas [we] pronounce are still poorly understood" and "[we] do not yet have the authority necessary to impose these ideas, nor the capacity necessary to support it."[150] While Madeleine's tone at the end of the 1930s communicated reflection and aspirations for the movement, it also articulated loss, perhaps for how far the women imagined their cause would be after a decade.

The women's organizational front was also evolving between wartime strategies and the transition in presidential leadership in Haiti. World War II started in September 1939, and Élie Lescot was elected president of Haiti in

May 1941. When Lescot ambitiously launched Haiti into war in support of the Allied Powers, he also launched the nation into several wartime projects that adversely affected the economy. These projects included a Jewish placement program for those escaping Nazi Europe and a rubber-planting and -extracting program to supplement the US rubber demand after Axis powers cut off Allied access to the Philippines rubber markets. The world war strains on the global financial systems put economic strain on Haiti. The nation faced an economic depression that disproportionately compromised women's livelihood with the continued lowering of already low wages alongside the increase in product prices.

The simultaneity of war, women's economic vulnerability, and the political volatility of the mid-1940s presented an opportunity for the women to hone a political agenda that was intelligible to more women's needs. This included cultivating a clear political outline that was reflected in the theories and practices of the organization, greater institutional power, and a strong working group of members. In particular, women's paid, underpaid, and unpaid labor took center stage as a political focus and rhetorical tool. Carrying Sylvain-Bouchereau's pronouncement that Haitian women were slaves into the 1940s, LFAS women used meanings of enslavement to indicate Haitian women's location, belonging, and value in society. Over the course of the 1940s, LFAS women's research and writing offered evidence to substantiate this claim.

Against the backdrop of war, ethnic cleansing, and international systems of unification (i.e., the United Nations), the women repeatedly referenced enslavement in terms of the historical and present vulnerability of Black women to sexual violence, unequal partnership, and their unpaid and underpaid labor. Similar to Marxist theorists of the period, the women connected their unpaid labor to global enslavement. Still, they were also deeply invested in capitalist participation and articulated a politics that accounted for how women experienced both capitalism and Marxism as Black women. As I will discuss in chapter 3 and chapter 4, women's understandings of themselves as subject and objects within these local and international theories and markets informed their politics. Both chapters are set in the 1940s. Chapter 3 follows Haitian women's rights organizers' local-global thinking about labor, family, and sexuality. Chapter 4 picks up in some of the same years as chapter 3 but follows the women's global-local travel and thinking that focuses on international alliances and performances of race.

A Pilgrimage

But her mother
had raised her
by the feet
told her
you are
you are a gazelle child
and even if the race has begun
you will
you will
run run
and
you will get there

—Stéphane Martelly, *L'enfant Gazelle*, 2018

There is always a place where, if you listen closely in the night, you will hear a
mother telling a story and at the end of the tale, she will ask you this question:
"Ou libéré? Are you free, my daughter?"

—Edwidge Danticat, *Breath, Eyes, Memory*, 1998

Black butterfly, sailed across the waters
Tell your sons and daughters
What the struggle brings
Black Butterfly, set the skies on fire
Rise up even higher
So the ageless winds of time can catch your wings
Let the current lift your heart and send it soaring
Write the timeless message clear across the sky
So that all of can read it and remember when we need it
That a dream conceived in truth can never die
Butterfly

—Deniece Williams, 1984

In September 1936, Jeanne Perez took the readership of *La Voix des Femmes*
(LVDF) on a journey north. If her editorial choice for the newspaper's cover
art was a map, the direction was clear. Like many who made the 120-mile trip

from Port-au-Prince to the old capital city Cap-Haïtien, Perez was taking the readers on an additional trek several miles south to Milot, and up the 3,000-foot Bonnet à l'Evêque mountain to the Citadelle Laferrière (the Citadelle). In the issue, Perez and Madeleine Sylvain both wrote about the nineteenth-century fortress, built by Haitian president and king Henry Christophe. They were responding to a *New World Almanac* essay that named the Citadelle an additional "wonder of the world." Sylvain celebrated the Citadelle, listed in the company of the Great Pyramids of Giza and the Great Wall of China, for the international recognition it brought to Haiti, showcasing "the incontestable truth of the genius of the black [*noire*] race."[1] Sylvain summarized the *Almanac* article with pride while imploring President Sténio Vincent to uphold his word, unlike past leaders who, she claimed, were negligent in their attention to the national monument. Like many celebrants of the Citadelle, then and since, Sylvain suggested that an asphalt road be paved from Cap-Haïtien to Milot and that tourists' investments be used to cover the cost of restoration of several rooms within the structure for a Henry Christophe museum.

While Sylvain wrote about the restoration of the Citadelle, Perez reflected on her encounter with the structure. She described the largesse of "the heroic dream of the Black [*nègre*] heart written in those high steps" constructed to watch for and ward off foreign and national enemies. Perez recalled feeling "a previously unknown emotion" when arriving at the foot of the structure and looking up. Humbled and overtaken with inspiration, gratitude, and reverence for the nineteenth-century fortress whose walls reached 130 feet into the sky, there was no other place for her to release the valve of her emotions except into the future. So she wrote a letter to her four-year-old niece.

À Marie-Madeleine Price-Mars

So, one Sunday, you will tell me when you want to commune with our ancestors through reflection and an immense will to climb the steep slope of Bonnet-à-l'Eveque. At the foot of the respected dungeon, stop for a moment, raise your head and watch the heroic dream of a Black [*nègre*] heart written in those high steps that have not been destroyed for over a century. A feeling that you've never known will humble you. Like the Fatherland, the Citadel was cracked, [and] wounded by the storm. Its wounds may be apparent, but all is magnificent in these things forged by Black [*nègre*] heroism that defies time and vultures. These things will live because they were the most beautiful reflections of our life, because they are our reason for being worthy heirs, because they represent what does not die: a noble idea.

Like the butterfly, lover of light, returns to the flame to burn its wing, if you go there one day, you will return, repeatedly, to re-immerse your soul again at the living source of the ancestors' faith.

The work is titanic. What have we done since? Do giants procreate dwarves?

The brazen eagle is bowed, stunned, before this prodigious conception. The Black [*noir*] mind, is it already so degraded that there is no hope?

May our sons go on a pilgrimage of love for the Fatherland, to this majestic present that a *bronzé* King bequeathed to us; let them climb, in the footsteps of the weeping Queen, the Princes and the Counts, [and] the great dilapidated stairs which saw the corpse of the beloved Monarch, King Christopher, pass for the last time; the stairs which knew the active life, the torments, and all the victories of Him who carried, to the tomb, the dream of a grandiose and magnificent Haiti!

May our sons greet the ancestors in the vestiges of yesterday's glory, and may they feel in their hearts the desire to be great and good Haitians![2]

Perez was in love—with her niece and with her country. Perez was moved by the memory of her experience at the Citadelle and by the anticipation of sharing it with the next generation. Published on the opening pages of the newspaper, her letter accounted for and shared her deep care and belief in the intergenerational transfer of ideas. This affect went beyond a *lien de sang* (bloodline). Instead, it was held in the unexpected feeling of being taken over by an ancestral call to arms.

Reared by her mother and sister in a woman-led working-class household, Perez took the practice of intergenerational care between women and girls seriously. Like many official and unofficial Haitian *matant/tante* (aunties) and *marraines* (godmothers), Perez cared for, thought about, and prepared the next generation. She engaged in the sacred calling that allowed her to spoil her niece and also serve as a safeguard for loss, an escape in the midst of confusion, and a fountain of unique marraine wisdom. In addition to a statement of care for the next generation, this type of divine mothering was also an extension of profound friendship. As Theodora Holly explained in her early twentieth-century reflections on Haitian godparents, "It is difficult for one who has not lived among the Haytians to realize to how great an extent the role of sponsor (godparent) can increase the affection already existing between two friends." Holly explained that some people said the relationship was "more binding than that of blood," and she agreed: "The assertion is hardly exaggerated. . . . To the Haytian mind, this friendly office performed towards a friend's child . . . creates a relationship" that "can best be gathered from the terms co-parents."[3]

Long before twenty-first-century terminology of nonnuclear, extended nuclear, blended, nontraditional, and multigenerational family structures, Holly communicated a Haitian co-parenting tradition. Perez shared the tightened bonds of friendship and this communal guardianship of her niece with her sister, Rosa Clara Perez, and Rosa Clara's husband, Jean Price-Mars. In her published statement in LVDF, Perez also placed Marie-Madeleine and her generation in the care of Haitian women writ large. This "othermothering" was not a biological or nationalist celebration of mothering that LFAS women both adopted and rejected at different moments in the organization's history. Rather, it was a sacred and simultaneous tending to the past and the present.[4] The public letter was an offering that archived Perez's experience and the revolutionary history that invoked it. The letter, like a *vèvè*, also called forth an ancestral impulse that Perez hoped would fasten to the hearts of the born and unborn.

With an emphasis on the material structure of the Citadelle and the physical exhaustion of the journey up the mountain, Perez was entrusting the readership with the future's maturation as an assurance that the revolutionary legacy of the nation would not be dwarfed by inaction. Interestingly, as she wrote to her niece, she explicitly invited their sons into the vision. They too, according to Perez, needed to be humbled by the dream, vision, and manifestation of the revolutionary cause. The attention to sons was not an acquiescence to a revolutionary future that would be led by men. Rather, as a statement to her niece, Perez reminds young girls and their co-parents to bring the boys along. This was not a women's project alone. Haitian women's politics of revolution, care, and belonging included and necessitated the political pilgrimage of Haitian boys and men as well. Thus, this practice of mothering, care work, and attention to history that Perez practiced toward her niece and printed in the periodical was, as Alexis Pauline Gumbs might say, "older than feminism; it [was] older and more futuristic than the category 'woman.'" Perez was "amplifying the nuances of practices that have existed as long as there have been people of different ages with different superpowers invested in each other's existence."[5]

Perez named this transcendent power and instructed her niece to be baptized by the heat of the revolutionary promise again and again: "Like the butterfly, lover of light, returns to the flame to burn its wing, if you go there one day, you will return, repeatedly, to re-immerse your soul again at the living source of the ancestors' faith." Curiously, Perez does not compare this ritual of soul immersion to a *papillon du nuit* (moth), but a *papillon* (butterfly) that is traditionally diurnal or daytime-flying. In so doing, she draws her niece's and the readers' imaginations to the unique family of butterflies that fly during the night toward light.[6] Born in Haiti and having traveled extensively throughout the country for her studies and research in law, education, literature, and theater, perhaps Perez was familiar with the rare Hedylidae butterfly whose dark brown-and-black wings carry it throughout Caribbean evenings seeking light.[7] According to Perez, these "lover[s] of light" were not singed by the flame. Instead, they were charged. Perez anticipated that the journey with her niece to the Citadelle (and through life) would be one of enlightenment. Her enthusiasm was not a calling into the euphoria of national mythology. Rather she hoped that future generations would be on a quest for an ancestral assessment ("What have we done since?") and an expanded application of revolutionary ideas. As the words on the front cover of the September issue implored, Perez wanted "more light!"

Touching the evidence of this shine, Perez also encouraged her niece to inhabit the Black history of the Citadelle.[8] As heirs of the *bronzé* King Christophe, Perez distinctly positioned herself, Marie-Madeleine, and Haiti's future as Black. She was the inheritor of Black thinking, Black dreaming, Black triumph, Black torment, Black sorrow, Black royalty, Black love, and care. Perez acknowledged the political climate of Haiti's modern history that weathered the revolutionary vision, leaving the nation with scars, but she still incited her niece to climb into the grief, the weeping, and the victories of revolutionary leadership.

In her zeal for her niece to dwell in the crevices of revolutionary possibility, Perez foreshadowed her own political and creative trajectory. When Marie-Madeleine was eight years old, Perez wrote and produced her first play, *Sanité Bélair*. The play was about the infamous woman revolutionary soldier of the same name (née Suzanne Bélair) who fought alongside her husband, Charles Bélair, under the leadership of Toussaint Louverture. The story of Sanité's skill as a fighter and her ultimate capture was legendary. And her courage to face her French colonial executioners without a blindfold so that she could look them in the eye as she screamed, "Viv libète! Anba esklavaj!" ("Long live freedom! Down with slavery!") had been told to children for generations. For this reason, some anticipated that the "subject [was] too well known" for Perez's theatrical staging of Sanité Bélair's life.

However, as one reviewer recounted the day after *Sanité Bélair*'s premier at the Rex Theatre on August 10, 1942, "This magnificent drama, with true events and feelings, hugging historical truth, had, through its reenactment of the past, the great success of not falling into what is called the 'false ideal.' On the contrary, a 'true' ideal emerges that was created by portraying these heroic and impassioned peoples' actions, hopes, defeats, and their immense and noble love of freedom." After the first act the reviewer stated, "Mrs. Perez is to be congratulated. . . . The performance is sober, clear, quick." And by the third and final act reviewers explained, "We all already knew that Charles and Sanité were lost. And yet, such is the intensity . . . that Mrs. Perez knew to give to her drama that in spite of our knowledge we were interested in their fate, we waited, we followed passionately . . . breathless towards what we knew had to happen."[9]

The inevitability of the twenty-one-year-old revolutionary's fate on October 5, 1802, did not stop Perez from telling the story again and again. In this performance ritual, Perez staged Sanité's care for the nation. As the reviewer recalled, "Full of enthusiasm and hatred against slavery, Sanité Bélair galvanizes [the soldiers] with her voice, filled with the accents of victory and freedom." Perez turned her audience to a newly lit revolutionary promise. This possibility had a sonic quality. Through young women's voices Perez orchestrated an emboldened women-centered past that touched the audience. The vocality that the audience collectively experienced in August 1942 was not just the dramatized battle cries of Sanité Bélair. Perez also scripted Haitian Vodou songs and dances into the play. While audience members may have been riveted by the portrayal of Sanité, Perez used the character of Sanité's goddaughter, Marie, to carry what would ultimately be the lasting legacy of the play. As dancer, choreographer, and Vodouisant Emerente de Pradines later recalled, "I played and sung there [at the Rex Theatre] the role of the goddaughter of Sanité Bélair." Similar to Perez, it was also de Pradines's first play, and "it was on this occasion that I sang my first two folk songs. . . . Never before had someone sung our folklore on stage."[10]

The historical weight of the play by a woman playwright, about a historical woman figure, with women singing and dancing songs from women's research and practice of Vodou cannot be overstated. In 1942 Haiti was experiencing the political transition of power from the Sténio Vincent administration (1930–41) to the Élie Lescot presidency (1941–45). Sténio Vincent was staunchly against the practice of Vodou and in his last year of office supported antisuperstitious campaigns led by the Haitian Catholic Church that criminalized practices of Vodou, resulting in a new wave of violent repression of the life practice.

Lescot inherited these anti-Vodou initiatives as well as the growing enthusiasm in scientific and philosophical study of Haitian folklore and cultural practices like Vodou dance, songs, and beliefs that Marie-Madeleine's father studied and espoused. Here, the distinction between spiritual practice and public performance was key. As de Pradines explained years after her 1942 performance, "When I am doing it [Vodou songs and dance], it is the truth. . . . It is the truth, it's real, except there is no ceremony, there is no calling the spirits. So that's the folklore."[11] As I will discuss further in chapter 4, this distinction between practice and performance often allowed urban Haitian politicians, leftist-organizers, intellectuals, and women's rights activists to use professionally choreographed spiritual performances and folklore as a marker of Haitian authenticity for their own ends in 1940s international relations, tourism, and political and professional advancement while rejecting "the truth" of these practices. Thus, Perez's delicate balance in staging the multiple sentient truths was profound.

The artistic praise and the novelty of *Sanité Bélair* in the early 1940s was significant. However, read alongside Perez's words to Marie-Madeleine, the play also signals and cites her feminist orientation. Enraptured by the skill and content of de Pradines's performance, the audience may have overlooked her actual character, Marie. Perez wrote a likely fictionalized goddaughter into the *Sanité Bélair* script. In the midst of song, dance, and rapid dialogue about military encounters, Sanité's *filleule* (goddaughter) reminds the audience that the revolutionary warrior was a marraine. Sanité's inevitable violent corporeal death was repeatedly refused by the presence of the future calling her name—"Marraine!"—in every act.[12] Their fates were linked. Between her letter in 1936 and her scripting of Sanité Bélair's goddaughter in 1942, Perez established an archival record of the sacred and political calling to care for women as a measure of Haitian citizenship. She choreographed women's relationship to one another and wrote Haitian women and girls into the national script as co-creators of a future with them in it, "even if the race ha[d] begun." Here, then, the octave of Sanité's cry of "Long live freedom! Down with slavery!" was elevated. The frequency amplified the possibilities and expanded the form of freedom. And the co-parenting that Perez articulated in her letter and in Sanité's mothering ultimately articulates, as Gumbs argues, "'the creative spirit' or 'love' itself."[13]

Between Marie-Madeleine's sixth and tenth birthdays, her marraine wrote a play and her father became a senator for the second time. While seemingly separate, these events were very much intertwined as contextual frames for the 1940s. As Price-Mars was a presidential candidate against Vincent in 1930 and then leading opposition senator against the president, Price-Mars's politics and work, particularly his study of Haitian African ancestry, were in conflict with the Vincent administration. When Lescot was elected president in May 1941, Price-Mars returned to the senate that same year. Additionally, as an outgrowth of Price-Mars's *indigéniste* philosophies regarding Haitian culture and thinking, Price-Mars and Jacques Roumain were also given government support to start the Institut d'Ethnologie.

The institutionalization of research on African traditions in Haitian cultural practices expanded the capacity for the Haitian arts movement to grow and be supported across national class and culture differences. The Haitian arts movement also resonated with the broader *négritude* movement that celebrated the study of global African cultures. In this regard, Perez and de Pradines were among a cohort of Black artists from throughout the region who studied, taught, and created art in Haiti, including Katherine Dunham, Zora Neale Hurston, Suzanne Césaire, Langston Hughes, and Lavinia Williams. Haitian artists like Lina Mathion Blanchet, de Pradines, and Perez also left the country to perform in the United States, and "formed," as was reported about Perez during a 1947 trip, "a great like for the amazing community of Harlem of which [Perez had] heard so much."[14] The shared affinity for African diasporic culture within and throughout the African diaspora was a legacy that Perez wanted to leave for her niece and other Haitian girls.

A year and a half after she published the letter to Marie-Madeleine, Jeanne Perez resigned as editor in chief of *La Voix des Femmes* (February 1938). She continued to be involved in the LFAS, which used her home in Pétionville as a school location to teach reading and writing to young girls from the urban center.[15] She also spent more time working on her journal of creative writing and poetry that she began in 1937 titled *La Semeuse* (The Female Sower). It is unclear how long Perez worked on *Sanité Belair* before its public production, and there are very few available issues of *La Semeuse*, but Perez likely tilled her thinking about the play through the journal.

As Perez moved forward with publishing, *La Voix des Femmes* remained a place for her to share and learn about women's different political thoughts and practices. LFAS women had relative clarity about the enormity of the systems of oppressions and political structures that informed women's dispossession,

R.B.R.
HQ
1102
F V5
v. 1
no. 12
1936

SEP 23 98

Plus de Lumière!

La Voix des Femmes

Vol. I   No. 12
Une Gourde.

Septembre 1936.

Revue Mensuelle

Organe de la Ligue Féminine d'Action Sociale

Un peuple qui se divise en deux catégories d'individus vivant chacune
de leur vie propre, d'un côté les hommes, de l'autre les femmes, sera tou
jours un peuple faible. Il nous faut arriver à une collaboration des deux
sexes pour le bien du pays.   MUSTAPHA KÉMAL.

"LA CITADELLE"
L'une des merveilles du monde. Construite en 1811 par le Grand HENRY CHRISTOPHE, Roi d'Haïti

The LFAS claimed its work as an extension of the Haitian revolution. The cover page
of *La Voix des Femmes* communicates this revolutionary legacy with the image of the
Citadelle framed by a future-facing feminist agenda. The contributing national and
international writers' essays represent topics in the Haitian women's movement, and
reflect the international connections between the US women's movement, Latin American
women's movements, and African American women's political organizing. Bryn Mawr
College Libraries, Special Collections.

and they conceded that not all would be reconciled in their lifetimes. But, as Perez's work reflects, they were committed to setting the scene for Haitian girls and women to "run," or fly like a black-and-brown butterfly in the way that love goes toward the light.[16] So when mothers who were storytelling in the night asked girls like Marie-Madeleine and her peers, "Oú libéré?" (Are you free, my daughter?), they would be able to answer, "Wi manman/matant/ marenn, M libéré" (Yes, mama/aunt/godmother, I'm free).[17]

CHAPTER THREE

The Right Sex

Political Geographies of Haitian Womanhood

In early November 1943 cases of a dangerous influenza virus were reported in Haiti, Europe, Canada, and the United States. Similar to the World War I–era spread of the 1919 world influenza pandemic that killed between 3 and 6 percent of the global population, this illness also moved fast across borders and bodies of water. Unlike the 1919 pandemic, this virus did not cause the same level of mortality, but it did disrupt livelihood. Jeanne Sylvain wrote to her siblings that "in almost every family you have a few days of fever accompanied by aches and a terrible depression that characterizes this disease. Some doctors believed they recognized dengue fever, others said it's a simple cold . . . others say that it is a flu that is not Spanish (maybe Dominican?). In any case the schools have only been open in the morning during the past month and this system will be maintained until January, so in the afternoon the children stroll around and the parents are furious!"[1]

As pandemics do, the end-of-year influenza outbreak brought on widespread speculation, fear, whiffs of underlying national and international conflict, business and school shutdowns, and frustrated caretakers. Jeanne's description echoed medical reports and journals of the time that identified a three- to five-day window of illness including "sudden onset, moderate prostration, fever, and general pains, followed by marked weakness."[2] Among the sisters, they wrote of their concern for the older members of their community, who were more vulnerable. And in the general confusion and lethargy caused by the virus running through the Sylvain home, Madeleine Sylvain-Bouchereau could not remember if she had informed her sister, Suzanne, who was conducting research in the Belgian Congo, of the death most close to their unit: "Did I tell you that Max's grandmother passed away?" Madeleine's husband, Max Bouchereau, whom she married after 1938, lost his grandmother during the epidemic.

In her description of the influenza symptoms, Jeanne referenced the mental health impact of the virus, accounting for the "terrible depression that characterizes the disease." This symptom gained less media attention, but it had a curious intersection with the second phenomenon of the period noted in Jeanne's letters, women's suicide and infanticide. In a family letter several months into the influenza epidemic, on January 6, 1944, Jeanne wrote, "The reports of death due to physiological misery and undernourishment, [and] reports of a birth on the street have become a commonplace story in the newspapers. And in recent months, we are starting to hear of infanticide."[3] Unlike mortality from the virus, these deaths were banally infused into the weekly news cycles, and it was casually insinuated that the pathogen in this epidemic was women themselves. As a reporter's question posed in the newspaper *Le Nouvelliste* alluded, "Is it misery that provokes these crimes of infanticide or is it a twisted mentality of these women?"[4] Haitian women and children were dying, and their deaths were interrogated as possible gender neurosis.

Although Jeanne did not know the exact cause for these losses or the most recent report of "a new born baby girl found near the shore in Cité-Vincent,"[5] she inferred that it was a crisis of resources. She explained to her sisters that President Élie Lescot lowered prices on food necessities but that the taxes levied on goods like oil, soap, and paper products from the United States increased, all while the minimum wage remained $1.50 goudes.[6] Her conclusion was women's basic needs were not being met. This had been the case for many women, for many generations before and after the world war or the Lescot presidency, but the shifting global markets were pressing on the precarity of local economies. While the merchant elite (factory owners and large import and export businesses) experienced an economic boom during World War II, these resources only trickled down to most workers as the local markets continued to extract labor from the growing working class and the peasant majority. In this scenario, Haitian women were being depleted.

Jeanne found that despite the wartime insecurity, fluctuating markets, the flu, and death, a third epidemic raged on. Informing her siblings of invitations to and her attendance at weddings nearly every week between November 1943 and May 1945, she shared a phrase from another friend who suggested that the incessant marriages were akin to an "epidemic." Other people may not have noted the frequency of marriage or framed it in terms of impending crisis, but Jeanne was thirty-seven years old and unmarried. To some in her social class, being unmarried was a crisis, and ameliorating this necessitated the urgent attention and care ascribed to an epidemic. Each time an invitation came to the Sylvain home or she attended a wedding, Jeanne was questioned about her marital status. According to her sister Yvonne, who was also unmarried at thirty-six years old, Jeanne's marriage status was a choice, since she had many people interested in courting her. Jeanne met the topic of her own marriage with sarcasm and skepticism. The wave of women getting legally married was a pattern to study, rather than a condition to be desired. Most practically, in adjusting to her first paying job, she felt that earning her own money was "a step up" for her and getting married would mean that her wages would legally no longer be her own.[7] From this perspective, marriage could have represented impending loss of freedoms and movement, something like a hovering disease.

The triad of epidemics happened at the end of World War II and through the midterm woes of President Élie Lescot (1941–45). The confluence of phenomena also tracked the path of Haitian women's political practice throughout the 1940s. During this same time, the LFAS crafted, supported, and won three major legislative victories, including the January 1944 women's wage law, which granted women the right to hold their own wages; the repeal of the child illegitimacy law in December 1944, which gave children born outside of legal marriage the same rights as children born in legal marriage; and the repeal of the marriage tax in January 1945.

The epidemics and the legislation, each a complex set of circumstances, were captured in Jeanne Sylvain's letters as she reported the goings on of the LFAS and the women's movement to her loved ones. Sylvain's correspondences echo the labyrinthine archival record and historiography of the 1940s that delineate the quickened pace of local grievances, national politics, and shifting global networks that collided into each other at warp speed by the end of the decade, producing, among other things, a revolution. Sylvain's catalogue and that of the LFAS remind us that the collateral outcome of these intersecting moments leading to the early 1946 revolution and the late 1946 constitutional assembly also named women's dispossession and political maneuvering.

Advances in wartime technology, the mass movement of people across the globe to play their wartime role in various parts of the world (not only in Europe), and the geopolitical restructuring of power as a consequence of the war impacted nation-states in subtle and spectacular ways. Haitian women documented and showed up in the record of this dynamic season. While the record captures the political intensity and legislative movements involving women, their archival curation offers that what was more intense than political debate or assembly grandstanding on any side of women's rights was the emotional hazing that women endured over the course of the 1940s. The continuity and even growth of misogynist discourse, disposability of women's lives, and general lack of care for women documented by women about women returns us to the opening narrative of this book and suggests that the "insults levied against Haitian women" toward the end of the decade at the 1946 assembly were not uncontrolled outbursts, but the continuation of years of attack on women as the nation navigated post–US occupation politics.

While Castel Démesmin and Emile Saint-Lôt words were the most aggressive recorded verbal attacks against women, their words were allowed and framed by a larger history of women's postrevolutionary citizenship. LFAS women repeatedly identified this context on conceptual and material grounds as an infantilizing, criminalizing, and maddening enslavement. Captured in Madeleine Sylvain-Bouchereau's 1937 assertion "Haitian women were minors, criminals, or insane" and her later assessment that "the woman is a slave," Haitian women's experiences and relationships to these respective epidemics echoed the truths of their social position and citizenship location. In particular, the fatality associated with the period, and women's experiences in it, communicated long-stated articulations of women's compromised freedom and choices in modern Haiti. And women's responses to their dispossession recalled the well-known acts of refusal by women during periods of chattel enslavement, including suicide, infanticide, and the rerouting of kinship and sexual relationships toward their own meanings of freedom. As women's rights organizers pursued clarity for the organization, they were attuned to the social and political circumstances that made women vulnerable to the volatility of the period.

The women's archive also recalls the limits of the revolutionary moment, challenges the historical inevitability of 1946, and reminds us that the possibilities of different outcomes for women at multiple intersections were constantly within reach. These possibilities walked in, of course, with the *femme du peuple* and LFAS women's documentation of her at the assembly hall. The unnamed woman walked into the assembly on the line created by the intersection of historical, political, and social planes in the 1940s. Along the lines of her entrance, this chapter moves with the realities of women of the decade. Like the unnamed woman's appearance in the LFAS archive, women like her show up in half sentences and brief encounters of these women's midcentury archives. And like the unnamed woman, these women's lives locate the stakes of the historical moments. The comments that were hurled at her, which I return to at the end of this chapter, were vulgarly recycled scripts that women recognized and improvised around in their everyday and public-facing organizing in the early 1940s. As documented in Jeanne's letter, women incorporated their physical and mental health and kinship networks into political thinking and into their translation of the historical moment, all of which were informed by women's wayfaring toward personal and collective sovereignty.

Thus, LFAS women paved alternative routes off the path of disposability, confinement, and containment that structured women's legal and social citizenship experiences. Following their course, this chapter ultimately leads to the 1946 postrevolution constitutional assembly.

AT THE BEGINNING OF JANUARY 1944, Jeanne reported to her sisters that the food prices fluctuated often, job insecurity was on the rise, and Haitians were being displaced from their land. Jeanne knew all of this because in addition to being the resident family reporter, while her siblings traveled the world during the 1940s, in mid-1943 Jeanne started a new job at the newspaper *A Propos de SHADA* [Société Haïtiano-Américaine de Développement Agricole]. After receiving her degree in social work from the University of Chicago in 1942, Jeanne returned home to work before continuing her studies. Her return home coincided with Lescot's wartime effort to build the Haitian economy and establish strong regional partnerships within Pan-American networks. In 1941 Lescot agreed to the agricultural development program with the United States called Société Haïtiano-Américaine de Développement Agricole (SHADA). Inserting Haiti as the solution to the United States' rubber supply shortage due to Axis powers blocking trade from the Philippines, one of the United States' largest sources of rubber, Lescot agreed to a partnership with the United States that included the importation and cultivation of *hévéa* (rubber) trees from the Philippines to Haiti.

Using the labor and land of the Haitian peasant class, SHADA also included the planting of cryptostegia vines (used for rubber making) and the extraction of lumber in southeast Haiti. The leaders of the program anticipated that the warm and aired countryside, mirroring the climate in the Philippines, would lead to significant yields in Haiti. For the *milat*, wealthy, internationally connected Lescot, this kind of partnership needed a media campaign. In the wake of the US occupation and in the midst of global war, Lescot had to dispel any suspicion of a backdoor US invasion through SHADA partners and US banks. Additionally, he needed the popular support or silence of the Black peasant population who inhabited the land needed for rubber cultivation. For these reasons, SHADA, Lescot, and minister of agriculture Maurice Dartigue spent time and resources on national goodwill campaigns and newspaper production to put a celebratory spin on the project.

Jeanne was the international translator for the SHADA newspaper, *A Propos de SHADA*. In her new position, she traveled throughout the country with other SHADA employees, including engineers, project managers, and surveyors, to document the efforts of thousands of peasant farmers who received subsidies to grow and cultivate rubber trees. When she completed her short work trips, she returned to the political and social news of Port-au-Prince, and back into another pandemic as she scrolled down the litany of marriage announcements when she took respite from her jobs.

Jeanne liked earning her own money and initially thought SHADA was a viable project, even if she was less enthusiastic about the work. Like many initial supporters of SHADA, including peasant farmers and urban dwellers, Jeanne likely trusted Lescot's capacity to leverage his international record of diplomacy for the nation's economy. The former minister of interior under President Vincent, Lescot had also served three years as the ambassador to the Dominican Republic, and in the final three years of the Vincent administration, Lescot was the foreign minister (1938–41). Moreover, his vision for the project was not idle musing. SHADA was infused with a $7 million loan from the Import-Export Bank of the United States to clear land and pay farmers to work the land and was provided administrators to navigate the many moving parts of crop development, production, and exportation. Over 90,000 Haitian and US citizens were employed to do this work. Yet the plan struggled from the beginning, as the agricultural ambitions did not match the ecological context. In addition to a drought in 1943–44, it took time to cultivate the land. The cryptostegia plant did not take root in certain key areas, and a fire at one of the SHADA locations all stunted the program. In the face of slow and low returns, the social failure of the project was the massive displacement of peasant farmers and clearing of food-bearing trees and crops for rubber cultivation.

When Jeanne committed herself to only one year of the "easy" job, she was not aware of the failing elements of the project. She explained, "My duties also include the assiduous reading of the daily and weekly newspapers that are sent to us, the cutting out of everything concerning SHADA, and the translation of articles or notes of any significance. As I said earlier, I have never read so many newspapers in my life." Although Jeanne had to "admit that the small insignificant work bores me a little," she became deeply familiar with the happenings of the country, allowing her to code, catalog, and account for women's lives in her messages. The frequency and matter-of-fact reporting on women's deaths must have been disheartening and thought provoking: what were the circumstances that would lead someone to surrender themselves and their children to the sea?

With the stories of women's lives circulating, Jeanne kept cutting and transcribing. Not quite grasping the "more or less painstaking" work of translation, her siblings enthusiastically requested that Jeanne send them copies of the papers, so that they could read and celebrate her work.[8] However, after some months of requests, with no action from Jeanne, she finally confessed, "I had not done it earlier because the fact that the newsletter has such a specialized interest does not make it very attractive to read and above all if it is the only Haitian publication that you can receive, you risk getting an inaccurate idea of things in Haiti." Jeanne did not want to waste her siblings' time or mislead them. Over the course of her year of employment, Jeanne learned that part of her job was to gloss over the inefficiencies of the SHADA work and spin a productive image to the country and their international partners. Her attempts to insert levity into the newsletter, once translating "a rather long humorous article," were blackballed by her supervisor, US agronomist Thomas A. Fennell, who said her work did "not fall within the scope of the newspaper."[9]

Beyond the rejection of her small attempts to insert an alternative voice into the SHADA narrative, Jeanne also got an uncomfortable firsthand look at the environmental damage and inefficiency of the SHADA project. By March 1944, a year into her position, most observers knew, despite Lescot's national and international tours, that SHADA was not viable. Three years into the project, Jeanne's letters accounted for the long-standing mistruths of the work: "The cryptostegia is more unpredictable, no doubt because we are not yet sure of the care that this young plant needs and we are demanding too much of it." That leaders on the project had not learned to care for the crops years into the project was concerning, but Jeanne's more astute observation was that the hypercapitalist, high-returns-driven financial desires were incongruent with Haiti's ecology.

SHADA forcibly removed peasants from their lands, destroyed homes, and cut down decades-old fruit-bearing trees. The project cleared 47,177 acres of land by 1943. SHADA ultimately controlled over 100,000 hectares of Haitian land.[10] SHADA depleted the land and the cycle of depletion extended to the people. Two months after Jeanne's observation, SHADA was forced to reduce its employment from over to 90,000 to 4,000. In three months' time, Jeanne was unemployed. And so were thousands of peasant farmers, many of whom had been displaced from their own lands for the advancement of the project. The massive unemployment of SHADA workers across the country "totally eclipsed the little economic revolution that [was] already half way done."[11] The failure and its poorly handled end also accelerated the criticism against Lescot and the timeline toward a social revolution to respond to what many felt was an example of his willingness to gamble with and dispose of land and the Black majority living on it.

As a multitiered and diverse class, not all peasants experienced the end of SHADA the same way. A few may have been able to financially break even if they were able to yield some *hévéa* growth and additionally move into an administrative position such as work leader or surveyor. However, many of the peasantry entangled with SHADA not only lost their land but also lost their capacity to withstand market fluctuation when the project uprooted and cut down food-bearing plants on their own small plots. Without their own minor provisions for daily sustenance and weekly changes in food pricing, women were in vulnerable spaces of existence. This vulnerability exacerbated what Haitian sociologist Alex Dupuy explains as the post-US occupation models that "unleashed a process of proletarianization" in which large mono-crop export farming and mining projects disrupted local, small-scale farming that allowed families to maintain their lives in spite of the growing powers of the state or strength of the merchant class.[12] This was not just a financial crisis for some displaced peasants, a violence unto itself, but by definition this caused a fundamental shift in identity, as landed or proto-peasants. Specifically, for young women, without access to land, the shift in family resources meant that they could be sent to the urban centers to earn money for the family through small jobs and domestic labor, swelling the urban population numbers but also making women vulnerable to the intimate volatility of the urban domestic space, including low wages, long hours, and sexual violence by employers.

The conditions of coerced or forced displacement were unquantifiable and far reaching. And as Haitian psychologists Guerda Nicolas and Casta Guillaume have shown in their work regarding environmental trauma, the rupture of women from the land and home space may have "caused immeasurable physical and psychological damage" to those who were caught in the winds of the international project.[13] SHADA was not a natural disaster, but it was a disaster that ravaged the environmental and rural social ecology of the country. A year after leaving her position at SHADA, Jeanne returned to one of the areas near Forêt de Pines with her sister and wrote, "The forest has been painfully exploited by SHADA."[14]

Jeanne articulated a tender truth of the deforestation of thousands of Haitian hectares. The leveled land also signaled a personal and historical discomfort: Jeanne had contributed to the narrative machine that kept SHADA running. The Haitian-American partnership hid behind the smoke screens of journalism to promote the project's unrooted and burning product. At the same time, Jeanne attempted to disrupt this work. In her refusal to share the newspaper with the theorists she held in the highest regard (her siblings) on the grounds of the periodical's unreliability and through her attempts to intervene in the information stream with her own humor, Jeanne communicated her unease with her participation in the project. Indeed, SHADA was one of several examples in the 1940s where the Pan-American visions of Haitians were soured by incongruent implementation of these visions with regional partners. At the same time, as Chantalle Verna reminds us, and as I will discuss more extensively in chapter 4, Haitians consistently used the apparatus of Pan-Americanism to achieve their own, varying, ends. Jeanne, like other educated or affluent Haitians, was able to leverage her foreign education into a high-wage-earning job during World War II, but as Jeanne documented, the work had a grave cost.

Jeanne responded to the deprivation by planting a new project. She was no longer being paid, but she was working. In the early days of the influenza epidemic, the LFAS opened the Foyer Ouvrier. The Foyer was a center for working-class women to study and learn technical skills and earn a remedial education. Before leaving SHADA, Jeanne would work all morning at her job and then leave to teach students at the Foyer. In her prediction for the new year of 1944, Jeanne concluded, "Madeleine and I will split our time between work, le Foyer, and home."[15] The target population for the Foyer was peasant migrant women–turned–urban working poor. They were the women of greatest concern to the government because of their unregulated movements, but the least considered in social services and educational programming. After its inauguration on November 3, 1943, the Foyer's pool of interested students topped four hundred, with one hundred students coming to the Foyer each day for lessons "on anything people ask for," including sewing, cutting, cooking, and typing classes, as well as French, Spanish, and English language courses. Working out of a room with a thirty-person capacity, Madeleine and Jeanne tried not to turn women away despite the fact that they struggled to find equipment and teachers to accommodate the interest. In offering what women asked for, the LFAS attempted to create a curriculum led by these women's desires and expectations for their lives in the capital city.

Le Foyer: Shifting the Social Terrain

The Foyer was a feminist response to women's needs. It was also an opportunity for Jeanne and Madeleine Sylvain-Bouchereau to translate their social work education to a Haitian context. The Foyer was an extension of LFAS women's research to curate and craft an alternative landscape for women in Haiti that invited women to circumvent the state. The new "home" for women was situated in the geopolitical space of a rapidly growing Port-au-Prince. Between 1921 and 1943, eight thousand new houses were built in the city with a total of 15,000 recorded dwellings when the country entered the 1943–44 season of epidemics. Between 1931 and 1949 the city population rose from 125,000 to over 142,208 in the geographic distance of 6.7 square miles.[16] Located across from the National Stadium south of Champs de Mars, the Foyer had an open invitation for women from across the city to make their way through the old city and the legislative plaza to gather together as working women.

Drawing women together under one roof was a project of care and an intervention in the social science of the period. In her 1939 study of leisure among girls in Port-au-Prince discussed in chapter 2, Suzanne Comhaire-Sylvain identified differences between girls and women in Port-au-Prince based on religion, language, education, and other social factors. In subsequent work she later concluded that based on these intersectional factors, housing was the most conspicuous index for studying differences among women. Over the course of twenty years of studying girls and young women, Comhaire-Sylvain ultimately argued that scholars had to attend to space in order to understand the social lives of women in Haiti. In an article published in 1959, she reflected, "Most visitors who have studied the Haitian scene have been Americans; and they have described the local society as split by cultures. This general insistence on the cultural cleavage between the two strata of Haitian society has made it appear the only important factor of social differentiation in the country."[17]

Comhaire-Sylvain argued, however, for a multi- and interdisciplinary approach that would be "neither easily accessible, nor could [the approaches] be used to the advantage of persons lacking experience in the country, since the sources are widely scattered and uncoordinated, and the data is incomplete." This alternative approach to understanding the urban landscape was necessary because, as she explained, the "figures show clearly that in urban Haiti the stratification is far less simple than that indicated by previous authors."[18] Comhaire-Sylvain did not identify these authors by name, but missionaries, international research groups, and leading scholars of Haiti including Melville Herskovits, Zora Neale Hurston, her co-collaborator Alfred Métraux, and Sydney Mintz, who was, by 1959, citing Comhaire-Sylvain's work, all articulated these "two strata" divisions to various degrees. In order to make women more visible, Comhaire-Sylvain poked holes at the thick descriptions of previous research that, as anthropologist John Jackson might say, "pretend[ed] to see everything and, therefore, sometimes [saw] less than it could."[19]

Comhaire-Sylvain's concern here was less to target specific scholars, but more to articulate that most research failed to see, account for, or locate Haitian women. Her call for nuance was an effort to expand the catalogue of women's experiences. She was particularly concerned with the labeling systems that used words like "caste" to describe Haitian social systems. Instead, she "insist[ed] on using impersonal references such as letters or numbers to describe the social classes" because "the word 'sub-proleteriat,' in particular, is objectionable because of its implicit value judgements." She explained that the "masses adhere to standards rejected by the upper classes; but this is not necessarily a mark of inferiority," but rather concepts to be understood.[20] Echoing her work and conclusions from her study in Kenscoff, Comhaire-Sylvain insisted that studying difference in Haiti required multiple and interlocking systems of measurement that ranged from the social to the quite literal use of metrics from within the community like pots and pans.

The gravity of this nuance for Comhaire-Sylvain was more than about research findings. The request for impersonal references, which she later established as Class Zones IV, III, II, and I, was in fact a personal intellectual request. Her social capital in Haitian and scholarly society allowed her to intervene in the language that often overdetermined political discourse and assumed research outcomes. She knew from her own research and from listening to her sisters' day-to-day work that the experiences of women in urban spaces were more complicated than a single axis social dichotomy. And the particular attention to producing new class names was an intellectual adjustment incited by the young women she worked with and studied. During her previous research projects, Haitian girls had refused presumptions about their lives and her access to them. As I will discuss further in chapter 4, Comhaire-Sylvain was influenced by her disciplinary training and assumed access to her "objects of study" when she started her research on girls in Port-au-Prince. But they refused her training and questions. They strategically walked around her intentions, avoided her inquiries, and taught her about their power and perspectives.

It was a schooling that girls kept giving LFAS women at the Foyer. In the first months of programming, the LFAS prioritized relaxation and play as pillars of the Foyer's function. Sylvain and Sylvain-Bouchereau made arrangements with neighboring businesses and the stadium to use their spaces so that the young women could spread out and relax. However, many women demonstrated more interest in the classes and often ignored the LFAS women's efforts to curate leisure for them. Sylvain-Bouchereau initially observed, "It seems the idea of entertainment is so distant"; attempting to address this she "bought all kinds of games, . . . cards, and dominoes, etc." Yet, when the girls and young women came to the Foyer after eighty- to ninety-hour work weeks with a minimum of ten hours a week committed to commuting (walking) to work, most women chose studying over games. Sylvain and Sylvain-Bouchereau quickly learned and adjusted. Leisure was about choice. And the women of the Foyer chose skills and language training that supported their intellectual curiosities and access to alternative routes of social mobility.

Comhaire-Sylvain's scholarly assertions were informed by these moments. She sought to name women's roles in the creation of social spaces beyond impenetrable tiered categorizations. Her concern was one of relation over evidentiary abundance. Comhaire-Sylvain observed that class labels and difference hurt people, held people, inflated people, left people unaccountable to one another and unaccounted for. Thus, Comhaire-Sylvain used numbers and letters not to flatten the context, but to expand the definition. Dividing the city into quadrants of population density, parish affiliation, housing style, and relationship to labor, Comhaire-Sylvain partitioned the city into four class zones. Class IV was the largest portion of the urban population, making up 49 percent (91,000) of people living in different types of homes across the "northern part of old city, near the business district. It includes Bel-Air Hill and the Cathedral, and a stretch of alluvial ground known as LaSaline, recently reclaimed from the sea." This class zone also spread across the southern half of old town to include Morne à Tuf (Tuff Hill). In this crescent cartography, Comhaire-Sylvain mapped eighty-seven *"humfo"* (*ounfò*, Vodou temples or convening spaces), seven Protestant churches, ten night clubs, and a "strong African influence" marked by celebrations and the singular use of Kreyòl. In LaSaline in particular, where she conducted 2,721 questionnaires, most of the "proud" respondents were illiterate homeowners of homes that they built, who documented a preference for "'common-law marriages' (*plaçage*)."[21] Most members of the community were self-employed, with three-fourths of the women naming "trading" as their profession.

Class Zone III made up 24 percent of the urban population (36,000 people) inhabiting areas north of Champs Mars including Poste Marchard and Bolosse. This group was most distinguished from Class Zone IV in that two-thirds of the population had permanent employment primarily in the industrial sector (food processing plants, hotels, and industrial crafts), with a smaller portion working as teachers, state employees, and retail trade staff. Within the St. Gerard's Parish, there were also twenty-one *"humfo"* and five Protestant churches. Comhaire-Sylvain explained that the presence of the *ounfò* and the preference for Kreyòl, although most people in Zone III spoke fluent French, made outside observers place the IV and III zones together. Comhaire-Sylvain also indicated that "one of [Zone III people's] outstanding characteristics is the extreme care which they take with the education of their children." They "nourish definite, thereby no means unreasonable, ambitions of their offspring." This class zone was also "swollen by well-to-do children who attended downtown schools" in the zone. Class III residents were also the "best patrons of the stadium, which [was] located near their homes."

Also near their homes and across from the stadium was the Foyer. The Foyer's location spoke to the LFAS's ultimate strategy. As Comhaire-Sylvain outlined it, Class Zone III had the most heterogeneity and class intersection of all the other class zones. It was a perfect meeting place. And it was different from Class Zone II, which made up 16 percent of the urban population within the Parish of Sacred Heart, St. Anne's, and St. Joseph's with no Protestant churches, or known *ounfò*. With the state being the largest employer, along with big import and export houses, retail, teaching, and clergymen, Comhaire-Sylvain surmised, "This is the 'middle class' of the Pan American Union inquiry." Comhaire-Sylvain's scare quotes connote her discomfort with the accuracy of class terminology for the group of people who included "families of humble origins, who have won some public recognition after one or two generations" and people "whose main ambition [was] to catch up with their wealthy relatives." Those wealthy relatives made up the multitiered Class Zone I, who lived southeast of Champ de Mars and in more distant suburbs and who made up only 9.7 percent of the urban population. Comhaire-Sylvain reported that "family property [was] common at this level" and that the communities were "less religious" with "university studies remain[ing] the most effective way to secure a high income" in the areas of state governance, banking, shop ownership, law, and medicine. The Sylvains, for example, were members of Class Zone I. However, Comhaire-Sylvain's purpose in using the spatial-class-culture descriptions was not to reinforce segregation between urban dwellers, but to foreground mobility between the urban population. Suzanne's class zones linked resource and culture to location, spatial intersections, and mobility.

Ultimately, women made up the majority of the Port-au-Prince population, and through their movements about the city, they were the interlocutors between zones. Comhaire-Sylvain did not explicitly name the arteries of connection between and among classes, but these intersections were referenced in the folds of each description. In Class IV she writes, "The rest of Class IV inhabit other quarters in some menial capacity, often as servants."[22] In Class II she notes, "Households are larger than in Class III, averaging 4 adults, and 5 children, but the fifth child is usually a servant." And in her

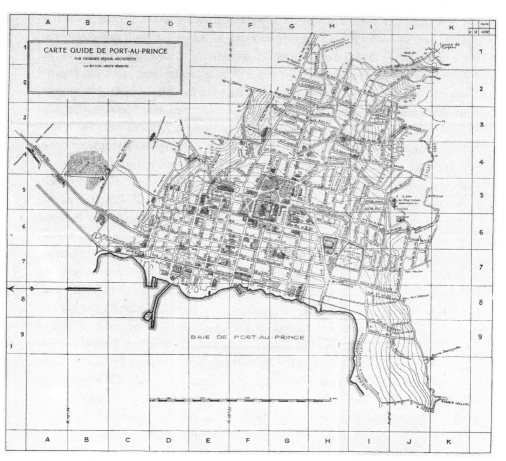

This map of Port-au-Prince is among several printed and sketched maps in Suzanne Comhaire-Sylvain's personal collection. In her research on urban demographics, she used maps like this one to chart the overlapping sociopolitical, cultural, and class dynamics in 1940s Port-au-Prince. "République d'Haiti Carte-Guide et Plan de Port-au-Prince," 1947. Courtesy of the Suzanne Comhaire-Sylvain Collection, Department of Special Collections, Stanford University Libraries.

statistics of Class I, only 6 of the nearly 10 percent of the population were wealthy, educated, and high wage earners. The remaining 3.7 percent "consist[ed] mostly of servants and other members of Class IV living outside of their densely populated wards."[23]

Nearly 20,000 women lived in the city at the intersections of Comhaire-Sylvain's class zones.[24] The women who moved between zones inhabited the city, but lived outside its visible cartography. These women went to work at

5 A.M. because their employers expected them to serve morning coffee at 7 A.M. These women were often forced to substitute their education for minimum-wage jobs. These women left, traveled, and returned to their homes in the dark of dawn *and* dusk. For other women, their commute from downstairs to upstairs was quick but often unaccounted for and subject to the whims of any person's desire. These women were lumped into their employer's household data whether they felt affinity for these families or not. Their statistical kinship only further obscured the archival record erasing women whose familial networks were not recognized by Catholic parish records because of their household beliefs, birth contexts, or partnering choices. These women accessed resources for their children's success (Class Zone III) and were self-employed (Class Zone IV), and their professional pursuits blurred the boundaries of class, culture, and spatial belonging.

The Foyer was a location for this group of ambulant women whose steps linked the cityscape of Port-au-Prince. These women were the femme du peuple. They were Amise, who nursed Comhaire-Sylvain back to health and took her to zones IV and III, where Comhaire-Sylvain learned to celebrate death. These women were Marguerite, the Sylvains' "young cook" who appears in the half-sentence of an announcement that the "whole house" caught the flu in 1943. Marguerite and the Sylvain sisters would have first introduced themselves in the foyer (entryway) of their home. Marguerite likely prepared countless meals for the LFAS leadership meetings at the Sylvain home on Rue Christophe. Marguerite was likely from nearby Poste Marchand or Bolosse. Or perhaps she was from farther north in Belair or LaSaline. If so, she may have passed Jeanne Sylvain on her way from work at the SHADA headquarters across the street from the Institute d'Ethnologie. In the afternoons she may have accompanied Sylvain and Sylvain-Bouchereau to the Foyer as a culinary arts teacher, or she may have been too busy with food preparations for the sisters' late return from the center. The women tried to close the Foyer before 7 P.M., but there were so many women "very anxious to learn, to learn anything" that they—Madeleine, Jeanne, and, perhaps, Marguerite—often stayed late. Crossing into their respective zones, the hundreds of women who left the Foyer as a group in the darkness of night could have offered the semblance of safety from the vulnerabilities of the evening hours.

The night also offered cover from eyes and opinions of those who may not have understood, decontextualized, or pathologized the limits of a parent's resource and capacity to see a future for her baby girl on the unsettled land of LaSaline. The road that ran parallel to the sea, just beyond the old city ports, was the same road that the women returning north from the Foyer

Silhouettes of two women walking through Port-au-Prince. Courtesy of the Suzanne Comhaire-Sylvain Collection, Department of Special Collections, Stanford University Libraries.

would have walked. Perhaps it was those groups of women walking home from the Foyer who heard the baby girl rejecting the care of the sea in the first days of the new year of 1944. Some ambulant group or lone commuter ushered the baby girl to the maternity ward at the general hospital back across town between zones IV and II. Yvonne Sylvain's future colleagues would have taken the baby into their care. Yvonne did not start her one-day-a-week shift at the general hospital until several months after this baby was found, but she worked in the neighborhood at Le Service d'Hygiene au Centre de Santé servicing La Saline and Cité Vincent, so she would have heard the details of the baby's rescue.

Yvonne would have witnessed how, although the LFAS established a home space for women, the urban space was still constricting—tight. The former French colonial city was growing beyond its capacity, but the gendered social confines were also stifling. So women accessed freedoms where they saw openings. In some cases, the Foyer was an opening, and in others the sea was more spacious. In other contexts, the invitation of a man from Class Zone II, who of possible Class Zone IV origins "may still marry women of lower social groups," was a possible opening.[25] In other cases, women woke up one morning and "vlan!" escaped the confines of their unseen labor. Women who left these domestic work jobs were often accused of theft on their way out of town. Guilt or innocence regarding accusations of petty theft were rarely determined, but these women were "stealing away" from the ambiguity of the intersects of urban life. These self-determining grabs at personal freedom were not toward rights. Rather as Carolle Charles explains, for many working-class women the body was "an important resource. It [was] a capital. As poor working-class and peasant women put it, 'kom se kawo tèm' (my body is a piece of land) or 'se lajam'm' (it is money)."[26] In this construction, rather than being the migratory, non-land-owning laborers who sociologists would identify as the "urban-proletariat," some women who left these domestic work jobs were more akin to the landed Haitian peasantry. Their body being their land in which "they controlled the rate of their exploitation."[27] Their bodies became the site and the mechanism of escape. The choice to come, go, love, or attend free classes in the afternoon revealed women's freedom to pursue "something" without destination or definition. In the meantime, the Foyer sought to intercede in the complexities of the urban landscape by slowly creating a context of recognition, care, and accountability. The Foyer was a space where one might see another woman looking out in the direction of the sea for too long and offer other possibilities.

As LFAS women developed their own curriculum and educational materials, they accounted for women's movements between spaces and social and cultural contexts. In mapping the urban space, LFAS research also charted the routes between urban and rural Haiti. Comhaire-Sylvain walked the mountains of Kenscoff in order to co-produce a series of handwritten maps of women's rural routes that lead to Port-au-Prince. In 1945, Sylvain-Bouchereau produced a series of beginner-level reading books that tweaked and highlighted the gendered landscape of women's mobility.[28] In the foundational grammar lessons, Sylvain-Bouchereau depicted a girl's day-to-day in which women moved between rural and urban space and stopped over at the foyers of aunties. The social work focus on home space was meant to redraw the cartographies of gender relation, work, and belonging.

Together, the family correspondences, research, and the Foyer demonstrated that women's social and political experience was "an alterable terrain."[29] Comhaire-Sylvain's analysis of space was evolving in the 1940s, but her research alongside the Foyer attempted to "[make] visible new, or unacknowledged, strategies of social struggle" because the LFAS women's action communicated that they knew what Katherine McKittrick has argued: "We produce space." It is not surprising, then, that while reflecting on the uprooted environment of SHADA, Jeanne Sylvain wanted to plant something, alter the space. In researching and writing over the course of two decades, Comhaire-Sylvain captured the transformation in this space. Most notably, she wrote of Class Zone III, which was made up of students and teachers at the Foyer. She asserted that they were the "most vigorous of all social classes in Port-au-Prince, the one likely to progress most rapidly in the future," noting that their zeal for cross-class connections made them "sympathetic to the peasantry."[30] Over the course of two decades, Comhaire-Sylvain had charted what many have called the Black middle class. In 1959 she concluded that this group's support led to François Duvalier's presidency.

The Foyer was one stopover for women's political wayfaring, but it was not uncomplicated. While Madeleine and Jeanne celebrated the history and intellectual study of Haitian folklore and visited the Institut d'Ethnologie, getting guided tours by Griot member "Lorimer Denis [who] enthusiastically provided [them] with the meanings of the collections," the education at the Foyer was also philosophically oriented toward a Catholic ethos of social conservatism that supported girls' piety and ultimate legal Christian marriage. At the same time, LFAS women used research to identify women's needs. Comhaire-Sylvain also acknowledged, "however, statistics have to be used with caution."[31] In this case, she specifically referred to the fact that the data for identifying population growth were based on Catholic baptismal records. The data did not include births outside of hospitals or outside of legal marriage. These silences in the archive foretold the LFAS's political focus on women's social and financial freedoms in 1944 and 1945.

The Marriage Epidemic

While the LFAS attended to the context of one epidemic by addressing women's needs in Port-au-Prince, they were also engaged with a national campaign to inform the legal conditions of the other epidemic—marriage. Within days of Jeanne Sylvain's early 1944 updates that included the flu, women's self-harm, and marriages, she also celebrated the passage of the 1944 marriage wage law, giving Haitian women the right to keep and control their labor earnings. The 1944 marriage wage law was one of the LFAS's greatest organizational victories vis-à-vis the state. The petition—known by the LFAS as the St. Aude Project because Senator Denis St. Aude originally sponsored the petition in the national legislature in 1936—called for married women's uncontrolled wages. When women were married by the state, they became the legal minors of their husbands, and as a result were required to give any earnings they made to their spouses. In addressing this particular law, Alice Garoute characterized married women's financial condition to enslaved people's unpaid labor or indentured servitude. The St. Aude Project, as one LFAS committee report communicated, "came to liberate."[32] The initiative was central to the LFAS women's early organizing, and their support of the law ordered the organizational structure for their first years of the movement in which the LFAS created a Justice Committee to specifically focus on the St. Aude Project.

The simultaneity of World War II and the political volatility of the mid-1940s presented an opportunity for the women to lobby for change in the rapidly changing political arena. For the LFAS, the marriage wage law was an issue of workers' rights. The members of the LFAS were among a number of Black women activists throughout the region who took up similar issues around women's wages. For example, a year before the LFAS put the wage law before the senate, Yvonne Sylvain's friend and member of the National Association of Colored Women Sadie T. M. Alexander put forth a domestic working women's bill in Pennsylvania that ensured that Black women's wages were issued fairly. In her work on Claudia Jones, Caribbean feminist scholar Carol Boyce Davies shows that the work of women like Alexander was a precursor to communist, feminist, intellectual Claudia Jones's organizing and thinking.[33] Interestingly, in 1946 when there was governing uncertainty for nine months, Alexander held Yvonne Sylvain's savings (several hundred dollars) in her US bank account.[34] However, most women did not have international friendships to buffer financial uncertainty, and with no labor unions legally sanctioned in Haiti until after 1946, the LFAS women used alliances with legislators like St. Aude to intervene on their behalf.

The law was crafted for legally married women. Thus, with less than 25 percent of women in state or church-sanctioned marriages, the law was conceptualized for a particular group of women. As the LFAS Justice Committee reported, "There is a category of women who will benefit the most from this law. . . . It is those who don't have the financial means to divorce, or cannot do it due to other reasons. They work and win their daily bread themselves, and sometimes support one or more children and cannot do with their salaries as they please; subjugated as they are to the unjust guardianship of their husbands. This law came to liberate them. It is justice."[35]

Women's social, economic, and political freedoms were informed by their labor and family networks. Concern for how and where the resources from women's labor were distributed was a particular interest of the growing professional and educated urban class of women in the mid-twentieth century. Although women owned businesses and earned money throughout the colonial period and nineteenth century, the early and mid-twentieth century witnessed growth in women's employment in the nonagricultural labor market. With greater access to secondary and university education for girls in the early twentieth century, young women were employed in greater numbers, making the issue of wage controls an issue of increased relevance for certain women.

For the majority of Haitian women, labor, marriage, and economic freedoms or restrictions were systems that had been navigated and negotiated since the colonial era. During her research on marriage in the Haitian countryside throughout the 1930s, Comhaire-Sylvain found that the majority of marriage unions in rural areas of the country were not legal.[36] Instead, women were in common-law unions known as *plasaj*, or in open relationships with partners with whom they were not legally bound.

Partnership and marriage across social differences were intimately connected to market fluctuation and mobility that revolved around women's relationship and accessibility to the resources of land. With access to land, via family relation or via marriage women cultivated plots that allowed them to sell produce throughout the nation, giving them relative access to income and movement. Marriage could jeopardize or enhance these financial and spatial freedoms. Legal marriage meant that women were subject to the economic will of their husbands, but common-law marriages or maintaining long-term plasaj contracts meant that women could extend their access to land without compromising their financial independence. At the same time, each form of union, even the less litigated relationships, involved compromise. Haitian economist Mireille Neptune-Anglade identified multipartnered, rural common-law unions as social contracts that often limited class mobility, and Haitian feminist Myriam Merlet cautioned against the romanticizing of peasant women's economic freedom given the high expectations of women's labor and resources that fluctuate within the diversified group of peasants or working-class women.[37] Many women selling foodstuffs made enough to supplement the basic needs of families on a weekly basis. Within the agricultural system, the majority of women were not *madan sara* (women commerce specialists) who brokered resources, pricing, and access to the larger national and international markets in Haiti. With international price fluctuations, madan sara often deferred the inflation in products and the high rates of their loans with larger factories and traders to the peasant women farmers who were buying their goods. In this regard, plasaj unions also highlighted not only women's access to resources, but how they were valued as an economic resource. Haitian feminist Sabine Lamour critically asserts that plasaj emerged as "a noninstitutional mode of union for the captive group" of Africans during the colonial era in which multiple women's labor was used on a single garden plot, so that men could maintain their land in the face of wealthy proprietors. In particular, as Lamour argues, plasaj normalized "the formation of a labor-intensive work ethic" in which "a woman must 'sacrifice herself' in order to be valuable."[38]

This self-sacrificing model of Haitian womanhood was disproportionately laid to bare on Black poor and working-class women.[39] Still, Francophone Caribbean scholar Marie-José N'Zengou-Tayo also shows that market women, farmers, day laborers, and domestic workers among working-class and peasant women were "far more advanced in terms of financial independence and entrepreneurial skills than their urban middle-class counterparts who were working."[40] This relative freedom and familiarity with finances was documented, for example, in Comhaire-Sylvain's story of Adelsia discussed in chapter 2. Comhaire-Sylvain's narrative of Adelsia's life also reinforces that women in wealthier classes had greater access to social mobility than that was afforded to peasant or working-class women. In the nineteenth century, women's long-standing central role in the strength of their financial management was acknowledged and written into law. For example, Article 201 of the 1840 civil code was created so that married women could hold their own wages. The law was repealed within several years, but the legislation was a state acknowledgment of women's role as significant actors in the flow of currency in the country and that marriage should not prohibit the flow of resources.

While the various types of unions and inter- and intra-class dynamics informed women's access to financial resources, weddings were also an important moment of financial adjustment, cultural retention, and celebration and were points of negotiation for peasant women. For example, in many plasaj weddings a *peye bônê* (payment of happiness) was given to the bride's parents on behalf of the groom. In this ritual, which included actual money and on occasion a cow or large offering of food, the payment was given to the father, "but immediately given to the mother who splits it between the couple and herself." Not only did the mother take the offering for herself, but the mother and the daughter's godmother negotiated the price if they found the payment to be too low.[41] Accounting for the exchange over women's bodies, which grounded the legal, religious, and nonlegal institutions of marriage, Comhaire-Sylvain's work highlighted that within the capitalist confines women were at the intersections of this financial and social exchange. As she recounted from her time with Adelsia, who married her plasaj husband as his second wife during World War I, when she earned money she kept it for herself and her daughters and "none of which she gave to her father."[42] Through marriage, women could also expand their access (if not ownership) to the lands of their family and that of their husband's family. But in addition to the financial navigation of wealth, marriage was also a context for cultural exchange, sustenance, and celebration. Comhaire-Sylvain wrote that everyone eats well at weddings and that ceremonies like the "water ceremony," in which parents asked the *lwas* for the couple's protection, revealed long-standing spiritual practices that moved across beliefs (practiced by Vodouisan and nonpractitioners) and urban and rural space.[43]

Thus while Jeanne and her friends referenced the perceived surge in marriages at the end of 1943 and beginning of 1944 as a unique contagion, it was more akin to a seasonal return. Throughout the twentieth century, marriage rates increased during the first coffee harvest in November and continued through February and during the corn harvest between August and October.[44] The financial resources that came from harvest season moved between the rural and urban areas and were governed by the agricultural seasons. For example, although coffee could not be legally sold in small markets and was strictly regulated by government and national processing companies, the success or failure of the mass-produced crop informed the economic stability of rural markets, which depended on the economic surplus of the coffee industry to purchase other goods.[45] This seasonal economic surplus also meant more resources to spend on weddings.

Long-term unions were a part of many women's lives, and as a result, LFAS women fought to change women's financial freedoms within marriage. As reflected in their organizational materials, LFAS women had different opinions about how women should operate in marriage and whether or not they should get out of it (divorce), but the organization directly and implicitly situated legal marriage (and motherhood) as ideal signposts for respectable Haitian womanhood. As the LFAS Justice Committee explained in its petition for the St. Aude law, "We have to make it clear that this law is not trying to insinuate an idea of rivalry between two beings called upon to live together to constitute this masterpiece, which is a beautiful family; the foundation of every society. We are only affording protection and more liberty to working women, knowing the new stages that they have reached on the road to progress."[46] Despite the inequalities for women under legal marriage, LFAS women maintained that it was a worthy institution and that the title "Madan X" held a social currency that counterbalanced the restrictions on personal liberties.[47] LFAS women were not alone in this valuation of state-sanctioned marriage over other forms of marriage unions. Women from across economic class and geographic locations in Haiti recorded some unique value for legal marriage.[48] Yet as evidenced in the marriage legislation passed between 1944 and 1945, the value that marriage had was measured differently by different women, and by governing institutions like the church and state.

In 1945 President Élie Lescot announced the reduction of the national marriage tax. Popularly discussed as the Marriage Tax Law, the law reduced the fees for marriage from a total minimum of 20 gourdes in the countryside to 0.50 gourdes nationwide.[49] In a message to the nation, Lescot explained that the law would "promote, as much as possible, the high and noble institution of marriage, while at the same time ensuring civil status to the children born in our country."[50] The president further explained that without a marriage tax more peasants would have the means to get married. Presenting marriage in a "noble" frame, Lescot clarified his position: "We have decided to combat polygamy among the peasants which is the source of the astonishing growth of our population and creates what some call overpopulation."[51] Lescot's association of peasant familial unions with the overpopulation and subsequent decline of the urban centers was misplaced. First, as a result of poor sanitary conditions and general health, infant mortality among the poor class meant that they were not having significantly more children than middle- or elite-class families in the urban centers.[52] Thus, childbirth outside of marriage, alone, could not have been the cause for rapid urban population growth. Second, Lescot's framing of peasant and poor people's presumed hyperreproductivity alongside overpopulation was an erasure of the increased patterns of rural-to-urban migration since the US occupation. Lescot's projection of urban population growth onto peasant women's reproduction and sexual practices also ignored his role in the disruption of rural geographies, like SHADA, that forced increased urban migration.[53]

Lescot's declaration also indicated that combating "polygamy" was a primary reason for the change in legislation. His term "polygamy" was a reference to plasaj, the common-law marriage that could but did not always involve multiple partners. In Lescot's formulation, plasaj was not an honorable union. He further argued that multiple-partnered marriages necessarily meant a family would have more children than a monogamous married couple. Lescot could not substantiate either argument. Like legal marriage, in the 1930s and '40s plasaj involved an extensive contract negotiation and gift exchange between families and a courting process that was often preceded by other noncontractual conjugal relationships including *rinmin* (to date) and *fiyansé* (to be engaged). In her research Comhaire-Sylvain asserted, "*Plaçage* is a form of marriage recognized in peasant society and also completely respectable from the sociological point of view as civil marriage."[54] Additionally, although infant mortality rates were not well documented, in her research Comhaire-Sylvain documented that families used plasaj to address infertility and infant mortality. In 1937 Comhaire-Sylvain interviewed a woman and her husband who lost seven children through miscarriages and infant death. As a fertility solution to their extraordinary loss, they extended their plasaj relationship to include an additional wife so that they could have children. Comhaire-Sylvain's research documented forms of loss and care that impacted women's decisions about partnering beyond economics or even sexual desire. Most profoundly, in her experiences with Adelsia, plasaj relationships were maintained because of women's care for and support of one another. Finally, in Kenscoff in 1938, for example, multiple partnering only occurred in about 9 percent of plasaj marriages.

Many plasaj marriages were viewed as interim partnerships insured by family-proctored contracts until legal marriage was desired. However, unlike the assumptions of the marriage tax law, fees rarely prohibit a couple's access to legal marriage. Most marriage celebrations, even in rural settings, cost more than the taxes. The wait to legal marriage was often in regard to a general capacity to house a family. Many plasaj women in marriages lived with their parental figures or families while they waited for their partners to establish greater economic security or to build their home. Thus, the hundreds of self-built homes in Class Zones IV and III in Port-au-Prince, for example, were often the material evidence of partnering contracts.

Lescot's true concern with plasaj was less about honorable partnerships and more about legitimacy. Sandwiched between the wage and marriage tax legislation was the December 1944 amendment that authorized research for children's paternity and gave children born out of marriage the same rights as those born in marriage, specifically the right to inherit land.[55] Until 1944, if a child was recorded as illegitimate, the child could not claim inheritance. While the child inheritance law authorized research for paternity and gave children born out of marriage the same rights to inheritance as children born in marriage, the law maintained that a married man could not legally recognize a child outside of marriage. Although the law held the possibility of bringing children into legitimate status, it did not necessarily, in the case of plasaj unions, promote a turn to marriage. If a man remained unmarried, he could continue to socially and legally recognize his children, but if he were married, he could only legally recognize the children of the first marriage. Children from second or third partnerships could not inherit land. And in the case of children born out of noncontractual or nonkinship arrangements in which the man was legally married, children were both economically and socially alienated.[56] Haitian women's rights activist Suzie Boisrond explains this type of legislation established not only hurtful practices of social and financial alienation for children and mothers (not married to the already married man) but also juridically tiered sexual relationships.

The regulation on legitimacy was anchored in women's reproduction, sexual practices, and labor to the land. In the promotion of the law, Lescot anticipated that a repeal on the marriage tax and the legitimacy laws would lead to more legal marriages and more legitimate children who could inherit land. If, he imagined, children were able to inherit the family land when their legally recognized fathers died, they would, in turn, stay in the rural districts and not migrate to the urban centers.[57] Cloaked under the discourse of morality, Lescot used the law to control sexual partnering decisions and family networks for the purposes of local and international markets. The role of women in the peasant economy necessitated that women simultaneously bear children, work rural plots, and sell that produce to urban markets. The overrepresentation of rural-urban migration disrupted the labor economy of the nation, and in a period of national economic uncertainty and the failure of large-scale international partnerships, women needed to stay in place—socially, physically, and sexually. Women having children was not a problem or a statistical burden on the urban economy. It was women's unchecked mobility between rural and urban space alongside their relative freedom of sexual partnering choices that produced outcomes—illegitimate children, migration, and personal income—that were outside the state's control. Thus, as feminist scholar M. Jacqui Alexander's canonical work reminds us, "morality within the context of translocal and transnational Caribbean markets is often communicated in terms of the monogamous conjugal family and is 'a euphemism for sex.'"[58] In this way, the marriage tax and legitimacy laws were used to "legitimate the exploitation of a predominantly female . . . workforce" and govern sexual relationships.

While the constitutional amendment was presented as a diplomatic deci-sion of national civility,[59] it ignored plasaj as a contractual union that for some women offered more freedoms than state- or church-sanctioned mar-riage.[60] Although legal marriage was seen by working-class, poor, middle-class, and elite women as the ideal union, it was not always a wise decision to make in order to remain economically independent and in charge of one's home and children.[61] However, money was not the only reason why couples chose not to get legally married. In her work on sexuality in Haiti, sociologist Carolle Charles has shown that historically some poor and working-class women also chose not to marry as a "counter-power" so that they could maintain control of their bodies and wages.[62] In these cases, Charles explains that women were celebrated for their decision to remain unmarried.[63]

Women in plasaj unions were not the only ones to recognize the power negotiation in the forms of familial and sexual unions. Elite socialization around marriage and multiple partnerships were evident in the lives of LFAS orga-nizers and their families. Alice Garoute's granddaughter, Ghislaine Charlier, was raised under these social complexities and illustrates the intersection these beliefs and the influence of Haitian feminism had on traditional elite social practice. When her husband Etienne Charlier, the leader of the Popular Socialist Party (Parti Socialiste Populair, PSP), proposed marriage, she jok-ingly proclaimed that she would prefer a plasaj union. She explained that in plasaj everyone would be free to do what they wanted. Although her interpre-tation of plasaj possibly revealed some naïveté about gendered power rela-tions even in common-law marriage, her statements illustrated the ways in which women were testing the legal institution of marriage. Ghislaine was playing on the social sensitivities of the time. The idea that Ghislaine would propose a nonlegal or non-Christian form of marriage was a slight to the so-cial expectations of her class and not to her love for her future spouse. It was an effort to address the performance of elite marriage. Ghislaine may have wanted the opportunity to entertain other partnerships, but she was also be-ing provocative. She was using the possibility of plasaj to gain control over what she suspected would be a union with double standards.[64]

The unequal gendered social standards were evident in intimate relation-ships and they were continually reinforced in the law despite incremental legislative gains. Among the marriage regulations of the 1944–45 legislative year, on April 19, 1944, the Senate voted to amend Article 8 of the constitu-tion, granting women the right to serve in all government positions except president. The legislation that Sylvain-Bouchereau identified as a "victory for feminism" was the least discussed among LFAS women, and it would not be implemented for over a decade. After earning the right to candidacy in government elections, the LFAS met with President Lescot in the national palace and listened to his thoughts on the legislation. Sylvain-Bouchereau wrote to her sisters, "The president received us and gave a long lecture sharing his feminist ideas. I believe that he will give us all that we ask for—that's to say civil rights. He said that on his last trip [out of the country] he was struck to see women's contribution to the war effort and that he would like to include women in his government."[65] It is possible that if he remained in office, Lescot would have supported women's inclusion in state governance; however, as he made his projections regarding women's rights, a worsening economic depression and a yearlong drought continued to adversely impact the nation and the perception of Lescot's leadership—all of which were compounded by Lescot's failed effort to establish a Haiti-US investment program to export rubber, and a campaign against the beliefs of the majority of the country through state-sponsored *antisuperstition* (anti-Vodou) campaigns.

In this uncertain climate, LFAS women were reluctant to get excited about a law that could not be enacted, since, as Sylvain-Bouchereau reflected, "there will be no elections during the war." Still, the women tried to remain hopeful, as Sylvain-Bouchereau later wrote: "Fortunately the war will be over soon and I hope a wind of love will pass over the world, but I fear after the war with all of its destruction and misery that it will require a lot of dedication, endurance, and above all justice!"[66] Indeed, Haiti's post–World War II political milieu was different. A radical context was cultivated in the decade following the US occupation in which intellectuals, activists, artists, and politicians reimagined the possibilities of modern Haiti. For many radical thinkers there was a call for the redistribution of wealth, valorization of African ancestry, and by extension peasant culture and knowledge, and a commitment to national sovereignty that cautioned against foreign, particularly US, involvement in Haitian law and economy. While urban radicals had varying beliefs, participation, and understandings of Vodou, many saw the displacement of practitioners as well as the hypersurveillance of their culture and way of living as a general assault on the peasant classes of the nation, both of which ran counter to the ideas of national progress espoused by various radicals. In this context radicals established activist organizations, political parties, reading groups, and newspapers to communicate their respective visions for Haiti.

All of this came to a climax in the first days of 1946. On January 7, students led by Jacques Stephen Alexis, René Depestre, and thirteen others left their schools and marched in the streets of Port-au-Prince demanding the immediate removal of Lescot from the presidency. Joined by other radical thinkers and sympathizers, including LFAS members, the crowds demanded Lescot's removal from office. Many known and unknown members of the LFAS participated in these protests. Most notably, future LFAS president Lydia Jeanty and her sister, Pauline, hid members of the revolution in their homes when the government sought to end the protest with police brutality and arrests.[67] And future Foyer director Léonie Madiou became the heroine of the revolutionary movement after being wounded and arrested by Lescot's police.[68] Madiou's participation in the revolutionary moment also signaled the presence of other emerging women's organizations and women's sectors of various political parties. For example, on January 8, 1946, in the midst of the protests, Léonie participated in a protest led by Nicole Roumain, Lilli Fortuné, and Jacqueline Wiener that marched to the National Cathedral. The archive suggests that this organization of women, known as the Comité Démocratique Féminin, was short-lived, but other groups, such as the women's division of the Mouvement Ouvrier Paysan (MOP), were revived after January 1946 through their Bureau d'Action Féminine and weekly journal *La Famille*, both directed by Carmen Jean-François Fignolé.[69] Interestingly, many of the women's collectives that emerged in the mid-1940s addressed women's labor. The precarity of women's work was recognized across political, social, and class divisions. By January 11, Lescot and his family were flown into exile in Miami. Lescot's pledge to see the LFAS's 1944 petition into fruition left with his departure and the crafting of a new constitution.

The 1946 Assembly

Per the terms of the Conseil Exécutif Militaire (CEM) transition government, a constitutional assembly was held before the national election for a new president. Starting in May 1946, newly elected senators and deputies drew the political volatility of January 1946 into their debates on the constitution. Although political factions had led to violent oppositions, and even some deaths, in the battle over the nation's future, the LFAS saw the 1946 assembly as another opportunity to have their legislative concerns met.[70] By August the political posturing and public debates had been going on for months, and the decorum waned as politicians used the assembly to vie for their own ambitions. At the same time, women were encouraged by the changes in the post–World War II international climate regarding women's rights. In 1945, at the United Nations Conference on International Organization in San Francisco, the conference issued a decree that women and men had equal rights. Although no nation was required to adopt the policies of the conference, women's rights activists maintained that any modern nation interested in participating in the geopolitics of the region would follow the example of the conference. With this argument and others, the LFAS leaders prepared themselves to present their petition at the 1946 Constitutional Convention. The topic, a petition for women to serve as candidates and vote in all national elections, was familiar, but the 1946 assembly was unlike any other mid-twentieth-century debate.

The long summer of debate had drawn politicians' attention inward, and long-standing national grievances and discourses about race, class, and culture simmered. After Lescot's exit, several radical activist organizations and political parties joined together to form a political base against those they identified as conservative elites and Lescot supporters. This group of activists established the Front Révolutionnaire Haïtien (FRH). As stated in the introduction, FRH had a mixed membership of *noiristes* and Marxist groups, but it was primarily led by noiristes, such as FRH president Emile Saint-Lôt.[71] Due to disagreements regarding the organization's focus on color differences over class differences in the nation, several months into the organization's existence the primary non-noiriste organization, the Parti Communiste Haïtien (PCH), withdrew its membership from the FRH.

In June 1946, the Black and *milat* members of the PCH temporarily aligned themselves with the predominately milat Parti Socialiste Populair (PSP). The PSP was founded in late January 1946 by Max Hudicourt, Étienne Charlier, Max Sam, Jules Blanchet, and Anthony Lespès. Established during the same time as noiriste groups such as the Parti Popular Nationale and the FRH, the PSP, as Matthew Smith explains, "represented the most stark contrast to the *noirisme* of the other [political] groups."[72] Smith further shows that when the PCH chose to collaborate with the PSP in mid-1946, "the noiriste assault on the PSP was harsh and personal."[73] These personal attacks were loosely divided along political lines between noiristes and non-noiristes. Most notably the majority of the pro-feminists in the assembly were also members of the socialist and communist parties, whereas the most aggressive denunciations of feminism came from assembly members who rhetorically and politically identified as noiristes. Yet assembly members on both sides of the discussion used concepts of national modernity, revolutionary nostalgia, moral character, and sexual honor to mediate radical leftist politics through their respective understandings of feminism.

As the grounds for debate were personal, proximity to any group could open one up to attack. In this regard, the LFAS leadership's relationships with several members on both sides of the suffrage debate left them vulnerable in the debate. As discussed in chapter 2, an early practice of the LFAS was to learn from and build coalitions with politicians and intellectuals from throughout the Haitian political world. Within the first year of the LFAS, the women asked several men to join a special committee to study Haitian women's legal and constitutional rights. These men included Dantès Bellegarde and Étienne Charlier.[74] The liberal conservative Bellegarde had shown his support for the women's movement since the beginning, and his support would continue throughout the twentieth century. By the summer of 1946, Étienne Charlier and Alice Garoute were family. In the 1930s, Étienne married Alice's grand-daughter Ghislaine, and he had proven to be a steady supporter of women's rights. In addition to Charlier, the LFAS had a long-standing organizational relationship with Max Hudicourt. Charlier and Hudicourt were both executives of the socialist PSP, and Hudicourt had signed the LFAS petition to establish his support of women's suffrage before the assembly. Hudicourt and Emile Saint-Lôt had in many ways become political rivals, and the women's rights debate only further divided these men and their respective sympathizers.

Like many assemblymen, Senator Rossini Pierre Louis, the sponsor of the women's suffrage petition, established his support for women's rights by drawing on the nation's memory of the Haitian Revolution. He reminded his senate colleagues, "Women were our companions for the Revolution," and as a result in a contemporary context, "We must bring them into party politics." Pierre-Louis's evocation of the 1804 revolution furthered the rhetoric of 1946, in which assemblymen repeatedly likened themselves to their national revolutionary heroes and sought to continue that tradition. Constituent Luc Stéphan added to the nostalgia by arguing that Garoute, Sylvain-Boucherecau, and the LFAS "continued the line of Marie-Jeanne, Claire Heureuse, [and] Défilée la Folle." In honor of these daughters of the revolution and "of women of all colors," Stéphen argued that their descendants should reap the reward of their ancestors' contribution to the nation.[75] Stéphan and Pierre-Louis's support of women's suffrage was a claim for social justice through the tenets of humanity espoused by their foremothers and fathers. As such, Pierre-Louis closed his remarks by stating, "In the name of the Revolution, I demand that we grant women the right to vote."[76]

While Pierre-Louis and Stéphen made claims for women's rights through revolutionary nostalgia, PSP leader Max Hudicourt attached his support for women's suffrage to the tenets of socialist philosophies regarding class equality. Hudicourt asserted, "My position, as the result of my socialist beliefs, obligates me to be in favor of the civil and political equality of women." He continued, "If we want to establish a proletarian government, we must make it with our other half, with the women who know how to read, write and think, these petites bourgeoisie. Can we logically refuse the right to vote to our daughters?" Recycling the rhetoric that recalled women's legal status as minors, Hudicourt unapologetically explained that the issue of women's rights fell under the larger need for an equalized social, political, and economic national government. Yet his comments also marked the limited parameters of participation for women. He qualified the right to suffrage to literate middle- and upper-class women. Additionally, he located himself and his statesmen as members of the petite bourgeoisie despite class differentiation among assembly members. In this context women's equal rights would serve a particular goal: to establish an informed and active proletariat. For these reasons Hudicourt clarified his understanding of women's work in the political economy of the nation: "I want women to vote, because women are a part of the education of our children."[77]

While Hudicourt established his support for women's rights as a step toward leveling class power, other constituents and women's rights sympathizers supported the amendment as a step in the direction of national modernity and inclusion in global (capitalist) diplomacy. When Senator Lanoix added his contribution to the debate, he asserted, "In every country, women have the right to vote. The international conventions demand it. Are our women inferior to the women of other countries?" Lanoix's concern for Haitian women's value was in part about women, but it was also a question about Haiti's international standing. Constituent Stéphan inquired to the impact of women's rights on Haiti's international reputation: "The institutions of a country have never progressed in ignorance of the trends of neighboring countries." Stéphan explained that Haiti was not formed in isolation and the founding fathers had not established the doctrine of the nation without understanding the doctrines of other nations.[78]

Senators Saint-Lôt and Démesmin were not swayed by the references to 1804, calls for class equality, or concern for Haiti's international standing. These senators sternly maintained that the assembly was gathered to handle the pressing issue of governance by the Haitian Black majority: "Not for sentimentality." They contended that "reasonable affairs must dominate. Matters of emotion must be neglected." Here, "sentimentality" and "emotion" stood in for women. Neglect, as established throughout the 1940s, was not a new relation between women and the state, but Démesmin further stated, "The reality of Haitians proves that all the problems of the country come from women. They corrupt male politicians, senators, and deputies. Women drive the country to ruin."[79] His comments elicited protests from the women in the

gallery. Despite their verbal rejection of these comments, Démesmin continued arguing that women had too many alliances with non-Haitians and that if
women were given the right to vote, the country would fall into the hands of
foreigners. Démesmin was questioning not only women's capability but their
loyalty and commitment to the nation.

Cautious of foreign alliances given Lescot's overinvestment in US companies, Démesmin believed that Haitian sovereignty was being threatened and
compromised by the influx of foreign interest groups including feminist
organizations and their thought. Thus, Démesmin used Haitian women's regional and international alliances and education as evidence of their compromised national allegiance. However, Démesmin was not only questioning the
women's international alliances; he also doubted the sincerity of the LFAS's
organizational platform to represent *all* women. Démesmin maintained that
"95 percent of the women of the masses will not claim these rights, they will
not profit from them. It's certain women, certain scheming women who will
benefit from suffrage. These women will say to them [the masses]: you are
some stupid savages."[80] The record of the LFAS's work proved otherwise, but
what was evident in Démesmin's comments was the extraordinary disdain
for and disbelief he and others had in women's civic, social, or political
participation.

While the attacks on LFAS women's authenticity as representatives of Haitian women and accusations of disloyalty to the nation were likely disheartening, from their responses to the assembly, the LFAS leadership was most
deterred by the attacks on women's character and capacity for full citizenship.
Démesmin and Saint-Lôt accused Haitian women of corrupting politicians
and leading the nation to financial and social ruin. Casting all women as bad
mothers and unprepared for leadership, Saint-Lôt turned on the very women
he proposed, as a noiriste, to represent, stating, "Working and peasant women
would not have the time to vote. Those that would: their sense of aesthetic
has been distorted, they are all in love with actors from films, not heroism,
not racial pride."[81]

The simultaneous dismissal of women's choices, reasoning, and taste were
announced just as the femme du peuple made her way to the section for women.
Deputy Castel Démesmin's voice bellowed across the "Doric-columned,
blue-and-gold-trimmed Chambre des Députés": "This peasant woman that
you speak of, she does not educate her five fatherless children, she does not
have an education, she cannot give any, she feeds five little pariahs to work as
domestic servants and she is a pariah herself. This is what we want to avoid."[82]
The assemblyman jettisoned verbal blows with the precision of a seasoned

attacker. The femme du peuple would not have had time to figure out if the deputy was talking about her or women like her, because moments later, she reached the section where the LFAS women were and was removed from the assembly hall.

Struggling to capture the intensity of the day, *Le Nouvelliste* simply reported that the women of the LFAS "were attacked." Among many reflections, one member of the LFAS wrote, "Obviously, good behavior and elementary courtesy are not required at the Constitutional Assembly."[83] And an essay in the US-distributed *Time* magazine later recounted that deputy Démesmin "let [words] fly with a hot blast of pure male chauvinism."[84] While potentially shocking, Démesmin's arguments, even if not their exact framing, were accepted by the majority of the assemblymen. Even though thirty-eight representatives signed a petition crafted by the LFAS leadership, promising to support their initiative, only eight honored their signatures. Thanking them in her "Open letter to the President, Vice President, and Members of the Constitutional Assembly and to Haitian Women," LFAS president Alice Garoute listed the supporters' names—Pressage Cajou, Rossini Pierre-Louis, Max Hudicourt, Luc Stéphen, Alphonse Henriquez, Philippe Charlier, Dumas Michel and Beauharnais Boisrond—and concluded, "Their names will be remembered for posterity."[85]

The open letter was presented in the bulletin *La femme haitienne repond aux attaques formulées contre elle à l'Assemblée Constituante* that the LFAS leadership produced several days after the assembly. As stated in the introduction, it was in this bulletin that the members wrote their grievances, offered a shared philosophical and political orientation, and documented women's presence in the archive. The opening essay, "Women's Rights and the New Constitution," was penned by Madeleine Sylvain-Bouchereau. She began by summarizing the detractors' points: "From their passionate closing statements based on arguments of sentimentality and sensuality, despite whatever they claim, we have tried to identify for you the reasons why the Constitutional Assembly did not grant political rights to Haitian women."[86] Sylvain-Bouchereau proceeded to list the arguments of assemblymen Démesmin and Emile Saint-Lôt:

1. All of the ills of the country come from women. . . . Save the revolution by saving the country from women. . . . (Démesmin)
2. All Haitian women are prostitutes. . . . (Démesmin)
3. The Haitian woman is the dictator of the confessional, with the white clergy ruling the country's affairs. . . . (Saint-Lôt)
4. Haitian women are bad mothers. . . . (Saint-Lôt)

5. The Haitian woman is not prepared. . . . (Saint-Lôt)
6. Those who ask for the rights and who would benefit from them are schemers, spoiled women who have everything: money, power, and would use these rights to steal the treasury of l'Etat. (Démesmin)
7. Working-class women would not have the time to vote. (Saint-Lôt)
8. Why would we import the prescriptions of Chapultepec or San Francisco? . . . (Saint-Lôt)

After listing each argument, Sylvain-Bouchereau then responded to each point in the juridical tone in which she was trained. At the end of her ten-page brief, she concluded:

Our national motto: liberty, equality, fraternity was trampled on by the same people who are supposed to protect it.

Liberty.—The woman is a slave in the civil and political order. She cannot defend her ideas, or appoint her representatives.

Equality.—All Haitians, naturalized, and 18 years of age, exercise the right to vote without class distinction. The Haitian woman has no rights.

Fraternity.—The constitution divides the people into two categories of individuals: on one side men and on the other women.

Sylvain-Bouchereau's conclusions of women's failed protections and different status under the state were popular critiques from a women's movement in the mid-twentieth century. However, beyond couching their grievances of gender inequality in the liberal rights of man, LFAS women turned to the language of enslavement to account for their location vis-à-vis the state. Surely crafted to jar the reader, Sylvain-Bouchereau's invocation of slavery after the constitutional assembly was an alarming assessment of the modern republic and the radical moment. As Matthew Smith convincingly argues, the 1946 revolution, the months immediately after the revolution, and the first months of the Estimé presidency were key moments in "a period of great importance in the advance of Haitian politics, as it was the country's first real attempt to create a stable government."[87] In the months following the 1946 revolution, the nation was certainly divided. Politically, socially, and rhetorically these divisions were between Black and *milat*, wealthy and poor, rural and urban. Yet, according to Sylvain-Bouchereau's assessment, the nation was divided between unfree and free, women and men. Women were civically and politically the unrepresented free labor and property of the state. Slavery, by Sylvain-Bouchereau's calculation, continued after *both* revolutions.

While the 1946 revolution was a faultline in the teleology of political governance in Haiti, the discourse circulated during the women's rights debates reveal underlying continuities of Haitian citizenship that were not predetermined by the radical moment or changed by political governance. Specifically, the LFAS's response to the constitutional debates of 1946 name unequal labor compensation, sexual violence, and asymmetrical standards of morality as continuities in women's experience across class, color, and culture that unsettled the radical promise of both the 1946 and 1804 revolutions. The LFAS's agenda here was not to undermine the historical significance of either revolution, but rather to invite the nation to learn from and improve upon those moments. In their response, LFAS women reframed the assembly and the conditions of their exclusion. The accusations of theft, sex work, and poor judgment each, not coincidentally, corresponded with the platform of the LFAS regarding economic independence, equal rights in marriage, and partnering practices in the years leading up to the assembly.

Sylvain-Bouchereau's assertion that "the woman is a slave" was echoed in Alice Garoute's theory of Haitian women's national belonging as well. Garoute extended the significance of the 1804 revolution as a contemporary guide for justice by invoking the legacy of enslaved women, "Here is a woman, very low on the social ladder, a humble slave who is mistreated and fondled by her master. She knew how to shape the soul of the little *mûlatres* born of the passing whim of the ruler who degraded their mothers." She continued, "The mothers watched and never let their sons become attached to those who martyred their brothers." Unlike the routine summoning of revolutionary militarism and might in 1940s politics, Garoute recalls the memory of the revolution through sexual violence against enslaved African women. Binding this violence with the birth of children whom the enslaved woman cared for, fortified mentally, and then supported during the revolution, Garoute cast women's role in the history of the 1804 revolution and pivots this history into a charge for the 1946 moment: "Will we make a place by his side for the one who helped him break his shackles?" In her assessment, "The victor [the Haitian man] gave himself civil and political status, whereas this woman was turned into a minor and mentally ill person. She has no rights, but is not exempt from any charge."[88]

During the 1946 assembly, women felt the intensity of these allegations as they were simultaneously hailed and rejected as national traitors and lascivious threats to the nation. Each of the LFAS respondents took particular time to address the accusations of prostitution, character, and general commitment to themselves, their families, and the nation. LFAS women were not necessarily or always opposed to the conservative application of the law that pro-hibited sex work. In the early years of the LFAS, the organization openly fought against brothels. However, in their 1946 response, LFAS women were less concerned with sex work and rather expressed a desire to shelter women from scrutiny around their sexual practices and from sexual violence. Sylvain-Bouchereau recounted, "We want women to be better protected in their honor and their freedom. We want all seducers to be punished by the law with a punishment proportional to the damage that he caused. It is not only legislation that must be modified: it is the prejudices that must be erased, it's the education that must be reformed. We want young girls' education to be more sound and straightforward, that it will prepare them against the perils that will menace them and that it will give them the moral strength to resist enter-taining their instincts."[89] LFAS women's public acknowledgment and de-nouncement of violence against Haitian girls and women was unprecedented. Their promotion of a "sound" and "straightforward" education program was a direct attack on the intergenerational silences about gender-based violence that predated and extended beyond the revolution.

The women were perplexed by the entangling of morality (read here as sex and sexuality) with voting rights. They questioned, "What does voting have to do with morality?" The discourse about voting masked the moral logics and economic desires about control over women's bodies and the conditions of acceptable Haitian women's sexuality, which in turn governed their place—economic, social, and political—in the nation. Sylvain-Bouchereau wrote, "In no country in the world has one ever asked for a certificate of morality from those who go to the polls. If this principle were adopted in Haiti a good num-ber of the parliamentarians would not sit in the gallery." Sylvain-Bouchereau was particularly taken with the accusation of women's prostitution. She ini-tially addressed the accusation within the scientific data the LFAS had recorded over the first decade of organizing. She maintained that from the organization's research she could testify that there was no more sex work in Haiti than in any other society.

Sylvain-Bouchereau's responses to the discussion of prostitution also dem-onstrated that sex work was used as a placeholder to address women's deci-sions about their sexuality. She went on to explain components of Haitian women's sexual practices and partnerships to the assemblymen. Establishing that women engaged in many different types of partnerships including, but not limited to, monogamous state-sanctioned marriage, polygamous unions, and common-law marriages, Sylvain-Bouchereau outlined a range of choices that women made about their sexual relationships. In their study sessions, the

LFAS had also identified what they called a double standard. Women not only experienced a double standard of excellence in their expectations as citizens, as sexually pious and loyal to their families, but they also had to remain silent as men were allowed to explore their sexuality, and exert physical and economic power over women. Sylvain-Bouchereau probed, if "Haitian women are all prostitutes . . . what about the young domestic girl who is trying to earn a living but is seduced by a man, likely her boss, is she a prostitute?"[90] Sylvain-Bouchereau turned the terms of the double-standard discourse of morality and, again, announced sexual violence against women. The formation of the question was not revelatory or a report of unknown information about assaults on young girls. Rather the question was an interrogation of the conditions by which sexual violence against women was normalized and in its discursive banality, ignored.

In her assessment of women's responses to sexual violence in Haiti in the mid-twentieth century, feminist literary critic Régine Jean-Charles shows that Haitian women writers "deliberately disturb[ed] the culture of silence that surround[ed] sexual violence in [their] portraits of sexual abuse and rape."[91] For the LFAS these portraits were crafted through a pallet of questions posed to the assemblymen. Refusing culpability in a moral economy that disproportionately robbed women of choice and silenced their experiences, how, then, Sylvain-Bouchereau asked, did the men of the assembly categorize violence against Haitian women? Not only did LFAS women ask about sexual violence of young girls, but they also questioned men's commitment to the institution of marriage through which the language of morality was scripted.[92] Sylvain-Bouchereau pushed her rhetorical questioning further: "And the petite bourgeoisie woman abandoned by her husband, who is responsible for her downfall?" She answered, "Here the man is responsible for both. He can get away with satisfying his passions without accepting the responsibility of paternity," concluding that families were left vulnerable in the wake of men's sexual choices as opposed to women's.[93]

Probing the logic of sex-work alongside the institution of marriage, the LFAS leadership gestured toward a thread between the radical moment and the allocation of rights based on sex (the act) and gender. In this formulation, the arguments by assemblymen in 1946 rehearsed and sought to codify sexual difference as a measure for citizenship rights. Women's sex—how, when, and with whom they had sex, not only their gender—was another measure of women's citizenship in Haiti.[94] It also, as Alexander might argue, "set the stage for the kind of repressive state rule" that was exercised to varying degrees in the nation's postcolonial history but that was foreshadowed in the political divisions communicated in the assemblymen's discussions about voting rights.

The legal management of sex and sexuality in 1944 and 1945 made Garoute's allegorical references to enslavement more compelling and drew a line between the pre- and post-1946 moment that troubled the presumption of radicality in the moment. Thus, when Démesmin proclaimed to save the revolution by saving the country from women, the threat that the women represented to the revolution was to blur class, color, and cultural logics of nationalism and division upon which politics rested and name how those divisions rested on women's bodies through sexuality. They were traitors to the nation because they were revealing the logics of sex and gender upon which the revolutions, both in 1804 and 1946, were held, that ignored and necessitated violence against women. As Sylvain-Bouchereau drew the two revolutionary moments together, she argued, "At the beginning of the Revolution it was the *mûlatre* who was the cause of all the problems in the country, now it's the woman!" Both categories of traitor were defined by sexual violence. As she quoted from Garoute about "the little mûlatres born of the passing whim of the ruler who degraded their mothers," she expressed a continuity in the experience of colonial and postcolonial contexts that scapegoated antinationalism with sexual violence against Black women.

Name calling, in this regard, only "obscure[ed] the state's complicity in sexual politics."[95] LFAS women, then, reminded their readership that feminism was a tool. As one LFAS member wrote, "Women did not need feminism to understand inequality."[96] They were deeply aware of their role in society and sought to record the inconsistencies in women's experiences and exclusion. In particular the discussion of sex-work framed within the historical context of labor, sex, and rural-urban migration revealed the shared conscriptions of women's citizenship. In her work on sexuality and the Caribbean, Kamala Kempadoo reminds us that from a Marxist perspective, prostitution is "sexual labor appropriation and distribution of surplus value" that does not focus on the selling of the body, "but selling the service of *labor power* in the production of labor sold."[97] As the service of labor power, sex work was what Charles identifies as the tangling of Haitian women's role in modern society as *machann ak machandiz*—meaning Haitian women "were both commodities and seller/trader of these commodities."[98] The LFAS queries and attention to "prostitution," then, called forth the understanding of sex work as a "gender-specific form of migrant labor."[99] The women also communicated that the work of sex was not limited to "prostitution." According to the LFAS arguments, women (married, unmarried, or practicing plasaj) having sex (in marriage, outside of marriage, by consent, compulsion, or nonconsent) were *machann ak* machandiz involved in an unequal exchange of labor.

Here, reading sex work not only as the profession but also interrogating how sex works returns us to the femme du peuple's entrance. The use and feminist querying of sex-work put all women's work in a shared political frame and compelled LFAS women to write the femme du peuple's presence into their story of that day. The woman's physical movement in the assembly hall, not necessarily any knowledge of her actual profession, recalled a particular association with women's mobility, labor, and sexuality. Haitian literary scholar Marie-José N'Zengou-Tayo offers that "at the bottom of the social ladder we find the recent female rural migrants who are unemployed and . . . very often have to resort to prostitution in order to survive."[100] While N'Zengou-Tayo distinguishes sex-work from employment, her attention to migration and labor remind us that these women's movements were often the interlocutors between women of rural and urban Haiti. They were women like the femme du peuple, whose near proximity to the LFAS women at the 1946 assembly presented a visual of women moving boldly within and beyond their social status. The possible intimacy between women of different social classes that "stray[ed] beyond the boundaries of existing gendered categories" was a threat to the laws and sociality that codified gender, sexuality, and class difference, for the ideological, philosophical, and economic sustainability of the nation.

The LFAS women staunchly critiqued sexual violence and developed a labor analysis about gender and sex, but they remained cautious of sexual pleasure. Girls' (and women's) "instincts," according to Sylvain-Bouchereau's statement, still needed to be governed. To this end, LFAS women commissioned mother's as trustees of girls' desires. "We demand that mothers have the right to also ensure the education of purity for their girls when the father is not there to ensure the point." Education and suffrage were tools for sexual violence prevention. The right to ensure education was a long-standing goal of the organization, as was the legal fight for women's recognition as guardians and citizens capable of bequeathing citizenship to their children. Yet as proxy protectors, the LFAS also reinforced patriarchal protections and ownership over other women. Women's preoccupation with purity at times even sidelined their labor concerns, as reflected in Sylvain-Bouchereau's further comments, "What women do with their money is their concern," but "if we are given the right to vote we will fight more than men to combat immorality." This moral fight taken up by the LFAS named violence against women, but it also adopted the patriarchal underpinning of a system that confined women physically, socially, and politically, and that the Haitian feminist actively challenged.

IN HER BOOK *Haiti et ses femmes*, Sylvain-Bouchereau wrote that the 1946 debates reignited the LFAS and the women's movement after World War II. Like the enthusiasm that comes when emerging from an epidemic, the women had newfound energy and seemed to be most transparent about their political goals.[101] The LFAS's 1946 pamphlet was the women's movement's (evolving) manifesto. In the collection of writings, the women produced a document that provided the greatest clarity and precision to their cause and meaning of feminism since the beginning of their movement for women's rights a decade before. The LFAS was interested in the right to vote and civil rights, but the organization was equally concerned with its self-definition. On this matter, the LFAS articulated a feminist message that saw women as a diverse class of unpaid and underpaid laborers.

The 1946 Constitutional Assembly also foreshadowed other attacks on the LFAS. Most notably, the assembly debate suggested that the LFAS had strong allies among Marxist activists. Several months later, in response to a lecture titled "The PSP and the Liberation of the Haitian Woman," Sylvain-Bouchereau was asked if she was a communist. She replied that she was not a communist because she did not share all of the opinions of the PSP but that she appreciated the goals of the party.[102] In the coming years, this ambiguous relationship between the LFAS and leftist organizations would put the LFAS and its members in the middle of violent political battles. In the final contribution to the 1946 pamphlet, feminist writer Yvonne Hakime Rimpel admonished the senators in an open letter aptly titled "To Those Who Insult Us." In her concluding statement, she reprimanded the senators for such horrible assertions about women who could be their daughters, sisters, or mothers. She suggested that rather than humiliating women publicly, they should "bow at the feet of the sex of your Mother." With these words, the women concluded the pamphlet. In the following decade, Hakime Rimpel would be one of the first popularly known victims of François Duvalier's efforts to silence the women's movement. While it would become a pillar of Haitian women's organizing in the late twentieth century to openly incorporate resistance to violence against women into feminist practice, in 1946 this forceful and public interrogation of sexual violence was unprecedented. The LFAS's prose bore witness to the decades of sexual violence against women and put the women writing at risk for physical violence.

Arthur O'Neill

FEMINIST GAROUTE (LEFT) & FRIENDS
Shooting, yes; little rooms, no.

Members of the LFAS, including Alice Garoute, Madeleine Sylvain-Bouchereau, and Lydia Jeanty, meeting at Sylvain-Bouchereau's home before a demonstration. *Time* magazine captioned the image, "Feminist Garoute (left) & Friends," March 1950. Courtesy of Sophia Smith Collection, Smith College.

In 1944 and 1946, LFAS women's petition for women's suffrage was met with the same outcome. Garoute encouraged the LFAS regarding their constitutional defeat: "We have lost the first battle, but the fight must continue, it must continue without failure and without fear until the final victory."[103] Despite the reality that the most aggressive opponents of women's rights during the 1946 constitutional convention were *noiristes*, in the years following the constitutional assembly President Dumarsais Estimé, a *noiriste* and the first Black president of the nation since the US occupation, was an ally of the LFAS's leadership. Lucienne Estimé, the president's wife, became an honorary member of the LFAS, and she drew more national attention to the women's cause. Lucienne's membership also revealed the political savvy and maneuverability of the women's movement. Unlike many of the other movements of the period that succumbed to the heightened political divisions of the moment, the women's movement gained more clarity, cohesion, and collaboration with other groups concerned with women's rights after the upsurge in radical leftist politics of 1946.[104] Also, in the midst of extreme racialized tensions and ideological polarization, leaders of the Haitian women's movement managed to organize without an explicit platform addressing color. However, within the time of the assembly and by the end of the decade, LFAS members were forced to critically consider their use and representation of race, color, and class within and outside the nation.

CHAPTER FOUR

Stage Right

Pan-American Pageantry, Diasporic Performance, and Feminist Play

During the first two weeks of April 1944, several small, thatch-roofed homes made of wood and dirt were transported from rural Haiti to the Military Circle in the center of Port-au-Prince. As the homes rolled down the streets of the capital, their shadows briefly eclipsed the front yards of the nineteenth-century gingerbread-and-stone constructions of the city's most prestigious residences and government buildings. An uncommon sight, the caravan bedimmed the geographic distance between rural and urban life and likely incited curiosity and queries from passersby.

The scene was designed to draw attention. The leaders of the Ligue Feminine d'Action Sociale (LFAS) commissioned the houses for their 1944 Pan American Day celebrations to showcase the conditions of Haitian women's lives. As Jeanne Sylvain professed in letters leading up to the annual performance of regional geopolitical alliance, "We are in the whirlwind of preparations for L.F.A.S.'s grand ball in honor of panamerican day." Referencing the homes, she continued, "It is a splendid idea." Similar homes would be donated by other American nations and each would be populated with "young girls in costume, choirs, dancing, etc."[1] Busied with staging the Pan American Day event, LFAS members from throughout the country coordinated the safe arrival of the Haitian domestic structures for display. Madeleine Sylvain-Bouchereau further explained in a correspondence days before the arrival of the homes, "There will be an authentic market in these shacks with the produce of the represented countries. We will also have a number of special dances and songs. We hope that this will get some publicity for the Foyer."[2]

In the 1940s the LFAS's annual Pan American Day celebrations were some of the organization's largest public events. They often included a day of educational speeches and performances by and for young people, public exhibitions, and an evening fundraising ball. The proceeds went to the LFAS operations, and as Sylvain-Bouchereau referenced, the 1944 events were designed to draw attention to the larger initiatives like the Foyer Ouvrier, the LFAS resource and community center for women. The women had orchestrated these events for several years, but they increased the pomp for the 1944 festivities.

With representatives from throughout the Pan-American Union joining the celebration, Sylvain later recounted that "we exhausted ourselves to insure the success of everything" because the 1944 Pan-American fête shared the political stage with the National Assembly's deliberation and decision about women's participation in electoral politics.[3] As the LFAS members prepared the homes for the April 14th presentation, they would have passed the government assembly hall where the newly instated President Lescot and the National Assembly were debating constitutional changes regarding women's right to vote and serve in government positions.

The women were using the fervor of the Pan American Day celebrations as a platform to promote a national agenda on a semi-international stage. While the homes may have provided an aesthetic contrast to the architecture of the city, the style of home was not foreign to the hundreds of women and men who worked in the urban districts of the country and returned to dwellings just like them at the end of each day, week, month, or year. The need for this type of display, then, was a strategic placement for a group of people, inside and outside Haiti, who were distant from or not familiar with the lifestyle of the majority of the nation. The consequential parading of the rural homes was a prop for audiences to witness the "real" conditions of Haitian women alongside the cultural currencies of food, song, and dance.

This presentation of homes was also curated within the evolving popularity of the *mouvement folklorique*. This culture movement originated within the intellectual project of Haitian *indigénisme*, and emphasized a celebration of Haitian history and national identity through cultural elements of Haiti's rural peasant class. In this frame, different parts of Haitian life were strategically conceptualized to stand in for the history and traditions of the nation. The homes signified the women who lived and worked in them, offering a folkloric costuming for national and international Pan American Day participants that was both conceptually familiar and experientially novel. With the surrogated presence of Haitian women through homes, food, and dances, the LFAS leadership created visibility for the organization in order to invite the country and the region into their discourse about women's citizenship, while absenting many of the women whose lives most intimately intersected with the artifacts of Haitian culture.

This kind of display was not unique to the culture of international conferences, exhibitions, and state celebrations. Similar displays were conducted throughout the Atlantic world in the nineteenth and twentieth centuries. For example, the Haitian Pavilion at the 1937 Universal Exposition in Paris had a similar presentation.[4] In Haiti this type of celebratory pageantry was written into the earliest constitutions, which included mandated celebrations of Independence Day, and presidential and presidential spousal birthdays. Moreover, during the interwar and World War II era, American countries used Pan American Day celebrations to communicate solidarity, alliance, and transnational indoctrination into a twentieth-century geopolitical identity that necessitated the consumptive performance of camaraderie.[5] Thus after Pan American Day was established as a Haitian national holiday in 1931, each April young girls donned the flags of the respective twenty-one countries of the Pan-American Union and walked to the sound of each country's national anthem, while reciting facts about the countries.[6]

The parading was a national project with established interlocking international implications. Six years earlier, at the 1938 Pan-American Conference in Lima, Peru, the Inter-American Commission of Women (IACW; the women's caucus of the Pan-American Union) made a resolution that all nations of the union would work for women's rights in all areas of political governance. As members of the IACW and participants in multiple Pan-American Conferences, members of the LFAS used the international platform to persuade the Haitian national assembly of the local and international implications of women's citizenship rights. They were particularly encouraged by the interwar suffrage gains of fellow IACW nations like El Salvador and the neighboring Dominican Republic that used the regional pressure and mandates of the international organization to advance and win their suffrage fights.[7] As the IACW pronounced, "The case [of feminism] is now before the jury of public opinion," and the LFAS designed its celebrations to draw legislators and laypeople, alike, to its side.[8] To this end, on April 19, five days after the Pan American fête, LFAS women were pleased to discover that the National Assembly adopted an amendment to Article 4 of the Haitian Constitution, granting women thirty years old and older the right to run for and hold all state offices except president of the republic.[9] It was not full suffrage, but as Sylvain-Bouchereau reported in a letter to her loved ones, it was a welcome victory:

> Great news, the constitution was revised and women were granted the right of eligibility for all functions except president of the republic. We did not get the right to vote, but that will come later[.] In any case, we will not have an election during a war. From here we will have the time to have more victories.[10]
>
> Our Pan-American fête went very well and there were a lot of people[.] We had very good jazz, but unfortunately we ended early. In the end, the

shacks were very pretty and it was a magnificent scene. We earned about $350. This is not extraordinary, but it is something.

I am in the process of planning another fête. . . . As you can see, one event comes right after the next and I do not have time to breathe. I had to prepare two lectures: one for the radio, while I prepared the [Pan-American] event, and the other on the day of the event. The day before [the event], Mme Garoute, Simone Hypolite, Lise Paret and I spoke on all of the radio stations in the capital, it was truly great.[11]

In the course of two weeks, Haitian women won the right to be candidates in secondary elections, celebrated intra-American relations, promoted their agenda on multiple media platforms, and earned "something" for their social projects. It is no wonder, then, that Sylvain-Bouchereau felt she did "not have time to breathe" and lacked interest ("in any case") in dwelling too long on the work that would be required to bridge the gap between the Article 4 amendment and full suffrage. While the rapidity of these events was not representative of the years of investment in these outcomes or an indicator of how the women would establish the wartime record of success with more victories, the letter does uniquely frame the interrelated interests of this chapter.

This chapter considers the relationship between performance, national legislation, and diasporic theaters of belonging to trace women's experimentation with evolving ideas of citizenship. It considers how the pageantry of regional wartime alliances persuaded, stifled, and propelled women's national political agendas and thought. Taking the 1944 staging of the rural homes as a departure point, this chapter looks at how LFAS women used public performances (fêtes, choreographed dances, congress presentations, and plays) to establish a political aesthetic that (perhaps artificially) drew different Haitian women toward one another in local, national, and international politics. Following LFAS women's political wayfaring from Port-au-Prince to the Belgian Congo, to Argentina, to the United States, Germany, and then back to Port-au-Prince, this chapter considers the LFAS Pan-American presentation, and ones like it, as a multilayered record of women's varying articulations of feminism as they navigated, experimented with, and expressed sometimes opposite or conflicting ideas about Haitian women's place in national and international politics. In these curated spaces, women's rights organizers witnessed and documented the subtle adjustments and limitations of their feminist practices. Most notably, by adopting the scripted forms of political performance that circulated in international political pageantries (presenting "a magnificent

scene" of "pretty" shacks), the chapter considers how LFAS women risked erasing Haitian women's lives, inserted their experiences, and expanded the possibilities of organizing across difference through the end of the 1940s.

Pan-American Politics and Folklore in Haiti

The Pan-American events held by the LFAS were not simple show and tell.
Haiti had a strong and arguably foundational roll in the conceptualization of
Pan-American alliances since the late eighteenth century, and the annual
events and organizational meetings were locations of regional and global political brokering. As Chantalle Verna explains, many Haitian intellectuals and
politicians of the 1940s located the birth of Pan-Americanism, "a regional
ideal celebrating connections between independent nations in the Western
Hemisphere," in the military support free people of color from Haiti (then
Saint Domingue) offered American soldiers during the United States revolutionary war (1775–83).[12]

Even more popularly argued throughout Haiti's modern history was that
Haiti's pioneering example of regional solidarity was further established
through Haiti's support of South American liberation campaigns, particularly
the early nineteenth-century political alliance between Haitian president
Alexandre Pétion and Simon Bolívar (1806). In this display of regional and
anticolonial solidarity, Pétion famously provided refuge and military arms to
Bolívar as he carried out his decolonization campaigns against the Spanish
Crown throughout South America, ultimately leading to his creation of the
Confederation of Latin American Nations at the 1826 Congress of Panama.
While many Caribbean and Latin American scholars argue that this confed-
eration was the inaugural articulation of Pan-Americanism, US-centered nar-
ratives of Pan-Americanism suggest that the concept was coined and solidified
three years earlier, in 1823, when US president James Monroe and Secretary of
State James E. Blaine planned the first Pan-American Conferences. In the
1940s, even when scholars conceded Bolívar's conceptualization of a unified
Latin America (that excluded Haiti) and Monroe's vision of a Pan-American
Union, many Haitians argued that these unions were precipitated and often
measured through, as this chapter shows, discursive relationships with Haiti.

The legacy of the relationship between Haitian and Latin American decolonial projects was foundational to Haitian politicians' and intellectuals' geopolitical understanding of the region in the 1940s.[13] In the early twentieth century,
Haitian women activists imagined themselves as politically connected to Latin
America. In particular, the postcolonial legacies of Latin American countries

alongside their navigation of early twentieth-century US diplomatic measures and military interventions bound the nations' regional affiliations.[14] Although LFAS members stayed abreast of feminist movements in France, England, Germany, and Russia, much of the "foreign" reporting that the women did in their newspaper *La Voix des Femmes*, for example, was about women throughout Latin America.[15] LFAS women studied the strategies, successes, and missteps of regional organizations for their national agenda. In March 1939, for example, the headline story in *La Voix des Femmes* read, "Lima's Declaration in Favor of Women's Rights." The article was written after the Eighth International American Conference and identified Peru as a leader in women's rights organizing in the Americas, explaining that "from as early as the first [Inter-American] conference in 1923, Lima heard and put the resolutions from the conference into action."

Querying their Haitian readership, the author, Sylvain-Bouchereau, then asked, "Will Haiti stay behind?" Recounting the history of Peruvian and Haitian solidarity harkening back to Pétion and Bolívar and the Haitian and Peruvian independence struggles, Sylvain-Bouchereau wrote that during the nineteenth-century revolutions, Haiti was a "pioneer" in abolition and independence fights, and Peru followed *its* example. Leveraging Haiti's revolutionary past against the contemporary moment, Sylvain-Bouchereau further provoked the reader, asking, "What will be the attitude of the Haitian government? Are they going to honor their signature [in the Pan-American Union] or continue the politics of the ostrich who closes his eyes to his own situation while recommending to others reforms that he does not care to undertake?"[16] Taunting the government with the nation's historical virility and inviting the leaders to proverbially take their heads out of the sand, the LFAS leadership challenged the Haitian government's revolutionary vision.

Drawing the Haitian government into a regional debate about women's rights made participation in Pan-American organizing compelling for the LFAS membership. Haiti was one of the original regional participants in the Inter-American Commission of Women.[17] Established in 1928 during the sixth Pan-American Conference, the Commission of Women was focused on conducting research on women's conditions throughout the Americas. During the mid-1930s, each nation was charged with collecting information about women in their country and presenting this to the larger assembly in order to collaborate and share resources between the countries. At each regional meeting, delegates were encouraged to report and expose the other delegates to key aspects of their country's culture and politics. The focus on research aligned well with LFAS's agenda for studying and theorizing Haitian women's lives.

Additionally, the Pan-American congresses provided a platform for the women to display their research beyond national newspapers and organizational programming. On the regional platform, Haitian women's research and reporting required a careful weaving of rich content, intellectual dexterity, and political savvy.

The LFAS leadership designed the local Pan American Day celebrations to celebrate women activists as interlocutors in regional geopolitics, turning the events into sites of transnational citizenship curation. For Haiti in particular, Pan-American presentations were opportunities for politicians, statespeople, and activists to collectively and respectively choreograph the image of the country. In the wake of the US occupation and still under the financial control of US banks, Haiti's international articulation of sovereignty in the 1940s was tenuous. Moreover, the gradual failure of US export programs that weakened the nation's economy meant that Haiti's capacity to contribute to regional initiatives was questioned. Following a Pan American Day celebration in 1937, Sylvain-Bouchereau published an open letter in *La Voix des Femmes* titled "Let's Organize Our University." In the text she revealed that during the previous Pan-American Conference in Buenos Aires in a discussion about regional student exchanges, someone commented, "What interest is there in sending students to Haiti?" Responding to the implication that Haiti did not have an educational or cultural base worth sharing with the region, Sylvain-Bouchereau surmised, "This delegate did not understand the moral message of the convention," which was in her view "to arrive at a better comprehension of different American peoples, and to build peace and friendship between neighbors." However, in the absence of geopolitical generosity, Sylvain-Bouchereau proposed that the LFAS lead an aggressive campaign to establish Haiti as the nexus for French-language education in the region.[18]

Sylvain-Bouchereau's proposition that the nation invest in French-language education and by extension maintain loose connections with France in order to establish regional alliances was echoed in the work of other Black internationalists from the French postcolonies. In her study of Suzanne Césaire, Annette Joseph-Gabriel shows that the Martinican writer and theorist also suggested French-language education in Haiti as a way to integrate the former French colony into the geopolitical sphere of regional Francophone countries.[19] Still, as evidenced in the conference participant's comments, the philosophy of friendship and neighborliness among nations was infused with other historically charged understandings of Haiti and its place in the region. In particular, Sylvain-Bouchereau was exhausted by the century-long debates about Haiti's capabilities to self-govern rooted in colonial and postcolonial philosophies of Black inferiority that specifically used Haiti throughout the nineteenth and twentieth centuries as fear-filled examples of failed postcoloniality, Black incivility, and inefficient governance. In the late nineteenth century these anti-Haitian and anti-Black assertions were met with the rise of writings like Anténor Firmin's *Essai sur l'inégalité des races humaines* that argued that Haitians were equal in their mental, civic, and governing capacity to Europeans.[20] Firmin's work greatly inspired Jean Price-Mars's thinking on *indigénisme*, and in the early 1940s *indigénisme* was infused into Haitian feminist, intellectual, and political discourses.

As Sylvain-Bouchereau and other LFAS women became increasingly frustrated with Haiti's treatment on the international stage, their writings reflected alternatives that focused on internal unity rather than appeals to regional actors. Several years later, in 1947, Sylvain-Bouchereau and Yvonne Sylvain co-authored the opening essay of *La Voix des Femmes* that reflected the political climate of the mid-1940s. Celebrating notable Haitian thinkers like Firmin and the emerging class of women intellectuals to exemplify the indigenous genius of the country, they lamented that Haitians who only sought foreign education or taught foreign texts had an "inferiority complex." Directing their essay to the young people of the country, they concluded, "Learn and respect Haitian values, fight for the stability of our country and for the unappreciated slogan: Haïti aux Haïtiens [Haiti for the Haitians]."[21]

In an interesting organizational evolution, the comments in 1947 echoed the sentiments that may have circulated in some of the organization's earliest workshops with Price-Mars. Other essays in the issue outlined a six-year research plan to develop the national education system, including a literacy program that would require that "the 20% of educated Haitian adults should each instruct 4 illiterate adults, or pay a professor to do so."[22] The inversion of resources through an "each one teach one" model was a call to claim sovereignty without having to cater to international models for Haiti's geopolitical participation. However, throughout the 1940s the women internationalists continued to balance the fine line between celebrating the nation's African ancestry and navigating preexisting racist performances of regional belonging.

Folkloric Dance and National Belonging

The most common performative display of Haiti in the 1940s was popular folkloric dance. Drawn from Vodou ritual dances, folkloric dance was a "superstition"-sanitized rendering of movements that were studied and performed to represent modern Haiti through "revivals of a transcended cultural past."[23] Institutionalized through a reevaluation of culture as social scientific folklore that could be studied, replicated, and performed, the *mouvement folklorique* presented Vodou ritual dance as evidence of Haiti's modern appeal.[24] The popular production of folkloric dance occurred alongside strict prohibitions on the Vodou spiritual practice and practitioners. In 1935, Haitian president Sténio Vincent passed the 1935 *décret-loi* that prohibited *les pratiques superstitieuses*. This law supported antisuperstition campaigns and encouraged renewed aggression by the government and the Catholic Church against Vodou that included the prohibition of ceremonies, dances, and spiritual meetings. Any act that appeared to "serve the lwa" could be responded to with prison time, legal fees, home invasion, and destruction of property.[25]

Simultaneously, in the 1940s, Vodun ceremonial dances were mediated through professionalization and choreography that scripted Haitian culture through the presumably nonsacred, choreographed popular dance. While in the 1930s and 1940s, there were strict and violent laws against practicing Vodou, the *sans* sacred performance of the dances became a popular commodity and "a sign of official national particularity."[26] In her study of Vodou and the law, historian Kate Ramsey shows that "the post-occupation state constructed popular practices, and particularly ritual dance, as indices of official Haitian identity and modernity."[27]

Using the particularity of popular dance as a reference to modernity was a common state practice throughout the Caribbean and Latin America. Countries often used settings like the Pan-American Conferences to solidify national identity through practices that were outlawed or highly surveilled in their quotidian and unchoreographed practice (Cuba, Puerto Rico, Venezuela, Trinidad, Jamaica, Argentina), establishing a unique lingua franca of national performance that was familiar to the Pan-American setting.[28] Thus, at Pan American Day celebrations members of the LFAS communicated Haiti's fluency in regional popular performance to establish their own national authenticity and unify Haitian women along culturally familiar lines. For example, during the 1940 Pan American Day celebrations, the LFAS had several events where young women performed popular dances. At one show, Jeanne Sylvain recounted that girls danced to Vodou songs and "negro spirituals" that were particularly moving: "The girls were dancing and laughing. The drum vibrating. A young 8 year old girl was singing, dancing, laughing, and her whole body was shaking. A commanding rhythm engulfed the room."[29] The collective arresting experience that Sylvain described, even in the largely performative and rehearsed presentation of spiritual dances, was a recurring response from dancers of the period who were aware of the porous line between the spiritual and performative.[30] In the context of this cultural consumption, the possibility of losing bodily or cognitive control was not only threatening to those who sought to choreograph the dances, but this embodied response could also be met with harsh social and legal responses.

While the blurred lines between what constituted popular and ritual dance were constantly negotiated, evidence that the choreographed dance had evolved into the spiritual was when performers seemingly lost control of their bodies, like the young girl had. Sylvain explained that after the performance an older woman was angry and exclaimed, "What! Parents are paying for their children to learn this stupidity?" Indeed, throughout the late 1930s and early 1940s some middle-class and elite families paid for their children to learn folkloric dance. Dance troupes led by LFAS member Lina Fussman-Mathon famously traveled throughout the region with mostly middle-class and elite students to represent the nation, and others like the troupe Mater Dolorosa, the troupe of the Bureau d'Ethnologie, was a mixed group of practitioners from the peasant class. Yet the spectator's frustrations were likely less about this learning and more about the ways in which the young girl's bodily response started to, as Ramsey has explained, "exceed the domain of representation."[31] Dancers and spectators alike feared that performers would not be able to control their responses to the music and choreography. But before Sylvain could respond to the critic's concern, the dance instructor defended the performance: "I love everything about it. It's that simple, it's Haitian and it's beautiful."[32]

This report on the Pan-American performance and potential presence of the sacred was recounted in the feminist newspaper *La Voix des Femmes*. The decision to document the dance instructor's sentiments of love and beauty for the folkloric and by extension Haiti as a foregone conclusion was significant. Folkloric dance, like rural homes, was a popular performative measure of beauty for the LFAS. Many LFAS women had been taught and reared by women and men like the displeased elder audience member. The women's experiences of the dances were informed by a long history of strict segregation and cultural appropriation in which elite and middle-class women masqueraded in "real" Haitianness but refused to share space with the women to whom the dances were attributed. The women activists' engagement with popular dance, then, teetered on the line between an aesthetic engagement with the embodied practice of Price Mars's *rapprochement culturel* and the dangerous satire and erasure of many Haitian women's spiritual and cultural life practices. As rapprochement culturel, the dance lessons and performances hosted by the LFAS and performed by members across classes could, as Verna has argued, "nurture connections between Haiti's privileged, urban minority and its rural majority [as an] essential to redressing the breakdowns in Haitian society that had made it possible for the US government to usurp political, economic, and social control of Haiti through a military occupation."³³ However, the government's legislated extraction of the sacred elements and conscription of women's (and men's) movements as authentic Haitian physical expressions more often rehearsed spatial and cultural differences between and among rural and urban Haitians. Through the dances' "beauty," not unlike the shacks' "magnificence," women were conscripted into a particular "genre of citizenship," in which performances kept different women in separate physical and conceptual spaces and particularly limited working-class, poor, and peasant women's possibilities to exercise multiple expressions of belonging in the nation.³⁴ In this way, LFAS women's performing and teaching of popular dance often served the Haitian state policies to isolate cultural and spiritual meaning from Vodun dance, making the former particular and the latter criminal.

At the same time, LFAS popular dances were *accoutrements* to their political practice that critiqued women's exclusion from citizenship through participatory governance. In this way, the dancing also offered possibilities for a different interrogation of national belonging. In particular, the study of dance performance as initiated through their own political practice and encouraged by international alliances offered a possibility of proximity that drew Haitian women closer—not as "studied" and "studying" or "authentic" and "masquerading"—at the intersection of research and reflexivity.

The field of folkloric study was an entry point for women's activists to account for women's lives in Haiti. In particular, the bodily experiences of dance offered a "flash point" for differing Haitian women to interrogate their relationship to one another on the grounds of varying claims to citizenship through signifying markers of bodily expression—dance and song. Much like the pulsing back movements of Vodun dances that popular performers rehearsed, through the discourse of dance, women moved closer and farther away from one another, navigating their proximity to one another and claims to Haitian citizenship through their familiarity with the movements. In this way the performances of Haitian dance and song against the backdrop of homes, like the ones on display in 1944, were also a stage for feminist inquiry.

This was most evident in the interplay between Comhaire-Sylvain's sociological studies of girls' "leisure" time alongside the performances of these rituals. In her research on leisure Comhaire-Sylvain studied young women's dance practices. When she asked the multiclassed sample of girls from Port-au-Prince about their leisure-time activities, they revealed that they danced samba, Lambeth walk, tango, rumba, and the Charleston. In many interviews, young girls accompanied their response to Comhaire-Sylvain's question with spontaneous examples of their expertise with certain dances. However, when Comhaire-Sylvain asked them about other forms of dance, such as Carnival dances, "in general there was a reluctance to admit."[35] She further noted that "many children also den[ied] attending *les veillées* [evening vigils]."[36] The girls' denial was likely out of an abundance of caution. In the 1930s and 1940s all acts that were associated with Vodou, including les veillées, sacred dance, spiritual songs, and ceremonial paraphernalia, could place a family or whole community at risk. For example, during rehearsals for Pan American Day in 1944, young women from the Foyer community center denied knowing folklore songs, and instead of wearing the colorful headscarves for their presentation on their heads, they wanted to wear the scarves around their necks like Guides (a form of Girl Scouts) and Parisian models. Jeanne Sylvain perceived these aesthetic choices in addition to the girls' insistence on "trying to speak French" over Kreyòl as cultural rejection and that the girls were "ashamed to be themselves."[37]

However, the girls' denial and feigned ignorance also communicated their apt assessment of their disproportionate vulnerability in the informational exchange with the LFAS women and further revealed an uncertainty about Comhaire-Sylvain's capacity as a researcher to accurately and safely represent them. While the girls refused to offer insight on sacred dances, Comhaire-Sylvain collected the "more valuable and sensitive data" of the girls' refusal to be conscripted into her feminist project.[38] Resembling what Haitian feminist scholar Gina A. Ulysse has called an *alter(ed)native* research approach of the native scholar to the subject-object frame of study, Comhaire-Sylvain not only tells how she comes to know what she knows but also publicly announces that she was not allowed to know, "as the subjects' gaze on the researcher caused a paradigm shift."[39] Rather than communicate frustration or attempts to further break the girls' silence on the subject, in an essay analyzing the results of her research Comhaire-Sylvain made a concluding aside: "Maybe someone else can do this [research] better." Pushing the form of the (all-)knowing observer, the well-published and respected Comhaire-Sylvain's comments were less self-deprecation and rather an instruction in reflexivity.[40]

The intersections between ritual dance, popular dance, and folkloric study presented a space for women to interrogate their place in and rehearsal of national scripts of belonging. There was no need to further dissect the girls' responses; rather, Comhaire-Sylvain interrogated the methods she used to ascertain and codify Haitianness. In studying her own research performance, as E. Patrick Johnson has presented, "black performance provide[ed] a space for black culture to reveal itself to itself—to come to know itself, in the process of doing."[41] In so doing, Comhaire-Sylvain and LFAS women were also confronted with the ways, as Johnson shows, that "black performance has the potential of simultaneously forestalling and enabling change."[42] While Comhaire-Sylvain was reflexive about her engagement and differences with the young girls and women in her work, the LFAS also used folkloric dance to restrict space, to mold taste, and to achieve conservative behavioral aspirations for young women. In this way, the LFAS performances were both the rehearsal of a radical celebration of African ancestry that combated global anti-Black discourse about Haiti and the women's participation and curation of transnational rituals that represented but also silenced some Haitian women. That is, dance, the shacks, or other representative performances all conjured the Black peasant, migrating urban poor, and the femme du peuple, but these performances did not always include these women.[43]

For LFAS women the performative space offered an opportunity to probe their relations to and culpability in upholding class and cultural differences. Ultimately, what made folkloric dance an authentic representation of Haiti was the dances' presumed retentions and reflections of a preslavery and precolonial African past that was articulated through girls and women and shared by all Haitians. It was this Africanness that buttressed the discourse on *indigénisme*. Thus, LFAS members were not just performing Haitianness, but they were also using the dance and other performances to interrogate their relationship to Africa and Africanness in and outside of Haiti.

Imaging Haitian Belonging in Africa

When Sylvain and Sylvain-Bouchereau were documenting their use of the shacks and folkloric dance in their Pan-American performance, they were writing to Comhaire-Sylvain, who was in the Belgian Congo. Comhaire-Sylvain spent her career studying the connections between African and Haitian language, and in 1943 she continued this work in Leopoldville (current-day Kinshasa). In her correspondences to family and colleagues throughout the Americas, Comhaire-Sylvain framed the unique context for her time in the Congo: "I have not come here to do any research on folklore, although I may bring back a good collection. I was called by my husband who, as you know, had been mobilized in the Belgian forces. They transferred him from England to Africa and he got permission from the Civil and Military authorities to have me join him."[44] In 1936, Suzanne Sylvain married Jean Comhaire, a white Belgian social scientist whom she met during her research at the London School of

Economics. In adherence with Haitian constitutional law, which revoked citizenship from women who married foreigners, her union with Comhaire, an immigrant and a noncitizen, meant that she lost her Haitian citizenship when she married. Thus, when Comhaire-Sylvain landed in Leopoldville, she arrived as a Haitian-born Belgian national accompanying her husband as a member of the Belgian colonizing project.

Comhaire-Sylvain was a direct descendant of nineteenth-century Haitian revolutionaries who fought French colonial rule and daughter of twentieth-century anti-United States occupation organizers, thus the irony of arriving in the Congo to contain and civilize Black bodies like her own could not have been lost on her. Her study of Haitian folklore and language addressed damaging cultural erasures and misrepresentations of African-descended people as a result of colonization.[45] Although her Belgian citizenship afforded her certain privileges in the Congo, colonial rule, racial segregation laws, women's curfews, and work prohibitions between "African" women and "European" men meant that Comhaire-Sylvain's movements were subject to policing. Her time in the Congo and ability to connect with African women was "badly handicapped by the segregation policy" and she was routinely frustrated by anti-Blackness articulated by the white European colonizers toward the Black African Congolese, but her letters suggest that when she was physically able, she moved around the country.[46] Like many Black soldiers and military personnel serving under European or American flags during World War II, Comhaire-Sylvain experienced dislocation and alienation as a Black woman estranged from home and excluded from the spoils of the colonizing projects to which she was attached. She was also surrounded by the rehearsal of colonial pillaging and the technologies of depletion that Jeanne had written about SHADA in Haiti as she watched Congolese men carry cut trees from the countryside into Leopoldville for export to Europe. In this setting, Comhaire-Sylvain regularly wrote of her longing for her home country.

Comhaire-Sylvain also expressed a desire for kinship with the Congolese. In a 1965 interview in the Congolese newspaper *L'Courrier d'Afrique*, Comhaire-Sylvain recounted, "From my arrival I wanted to merge with the life of the natives. I spent my days in . . . the indigenous society."[47] Her reflective assertion of a blended life with the Congolese rings similar to the familiar late nineteenth- and early twentieth-century anthropological practice of "going native." Yet contextualized alongside her photography the desire for proximity was different from the brand of performative mimicry in dress, comportment, and culture. Rather, her photography suggested a desire to engage, situate, and

Suzanne Comhaire-Sylvain standing among thatched roof homes in the Belgian Congo, 1944. Courtesy of the Suzanne Comhaire-Sylvain Collection, Department of Special Collections, Stanford University Libraries.

even showcase her life and work among and within a kinship frame of Congolese labor. Alongside the images in Comhaire-Sylvain's archive of women weaving baskets and preparing meals and men carrying lumber throughout the Congolese forest, there are also images of Comhaire-Sylvain at work. Because there are few pictures of Comhaire-Sylvain, the photograph of her dressed in pants and a white blouse as she stares directly at the camera while forcefully leaning toward the photographer stands out. In the canon of Black women anthropologists of the early twentieth century, the image also rings similar to pictures of Zora Neale Hurston in "the field," staring down a camera showing her working in her discipline and conveying a disciplined command of the space.[48] Like Hurston, who studied in Comhaire-Sylvain's home country and claimed proximity with Haitians through a shared African ancestry and spiritual aesthetics, Comhaire-Sylvain also sought to draw herself into closer proximity with the Congolese through aesthetics.

Instead of dance, homes, or folklore, however, Comhaire-Sylvain used photography. The image of Comhaire-Sylvain "in the field" ensured that the viewer saw her work as a part of the image of the colonized Congo. At the same time, here, as in her research connections with Haitian girls, the tensions of difference between herself and the world to which she desired proximity were evident. The Congo remained distant even as she became familiar with the landscape and made long-lasting friendships, as evidenced in her letters to Haiti, where she continued to professionally categorized the Congolese as either "progressive or primitive natives."[49] Yet, similar to her practice of self-reflexivity with the girls in Port-au-Prince, Comhaire-Sylvain again used her research methodology to trouble the boundaries of the subject-object frame and her own possibilities of belonging.

The dissonance between her aspirational connection to Africa and her diasporic difference(s) appear most clear in Comhaire-Sylvain's use of "type" photography during her time in the Kasai region. At the end of the nineteenth and into the turn of the twentieth century, this imaging style focused on cranial measurements and helped scientists draw racist conclusions through physiognomy and phrenology. Ethnographic photography in this region of the Congo was central to the circulation of type photography.[50] By the 1930s a growing body of cultural anthropologists frowned on this practice, but when Comhaire-Sylvain arrived in 1943 the images, popularized by Russian photographer Casimir Zagourski, were on postcards and magazines that claimed to "document all contemporary aspects of life" in Africa, while being used to "classify and control colonial subjects."[51] A Zagourski postcard became a staple of gifting among tourists, scholars, and residents alike.[52]

In the 1940s Comhaire-Sylvain participated in the circulation of these images. During her first months in Leopoldville, she obtained several of these postcards and sent them to friends and colleagues in the Americas. In sharing the images, Comhaire-Sylvain showcased a particular Congolese artistic aesthetic to her family and friends. Professionally, she capitalized on the race discourse that allowed her to showcase her anthropological training as she categorized images of Congolese people as "Negroid," "pure blood," and "mixed bloods" and encouraged her colleagues receiving the postcards to do the same. However, at some point, just as in the moment when she questioned if she should be studying Haitian girls, Comhaire-Sylvain's archival record communicates her disquiet with her participation in what Laura Wexler calls the "tender violence" of colonial image exchange.[53]

Thus, as Comhaire-Sylvain shared the postcards, she also experimented with taking her own "type" pictures. There are a dozen forward-facing and profile pictures of Kasai women and men in her photo collection. Within the context of the over two hundred photos in Comhaire-Sylvain's archive, the developed profile pictures represent a small fraction of her work. However, the negative sheets in her archive reveal that she did not develop all of the type profile images. Among the developed photos of the Kasai women and men were undeveloped photos of Comhaire-Sylvain in the same type photography poses. In this series there are five photographs, three front-facing photos taken at varying distances, one left-profile photo, and one photo of the back of Comhaire-Sylvain's head. Blurring the record of her type photography of the Kasai people with type images of herself, Comhaire-Sylvian fused her body into the object position, and in so doing, she marked herself as a member of the available bodies inserted into the race science of this imaging method. Joined with the Congolese photos, the images of Comhaire-Sylvain trouble the historical understandings of her subjective and political sympathies. Appearing in the archive only a few images away from the type photographs of Kasai men, these photographs frame her life as deeply intertwined with, and perhaps "merged" with, the moments of colonization, race science, and anthropology in the Belgian Congo. She constructed her photographic relationship to the Congo through the means of bodily classification and produced an image that adhered to her own political aspirations.

The photo negatives put Comhaire-Sylvain in the lineage of the studied. Her presence in the images suggests an acute awareness of the slippage between inquiry and harm in the representational practices used by scholars and activists in the Belgian Congo and in Haiti. Through these photo negatives, Comhaire-Sylvain's already-alienated status of belonging, as noncitizen (of either Haiti or the Congo) was drawn into the larger spectrum of racialized and gendered global othering. Her insertion of her body in the type photography form located her multiple sites of belonging within Africa and the Haitian and African diasporas. Here, tracing the catalogue of Comhaire-Sylvain's "negatives" expands the frame for witnessing her intellectual and political thought. Her undeveloped photos reveal a haunting pleasure and satisfaction in her play with imaging. In the first undeveloped photo, Comhaire-Sylvain looks straight into the camera, no smile. In the second photo she is smiling at the camera. However, in this negative not only is she smiling, but the movement captured in the image's blurriness records laughter. Perhaps she was bored or playing with her camera, but even in jest her photography suggests a realization that she, too, could be, and should be, the object of her intellectual gaze. She had received a similar message from the girls in Haiti.

Photo negatives of Suzanne Comhaire-Sylvain "type" photography images in the Belgian Congo, 1944 (not smiling in the negative on the left, smiling in the negative on the right). Courtesy of the Suzanne Comhaire-Sylvain Collection, Department of Special Collections, Stanford University Libraries.

Their unwillingness to play her research game turned her inquiry back on her. And thus in the Congo, she was not simply looking at the camera; she was toying with the camera, the photographer, with herself, and her own subject positioning.

Comhaire-Sylvain's laughter also disrupted the assumed objective science in the type form and refused the spectacle of Blackness and race science of the early twentieth century. Her smile breaks out of the dehumanizing parameters of the racist technologies that othered and alienated Black experiences by forcing subjects to offer stoic looks void of emotion and humanity.[54] Her smile additionally points toward a particular Black diasporic performance that played and rehearsed belonging. In her 1930s work in Haiti, Comhaire-Sylvain was not visually captured in her study of Haitian women. However, the unique experience of Black women's international and local traveling brought Comhaire-Sylvain's articulation of belonging into greater focus. In the Belgian Congo and in Haiti, she framed her citizenship by putting herself into the overlapping frames of racialized and gendered meaning while interrogating her own actions. Several years later in Argentina, however, her role in representing Haiti and feminism in the Pan-American milieu invited even further interrogation and frustration with representational politics.

Political Modeling in Argentina

On August 7, 1949, Comhaire-Sylvain arrived in Buenos Aires for the Inter-American Commission of Women. According to Haitian newspapers, Comhaire-Sylvain, "the Haitian Erudite," was an ideal candidate to represent Haiti because "she was very well qualified as a Ph.D. from the University of Paris and the recipient of graduate studies diplomas from Oxford and Columbia Universities" who also "had numerous international relationships."[55] "Wherever she has been," announced the Haitian newspapers, "she has endeavored to make her country loved and respected and also defends the interests of colored races in general."[56] Her high praises in Haiti seemingly resounded in Argentina, where upon arrival she was escorted through the city passing the Palace of the Argentina's congress and national monuments. Comhaire-Sylvain was most impacted by the physical appearance of the city. "The old streets are exact copies of Paris, apart from the writing in Spanish," she remarked, and the city had a "French air" in which "the women are dressed like European women without any influence of North America."[57]

The feeling of a limited North American—read US—influence in the city's aesthetic was echoed in Comhaire-Sylvain's assessment of the conference as well as through her remarks on the sentiment of "mutual respect" between participants that she attributed to the conference's location in Latin America rather than in the United States. During the first days of the conference, Comhaire-Sylvain expressed her excitement to represent Haiti in Latin America. In this milieu she felt she was making a contribution as a delegate. As the leader of the publicity committee and member of the economic, political, and cultural committees, her enthusiasm for the camaraderie within the conference grew as she was invited to attend an additional conference the following week in Uruguay, about which she wrote to her husband, "Everyone says I can miss Rio, but not Uruguay." While she was intrigued by the goings on of the conference, Comhaire-Sylvain was committed to the promotion of the LFAS's work while there. She attended committee meetings and negotiated a brief face-to-face with Eva Perón, following which she later reported that the first lady of Argentina sent regards to her sister Madeleine and committed to strengthening the ties between the Haitian and Argentinian women's movements. These interactions were so productive that Comhaire-Sylvain even wrote during the first days of her trip that she was thrilled about the positive reception and felt the Haitian Women's Congress scheduled for the following April would garner a large Latin American crowd: "The participation at our Exposition will be magnificent!"[58]

However, a week into her trip, the tone of her letters shifted. She was suddenly displeased and refused to attend conference sessions. Then, in a letter
to her husband, she explained, "I hate the way they consider me a *mannequin*,
shuffling me to the left and right."[59] Communicating this frustration with a
further disengagement from the Pan-American collegiality, she revealed to
her sister Jeanne, "I am not going to Montevideo or Rio . . . not in a mood for
tourism." Comhaire-Sylvain's conference schedule was exhausting as she
worked from 6 A.M. to 6:30 P.M. each day, which likely pushed many delegates
toward fatigue. But Comhaire-Sylvain's early letters had suggested not only
that she was pleased with her trip but that she took every opportunity to engage with the conference. By mid-1949 the *La Voix des Femmes* was no longer
in circulation, but LFAS members frequently published in other journals,
particularly *La Semeuse*, run by LFAS member Jeanne Perez, and the Christian paper *Phalange*. In *Phalange*, reports of Comhaire-Sylvain's travel did not
mention her frustrations, although they did report a rigorous, but rewarding,
travel schedule. Yet her disdain for and use of her *mannequin* (model) status
communicated more than exhaustion. Comhaire-Sylvain was frustrated. Her
leadership on multiple committees and the general enthusiasm of conference
leaders toward LFAS representatives at previous conferences suggested that
Comhaire-Sylvain's initial feelings of mutual respect were shared. However,
Comhaire-Sylvain's use of *mannequin* and her emphasis on being "moved
from left to right" point toward the disembodied, nonhuman, replica of a person. By her definition, she was a "model" form that represented and showcased Haiti. She was a Black woman on display. Or, as performance studies
scholar Joseph Roach might say, she was a Haitian Pan-American surrogation
that "perform[ed] effigies to evoke an absence, to bring something forth, especially something from a distant past."[60] Her frustration, then, was a dissonance between how Comhaire-Sylvain figured herself and how Haiti was
figured into the Pan-American project.

In his work on Haiti and Pan-Americanism, historian Millery Polyné explains that for Haitians in the early nineteenth century, Pan-Americanism
meant the support of a radical antislavery program and the defense against
European threats to recolonize independent Caribbean and Latin American
states. By the twentieth century and in the period of post–US occupation of
Haiti, the promise of Pan-Americanism was a collaboration between Latin
American countries that decentralized the United States and provided the
potential for geopolitical alliances with non-white people in the Americas.
Comhaire-Sylvain had expressed enthusiasm for this promise when she ar-
rived in Argentina. This decentralization of the United States also supported,

as many Haitian thinkers of the mid-twentieth century hoped, a deemphasis on race in regional Pan-American discourse and rather a focus on the universality of Haitian leadership and republican ideals while highlighting the nation's cultural particularity.

Despite the strategic use of Pan-America by Haitian presidents Sténio Vincent and Elié Lescot and intellectuals across the political spectrums, like Jean Price-Mars, Dantes Bellegarde, and Max Hudicourt, the representations of Haiti in Pan-American spaces often reinforced the racialization that many theorists sought to neutralize. Folkloric dance was one arena of slippage in which the performative reinforced the very ideals—primitivism and incivility—that some Haitian politicians sought to reject. All of the Pan-American nations participated in this showcasing of a premodern heritage that anchored their respective nationalist projects, but for Haiti, representations of precolonial and colonial artifacts and folktales threatened to present a mockery of the nation. For example, in a review of Pan-American brochures and paraphernalia, Haiti's racial and ethnic uniqueness was often overrepresented in comparison to other countries, overshadowing evidence of leadership and participation in the regional markets. When Haitian delegates had not been present at the conferences, Comhaire-Sylvain's own work was used to represent Haiti's rich cultural tradition. Comhaire-Sylvain submitted a Haitian folklore story, "Thezan," to the 1939 Pan American Conference bulletin. Yet, in 1949, in her self-defined inanimation Comhaire-Sylvain was the cultural artifact of Haiti.

As both Polyné and historian Brenda Gayle Plummer highlight, although variations of regionalized understanding of Pan-Americanism deemphasized race and color and encouraged a transnational egalitarianism, the regional nations constantly used racial primitivism to determine their collective agenda. Throughout the Americas, Plummer argues, the nation-state under Pan-Americanism was racially constructed as white. In this configuration Haiti, the Black nation, was misaligned. This asymmetry had been communicated since the early mid-nineteenth century with Haiti's exclusion from the Panama Conference on the basis of linguistic and racial difference. At the 1949 congress in Argentina, the performance of this difference was wrapped into what Diana Taylor names "the pseudo-carnivalesque quality of the Perónist production" of nationalism that emphasized the "commingling of bodies (class, race, gendered)" to promote images of unity.[61]

This performative quality transferred to the conference, which was largely orchestrated by Eva Perón. Comhaire-Sylvain walked into this additional layer of pageantry and was (for a time) captivated by it, even writing enthusiastically that Perón sent a bouquet of flowers to her room after their brief interaction. Yet, as Plummer has argued, non-US Pan-Americanists "found both their estrangement and their ambitions understood by persons who shared their optic." This estrangement was resonant in Comhaire-Sylvain's "model" assessment and recalls Black feminist literary critic Daphne Brooks's assertion that "black women's bodies continue to bear the gross insult and burden of spectacular (representational) exploitation in transatlantic culture. Systemically overdetermined and mythically configured, the iconography of the black female body remains the central urtext of alienation in transatlantic culture."[62] In this light, the bouquet of flowers from Perón only further adorned the political pageantry and fictive configuration of the Pan-American performance. Moreover, being paraded around as a mannequin suggested that Comhaire-Sylvain's presence was valued as representational, rather than contributive.

Polyné's work attends to Comhaire-Sylvain's sentiments of estrangement and alienation in the Pan-American context, and he has argued that for these reasons Haitian politicians, activists, and intellectuals moved toward a Pan-Africanist discourse with people of African descent in the British Caribbean and specifically with US African Americans. While LFAS members did not make explicit Pan-African statements of alliance, their international networks suggested an affinity to this discourse. Several weeks before Comhaire-Sylvain arrived in Buenos Aires, African American women's and civil rights organizer and National Council of Negro Women (NCNW) president Mary McLeod Bethune arrived in Port-au-Prince.

Throughout the 1920s, 1930s, and 1940s, women's rights and nationalist organizers from Haiti developed political alliances with US Black women. From anti–US occupation organizing in the 1920s to the creation and participation of Haitian and African American women in the International Council of Women of the Darker Races (ICWDR, 1922–40), these women developed a transnational women's coalition of mutual affiliation and national concern that included interests in women's education, families, and rights. As related to the state, each wife (or sister) of the postoccupation Haitian presidents were members of the LFAS and had their own extensive relationships with African American clubwomen and rights organizers, including Bethune and the NCNW. In the late 1940s, Lucienne Estimé (wife of President Léon Dumarsais Estimé) and Bethune were friends, corresponded frequently, and encouraged collaboration between their respective organizations. As activist Ruth Clement-Bond explained in a letter referring to Bethune and Estimé's relationship, "the Negro women of the United States, who feel a kinship with the people of this black republic . . . [believe] that through collaboration, even on this small project, there can come a wider knowledge and a better understanding of each other."[63] Both women had the ear of the most influential activists and politicians of their respective nations.[64] In 1948 Estimé became a member of the NCNW, and in 1949 Bethune made her first and only trip to Haiti.[65]

After her trip to Haiti, Bethune wrote to future LFAS president Fortuna Guery, "Your Haiti has stirred me as I have never before been stirred." After referencing some joint public health initiatives between the groups of women, Bethune enthusiastically concludes, "Oh I can see it now the thousands and thousands of [Haitian] women with a swing and a poise like princesses of Africa lifting themselves by their own bootstraps!"[66] She further proclaimed that Haiti was "a land of peoples of my own color—ruled—and ruled NOBLY— by black men; your lovely women, awakening to your needs,—aspiring to greater levels;—wanting the franchise."[67] The support for Haitian women's rights and the affinity shared between Bethune and members of the LFAS reflect the promise of diasporic belonging echoed in Pan Africanism. At the same time, from mannequin to princesses, the allegorical characterization of women like Comhaire-Sylvain resembles Plummer's ultimate conclusions that Haiti was the antithesis to both Pan-Americanism and Pan-Africanism. While Plummer's and Polyné's work is instructive, situating Haiti beyond both Pan-American and Pan-Africanism within a milieu of cultural and somatic plural-ism, this framing does not account for the ways that women performed a particular kind of work within and about Pan-Americanism and Pan-Africanism to achieve their own political goals. For Comhaire-Sylvain this was reflected both in her experimentation with picturing herself merged with Africa as well as her desire to be viewed as an equal contributor to regional geopolitics. Thus, being cast as a fiction dashed her fantasies for the efficacy of being seen as simultaneously African (descended), *femme*, Haitian, American, Latin Ameri-can, researcher, researched, and feminist.

The antiromance of Comhaire-Sylvain's Pan-American moment and Pan-African characterization echoed the unease of the LFAS's parading homes and dances at their national fêtes.[68] LFAS leaders similarly used, erased, and surrogated the women with whom they claimed co-curation of a feminist practice. In particular, LFAS women's performances and Comhaire-Sylvain's figuring hinged to "the memory of otherwise forgotten substitutions," of ur-ban working-class and rural peasant Haitian women.[69] The translocal experi-ence of Blackness for internationally affiliated Haitian women presented opportunities for them to interrogate their power among and representation of Haitian women and experiment with alternative lines of inquiry that were not articulated through shared claims to women's rights. These regional performances also point toward some of the ideological ambiguities of the Haitian women's movements' organizational practice that had a calculated deemphasis of race and color within the country, but in the process of being "strategically hailed" in the international arena, the women began to rely heavily on their understanding of African diasporic belonging and tinker with the scripts of Blackness and citizenship in Haiti.[70]

Playing with Politics in Tennessee and Germany

Thus in the same year that Suzanne became a mannequin and Haitian women were proclaimed African princesses, Madeleine Sylvain-Bouchereau staged a play. Serving as a visiting professor of French Language and Literature at Fisk University, Sylvain-Bouchereau finished her semester at the US historically Black college with the Greek tragedy *Antigone*. The play was a culmination of Sylvain-Bouchereau's work and professional collaboration with African American scholars such as Arna Bontemps and Charles Johnson (Fisk president) who studied Haiti and sought to establish relationships between the "Black republic" and the Black world.[71] During her time at Fisk, Sylvain-Bouchereau advanced her own regional initiative and sponsored Black students from the United States to travel to Haiti, as she worked to formalize a language exchange program. In this measure of Haitian cultural exchange, her performance of *Antigone* was significant. In the mid-twentieth century, *Antigone* was routinely performed by activists when they were protesting a government or imperial power. The story of Antigone, the Greek princess who defies King Creon's order and insists on burying her brother Polyneices's body has, as Haitian novelist Edwidge Danticat reminds us, been historically used as an act of "creating dangerously" in response to restrictive governments in Haiti.

In her book of the same title, Danticat shares, "The legend of the underground staging" of Greek plays during the François Duvalier period [1957–1986], for example, reverberated throughout the late twentieth century so emphatically that when there was a political murder people would say, "Someone should put on a play."[72] In the 1940s LFAS women were not under the imminent physical danger that propelled staging plays into legend. They were, however, co-creating new ways of knowing that threatened the gendered and social order of politics and the nation.[73] For Danticat, understanding the utility of the Greek tragedy in Duvalier-era Haiti focused on Haitian women's desire, like Antigone's, to bury their loved ones despite the threat of their own deaths if they did so.[74] However, in 1949 Sylvain-Bouchereau's use of

Antigone may have asked the audience to dwell in a different corner of Antigone's desire—the agony within Antigone's calculations, the many times she almost rebels against King Creon but does not (yet) make the move. This space echoes the torment discussed in the next dwelling space of the book as well as a nod to the generous space of "we will have time to have more victories" that Sylvain-Bouchereau assumed in her letter about the 1944 shacks and legislative victory. This was the space of not quite getting it right, almost connection, reflection, negotiation, experimentation, failure, and rehearsal that LFAS women took advantage of, documented, and refused.

Only two documents remain from Sylvain-Bouchereau's production: a request for production funding and the campus advertisement. Yet the version of the play that Sylvain-Bouchereau chose was Jean Anouilh's 1944 script, which was an open critique of the Nazi occupation of France. In the context of global attention to racial cleansing and national examples of gender activism, Sylvain-Bouchereau's play could be read as both a declaration of frustration and a projection into the future in which she "[knew] in part that no matter how trivial [her] words may seem, someday, somewhere, someone may risk his or her life to read them."[75] Within the possibilities of this reframing of women in Haiti, the play was in the lineage of a dangerous (diasporic) creation. More imminent danger would loom heavier in the coming decade. But this play was, perhaps, a preimplantation of "maxims and phrases [that] would keep coming back, buried deep in memories by the rote recitation techniques that the Haitian school system had taught so well."[76] In this rehearsal space, Sylvain-Bouchereau played with the possibilities of women's political wayfaring.

Sylvain-Bouchereau's space of almost rebellion continually ebbed and flowed through allegory. The story of Antigone cloaked Sylvain-Bouchereau's civil disobedience and highlighted her love for family, both being foundational components of her feminist practice. In this space Sylvain-Bouchereau also continued to recite and play literal roles in the global scripts about Haiti. On the occasion of Haiti's 150th celebration of independence, Sylvain-Bouchereau was on a diplomatic trip to Germany. She traveled to Germany almost a decade after her nine-month deployment as a principal welfare office worker for the United Nations in 1944. Upon her return to Germany, she styled a fictive Haitian homecoming. The German newspapers reported that at her welcome ball, through folkloric dance and drumming, "the discreet, social whisper [of the evening] was replaced by the sound of the Negro drums. Very black and more chocolate-colored guests from Haiti gave . . . an enthralling show, in which musical, dance and pantomime mixed. . . . Swords of

Negroes in war jewelry crossed. And a graceful mulatto in colonial costume threw fruit into the audience during the dance."[77]

With weapons, colors, and bodies swirling about the room, the description of the dizzying spectacle that welcomed Sylvain-Bouchereau to Germany reflected every well-known exotic image of the far-off Haiti to the captivated European audience. The folkloric dances, seasoned with a sprinkle of tropical fruit, satiated the European desire to be "enthrall[ed]" by the proximity of Black culture in the comfort of a ballroom. However, despite the foreign intrigue, the show was crafted for Sylvain-Bouchereau. The dancers came with her. The dancers were the entourage that she chose to represent her. Together the dancers and Sylvain-Bouchereau staged the movements of national belonging. Again, Haitian women—Sylvain-Bouchereau and the "graceful mulatto"—were drawn into the frequently rehearsed steps of "authentic" African diasporic ancestry. But unlike the LFAS's showcasing of shacks or even Comhaire-Sylvain's refusal to participate as a Haitian effigy, Sylvain-Bouchereau was in the foreign ballroom as a spectator and a performer. Through the lens of the German newspaper's reporting and photography from the night, the archive reminds us that she not only was spectating, but she was also being watched. Sylvain-Bouchereau's performing-spectating-performing aligns with Michelle Stephen's interrogations of the diasporic meanings of gender and race constructed between performer and audience. What if, as Stephen's asks, we "think about radical politics in terms of an audience, and in terms of what the expectations of particular audiences might be at different times"?[78] What did Sylvain-Bouchereau expect from intertwining her presence with the performance of the folkloric?

Still on the outside of legislated Haitian citizenship, Sylvain-Bouchereau used the politics of her audience position in a similar way that her sister used photography, to draw close to a national belonging that she was repeatedly denied by the politics of the period and by the state. If we understand pageantry as a space of civic ritual and play that represents a country, culture, and nation-state, the ensemble of dance, theater, photography, conferences, and women's participation in them communicated the ways in which women used and refused performance to delineate their political and social visions of citizenship. Here, Haitian women's performances were not always synchronous. For example, Comhaire-Sylvain refused to be paraded within the terms of Pan-American audiences, even as LFAS women expected other urban working-class and rural peasant Haitian women to be showcased for women's rights. And as Sylvain-Bouchereau explicitly and powerfully claimed Blackness as a

Dancer representing Haiti in Germany at a reception honoring Madeleine Sylvain-Bouchereau, January 1954. Courtesy of the Suzanne Comhaire-Sylvain Collection, Department of Special Collections, Stanford University Libraries.

A split image of dancers performing at a reception in honor of Madeleine Sylvain-Bouchereau's visit to Germany and Madeleine Sylvain-Bouchereau in receiving line being greeted by guests, January 1954. Courtesy of the Suzanne Comhaire-Sylvain Collection, Department of Special Collections, Stanford University Libraries.

part of her national identity, even when the performance of that Blackness fell back on old scripts of exotic Africanness.

If national representation and inclusion in the vision of Haiti were Sylvain-Bouchereau's expectations for the German presentation, the dichotomy between the nearly naked dancing Haitians and her evening attire graphically illustrated the failure of that merger and the differences among Haitians even in diasporic spaces. Yet in the context of this well-worn choreography and gaps in connectivity between Haitians, we might turn our attention back to the dancers at the reception. In her scholarship on African diasporic dance, Jasmine E. Johnson argues that the "casualties" of a perfectly choreographed belonging are in fact opportunities to turn our attention to "what falls away rather than what echoes." Or in the historical context of these political wayfarers, there is an opportunity to dwell in the space of almost touching. Johnson explains: "Focusing on what is lost in translation is not to say that there is no cohesion, community, or family formation being constituted. Rather it is to say that the proof of diaspora is where the body fails, does differently, or does extra."[79] Thus, the "extra" of bringing an entire Haitian dance troupe to a foreign reception to perform worn choreographies of Haiti was also Sylvain-Bouchereau's opportunity to improvise a step closer to a Haiti that she longed for. Sylvain-Bouchereau's familiarity with the centuries-old choreography of "authentic" Africanness allowed her to recognize a gesture done differently or an extra flare that created a shared space of connectivity for both Haitian audience and performer in the midst of foreign onlookers. It is the space among the Haitian audience and the performers that revealed the creativity and fragility of women's evolving political consciousness and feminist thinking. The space was the political location of almost touching, but not quite.

Haitian Women's International Stage

The national and global sites that these women moved through allowed Haitian women to consider and reject aspects of themselves and their political practice. Haitian women activists used performance mediums to interrogate their national, regional, and diasporic belonging as well as push the possibilities of different women's gendered citizenship. In this regard there may have been no bigger stage than the first Haitian Women's National Congress in 1950. The women's international performances and strategic alliances throughout the 1940s primed the region and the world for Haitian women's rights organizers' campaign for suffrage. On Monday evening, April 10, 1950, two hundred women from Haiti, the Caribbean, and the United States representing forty-eight women's organizations and five labor unions filled the main reception hall of the Haitian National Palace for the opening ceremony of the Congress. Before being offput by her experience at the Pan-American Conference in Argentina the year before, Comhaire-Sylvain was enlivened by the regional enthusiasm for the LFAS's work and wrote that she anticipated a regional outpouring of support for Haitian women in the coming year. The conference, as Comhaire-Sylvain predicted, was a large showcase of regional feminist camaraderie. The LFAS organized the congress as an extension of Port-au-Prince's Bicentennial Exposition and as a platform for women from throughout the region to debate issues of gender equality, women's rights, and most specifically, Haitian women's suffrage.

As the sun set outside the room of the first day of conferencing and guests waited for the week of festivities to begin, Lucienne H. Estimé, the host of the venue, first lady of the nation, and LFAS member, gave the opening address in her official duty as president of honor for the congress.[80] Combining the LFAS organizational agenda with the then president Dumarsais Estimé's needs to showcase a forward-thinking government with national and international alliances, Lucienne Estimé welcomed the international guests. As leaders of the republic, Lucienne and President Estimé had both put extensive time, energy, and government resources into the exposition and the congress. They engineered the exposition to reignite the excitement of their supporters, who had enthusiastically ushered them into the presidency following Haiti's revolution of 1946.[81] Yet, four years into their leadership, the Estimé's were unable to ignore the cloud of criticism and suspicion from politicians and citizens that had befallen them.[82]

Under their administration, political divisions intensified and the nation had fallen into an economic crisis. Estimé needed to resuscitate the nation and his popular image. The First Family of the Republic were, as a result, straddling the line between desperation and enthusiasm when they planned the exposition and invested over 60 percent of the nation's annual budget on pavilions, bridges, and beautifying the capital city.[83] Lucienne and President Estimé anticipated that this extravagant showcase of the nation and the Women's Congress would rally support around the presidency and be a part of their lasting legacy as first family.[84]

With her family's political future in mind, Mme. Estimé rose to speak. Until this point Mme. Estimé, like many of the wives of the republic before her, had limited public speaking appearances. Yet as the murmurs of the distinguished audience settled into silence, the first lady greeted her guests with executive poise and "a subtle simplicity of emotion."[85] Mme. Estimé proclaimed, "In my role as President of Honor, it is my pleasure to cordially welcome the delegates from the friendly nations and our sisters from the province who immediately accepted [the invitation] to attend this beautiful manifestation of female effort. Their presence permits us to say that despite the distance, common feelings connect our hearts and that we are guided by the same ideals."[86]

The delegates traveled from as near as Croix-de-Bouquet (Haiti) and as far as Detroit, Michigan, to attend the congress. The women gathered in the national palace represented Haiti's leading feminist activists and Lucienne's co-collaborators on philanthropic and social service projects including her own orphanage, l'Abri des Orphelins. Her international guests were equally accomplished. Traveling from Puerto Rico, Cuba, Jamaica, and the United States, these women included some of the most active and politically influential women from the region, including Dorothy Irene Height, US Black women's activist and president of Delta Sigma Theta Sorority Inc.; Vivian Carter Mason, president of the US National Council of Negro Women; Layle Lane, educator and US Socialist Party member; and Felisa Rincón de Gautier, San Juan mayor and Caribbean social activist. Additionally delegates from the United Nations, the International Labour Organization, the United Nations Educational, Scientific and Cultural Organization (UNESCO), and the Women's International League for Peace and Freedom (WILPF) attended.[87]

Many of the Haitian women present had traveled both geographic and ideological distances to the congress. As Lucienne Estimé stood before the congress, she was aware of the past successes of the movement, having participated in them, yet the reality of women's "distance" from one another and their continued social and political subordination still loomed over the union. Haitian women were not only denied political and civil rights, they were also disproportionately affected by fiscal downturns in the country following her husband's administration's failed domestic and international economic ventures.[88] Day-to-day, women's life experiences teetered between life and death with disproportionate numbers of sexual assaults, communicable and sexually transmitted diseases, and extreme poverty.[89] Indeed one of the speakers at the congress was the former minister of public health and labor, Dr. François Duvalier who was invited to share information about the spread of bacterial infections like yaws. While many women were struggling to feed, clothe, and educate their families, it is certain that many were indifferent to what some critics saw as a crusade for affluent women's rights and perhaps would have seen the money and effort for the congress better spent on national programming to improve social services.[90]

Among the international attendees at the 1950 congress, there was less critique. In the three decades proceeding this "female effort," the region was bustling with feminist and woman-centered activism including several Pan-Caribbean and international women's congresses.[91] During this period LFAS founders Garoute and Sylvain-Bouchereau established relationships with women in political movements throughout North America, the Caribbean, India, and Europe. Representatives from each of these areas joined the LFAS in Port-au-Prince for this final push to the vote.

First Lady Estimé was cognizant of the affinity the international delegates had for her husband as the first Black president since the US occupation. Despite differences in class, color, political ideology, language, or nationality, the women who converged in Port-au-Prince were committed to what they saw as a shared purpose to advance and improve the condition of women in Haiti and the world. Narrowing in on their commonality, Mme. Estimé impressed upon her guests that women's rights and improved social status were a matter of "life and death."[92]

Lucienne Estimé's celebration of camaraderie coupled with her direct messaging spoke to the immediacy of the moment. In the weeks before the congress, leaders of the LFAS received a verbal commitment from President Estimé that Haitian women would be granted the right to vote within the coming months.[93] With his political influence waning with senators by the middle of 1950, this was a premature commitment, but Estimé attempted to remain true to the promise he made to his wife, closest advisers, and several international allies.[94] Although members of the LFAS were encouraged by Estimé's support, they also recognized the power of national and international enthusiasm for their suffrage campaign. The Haitian Women's Congress was a stage to put unified national popular and international pressure on Haitian senators to pass women's suffrage legislation.[95] When the conference came to a close, the women had earned the support of President Estimé and fully expected to win the right to vote within months. However, weeks after the Congress, on May 10, 1950, President Estimé was ousted from the presidency. It may have seemed that the women's hopes of suffrage were cut off at the moment of Estimé's removal, but the women incorporated this setback into their political plans. Out of the convention the women had gained momentum that propelled them despite the volatility of the political moment.

In August, Sylvain-Bouchereau wrote a public letter to the leader of the new Junta Government, Paul Eugene Magloire. She admonished the military for not granting women suffrage in 1946 following Lescot's failed presidency four years earlier. Then, she encouraged the military administration to grant and enforce women's right to vote, inviting them to

> finally abolish the discrimination that has weighed on the Haitian woman since independence. How can you talk of the Free People of a completely democratic state and universal suffrage when more than half of the population is left out! We hope that the members of the junte will not let themselves be influenced by subversive ideas only to commit the same grave mistake of further slowing the evolution that is already slow in our dear Haiti. We hope that they will be deaf to the voice of those who say that Haitian women are not prepared to exercise their rights.[96]

As the Junta Government navigated the transition in executive power, it was impossible to ignore the quickened pace of the women activists' organizing as they joined with new women's organizations in Haiti and formed strategic international coalitions.

As the women's movement gained more strength and supporters after the Women's Congress convention, the leaders were also attending to a potential momentum breaker: their leader and LFAS president (1945–50) was fatally ill. In the early hours of October 2, Alice Garoute died. The resonances of Garoute's influence on the country could be felt within hours of her death when a spontaneous "feminist demonstration" entered into the streets of Port-au-Prince. In perhaps the most improvisational performance of Haitian women's political orientation, women of all classes, colors, and cultures moved and mourned the fallen leader.[97]

DURING THE FIRST DAYS OF OCTOBER 1950, leaders of the LFAS met in a Port-au-Prince cemetery. The women convened at the grave of Alice Garoute, the second president of the Ligue Feminine d'Action Sociale and the "mother" of the Haitian feminist movement. On October 2, Garoute succumbed to months of illness and died in the countryside of Port-au-Prince. The women's immediate attention was likely focused on their shared grief, but they were equally consumed with the work of the movement and how they would proceed without their leader. Encircled around Garoute's final resting place, the women recommitted to fight until women achieved their full rights as Haitian citizens.[98]

Many of the women who recommitted themselves to the movement in the name of Garoute also witnessed her last public moments as she declared, "We will have the victory" and "On the day when women vote for the first time, I hope that a delegation will come and place flowers on my grave."[99] The gathering in late 1950 was not the victory delegation come to adorn Garoute's grave. Seven more years would pass before that delegation would arrive to celebrate Haitian women's first journey to the polls. Instead, the feminists came to have a moment of solace away from the queries of the press and onlookers who questioned the future of the movement without Garoute.[100]

The decade and a half of organizing had taken a toll on the women organizers. While advancing their own careers and projects, often caring for children and extended family, Garoute and her comrades ushered a nation from a time where "feminism was unknown" to a moment where every major political organization and citizen was forced to reflect, even if briefly or negatively, on women's role and impact on Haitian society, politics, economy, and national identity.[101] With Garoute's counsel the LFAS strategically incorporated international discourses about gender and race into their practices of feminism and repeatedly revised a political plan that was nationally focused and incorporated multiple national women's groups.

Months into the Junta Government, a constitutional convention was held in Gonaives. The women planned marches and established a coalition of the women's organizations called the Comité des Droits de la Femme. The Comité des Droits included members from the LFAS, the Bureau d'Action Feminine, and other prominent women's organizations. The coalition of these women's organizations was evidence of an evolution in the movement. Leaders and members of the coalition were the family and friends of men on competing ends of the political spectrum who refused coalition building. In their commitment to women's rights, however, different groups of women interested in women's rights maintained their particular political doctrines, while still finding points for collaboration. On November 4, 1950, the constitutional assembly ratified Article 8 of the Haitian Constitution, granting women twenty-one years or older the right to vote in all national elections. The LFAS with the support of countless other women, seen and unseen, represented and performatively presented, achieved legislative victory. Paul Eugene Magloire was elected president five weeks after Alice Garoute died, and although he was initially publicly supportive of the women's movement, he was slow to bring her vision to a reality.

A Feeling

Feminism is not an empty phrase, but a reality. To be a feminist, one must have an ideal and be tormented by the need to help others. Feminism is, in short, the collective efforts of women for the betterment of women.
— Marie-Thérèse Poitevien, "Le Feminisme," 1946

I mourn the women whom I have betrayed with my own ignorance, my own fear.
—Cherríe Moraga, 1981

In 1946 Marie-Thérèse Poitevien defined *feminisme*. In a short essay, the long-time Ligue Feminine d'Action Sociale (LFAS) member wrote, "Feminism is not an empty phrase, but a reality. To be a feminist, one must have an ideal and be tormented by the need to help others. Feminism is, in short, the collective efforts of women for the betterment of women."[1] Coded in the political vernacular of uplift, Poitevien defined Haitian feminism as altruistic. Feminism was a collective effort to "help." Throughout the 1930s and '40s this definition was articulated in the LFAS's organizational programming and outreach. It materialized in night classes for working women in Port-au-Prince, Jacmel, Cayes, and Port-de-Paix, milk and food distribution to children in Mirogoâne (L'Oeuvre de la Goutte de Lait and L'Oeuvre de La Bouchée de Pain), medical transportation services in Cayes, weekly food deliveries to women in prison, and literacy and recreation services for working women at Le Foyer Ouvrier. In this work the ideals of the LFAS were communicated in their national and international alliances, government petitions, and political initiatives to improve the social and political condition of all Haitian women. In addition to shared philosophies and action, Poitevien's definition privileges a prerequisite: to become a feminist, "one must have an ideal and be tormented." A feminist had to feel deeply. If drawn from a Catholic context, the torment that Poitevien references could connote the sentiment of being grieved by injustice or sin. Indeed, many of the LFAS leadership were educated in Catholic schools, and some espoused these beliefs in their political rhetoric.

Rivarol Lemaire, the president of the Jacmel chapter of the LFAS, articulated some sentiments that met a possible Catholic-oriented definition of torment in a *La Voix des Femmes* editorial. She advised that, "devotion is women's destiny. What is it to devote oneself? To devote oneself is to commit oneself either to a cause, or a being, or some kind of art. It's to sacrifice oneself for the well-being of others . . . to wear . . . the martyr crown, to charge one's cross and say: my happiness will be that of a people! It is to be a star in the dark night, a sunray under a crumbling roof, a lamp in a slum. To devote oneself, is to be an apostle."[2] Resonating with themes of predestination and self-sacrifice, this frame for women's organizing was circulated among LFAS members through the newspaper and through their organizational rhetoric. It was also a familiar gendered expression of radical martyrdom in which women were implored in colonial and post-revolutionary Haiti to sacrifice themselves for the people.[3]

However, witnessing the letters exchanged between LFAS members between 1935 and the late 1940s, an alternative orientation to torment emerges. In the midst of talking about politics, research, and international travel, women's rights activists also expressed uncertainty, melancholy, joy, ambivalence, and even regret about their lives as organizers. In a letter in early 1944, Yvonne Sylvain wrote, "Until now I have not rejected the idea of a Haiti transformed by our efforts. [But] maybe it would be wise to make a fortune and leave it to the future generation to climb these mountains."[4] It is unclear what prompted Yvonne's uncertainty regarding the movement's efficacy. She wrote these words as the organization was celebrating the Senate vote in favor of the 1944 St. Aude Project (Married Wage Act). Yet Yvonne was considering leaving the project of women's rights to another generation. Midway through her writing, she assessed, "This letter seems pessimistic," and she changed the topic.

Pessimism also hovered over Madeleine Sylvain-Bouchereau as she wrote to her siblings several months later, "I don't know if it is our destiny but it seems that our lives have become, after all the freedoms, more and more dismal and our joy is only found in the satisfaction of completed tasks, when this task itself is thankless. Without reason, I am lingering in this cloud of pessimism."[5] In recounting her pessimism, Madeleine questioned the methods of their work and revealed the seeming futility of their actions. She was not alone. Jeanne Sylvain found that even though the LFAS's greatest legislative victories "made a ruckus" and caused lots of "gossip" it was still difficult to keep people engaged with organizing.[6] Cautious not to continue this tone, Jeanne stopped writing to her sisters for a short period at the end of 1945. When she resumed writing, she confessed to Suzanne Comhaire-Sylvain that she had not written because she felt "melancholy" and "a defeatist spirit" and that she "did not want to transmit the spirit across the distance."[7] Turning her pen to other subjects, she wrote, "Now I will give a little chronicle of the mundane."[8] Jeanne wrote of weddings, deaths, babies born and died: "The Pierre Montes' lost their baby."[9] In each letter Jeanne measured her melancholy with a narration of the everyday. She narrated the calm over their family home in the "heavy and exhausting" heat of summer, as well as the laughter that bellowed through the space as Madeleine and Marie-Thérèse were "happily talking in the kitchen."[10] The women's rights organizers laughed so loud that Jeanne apologized for the incongruency in her letter because "it [was] very difficult to hold a line of thought in [the] house" with all of the lively conversation. Her social life never made it into her chronicles, because, as her sister Yvonne wrote, "Nothing has changed on the subject of family—Jeanne continues to have some admirers, but has not yet renounced her liberty."[11] As a result of these refusals and her "very hard [work] to maintain the regular publication of *La Voix* [*La Voix des Femmes*]" and administrate *Le Foyer* that kept her busy during weddings and parties, Jeanne feared that she had been deemed a "woman hater."[12] While this would have been an ironic characterization for a feminist organizer, Jeanne's concerns communicated the disconnect between her desired and the perceived outcomes of her actions. She did not want to be misunderstood or worse communicate that she did not care for friends, loved ones, or women. Thus, while she criticized those who did not support the women's movement, she wanted her friends to know that she supported their happiness. Navigating the matrix of the mundane and the hum of the evolving movement, Jeanne also found herself feeling isolated and uncertain about her future as if she were simply "living day-to-day" ("like a bird on a branch").[13]

In recounting the isolation and mundanity of their lives and political work, the women's correspondences relay a feminist practice that was labored and contemplative. As women who were hurried with the business of feminist work, they also questioned the efficacy and redundancy of their efforts. Taking Poitevien's assertion of torment into account, the women's simultaneous disenchantment and commitment to the political project correspond with an alternative definition of torment that names "incessant repetition of vexations or annoyances."[14] This torment captures the tasks and "the same circle of hours, days, weeks, and months" of feminist work.[15] It articulates a feminism that has tangible and affective movement and inertia, leaving women with wings flung into trees. In their 1976 Combahee River Collective statement, Black feminist intellectuals penned a section called "Problems in Organizing Black Feminists." Many of these problems were unique and specific to the Black women's experiences in North America, but they also shared, "During our years together as a Black feminist collective we have experienced success and defeat, joy and pain, victory and failure." They go on to write, "The psychological toll of being a Black woman and the difficulties that this presents in reaching political consciousness and doing political work can never be underestimated. . . . We are dispossessed psychologically and on every other level, and yet we feel the necessity to struggle to change the condition of all Black women."[16] The LFAS members' writing echoed a similar dispossession.

Still, psychological dispossession was not martyrdom. Rather, these feminists continued to work, if not with the expectation of "victory," with the commitment to care for one another. To be tormented, then, was not simply a psychic quandary. Rather, it was a corporeal articulation of an incongruent relationship to the nation, citizenship, and gender relations that was felt. In her 1981 preface to *This Bridge Called My Back*, feminist pioneer Cherríe Moraga writes, "What brought me to feminism almost forty years ago was 'heart.' Feminism allowed 'heart' to matter."[17] In Haitian women's rights organizing, "heart" was evidenced in the care *not* to spread melancholy. These tormented feminists engaged in a political practice that understood bodily possession and transferral.

This type of exchange pressed on the conscience of women who wondered if they should be the ones to do their political work, not only because of exhaustion but also because of the uncommon drawing together of women's life experiences. In a letter celebrating the end of World War II, Jeanne shared that when she expressed her anticipation for peace with a working-class woman at the Foyer, the woman replied, "La paix, cé bagaille pou moune qui gain lagen."[18] In her 1940s translation of *Lapè se yon bagay pou moun ki gen lajan/ Peace is a thing for those who have money*, Jeanne announces the reality of two simultaneous translations. First, the Foyer woman's translation of *lapè* tempered Jeanne's expression of *la paix* and called on Jeanne to account for and co-create measures to fill the gap between her experience of peace and the woman's. The second moment of translation was in Jeanne's documentation and actual script. Here Jeanne writes this woman's Kreyòl words in a 1940s French approximation of the language that would not be formalized until nearly half a century later.[19] The collapse of experiences, sentiments, languages, and archival time translates parallel feelings and connotes proximity and distance between Haitian women's lives. The decision and uneasiness of women translating different women's experiences was, perhaps, the torment that Poitevien explained. In this tormented (feminist) space there were both the effort and acknowledgment by women that all could not be translated and still a belief in the possibility of transmission across distance.

CHAPTER FIVE

The Right Candidate

Gender, Race, and Political Violence

On November 21, 1956, the Ligue Feminine d'Action Sociale (LFAS) sued the Haitian government.[1] Six years after their suffrage legislative victory, women had not voted in a national election.[2] Still waiting for their first national electoral experience, women did vote in municipal elections for the first time in January 1955. In their inaugural voting experience, eight women were elected as city mayors and government officials.[3] In preparation for these local elections, the LFAS developed a civic education campaign to help women understand the voter registration process. A year later they transferred this strategy to prepare women to register for the national election that was scheduled for November 18, 1956.

These preparations came to a halt, however, on October 5, 1956, when the local Port-au-Prince government issued an announcement: "Male citizens of the municipality of Port-au-Prince benefiting from the electoral process are invited to register."[4] Women were not included. Recognizing this bureaucratic attempt to deny women their civil rights, Lydia Jeanty, then president of the LFAS, along with former president Madeleine Sylvain-Bouchereau and fourteen other co-defendants sued the municipal government of Port-au-Prince for failure to apply the suffrage amendment within the three-year time frame stipulated by the 1950 constitution.[5] In a written statement, LFAS leadership asserted that as defenders of women's rights, they "found it necessary to act in the name of the Haitian woman, and to sue the municipal government that [was] trying to steal the political rights recognized by the constitution of 1950 and the electoral law of 1954."[6] The lawsuit should not have come as a surprise to the government.[7] Sylvain-Bouchereau repeatedly warned the government that she and her fellow activists expected the suffrage legislation to be taken seriously.

When the women brought the case before the Civil Court in November, LFAS members had every expectation that the hearing would be quick and the verdict would fall in their favor. Yet the lawsuit proceedings drew out for weeks as the attorney for the government, André Chérilus, tried to stall the proceedings with claims that the LFAS followed improper procedures when it filed its suit. Although the presiding judge, Roger Charmant, feigned an interest in following procedure, it was clear that the government was using the bylaws of procedure to draw out the hearings beyond the voter registration period and ultimately thwart women's opportunity to vote. Yet after two decades of legal confrontation with the government, the LFAS was well represented by prominent legal counsel including Stuart Cambronne, Franck Sylvain, Etienne Charlier, Max Bouchereau, and Antoine Rigal.

Strong legal representation was of critical importance, as the LFAS was also facing media relations that questioned its case's legitimacy. The day after the hearings began, the organization's vice president, Maud Desvarieux, released a written statement that she did not support the lawsuit.[8] The shocking disavowal made the LFAS appear divided and unorganized while also giving opponents fodder for their campaign against women's rights. Over the course of several days, a public debate arose through statements in *Le Nouvelliste* that ultimately revealed that Desvarieux was not necessarily against the legislation but that her husband had not given her permission to participate in the lawsuit. In a public assertion of his legal and patriarchal authority over his wife, Mr. Desvarieux explained that he did not support the LFAS's legal actions and thus his wife had to follow his position. For many LFAS members, the public bridling of their vice president and the confusion that they brought to the organization were evidence of why they had to pursue the lawsuit and insist on their right to vote. Enfranchisement and the ability to hold public office would afford women the opportunity to challenge laws that made women the political and social pawns of their husbands and fathers.

Fortunately for the LFAS, the retraction of their vice president's support appeared to have no lasting impact on the court's final decision. Three weeks after they filed their lawsuit, Judge Charmant decided that the municipal government was guilty of violating the constitutional and electoral laws of 1950 and 1954. With this decision the judge passed a provisional judgment so that women could immediately register to vote. The legal loopholes and obstacles that the representatives of the municipal government used to inhibit the smooth legal proceedings were surprising, as most people, including Jeanty, expected that the case would be heard and closed in one day. Yet the efforts to stall the legal proceedings were not as alarming as the municipal government's psychological and physical scare tactics. During each session of the proceedings, LFAS members were taunted by armed military guards outside the courthouse and inside the tightly packed courtroom. As Sylvain-Bouchereau later reported, the unnecessary presence of the armed men were obvious "measures of intimidation" used to dissuade the women from their legal pursuits.[9]

The suggestion that government officers would pose a threat rather than offer protection to civilians in pursuit of a fair application of the law reflected the political culture of the moment. At the end of November 1956, President Paul Eugene Magloire was failing to maintain his political power. Since his election in 1950, Magloire had been more of a charismatic leader than an implementer of civil rights law. Although he inherited a declining economy, his persona and perceived concern for the nation's masses as their "Bon Papa" and his support of the tourist industry earned him popular support. In addition to popular support, Magloire held strong ties to the business class and the Catholic Church at home and abroad.[10] Like Estimé, Magloire used the performance of national prosperity through building urban infrastructure and funding elaborate celebrations of patriotism to mask the misgivings of his administration.

Ultimately, the pristine image of the calm 1950s government by a level-headed leader gave way to Magloire's frenzied attempts to maintain executive power. In his slow decline as a political authority, Magloire increased his physical control over the city of Port-au-Prince and the nation as he routinely turned to exile, imprisonment, and assault to stop his opposition. Although Magloire made a shift in his political rhetoric by the end of 1955, announcing that he was a champion of Black nationalist thought and the legacy of Estimé (the president whom his military coup ousted), Magloire's last efforts could not abate the widespread public frustration with his leadership.

At the point of their lawsuit, the leadership of the LFAS had expressed public discontent with the president, placing the organization in the government's crosshairs. As Michel-Rolph Trouillot asserts, the end of the Magloire presidency "presaged the era of François Duvalier" in its increased used of totalitarian governing, sanctions on organizations and the press, and a politics of personal vendettas.[11] In the last two years of his presidency he was known less for his paternal benevolence and more for his "iron pants" (*kansonfè*) approach that was exemplified in his use of brutal force, a strong military presence, and politics largely driven by personal conflict.[12]

Although Magloire had publicly supported women's rights in the early days of his presidency, the impact of newly enfranchised women on the election was unpredictable and posed a threat to the president's already uncertain political future. While Magloire's involvement in voter registration was unclear, his support of the municipal government and its use of armed force to intimidate members of the LFAS was almost certain. Although the lawsuit was to the municipal government of Port-au-Prince, as the nation's capital city, the administrators of the city were intimately intertwined with national officials.[13] At the end of the year, LFAS members were among the demonstrators from different factions of the social and political milieu who initiated a massive urban protest against the Magloire government in early December.[14] Magloire initially attempted to imprison his critics and political opponents, but within days of the protest, Magloire conceded his power to the Supreme Court, and he resigned as president on December 6, 1956.

As control of the country's executive position sat in the balance of military coups and provisional governments, the LFAS kept political pressure on the changing governing powers. On December 13, 1956, LFAS and members of the women's collective organization, planned a march and prayer vigil to be held at the National Cathedral. As the women were peacefully marching and chanting phrases and songs of equal rights, they were attacked by government military officials. The women were brutally assaulted with batons and beaten with objects as they ran into the shelter of the church, where the military followed them and continued their ambush. Despite the uncommon brutality of this large-scale violence against women, the LFAS continued to insist on women's rights legislation. As a result, on January 26, 1957, the provisional president, Joseph Nemours Pierre-Louis, granted women the full rights of citizenship and political representation. As *La Semeuse* announced, "We are voters and we are eligible. And married women can vote without their husband's authorization. Glory to the Government of Mr. Provisional President Joseph Nemours Pierre-Louis!"[15]

New Political Tides

Women's access to the full rights of citizenship coincided with the chaotic and politically violent election season of 1956–57.[16] The intimidation that LFAS members experienced regarding their access to registration would become normalized throughout the country as voter registration was plagued by violent attacks, tampering, and blatant intimidation tactics by all candidates.[17] Despite the increasing physical attacks against politicians and voters, many women throughout the country celebrated and prepared themselves for their first national voting experience.

Evidence of the rejuvenated political interest and participation in the women's movement was palpable on January 29, 1957, when Madeleine Sylvain-Bouchereau announced her campaign for national senate. Speaking to a crowd of some five hundred women from the rural and working class, the pep rally atmosphere of the campaign launch mirrored the enthusiasm of the crowds gathered by labor organizer Daniel Fignolé in the 1940s.[18] Unlike

Fignolé, Sylvain-Bouchereau's class status did not characterize her as a champion of the Black urban working class but as a rumored Marxist concerned with labor issues; she was not considered a foe. She incited enthusiasm in her audiences as she highlighted her longevity as a champion of women's rights and explained her political platform to defend women's citizenship rights, children, and the elderly.[19]

The presence of supporters from all classes boded well for Sylvain-Bouchereau's assertion to represent all women.[20] In her capacities as educator, attorney, and social worker, her public recognition as a woman politician was unparalleled. Her celebrity could only be matched by her sisters', who in their own semistardom only increased Sylvain-Bouchereau's familiarity throughout the country. Moreover, her international work with the United Nations as a principal welfare officer in Germany (1945) and her position on the Commission of Women's Affairs (1951–52) in New York cemented Sylvain-Bouchereau's national and international legitimacy as a competent leader. With her record of activism, some supporters argued that Sylvain-Bouchereau was worthy of support from both women and men but that women in particular should give their support as "a tribute [to Sylvain-Bouchereau] for being a crusader in their service."[21] Sylvain-Bouchereau, according to these supporters, "deserved the endorsement" of Haitian women because of her twenty-year commitment to the women's movement.[22]

Yet Sylvain-Bouchereau's record of benevolence and familiarity did not necessarily garner enough support for her to win an election. For this, she had to establish an appeal and significance larger than herself. Thus, Sylvain-Bouchereau encouraged her supporters to vote for her based on a shared identity as Haitian women and mothers of the nation, a distinction that she claimed permeated through divisions of class, color, and culture. Sylvain-Bouchereau declared, "We must be united to continue the fight for the rights of women and children."[23] In her campaign addresses and public writings, Sylvain-Bouchereau maintained that women needed to vote as a political block. In a letter in the women's journal *La Semeuse* she further emphasized that the power of women's collective vote did not just pertain to the senatorial election that she was in but also applied to the presidential election. Moreover, she impressed upon her audiences the importance and uniqueness of their citizenship as women.[24] She explained that women should decide and vote as a cohort for one presidential candidate. This candidate, she suggested, needed to support women's rights and thus women did not necessarily have to vote based on their class or color group. This strategy, if successful, had the potential to categorically change the political arena. Haitian feminist scholar

Myriam Chancy asserts, "women's demand for equal rights thus not only defie[d] the society's traditional sexism but also present[ed] a challenge to the colonial tradition of exclusion: the demand for women's equal rights expose[d] the non-existence of civil rights for most of the country's inhabitants."[25] No group until Sylvain-Comhaire's campaign had held such a gender-defined political base.

Sylvain-Bouchereau explained, "The color of skin does not have a place in a question of where the future of Haiti goes." She continued, "Although we are, *noir* and *mûlatre*, we are all *nègre*."[26] Sylvain-Bouchereau strategically used *nègre* as a "framing gesture" to privilege the concept of Blackness apart from skin color. If women voted based on color, they had the potential to divide her desired feminist block. Thus Sylvain-Bouchereau rallied women around a collective African ancestral identity. Sylvain-Bouchereau later explained that she was concerned with "the lived application of the nation's democratic principles without distinction of sex, class, or race."[27] Her insertion of race into her trilogy of equality was noteworthy. For two decades Sylvain-Bouchereau, and the LFAS leadership, had only directly addressed national color dynamics several times.

However, Sylvain-Bouchereau and the LFAS were acutely aware of the intersections of color and class conflict in the nation in the heat of the 1957 election season. Sylvain-Bouchereau also recognized that the majority of the women who would earn the right to vote would be members of the Black (*noir*) majority, a majority that was being heavily courted by prominent presidential candidates. By the summer of 1957 the front-running candidates were Clement Jumelle, a Black former Magloire supporter and minister of finance; Louis Déjoie, a *milat* businessman; Daniel Fignolé, a Black labor activist and popular icon of the urban working-class; and François Duvalier, a Black *noirist* doctor, meek in stature but skillful in political pontificating and prose.

Although Sylvain-Bouchereau was not running for president, the national election discourses that fueled the class, color, and cultural debate drew voters to candidates that they felt best represented them. If Sylvain-Bouchereau did not address race or culture in her campaign, she ran the risk of alienating women who had a heightened sensibility to national division as witnessed and experienced in campaign politics. As Trouillot explains of the 1957 election, "Control of the Executive was not merely the main issue; it was the only issue."[28] Those seeking executive office were also recruiting and courting Haitian women's vote. For example, when François Duvalier announced his official candidacy for president in September 1956, he celebrated women's right to vote and established a women's department within his campaign called the Faisceau Feminine (Feminine Torch).[29] In amassing women's support, Duvalier was also galvanizing the Black middle and poor classes. He situated his campaign as a continuation of the political revolution of 1946, and championed recovering the executive offices for the Black majority. Since Estimé had died a few years after the military coup that removed him from office (1950), Duvalier used his wife, Lucienne Estimé, to solicit votes. Mme. Estimé, the first lady who seven years prior brought the nation and international women's movements together by appealing to their "common feelings," was on the campaign trail with Duvalier. According to journalist Elizabeth Abbott, Mme Estimé "supported Duvalier so wholeheartedly that she appeared beside him like an approving shadow on his entire campaign trail."[30]

Madame Estimé was not alone in her support of Duvalier. Many women of the Black poor and non-land-owning rural classes responded to Duvalier's promises to equalize the power differential between the majority and the minority.[31] Duvalier supporters would have also had crossover with the demographic of women who were participants and students of the LFAS's Foyer. Suzanne Comhaire-Sylvain observed in her urban analysis that although Class III Zone folks were "a minority in the nation as well as in the capital city, they won the day for Dr. Francois [*sic*] Duvalier, their favourite candidate for the presidency."[32] As one activist later explained of her mother, whom she defined as a feminist "in her own way," "She voted for him because she thought he was for black people."[33]

Duvalier, however, was not only appealing to the Black middle and poor classes. His grasp of culture, politics, and international relations also earned him the respect, if not political support, of some members of the milat classes. For example, Alice Garoute's granddaughter, Ghislaine Charlier, recounted that early in the campaign season she supported Duvalier because he appeared to be a family man with a solid education and a respect and care for the nation's people. She explained that "for two years he rented a house in front of ours in Pétionville. And I saw Duvalier and his wife come and go from their home. I admired them! I saw a couple that was nice. Their children were well behaved and I never heard a person talk aggressively, or hit, or domestic violence, or say negative things to passersby. No, I never heard that. Everything was perfect."[34] Yet, by the time Charlier went to cast her vote for president, she had heard rumors that he was a different man.

Charlier's fleeting support of Duvalier revealed her admiration for the candidate's perceived character. Character and comportment were a centerpiece of successful campaigning in the 1957 election. Trouillot expounds on this dynamic, explaining that with party politics in a state of confusion and absentee leaders, "in 1956–1957, the candidates' personalities dominated political discussion more than ever before . . . in part because universal suffrage had just changed the rules of the electoral game." To this end, Charlier's opinions were not passive observations or the opinions of a nosey neighbor. Rather, Haitian women throughout the country took their responsibility as voters seriously and made their judgments based on the perceived quality of the candidates' character. They discussed the candidates with friends and weighed the personal attributes of each candidate. It was not a given that women would vote along racial or class lines, and to ensure this, the LFAS and Sylvain-Bouchereau focused on individual qualities.[35]

The LFAS, as was its tradition throughout its organizational history, had never advocated for or campaigned as an organization for any particular candidate. In her call for women to conceptualize themselves as African-descended patriots for their country, Sylvain-Bouchereau emphasized the need for a president who was devoted to family and leadership. She challenged women to consider whether their choice for president was "moved by the grand winds of Christian Charity." She asked them to assess the candidates: "Did he ever attempt to sell the country?" "Does he possess valor?" The readers were instructed to "reflect" on a candidate. However, the questions were leading and indirectly excluded certain candidates as viable options for president.

Although there was no public endorsement, many leaders of the LFAS, including Yvonne Hakime Rimpel, made their way to the Louis Déjoie Women's Bureau, where they provided support to the Déjoie campaign.[36] At the height of the campaign season when Déjoie and Duvalier were the clear leaders of the race, a decision to support either candidate was for most women a long, thought-out process that considered the candidates as people. However, by midsummer and early August, each of the candidates revealed significant flaws as the nation marched toward election day and candidates used the election to torment each other's supporters. Under a repressive interim military rule, largely supportive of Duvalier, all of the candidates were guilty of inciting riots, mob attacks, and bombings.[37]

Despite the tumultuous political atmosphere, September 1957 remained an exciting time as women went to cast their votes for president for the first time. In the days leading up to the election, the radio waves were full of election songs for the various candidates. Children hummed the lyrics on their way to school.[38] One observer remembered that when she was a child, election day was a thrill. She recalled that her parents were away from the house all day, shuttling friends and neighbors back and forth from the polls.[39] Yet some people never made it to the polls, as they were physically restrained at home or threatened by Duvalier's campaigns to abstain from voting. According to Trouillot, "Duvalierist terror came into its own during the campaign, in part because of the support of the influential *noiristes* within the army," who could intimidate and mandate policy in favor of the candidate.[40] When the ballots were counted, François Duvalier was named president of Haiti on September 22, 1957.[41]

The senatorial race results were also announced. Despite her efforts, Sylvain-Bouchereau was unable to establish the feminist voting block that she needed to win. Her loss was disheartening, but most of her supporters were proud of her courage as the first woman to run for a nationally elected office.[42] In the weeks after the election, supporters also realized that the nation was winning and losing much more than elections. Immediately following his inauguration, Duvalier systematically imprisoned, tortured, exiled, or killed his political enemies and their supporters. In the process of these "inaugural acts of terror," Duvalier's armed men made their way to Rue Camille Léon and forcefully entered LFAS member Yvonne Hakim Rimpel's home.[43] On January 7, 1958, the front page of *Le Nouvelliste* read,

> *Mme. Yvonne Hakime hospitalisée.* In the night between Sunday and Monday, Madame Yvonne Hakime Rimpel reports that her house on Rue Camille Léon was invaded by a half a dozen armed men who violently attacked her and her two daughters Rose May and Gladys. Madame Hakime was then taken in a car in the vicinity of Delmas where she was found the next day in an extremely bad condition. She had to be hospitalized at the St. François de Sales Hospice. We ask that the police lead a serious investigation into this event, into not only of what happened on the day above, but to find the culprits and we send our sympathies to Madame Hakime and her daughters.[44]

As details of the attack were revealed and spread among family and close friends, Hakim Rimpel's colleagues from the LFAS wrote a joint letter of condemnation.[45] The letter was signed by thirty-six women, including Sylvain-Bouchereau, and published in the Catholic newspaper *La Phalange*.[46] The letter did not name any specific assailant, but the women suspected that the attack was orchestrated by the newly instated president, Duvalier (1956–71).[47] In the weeks before her attack, Duvalier announced that he would change the colors of the Haitian flag from blue and red to black and red to reflect the national flag under independence hero Jean-Jacques Dessalines and to represent the Black majority.[48] In response to Duvalier's proposal Hakim Rimpel wrote an article in her newspaper *L'Escale* that harshly criticized the president's plans, suggesting that it was divisive political gesturing.[49] According to oral history, Hakim Rimpel was repeatedly threatened with violence because of her provocative articles against the new president.[50] But even with those cautionary directives, few people could have conjured the vision of Hakim Rimpel beaten so brutally that she almost permanently lost her eyesight.[51]

Hakim Rimpel was released from the hospital two months after her attack. When she emerged from her recovery, the writer and activist went into isolation. She made no public appearances or statements until 1962, when *Le Nouvelliste* published an open letter from the former editor-in-chief of *L'Escale*. In the statement Hakim Rimpel reiterated that she could not identify her attackers and emphasized her certainty that they were not the president or members of his personal police. If Hakim Rimpel could not identify her attackers, it would be unlikely that she could definitively claim that they were not members of the president's personnel, but her public statement would hopefully reduce the prospect of further harm to her family. Hakim Rimpel's statement publicly absolved the president of responsibility, but it left many questions unanswered.[52] The statement was also Hakim Rimpel's final public communication.[53]

The Politics of Gender-Based Violence

The inconceivable attack on Hakim Rimpel, her daughters Rose-Marie and Gladys, and others who were arrested, disappeared, or killed by the Duvalier regime left the nation in a psychological hold. Citizens routinely questioned their safety and sought ways to negotiated their relationship to state power. The "dictatorship of fear," as a former supporter-turned-critic described the presidency, was directly related to Duvalier's invasion of private space.[54] In his analysis of the qualitative differences of the Duvalier presidencies in comparison to other Haitian presidencies, Trouillot asserts that bodies and spaces that were traditionally the domain of the "innocent" were targeted as sites of control and conquest.[55] The home was the nexus of women's political consciousness and organizing as well as the site of patriarchal oppression. Yet in its multiple meanings, the home was also a place of respect in which the woman was often understood as the domestic manager.[56] Women physically and spiritually held up the framework of the domestic space. However, Duvalier's control over the nation made some homes prisons that could be penetrated.

As the nation learned from the invasion of Hakim Rimpel's home, the *tonton makout* (military police) disrupted the codes of civility, domestic sovereignty, and respect when they entered homes uninvited. Haitian author and feminist activist Marie-Célie Agnant explains being terrified as a child when she realized the tonton makout could enter her home. "I remember the military coming in my house at night. They said they were searching for something. . . . I remember being in my bed at night and watching the military opening the closets, searching, and terrifying us."[57] Government repression was not unique to Duvalier's presidency. Historically, presidents who saw journalists, activists, and politicians as a threat to their governing power had punished them. However, under Duvalier, even the traditional forms of government surveillance and repression were changed. Ghislaine Charlier explained this new invasion of home and respect in her reflections on her husband's arrests:

> All of the other governments had arrested my husband several times because he said the truth in his newspaper. But the people would come, they would get out of their jeep, and I would see them coming from the street and I knew that they were coming to arrest Etienne. So, each time, I would go down the steps, I would arrive at the bottom of the steps and I would say, "My husband is getting dressed." And they would wait. They wouldn't go up the stairs because they heard me say that my husband was getting dressed. One time, I was supposed to be going to the United States, so he [Etienne] took off his watch, put it on the nightstand, and he said to me, "Give me a pen so that I can make my signature." Because at that time a woman had to have the authorization of her husband in order to travel. Then he calmly came down the steps. He greeted the men and they followed him out. They did not walk next to him because my husband was very respected. But when you talk about Duvalier, when he arrested you, they beat your workers, they knocked your children down, sometimes they even arrested your wife, still dressed in her nightgown. They will arrest you in your boxer shorts, or completely naked.[58]

Trouillot explains that Duvalier erased the concept of "respectable opponents" or civil treatment of popular figures. According to Trouillot, "Duvalier violence took away that respectability by forcing the 'notables'—judges, clergymen, physicians, prominent writers, village elders, and other pillars of civil society—to participate in the repression, either as its victims or as accomplices of the state." Thus, the practice of humiliation and exposing the intimacy of domestic space in public, through violent apprehensions in the home or through embarrassing displays of nakedness, was an articulation of Duvalierist control. Clothed only in nightclothes or the tattered clothes from the day of their arrest, people made the uncertain journey from their homes into the hands of the state.

The sanctity of freedom and of self-governance in one's living space was ruptured by the attack on private space, but it was also severed through assaults on the symbolic referents of home life—women and girls. Author Marie Vieux Chauvet captures this dismantling of respectability and the convergence of private and public space through violence against women in her depiction of Dora Soubiran. In the first volume of her 1964 trilogy, *Love, Anger, Madness*, Vieux Chauvet fictionalizes the trauma she witnessed during Duvalier's presidency. The fictional character Dora Soubiran was attacked in response to her "show of antipathy" for the governing president. The protagonist, Claire, narrates, "I saw Dora passing by. She hobbles along with legs spread apart like a maimed animal. What have they done to her? What awful torments has she endured that for a month now she has been unable to walk normally?"[59]

Vieux Chauvet's depiction of Soubiran, the woman who refused to hide her antipathy for the president, bears a strong resemblance to oral histories of Hakime Rimpel the days, weeks, and months after her attack. Like Hakime Rimpel and her daughters, many women were forced to walk into invaded and disheveled homes after government-sanctioned attacks. In Vieux Chauvet's construction of a Haiti that is simultaneously occupied by the United States and by a homegrown dictator who wears the infamous wardrobe of the tonton makout—khakis and black glasses—readers are reminded that violence against women did not begin with the Duvalier regime. As Trouillot aptly discerns, "what characterizes Duvalierist violence is not the fact that it also touched women, and not even the fact that it touched many more women than preceding regimes; it is, rather, the complete disappearance of the protection traditionally conferred by femininity."[60]

This traditional system of protection, although patriarchal at its root, provided the semblance of safety. Women had never been exempt from violence, but the disruption of traditional protections for women erased any concept of safety. Moreover, women, particularly those who spoke out against the government or questioned its structure in relation to civil rights, were seen as aberrations of womanhood. These women, according to the new gender order, no longer needed protection and had to be put back in their place.[61] For these reasons, Hakim Rimpel and other outspoken leaders of the LFAS were targets of Duvalier's regime. Several members of the LFAS were accosted and tortured, and their families disappeared. For example, Sylvain-Bouchereau was arrested in July 1959 because she refused to sell a weekly newspaper published by a Duvalier supporter in her bookstore.[62] She was interrogated and released from police custody, but after Sylvain-Bouchereau's arrest it was clear that the organization would be perpetually terrorized.

Although the violent invasion of home space was unique to the Duvalier regime, members of the families that were being accosted in the above examples were politicians, activists, and writers who were in open dispute and disapproval of the president. Yet in the attack on Hakim Rimpel's daughters and the experiences of the close observers to other home invasions, one did not have to be openly antagonistic toward the government to experience violence. The regularity with which people were targeted by the government deteriorated familial relationships. Providing more insight into this phenomenon, Trouillot writes, "Duvalierist violence recognized as legitimate targets *all* individuals who had a relationship with a political suspect, regardless of the nature of that relationship. It thus succeeded in casting a pall over most relationships. Fathers repudiated sons, sometimes publicly. Neighbors denounced neighbors."[63] The traditional systems of protection were compromised by breakdowns in interpersonal relationships.

Often the disappearance of protection manifested into silence. For many, silence offered a measure, or semblance, of coverage from the violence. However, as silence began to cover everyday lives for many young people this silence represented a betrayal in their understanding of communication with parental figures. As Agnant explained, "The silence. People would not talk about what happened. . . . I was nine-years old when they [makout] burned down a house not far from where I was living. There were people in the house, and the people died. I saw the house burning down and I saw the military in the street [watching] as the people died."[64] After a pause, she continued: "But in my family, they didn't talk about it." As several oral histories and memoirs recount, this silence, particularly for the generation of youth who grew up under Duvalier, revealed a withholding of vital knowledge on the part of their guardians. In this way the deterioration of the home did not require Duvalier's men to physically enter. The threat of violence and fear of invasion were enough to elicit self-censorship.

Families were also often forced to enshrine their homes with paraphernalia that performed their allegiance to the president through photography or signage. In this way, not all brutality of the government was enacted by Duvalier's men or by his order. Rather the atmosphere of fear meant that citizens terrorized other citizens to preempt even worse assaults. In this sorted protection, children could be the unassuming victims. The deterioration in communication within families was what Trouillot might classify as the "perversion of the very notion of innocence" under Duvalier.[65] In *Memoirs of an Amnesiac*, author J. Jan Dominique writes extensively about Duvalier's impact on her relationship with her "mothers" and father. Throughout her reflections she, who "appears as actors in [her] texts," repeatedly returns to a moment where her father hit her in order to prevent a makout from punishing her.[66] "One evening, the pain struck. She has never understood what happened. She was listening to them speaking, a conversation between grown-ups, with harsh words. The little girl knew that it was about those things one does not repeat, even to one's best friend." The two men in the conversation were her father and a makout. When she saw the makout, "She moved, looked at the man." And then, in a matter of seconds, "the slap. Paul [her father] had struck her." Later in the night, the father tried to explain and apologize for his actions: "I beg your pardon. Try to understand, if you can. . . . You looked at him with such contempt. I saw you dead. . . . He was killing you. You had to be protected."[67] While Dominique's narrative is drawn from her relationship with her family, Dominique cautions that *Memoirs* is not autobiographical because "at that time, it was the autobiographical experience of the whole country!"[68]

The phantomlike power that Duvalier had over the nation's households disrupted the nuclear governance within families. No longer were children and parents reprimanded for the rules made in their home; they were also subject to arbitrary and shifting rules from the government.[69] Disobeying Duvalier's parental command resulted in public humiliation or fatal punishment. As the primary provider and disciplinarian of the nation-family, Duvalier supplied those who obeyed his rules with the benefits of parental favoritism in business, security, and private education. As one community activist stated, "I cannot talk bad about Duvalier. I know he was evil. But because of that official [who helped me], I cannot talk bad about him." She explained that her family's life was put under surveillance in the early 1960s when two mistresses of the tonton makout moved next door.[70] When the women arrived, her family was afraid they were being watched, so "we whispered in the house." At the time, the woman could not find work. She explained, "You could not find work unless you knew someone."[71] So she began tutoring the son of an official in Duvalier's administration. The minister was extremely appreciative of the young woman's work with his son, and for her stewardship, she and her family were protected. When the makout came to "check on panties," an insinuation of the regular sexual assault of young women and girls, they never stopped at her house.

Duvalier's image as the sovereign father of the nation was crystallized in his appropriation of traditional religious tropes and control over the tone of households.[72] While physical assaults on the body and psyche were the historical legacy of the Duvalier regime, the fear of assault, and, as a result, the efforts to avoid this violence through displacement from the home were equally traumatic on the country. In certain cases, this displacement occurred because the home was physically destroyed—for example, in Agnant's account of makouts burning a home and its inhabitants. In other cases, it was a forced or self-imposed evacuation.

The assault on the home—the sovereignty of a particular family unit—was codified in the forced displacement from home and space. Although the threat of indiscriminate violence compromised interpersonal relationships, this threat also meant that families went to great lengths to protect each other from harm. Many families chose to uproot their homes because they wanted to protect their children. They particularly wanted to protect their girls.[73] Violence against young women destabilized the familial and national meaning of home and citizenship. In the aftermath of Rose-Marie and Gladys's experience of violence with their mother, it became clear that children were not exempt from retribution. Instead the tonton makout emphasized that young girls were the property and collateral to be owned and bartered for the government's purposes. Most often, families feared that their daughters would be summoned as sexual servants of the tonton makout. Agnant recalls that on the way to and from school, men with "black sunglasses" would harass the girls with sexual taunts and threats. Under these circumstances, families chose to quarantine their young girls, imprisoning them in the walls of their own homes.[74] As several women later recalled, "We were not allowed to go outside" or play with other children. When this isolation became impractical, families abandoned their homes.

For several families, the first move was from the urban center of Port-au-Prince, where Duvalier was perceived to have a more significant stronghold and capacity to monitor families, to the countryside or mountains where it was believed that this surveillance was not as pervasive.[75] When discussing the defining moments of her life, a prominent feminist activist replied that she was most traumatized "when we moved from the city to the mountains."[76] The urban-to-rural move disrupted her sense of security and community. Many families became what Chantalle Verna calls "contemporary maroons"— moving from home to the next home, hiding, and establishing clandestine community.[77]

Yet many "maroon" families quickly discovered that Duvalier's governing strength was his ability to maintain control over both the urban and rural regions of the country.[78] It was in these more rural communities of the country that certain families realized the pervasiveness of Duvalier's power and then chose to make a second move out of the country. Even for those who were protected through relationship with the government, the volatile and fragile line of remaining in the president's favor was not enough to ensure their peace of mind in the country. One younger activist remembered, "One day I was teaching my class and about forty armed men came in." She was not clear on why they came to her class, but after this intrusion she decided, "I need to leave this country." The government official who had protected her and her family from physical violence prepared her papers for departure.[79]

As the number of girls and families displaced from their homes grew, so did the gap between a generation of women's activists and the women they claimed to represent. The culture of repression, silence, and transience dislocated the continuity of the women's feminist organizing. In the face of threats to their homes, family, and girls, women activists were less vocal. Dominique even asserts that the disruption of home culture was evident in the practice of storytelling and sharing information among mothers, aunts, and daughters. She explains that because "the night had become hostile" under the dictatorship, women did not share their histories with one another. This assault on home space and the dissemination of knowledge created a rupture in the link between a history of women who fought for women's rights in Haiti and a generation of girls who were forced to leave their home nation. The strain on carefully woven connections between different Haitian women over the prior two decades were also frayed as distrust and silence undid organizing networks.

The LFAS spent nearly three decades attempting to shift the meanings of women's place and movement in political, social, cultural, and feminist spaces. Their research, support of legislation, and programming considered women's belonging in the nation. The Duvalier regime, however, forced many women to consider other alternatives for home and belonging. From the late 1950s through the mid-1980s, women affiliated with the women's movement reconfigured their spaces and kinship networks to make them less vulnerable to political attack, and many made new homes abroad. In the diasporic locations that included the United States, Canada, the Democratic Republic of the Congo, and various countries throughout the Caribbean and Europe, these women organized and made new activist agendas toward Haiti. Similar to the way the Foyer was designed to create a haven for the multiple experiences of Haitian women, the organizations and centers that emerged throughout these diasporic new homes continued this lineage of creating shared space for the different experiences for women: Maison d'Haiti (Montreal), Kay Famn

Femmes   Haitiennes   Votez pour
LÉONIE MADIOU   Magistrat
MAUD DESVARIEUX   Assesseur
LYDIA JEANTY   Assesseur

Vous assurez par ainsi:
L'Entretien des rues et des marchés,
La protection de l'enfance
Et l'organisation du travail.

Candidates aux élections de 1955

Campaign flyer for women candidates in 1955 elections. Lydia Jeanty and Léonie Madiou were leaders of the LFAS and participants in the 1946 revolution.

(Port-au-Prince), Haitian Women for Haitian Refugees (New York), MUDHA (Dominican Republic), and many more.

At the same time, some homes remained. By 1962 the name and location changed, but the newly named Foyer Alice Garoute, that the women initially established in the 1940s continued its operation throughout the Duvalier regime. During the twenty-nine-year reign of the Duvalier father and son much of the LFAS women's practice and the larger movement of women's organizations as vocal and visible critics of gender politics in Haiti went underground or moved out of the country. However, in their new location in the southwest suburbs of Port-au-Prince in Bollose the LFAS women attempted to keep their doors open "for the training of rural girl leaders."[80] The new project was different from the one strategically located in Port-au-Prince that would allow different Haitian women to wander into one another's political presence. Yet, if information of the Foyer Alice Garoute made it far enough, LFAS women hoped that another young woman, like the woman at the assembly hall, might, again, make her way toward an ever-changing Haitian women's political practice.

Conclusion

Filling the Bottom Right Cabinet

"Does the Ligue have a library or an archive?"
"My dear child, you are coming into politics."
—Chantalle Verna and Paulette Poujol Oriol, 2002

The violent eviction happened in the early 1970s. Paulette Poujol Oriol re-membered it was before President François Duvalier's death in April 1971. On that day, a group of the president's paramilitary police arrived at the office of the Ligue Féminine d'Action Sociale (LFAS). Without notification or expla-nation, the men, led by Luckner Carbonne, barged into the building on Rue Bicenntaire. They ransacked the office and threw the LFAS's documents into the street. When they finished, Carbonne claimed the feminist headquarters as his own. In the mysterious way that information spread while silence was maintained during the Duvalier regime, members of the LFAS were quickly notified of the property invasion. When they reached the organizational head-quarters, they found a mound of office supplies and papers littering the street. As the women scrambled to recover the materials, hurried passersby and ur-ban traffic muddied the organization's historical record. The women salvaged the remaining soiled fragments of their collective history and returned to their homes.[1]

Paulette Oriol shared this story with me in the summer of 2007.[2] As she vividly recounted what she knew of that day, she opened the bottom right drawer of a file cabinet in her Bois Verna office where we met. She explained that when she became president of the LFAS in 1987, she went door-to-door in search of the LFAS's written archival legacy. When she completed her re-trieval expedition, the entire collection fit into the bottom drawer of a metal file cabinet in her office.[3]

As Oriol told me the story of what she called the scattered archive of the early women's movement, my gaze traveled back and forth between this intel-lectual icon and the encased history against the wall. I imagined the activists' frantic efforts to recover documents from the streets and Oriol's door-to-door search in LFAS members' homes. The urgency likely mimicked the frenzied search for knowledge and self-representation that literary scholar

Myriam Chancy describes in the illustration of her character Solange, desperately searching for a book, any book, that would tell Haitian women's history.

During the interview, Oriol would gesture toward the cabinet. And as I listened to the stories and waited for her to open it, I could only imagine what was inside. When she finally opened the bottom drawer, I was shocked. The sound of a nearly empty steel cabinet is unforgettable. There were a few papers and some photocopies of photographs. The quantity of the contents was unclear, but the position of the papers laid horizontally on top of one another with a slight incline suggested that there wasn't enough material to "file" the material vertically. There was no need for dividers; the full contents of the cabinet could fit in two large manila folders.

Oriol's foreshadowing and enthusiasm before the "reveal" did not match the partially filled cabinet space. The way she talked about the LFAS archive was the way a grandmother responds when she is asked how her grandchildren are doing (pre-smartphone), pulling out her photo book from her bag and showing off pictures of little faces smooched by plastic coverings. Oriol did have that archive as well. Under a hard plastic cover on her desk, she had images of her children, grandchildren, extended family, and friends shining through her workstation. But as I returned my gaze to Mme. Oriol and then back to the cabinet, her enthusiasm was instructive. Of course she was thrilled by the contents of that drawer. There could have been nothing there, but because women moved fast, and risked their lives in some cases, to collect what they could, there was something to file, and that something was worth the hype. The effort to hold all of these little fragments together over generations in the hope that someday they might all come together and account for something was unquantifiable.

The presence of the unfilled drawer certainly reflected the alarming absence of women in Haitian historiography. The storage space reverberated Michel-Rolph Trouillot's words that archives "are not mere presences and absences, but mentions or silences of various kinds and degrees."[4] The paucity of Haitian women in public archives then is not merely an oversight in documentation, but as Trouillot explains, silences in archives are also a reflection of the history in which "inequalities experienced by actors lead to uneven historical power in the inscription of traces."[5] However, confronted with the contents at the bottom of Oriol's metal drawer, I found *other* significance in the story of Haitian women's activism.

I initially conceived my research and writing for this book as a project of filling that drawer. I thought the work was to fill in some of the historical gaps.

And to a degree it is. But as my time with Mme. Oriol went on, I realized why the cabinet was empty. It was not only because of violence that damaged the material archive or because of the mutilations in the archive; it was also because of years of gifting the information.[6] During my time with Oriol she gave me a copy of Madeleine Sylvain-Bouchereau's book *Haiti et ses femmes* (1957) and then asked me if I thought I could use anything else in her collection. After most interviews for this project, someone would say, "Here, this might be helpful," or "I found this; maybe you could use it." I received papers with notes on them, drafts of projects, old newspapers, and an entire matrilineal family tree that extended to the nineteenth-century Haitian Declaration of Independence all written on the dog-eared pages of a book. This was a circulating archive that was not preoccupied with possession. There were no sign-in sheets, surveillance from cautious archivists, or white gloves to protect the material from my touch. These women insisted that the archive be used, held, and experienced now, and then passed on. This book is indebted to this practice of archival offering.

This practice of care included the work and deep intentionality of LFAS members cutting newspaper articles of their friends, requesting news from their siblings, and then carrying these pieces between cities and countries, storing them just safely enough so that they might land in a friend's file cabinet or a university archive. These women's work was not just making or storing material. It was also the work of moving the material and ensuring that it kept moving. It was the agile practice of a political wayfarer, picking up what needed to be carried to the next generation and releasing the material with the expectation that someone else along the road might use and retool it. This archiving was a fragile currency exchange between family, friends, colleagues, loved ones, and strangers. Reflecting on the women who picked up the LFAS papers in their rain-soaked hands in the 1970s or considering the Sylvain sisters carrying books and newspapers to share with one another in the midst of occupation, world wars, revolution, and migration, Oriol's enthusiasm was evident. And the invitation was clear: leave the drawer open, because the politics, the theories, the histories, and the women are en route to the next reconfiguration of an anticipated, but unknown future.

Acknowledgments

In the histories of women's organizing and feminist practice, the word "sister" has been misused, overused, and in some cases justifiably rendered insignificant through its uncritical application to flatten difference and limit the spectrum of gendered sibling identification. However, I love the word "sister" and claim it for all of its cozy, loving, check you when you are out of line, and cheer from the mountain tops when you are flowing in your zone parts. "Sister"/Sè/"Sista"/sœur has many meanings, but my favorite definition is "a congregation of women." It is a sacred cohort or gathering. "Sister" resonates a care that conjures something so inspiring that it can will a book into existence and move across multiple living realms to open and close a chapter. Sisters show up in your dreams and on your doorstep and tend to the doubt, the exhaustion, the enthusiasm, the new idea, the old thought, and all the possibilities. Big sisters are seasoned and even anticipate the needs, while little sisters charge our imaginations. There are the sisters you are born with and the ones you choose and all, for me, live in the category of the divine. If I have learned nothing else from siting with the catalogue of these women's lives, it is that sisters are powerful and sisterhood is a world changing force.

So my gratitude begins and ends with the congregation. As gatherings of sisters go, there is no order here, just many constellations of love. Mia Woods, Ranetta Perkins, Pamela Shepard, Stephanie Schiavenato, Talisha White, Amber Moore, Anne M. Graham and Rachelle Valentine, thank you for guarding my physical and emotional safety during this journey. Together you all practice a sisterhood that makes my mind and heart glow. Ariel Gyandoh, thank you for counting me among the writers whom you love and gifting me your best gift yet, your friendship. Yveline Alexis, Manoucheka Celeste, and Casta Guillaume, you faithfully leave me stitched in laughter, inspired by your intellect, and in awe of your care and generosity. Casta, thank you for keeping me company as I wrote in the early morning hours and for literally keeping the candle burning for this project. Thank you for sitting through grown folk and baby graduations in chairs that put your knees nearly to your chin and for showing up for all of my intellectual experiments. Yveline, thank you for being attuned to the faintest weakness in my spirit and strengthening it with an epic voice memo comedy sketch. Manoucheka, thank you for reminding us all that the work must be rigorous but that the journey can be rewarding and smell good. Tayana Hardin and Maria Paz Esguerra Johnson, thank you for holding my hand and vigils since the very beginning. Yana, thank you for encouraging me to keep showing up to the work and for literally lighting my path. I am grateful to Moya Bailey and Eunsong Kim: twenty-five minutes have never gone so fast or been so sweet. Jacquie and Nadine Mattis, thank you for opening your home and your hearts to my family. I am incredibly grateful to my Northeast Corridor family for being so patient with me when I postponed hanging out or simply disappeared. Thank you for the hikes, childcare, pop-ups, messages, meals, sleepovers, workouts, parties, and phone calls: Tracee, Aiesha, Sirein, Kia, Shanise, Amelia, Tajah, Alicia, Joanne, Emily, Pam,

Martina, Andrea, Jenna, Tolu, Mama Kim, Leashia, Ariel, Jasmine, Hannah, Kassidi, Josslyn, Nora, and Afiya. Also thanks to Vernon H. Dixon, Jason, Vasco, Mark, Bets, Hezekiah, and Mark. I completed this book in a small place. Thank you Mama Jacquie, Tyrelly, Shelly-Ann, Davitia, Josia, and N'Jelle. So much of this work was formulated between Montreal and Haiti. I am grateful for the Concordia University Oral History Department and the members of the Haiti Group and Rwanda Group at the Histoire de Vie Project. Thank you to everyone at Maison d'Haïti, who pulled me from a dark place in the early moments of this project. Thank you, Stéphane Martelly, for asking pointed questions, giggling with me in three languages, and constantly saying, "Go, Gracie, Go!" For the women of the Cercle des Femmes Endeuillées de la Maison d'Haïti, thank you for making me whole again. Wani Coriolan, thank you for being my traveling partner and reminding me to prioritize fun. I offer my sincere gratitude to all of the women in Haiti and Montreal who offered their words of support, feedback, interviews, archives, and creativity especially Myriam, Monique Dauphan, Marjorie Villfranche, Mireille Métellus, Mme. Suzie Boisrond, Marie-Célie Agnant, Nadine Modestine, Pascal C. Annoual, Adeline M. Chancy, Clorinde Zéphir and ENFOFAMN, Rose Desilus, Yolette Jeanty, Alexandra Philoctète, and Lorraine Mangones. I am particularly grateful to the Cazeau, Vieux, Michaud, Surpris, Dauphan, and Charlier families for giving me a place to lay my head, fill my stomach, hear good stories, laugh hysterically, and dance. Claudine Michel, thank you for calling me every day on my first research trip to Haiti years ago and making sure the contacts were made. I am eternally grateful for Yveline Alexis, Chantalle Verna, Manoucheka Celeste, Guerda Nichols, Nadève Ménard, Évelyne Trouillot, and Gina A. Ulysse. In the end these women came out of the crowds of the marathon and ran across the line with me. My gratitude cannot be translated into words.

This work was enhanced and supported by several fellowships and workshops. I am grateful for funding provided by the Andrew C. Mellon Foundation, the Ford Foundation, the Canadian Embassy and the Canadian Studies Association, the Conference on Latin American History, the Haitian Studies Association, the Woodrow Wilson Fellowships, the Schomburg Scholars-in-Residence, and the History Department, the Women's Studies Department, the Institute for Research on Women and Gender, and the Horace Rackham School at the University of Michigan. The Department of Africana Studies, the Wolf Humanities Center, the Center for Latin American and Latino Studies, and the Center for Gender, Sexuality, and Women's Studies at the University of Pennsylvania also sponsored workshops and guest lectures where I shared and revised the book. I am particularly grateful to Karen Redrobe and the "First Book" Workshop Grant—the feedback from this session made the book exponentially better. I am also grateful to Reena Goldthree, Takkara Brunsen, Mary Renda, and Lara Putnam for their feedback during conference panels and invitations to speak. Of course this project has grown most through the incredible constellations of folks who make up the Haitian Studies Association. Special thanks goes to Carolle Charles, Claudine Michel, Gina A. Ulysse, Kate Ramsey, Régine Jean-Charles, Matthew Smith, Millery Polyné, Chantalle Verna, and Charlene Désire for listening to, reading, and providing feedback on different components of this project along the way. Chantalle, I am especially grateful for your generosity and genius that are woven all throughout this text. You have cared for and inspired my mind and heart in the most profound ways.

I am honored to have the support of my Career Enhancement Fellowship mentor Marisa Fuentes, who generously offered her time and wisdom as I juggled many parts of this project. I am also grateful for my Schomburg Scholars-in-Residence cohort, including Melissa Cooper, Malachi Crawford, Anasa Hicks, Ebony Jones, J. T. Roane, Kali Tambree, Andrew Anastasi, Rebecca Hall, Eve Meltzer, and Namwali Serpell, who read and offered valuable comments on key parts of the introduction. I am particularly grateful to our director, Brent Hayes Edwards, for being the supreme example of a thoughtful, engaged, and critical scholar. It was a pleasure to witness your care in smoothing the edges of our loosely formed ideas. I am also grateful to the archivists who continue to amaze me with their enthusiasm and commitment to history. I owe a special thanks to the librarians and archivists at the Bibliothèque Nationale d'Haïti, the Canadian National Archives, Moorland-Springarn, Stanford University, Smith College, and Bryn Mawr College, who were particularly helpful. I am especially thankful to Jean Felix and Katherine Gyssels for answering my questions about the Sylvain family archives. I am also grateful to Frantz Voltaire at the Centre International de Documentation et d'Information Haïtienne Caribbéenne et Afro-Canadienne (CIDIHCA), who has supported this project since its infancy and has provided so many archival gems. I am excited and thankful for the new generation of historians who went into the archive with me each semester, including my incredible research assistants Wilnaphekie Taloute, Nakeeta Garland, and Roberta Nin Feliz. The classroom was also where I had many of my most revelatory moments about this project. I am grateful to all of my students, especially the members of the Black Culture Studies Collective, and multiple semesters of Black Feminism in History and Memory students.

I am grateful for the support of my colleagues in the Department of Africana Studies and the Center for Africana Studies at the University of Pennsylvania. I have learned so much from being in this community of scholars. As we all know, nothing happens in our department without the faithful work of Carol Davis and Teya Campbell. Thank you for staying on top of every detail and for your constant care and support. I am also grateful to my colleagues throughout the University of Pennsylvania who generously read or listened to parts of this project and offered feedback, including Barbara Savage, Heather Williams, Tim Rommen, Deborah Thomas, Kathleen Brown, Ann Farnsworth-Alvear, Tulia Falleti, Gwendolyn Beetham, Amy Offner, Evelyne Laurent-Perrault, Paul Farber, Jasmine E. Johnson, Krystal Strong, and Gutherie Ramsey. Paul Farber, thank you for constantly traveling with me to the farthest parts of my imagination and catching my Hail Mary passes in the final minutes of the last quarter.

I am sincerely grateful to my editor Mark Simpson-Vos and the editorial team at University of North Carolina Press. Mark, thank you for shepherding my work through this process and for your constant encouragement. I am also grateful to the anonymous reviewers whose close reading of my work and pointed feedback truly humbled me and exemplified the beauty of intellectual exchange.

I have had many mentors and teachers on this journey who have encouraged this project through many stages of maturation. I am indebted to Kathleen Phillips Lewis, Bahati Kuumba, Beverly Guy-Sheftall, Veta Goler, Cynthia Spence, Dona Akiba Harper, Shirley Toland-Dix, and Rhoda Rheddock, who first encouraged me and taught me how to share women's stories. I am grateful to Sueann Caulfield, Nadine Naber, Jesse Hoffnung-Garskof,

Julius Scott, Martha Jones, and Laurent Dubois for guiding me through the scholarly world of research and writing. Over the course of this project, I have been truly blessed by the gentle and humble support of Matthew J. Smith and Tiya Miles. Matthew J. Smith, your commitment to excellent scholarship about Haiti alongside your unmatched generosity and kindness are a constant example to me. Thank you for reading so many versions of this project along the way. Your encouragement and suggestions are all over this book and have made it a much better text. Tiya Miles, thank you for being a compassionate mentor and an inspiring visionary. I have learned volumes from your example. Thank you for every note, invitation, and random check-in, and for encouraging me a long time ago to follow the thread of love in the book and to keep pulling at it.

In the end, it all comes back to love. I am blessed to walk in the footsteps of Margaret Hampton Bowers and Jesse LaRosa Sanders Greene, and their extended crew, Johnny Jones and Lulu Mortley. These women cleared the way and left so many lovely treasures behind. No one could ask for a better set of aunties, uncles, and cousins than the Sanders, Bowers, Grant, Mizzell, Jones, Thomas, Johnson, and Mortley families. Your messages, questions, and expertise in *all* things motivated me during this process. Cuz, thank you for answering every 3 A.M. phone call and receiving whatever tears, laughter, or random thought that I had at that perfect hour. Simunye, thank you for being my first teacher. You taught me what it means to be a compassionate, critical, and loving educator. Your prayers saved me. Joseph, thank you for being my first student. It is a blessing to have a "twin" who loves unapologetically and expects the extraordinary. Ilana thanks for joining the crew. Jeff and Crystal, thank you for being my dear siblings and managers of the Johnson Family fan club. To the littles, Jeffrey, Niko, Nevaeh, Aylana, Noelle, Makai, Aurora, Libertad, Kofi, Addae, Taya, Renase, Macaya, Heze, Zekai, the Fabien 4, the Jackson 4, the Lion, the Light, Ivy, Luna, Harriet-Noni, and Kazi: I love you dearly, and it is my true honor to be a part of your beloved community. Mona and Turner, I am blessed beyond measure to have found your parental love along the way. Thank you for cheering me on at every step. Billye and Edwin, the dancer and the fisherman, thank you for loving me in a way that I may never fully comprehend but that I feel every day. I am constantly amazed by your commitment to my happiness. To the "twins": there is no gathering of words that could express the all-consuming warmth and light that I feel for you and that you bring to this side of living. Thank you for choosing me, cheering me on, leaving sweet notes on my desk, encouraging me to play, begging me to finish, and showering me with so many perfect hugs and kisses. We have all grown up during this journey, so this book is yours as much as it is mine. Amari, thank you for being my home base. I am grateful for your unyielding support and constant sacrifice to ensure that all the desires of my heart come to fruition. I could not have dreamt of a greater love, but I am grateful God has a bigger and wilder imagination.

To those who have gone before and to those who are to come, thank you for paving a way.

Offering

Early in this project there was a two-month period where I believed Madeleine Sylvain-Bouchereau had been in my childhood home. Aside from the feeling that I was carrying this woman's story with me, I thought there was a strong possibility that the co-founder of Haiti's first women's rights organization had partied inside my parents' home in Nashville,

Tennessee. In 1946 Sylvain-Bouchereau was a visiting professor at Fisk University. During these two semesters the university's few Black faculty had regular social gatherings at their homes. This partying was a function of southern hospitality, but it was also a truth of a segregated South in which Sylvain-Bouchereau and her colleagues would not have been granted entry into any city bar or social club. As a result, these intellectuals would have found themselves on the Black side of town at the end of historic Jefferson street socializing on "the hill." I remembered my parents saying that the Black architects who originally designed our home (and many others in Black northwest Nashville) created it in an open layout (long before it was a twenty-first-century architectural trend), so that their neighbors and friends could easily flow in and out of their parties. The houses were not huge, but they had a large function, to bring community together, freely and safely. One of the neighbors on the hill was Arna Bontemps. Bontemps the literary scholar, poet, and theorist was one of the faculty members who petitioned for Sylvain-Bouchereau's position, and so when she documented having socialized with him at his home, I thought it was possible that they made their way down the street to the "party house." Expectantly, I asked my mom to go to Fisk University's Special Collections and Archives to ask the legendary archivist Ms. Beth Howse for help. Ms. Howse was a Fisk icon who taught generations of Black children in North Nashville to love not only books but also archival research. With her special key that she wore on her wrist with a neon-colored plastic spiral band, she opened up worlds. She who held the key to original shackles from slave ships, and Frederick Douglass's Bible, Ms. Howse could certainly find out if there was any trace of Madeleine Sylvain-Bouchereau's time at Fisk. She found the boxes I requested, and my mother and I started searching. Until this point, my mother had little idea of what I did as a historian. And now she was my research assistant. As a Fisk alum, my mother was easily distracted by the names, letters, and salaries of her old professors. After some time, we finally found Sylvain-Bouchereau's name. This was surreal, as the only places I had ever seen Madeleine's name were in places in or close to her homes in Haiti, France, Canada, Germany, and New York, and now her life was about to come inside my home. But it didn't. We found her pay stubs, letters, and an announcement for her end of the semester play (discussed in chapter 4), but no evidence that she ever partied in our home. Later we looked at the building records and discovered that the house I imagined her flowing through was not completed until shortly after Sylvain-Bouchereau left Tennessee. But she had been on the hill, and that was enough for me to keep going at a moment when I doubted whether I could or should tell these stories.

I wanted Miss Howse to see this book on one of her Fisk library bookshelves almost as much as I wanted to find out that Madeleine had walked into my childhood home. Neither happened. Miss Howse died shortly after our library adventure, but I am grateful for the push of possibility that fueled my imagination. I am most grateful however, for the opportunity to work with my mother (on a project that at first glance had little to do with her or us). This process attuned me to the intergenerational quests that were so evident in the family stories of Madeleine and her family of organizers, as well as the traces of connectivity that were written throughout the archive between political organizers and their families, students and their teachers, or young girls walking alongside their grandmothers vending, caretaking, and living in the early twentieth century. This book is an offering to those ways of knowing that come from the work of mother(ing)-child becoming and kinship loving while navigating the limitations and possibilities of different close by and far away homes.

Notes

Introduction

1. In an urban setting this would translate to a woman of the urban poor or working class. The term *du peuple/pèp la/*"the people" assumes Blackness and refers to the Black Haitian majority. Ligue Feminine d'Action Sociale, "La séance du 9 Août de l'Assemblée Constituante," *La femme haitienne repond aux attaques formulées contre elle à l'Assemblee Constituante*, 1946.

2. See Hudson, *Bankers and Empire*; Dalleo, *American Imperialism's Undead*.

3. Smith, *Red and Black in Haiti*, 2.

4. Sylvain-Bouchereau, *Haiti et ses femmes*, 84.

5. "Les membres de la L.F.A.S. protestent soutenues par la foule," in *La femme haitienne repond*, 36.

6. "Un signe de ce que je viens de dire la femme du peuple sera toujours repoussée par ces femmes," in *La femme haitienne repond*, 36.

7. "Je vous demande de ne pas voter cette proposition, car seules les intrigantes demandent à bénéfiier de ce droit. Sauvez la révolution en sauvant le pays des femmes d'abord," *La femme haitienne repond*, 36.

8. *Le Matin*, "En feminisme." Although Jean Price-Mars was an open supporter of the LFAS, he was also critical of these women's peers for their elitist attitudes and treatment of the peasant majority; *Vocation d'elite* (1919).

9. "La séance du 9 Août de l'Assemblée Constituante," *La femme haitienne repond*, 36.

10. There is a large body of Black feminist, Caribbean, Latin American, and transnational literature that addresses the history and legacies of these class and anti–Black feminist practices. Some examples include Alexander, *Pedagogies of Crossing*; Basch, Schiller, and Szanton Blanc, *Nations Unbound*; Hull, Scott, and Smith, *All the Women Are White*; Davies, *Black Women, Writing and Identity*; Higginbotham, "African-American Women's History"; Crenshaw, "Mapping the Margins"; Carby, *Reconstructing Womanhood*; Newman, *White Women's Rights*; Findlay, *Imposing Decency*.

11. Sylvain-Bouchereau, "Les droits des femmes et la nouvelle constitution," *La femme haitienne repond*, 6–7.

12. There is a vast canon of literature on gender, race, and nation. Some examples include Alexander, *Pedagogies of Crossing*; Grewal and Kaplan, *Scattered Hegemonies*; Kempadoo, *Sexing the Caribbean*; Mohanty, "Under Western Eyes"; Moraga and Anzaldúa, *This Bridge Called My Back*; Reddock, *Women, Labour and Politics in Trinidad and Tobago*; Stoler, *Race and the Education of Desire*; Thomas, *Modern Blackness*.

13. Anonymous author (Une qui ne se rend pas), "En marge d'une Conférence," June 22, 1935, newspaper clipping from Ester Dartigue Personal Papers, courtesy of John Dartigue.

14. *Le Nouvelliste*, "Des membres de la Ligue Feminine molestés," August 10, 1946, no. 21,765, 6. See also for more media coverage of the women's congress, "Haiti: Ladies Day," *Time*, March 27, 1950.

15. LFAS, *La femme haitienne repond*, 36.

16. Trouillot, *Silencing the Past*, 50–51.

17. Trouillot, *Silencing the Past*, 50.

18. "All" of them.

19. Thomas, "witness 2.0" in *Political Life*.

20. Sylvain, "Feminist Movement in Haiti," 321.

21. Kelley, *Freedom Dreams*; da Silva, "To Be Announced"; Robinson, *Black Marxism*.

22. Trouillot, *Silencing the Past*; Fuentes, *Dispossessed Lives*, 7; Johnson, *Wicked Flesh*, 5; Thomas, *Political Life*.

23. Paulette Voltaire (pseudonym), interviewed by author, June 7, 2008, Montreal, Canada.

24. Trouillot, *Haiti, State against Nation*; Ulysse, *Why Haiti Needs New Narratives*; Bonilla, "Ordinary Sovereignty"; Bonilla, *Non-Sovereign Futures*; Puri, "Beyond Resistance."

25. Madeleine Sylvain, "Pour le moment, c'est une reforme de notre statu civil que nous réclamons," *La Voix des Femmes* 1, no. 6 (March 1936): 2.

26. Fernande Bellegarde, "Rapport de la secrétaire generale," *La Voix des Femmes* 1, no. 2 (November 1935): 7.

27. Paravisini-Gerbert, "Decolonizing Feminism," 7.

28. Alexander, *Pedagogies of Crossing*, 6.

29. Trouillot, *Haiti, State against Nation*, 83.

30. Other members were *noiriste* sympathizers such as labor organizers and FRH vice-presidents Daniel Fignolé and Juste Constant.

31. Smith, *Red and Black in Haiti*, 87.

32. Smith, *Red and Black in Haiti*, 92.

33. Trouillot further explains, "Race and color are always gendered." Trouillot, "Culture, Color, and Politics in Haiti," 159.

34. Dupuy, *Haiti: From Revolutionaries Slaves to Powerless Citizens*; Verna, *Haiti and the Uses of America*; Smith, *Red and Black in Haiti*; Polyné, *From Douglass to Duvalier*; Nicholls, *From Dessalines to Duvalier*. As anthropologist Michel-Rolph Trouillot aptly explains, "the danger of taking Haiti for a caste society lies not in the observations upon which this analysis is based—Haiti is undeniably a society split in two—but in focusing on the split between elites and masses, rural and urban, mulâtre and black, French and Creole, or Christian and Vodoun believer, we run the risk of masking the exchanges and contacts underlying these oppositions." Trouillot, *Haiti, State against Nation*, 81.

35. Trouillot, *Haiti, State against Nation*. My thinking here also benefits from scholarship that looks at space as an aesthetic and corporeal social marker of degrees of citizenship. See Ulysse, *Downtown Ladies*, "questions concerning the relationship between gendered identity and spatial orders," 14.

36. Here Blackness is both a national orientation that is written into the constitution that all Haitians are Black, as well as a racial color. Colin Dayan has argued that "intentionally or not, they [bourgeois poets and other elite, urban writers] press the *négresse*, eulogized as the 'woman of the people' or the erotic symbol of racial recovery, into serving their myths and sanctifying their imagination." *Haiti, History and the Gods*, 135.

37. Sheller, *Citizenship from Below*, 25, "Movements of citizenship, performances of citizenship, and the spatial relations that arise from contestations over citizenship are irrevocably grounded in the intimate domains of bodily practice."

38. Manigat, *Etre femme en Haiti heir et aujourd'hui*, 281.

39. Desgraves-Valcin, "Notre congrès," *La Voix des Femmes* 1, no. 10 (July 1936): 12.

40. Madeleine Sylvain, "Pour le moment, c'est une reforme de notre statu civil que nous réclamons," *La Voix des Femmes* 1, no. 6 (March 1936): 2. Car nous pensons qu'il ne suffit pas de former une élite féminine capable de rivaliser avec l'élite masculine, mais qu'il importe surtout d'élever le niveau intellectuel de la femme du peuple qui constitue la majorité de la population féminine et en dehors de laquelle aucune réforme ne saurait être durable.

41. Marie Louise Barou, "Life in the Countryside," *La Voix des Femmes* 9, no. 3 (February 1947): 5.

42. Smith, *Red and Black in Haiti*, Table 8, 62. This is the 1949 survey for women's labor positions.

43. Jeanne Perez, "Chronique féministe," *La Voix des Femmes* 1, no. 2 (November 1935): 3.

44. Fernande Bellegarde, "Rapport de la secretaire générale," *La Voix des Femmes* 1, no. 2 (November 1935): 5–7.

45. Marxist women affiliated with the PCH created "the Comité d'Action Feminine," under the direction of Jacques Roumain's wife, Nicole. Direction du Comité d'Action Féminine: Mme Jacques Roumain, présidente, Mme Max Sam, vice-présidente, Jacqueline Wiener-Sylvera, secrétaire, Léonie Coicou-Madiou, secrétaire-adjointe, Mmes Edmond Gaetjens, Claire Jaeger-Pressoir, Odette M. Roy . . . conseillères. Claude-Narcisse, "Le vent du féminisme."

46. Sabine Lamour, "Between Intersectionality and Coloniality," 145.

47. James, *Black Jacobins*; Dubois, *Avengers of the New World*.

48. Trouillot, *Silencing the Past*, 95.

49. Fischer, *Modernity Disavowed*; Fick, *Making of Haiti*; Geggus, *Haitian Revolutionary Studies*; Dubois, *Avengers of the New World*; Polyné, *From Douglass to Duvalier*; Popkin, *You Are All Free*; Scott, *Common Wind*. As I was finishing this manuscript, Julius Scott transitioned. Scott's work and kindness toward me as a graduate student had a profound impact on my understanding of the eighteenth- and nineteenth-century Caribbean archipelago and on how to be a thoughtful and kind person in the world. Mèsi anpil, Dr. Scott.

50. Daut, *Baron de Vastey*.

51. See Wynter, "Unsettling the Coloniality."

52. For more on this article as it relates to national reproduction, sexual futures, and the exclusion of African-descended women, see Francis, *Fictions of Feminine Citizenship*; Sheller, *Citizenship from Below*.

53. Women fought and participated in the Revolutionary War, and in the Caco wars against independence. However, women could not be formally enlisted in the military. See Bayyinah Bello, *Sheroes of the Haitian Revolution*; Alexis, *Haiti Fights Back*.

54. Morgan, *Laboring Women*; Fuentes, *Dispossessed Lives*; Lowe, *Intimacies of Four Continents*; Wynter, "Unsettling the Coloniality"; Sheller, *Democracy after Slavery*.

55. Dayan, *Haiti, History, and the Gods*; Sheller, *Citizenship from Below*.

56. Women who married lost their rights to self-govern. They were classified as minors and needed the permission of a husband or male guardian to conduct business, travel, or hold their own employment wages.

57. Madeleine Sylvain, "Notre conception du féminisme," *La Voix des Femmes* 1, no. 10 (July 1936): 2.

58. Hanchard, "Afro-Modernity," 256.

59. In addition to Hanchard's articulation of "racial time," see King, *Why We Can't Wait*.

60. "Evasion," *La Voix des Femmes* 2, no. 19 (April 1937), 8.

61. Cléante Desgraves-Valcin, "Notre congrés," *La Voix des Femmes* 1, no. 10 (July 1936): 12.

62. Trouillot, *Haiti, State against Nation*; Sheller, *Citizenship from Below*.

63. Sylvain, "Notre conception du féminisme," 2.

64. Trouillot, "The Three Sans Souci," in *Silencing the Past*; Fischer, *Modernity Disavowed*; Fick, "Emancipation in Haiti." Régine Jean-Charles addresses the terms of violence against Haitian women as a trope and foundational script within the Haitian national narrative in her work *Conflict Bodies*, 22.

65. Jean-Charles, *Conflict Bodies*, 9.

66. Garoute, *La femme haïtienne répond*.

67. Jean-Charles, *Conflict Bodies*, 26–27.

68. Scott, "Re-enchantment of Humanism,"158.

69. Glover, "'Black' Radicalism," 8.

70. Dayan, *Haiti, History and the Gods*.

71. Smith, *Red and Black in Haiti*; Nicholls, *Duvalier to Dessalines*; Polyné, *From Douglass to Duvalier*; Trouillot, *Haiti, State against Nation*; Verna, *Haiti and the Uses*; Glover, "'Black' Radicalism."

72. Sheller, *Citizenship from Below*, 145.

73. Glover, "'Black' Radicalism," 11.

74. Glover, "'Black' Radicalism," 11. The analysis ranges from casting the LFAS as "reformist" with what feminist scholar Carolle Charles calls a "narrow class perspective," to global feminists. Charles, "Gender and Politics," 147.

75. Charles, "Gender and Politics," 147.

76. Charles, "Gender and Politics," 147.

77. Chancy, "Nou là!," 44.

78. Chancy, "Nou là!," 44.

79. Manigat, *Etre femme en Haiti heir et aujourd'hui*, 273–74. "Avec le recul du temps qui tamise les sentiments et les reactions, il est difficile de mesurer l'impact de la creation de la Ligue et les caractères du context qui lui a servi d'adjuvant. D'autres mouvements feminists ou féminins ont pris place depuis dans le pays, plus radicaux sinon plus opérationnels, et ont relégué la pionnière du movement féminin à une place où elle demeure parfois embaumée, louangée, certes, pour avoir trace le chemin de la revindication politique, d'autres fois critquée pour n'avoir pas emboîté le pas de la stratégie radicale."

80. Césaire, *Cahier d'un retour au pays natal*, 24.

81. Jeanne Sylvain to Suzanne Comhaire-Sylvain, August 16, 1944, SUA.

82. Jeanne Sylvain to Suzanne Comhaire-Sylvain, October 7, 1944, SUA.

83. Joseph-Gabriel, *Reimagining Liberation*, 39.

84. When I considered other political actors of the period, the primary political figure whose comportment became a historical point of discussion was the leader of the intellectual *noiriste* group Les Griots and former president François Duvalier. With his black top

hat, suit, and sunglasses reminiscent of the Haitian Vodou *lwa* (spirit), Baron Samedi invoked cultural authenticity and political-spiritual omnipresence.

85. Ulysse, "Going Home Again and Again," 265; Ulysse, *Why Haiti Needs New Narratives*. For other information on the history of representation in Haiti, see Dash, "(Un)Kindness of Strangers."

86. Trouillot, "Odd and the Ordinary."

87. Trouillot, *Haiti, State against Nation*; Ulysse, *Why Haiti Needs New Narratives*.

88. Ulysse, *Downtown Ladies*, 11. Also see Trouillot, *Global Transformations*. For other conversations about women's intellectual production, see Bay, Griffin, Jones, and Savage, *Toward an Intellectual History of Black Women*.

89. Verna, *Haiti and the Uses of America*, 2.

90. Price-Mars, *Vocation d'elite*, 99. The 1917 speech was published among a series of speeches from 1906–1907 in *Vocation d'elite*, 1919.

91. Lamour, "Between Intersectionality and Coloniality," 145.

92. Haitian scholars: Jean Price-Mars, *Ainsi parla l'oncle*; Dartigue and Liautuad, *Géographie locale*; Dartigue, *L'enseignement en Haïti*; Romain, *Masters of the Dew*; Foreign scholars: Herskovits, *Life in a Haitian Valley*; Métraux, *Voodoo in Haiti*; Hurston, *Tell My Horse*; Dunham, *Island Possessed*; Mintz, "Caribbean as a Socio-Cultural Area"; Lundahl, *Peasants and Poverty*.

93. Herskovits, *Life in a Haitian Valley*; Hurston, *Tell My Horse*; Métraux, *Voodoo in Haiti*.

94. Fuentes, *Dispossessed Lives*, 7.

95. Trouillot, *Silencing the Past*, 48.

96. Fuentes, *Dispossessed Lives*, 6.

97. Sheller, *Citizenship from Below*, 21.

98. Trouillot, *The Infamous Rosalie*; Miles, *All That She Carried*; Williams, *Help Me Find My People*.

99. Thomas, "Caribbean Studies," 42.

100. Blain and Gill, "Introduction: Black Women and the Complexities of Internationalism," 7; Farmer, "In Search."

101. Rochat, "Archiving Black Diasporic Activism," 15 and 21.

102. Tina Campt, *Listening to Images*, 17.

103. Many authors have devoted deep attention to this genre of Chauvet's "Amour," including Stéphane Martelly, Edwidge Danticat, and Kaiama L. Glover.

104. Thanks to Tiya Miles, who nudged me to push this framing forward when I only hinted at it years ago.

105. Jeanne Perez, "Chronique féministe," *La Voix des Femmes* 1, no. 2 (November 1935): 3. "Que la femmes peut-être une personnalité autre que celle qu'on a si souvent ravalée."

106. Charles, "Sociological Counter-reading," 68.

107. Alice Garoute, "Lettre ouverte aux Président, Vice-Président et aux Membres de l'Assemblée Constituante et aux Femmes Haïtiennes," in *La femme haïtienne répond*, 22.

108. Garoute, "Lettre ouverte aux président," 22. "Le fumier est un fertilisant de tout premier ordre."

109. Garoute, "Lettre ouverte aux Président," 22. "Le fumier est un fertilisant de tout premier ordre . . . Il n'y a que la boue qui salit tout ce qu'elle touche."

110. For example, at the historical moment where this narrative begins (the early twentieth century), terms like the "Haitian *dyaspora* (diaspora)" did not exist as they did by the end of the century.

111. Ferrer, *Insurgent Cuba*, 10.

112. Trouillot, *Haiti, State against Nation*, 117.

113. In the archive this meaning of Black is most often understood as *nègre*; however, the political meaning of this term changes over time and space. For more on the political evolution of this term in Afro-Francophone discourses of the mid-twentieth century, see Edwards, *Practice of Diaspora*, 25–28.

114. Edwards, *Practice of Diaspora*, 25–28.

115. Ramsey, *Spirits and the Law*; Smith, *Red and Black in Haiti*, 198.

116. Smith, *Red and Black in Haiti*, 198.

117. Charles, "Transnationalism in the Construct of Haitian Migrants' Racial Categories of Identity," 108.

118. Dominique, "Mme Ghislaine Charlier, écrivaine et veuve de l'historien Étienne Charlier (1)," *Face à l'opinion*, March 14, 1997, Port-au-Prince, Haiti.

119. Alexis, *Haiti Fights Back*, 116.

120. I use "outside" here to reference Ntzoke Shange's choreopoem *For Colored Girls Who Have Considered Suicide When the Rainbow Is Enuf*. In the opening scene, women come on the stage from different geospatial locations. Shange writes, "i'm outside chicago," "i'm outside detroit," "i'm outside houston," etc. I use "outside" as a way to hold and tell different stories of different women from different times and spaces onto the same stage and within the same history.

121. McKittrick, "Mathematics Black Life."

122. Brereton, "Gendered Testimonies"; Ulysse, *Downtown Ladies*, 11. Ulysse's eloquent summary of Trouillot's work is worth citing here. In particular, "how contempt for local scholarly discourse often viewed as elitist only allows anthropologists to erase the knowledge that societies produce themselves. In so doing, [Trouillot] argues, we not only homogenize the native, but also treat her as a noninterlocutor," 11. Also see Trouillot, *Global Transformations*.

123. I read Sylvain-Bouchereau's theory of literal transformation alongside Hortense Spillers's distinction between flesh and the body. Spillers, "Mama's Baby, Papa's Maybe," 67.

124. McKittrick, *Demonic Grounds*, xvii. In her intervention on the landscape of enslavement, Katherine McKittrick invites us to consider "the ways in which geography, although seemingly static, is an alterable terrain."

125. Alexander and Mohanty, "Introduction: Genealogies, Legacies, Movements," in Alexander and Mohanty, *Feminist Genealogies*, xxviii.

126. Charles, "Gender and Politics"; Glover, "'Black' Radicalism."

127. Lorde, *Zami*; Crenshaw, "Mapping the Margins"; Davis, *Women, Race and Class*; Davies, "Beyond Unicentricity"; Moraga and Anzaldúa, *This Bridge Called My Back*.

128. Alexander and Mohanty, *Feminist Genealogies*; Alexander, *Pedagogies of Crossing*; Bonilla, *Non-Sovereign Futures*; Haynes, "Interrogating Approaches to Caribbean Feminist Thought." Also see Blain and Gill, *To Turn the Whole World Over*, 7.

129. Allen, *¡Venceremos?*, 7.

Chapter One

1. Charlier, interviewed by author, September 17, 2010, Montreal, Canada.

2. See Plummer, *Haiti and the Great Powers* and Renda, *Taking Haiti* for other US attempts at military intervention.

3. Castor, *L'occupation americaine d'Haïti*; Plummer, *Haiti and the Great Powers*; Sylvain, *Dix années de lutte*; Bellegarde, *L'occupation américaine d'Haïti*; Corvington, *Port-au-Prince au course des ans*; Ménard, "Occupied Novel"; Renda, *Taking Haiti*; Schmidt, *United States Occupation of Haiti*; and Hudson, *Bankers and Empire* for other US attempts at military intervention. The dissolution of the Haitian legislature (1917) and implementation of the U.S. Martial Law (1915–29) made the court martial the only legal recourse in response to military misconduct.

4. Charlier, interviewed by author, September 17, 2010, Montreal, Canada.

5. Sylvain, *Dix années de lutte*.

6. "Madeleine Sylvain to attend Bryn Mawr," *Chicago Defender (Big Weekend Edition)*, October 3, 1936, vol. 31, no. 2324, Suzanne Comhaire-Sylvain Papers, Stanford University Archives (from here on, SUA). See Sylvain, *Dix années de lutte*, 6–8.

7. Sylvain-Bouchereau earned her law degree from the Faculté de droit de Port-au-Prince.

8. "Haitian Girl in Bryn Mawr on Fellowship; Miss Madeleine Sylvain to Exclusive School for Graduate Work," *Chicago Defender*, October 2, 1937, vol. 33, no. 23. Cover page has picture of Madeleine Sylvain. "Haitian Women Score Meritorious Victory When Mlle. Sylvain Wins Bryn Mawr Fellowship," *Pittsburgh Courier*, September 26, 1936, 2, SUA. "US African American" is a reference to Millery Polyné, who uses the United States to disrupt and name the presumption of African Americans only being those in the United States.

9. Sylvain-Bouchereau, *Haiti et ses femmes*, 82. For more on women during the occupation, see Alexis, *Haiti Fights Back*; Renda, *Taking Haiti*.

10. Sylvain-Bouchereau, *Haiti et ses femmes*, 82.

11. Manigat, *Etre femme en Haiti*, 277. Feminist scholar Carolle Charles affirms the connection between the occupation and political organizing, stating, "It was during the last years of the U.S. occupation of Haiti that Haitian women began to formulate their specific demands in an organized way." Charles, "Gender and Politics," 146. For many scholars, women's political transformation is legible in the formal creation of organizations like the Ligue Feminine. As Charles explains, "The development of the Ligue, between 1934 and 1957, was closely linked to the political crisis resulting from the U.S. occupation and the emergence of the nationalist movement" (147). Also see Castor, *L'occupation americaine d'Haïti*. Early twentieth-century Haitian feminist politics followed a similar trajectory of other women's movements across the post–World War I era as gender-focused politics were included in or operated defiantly against nationalist movements.

12. Maud Desvarieux, "Lived Pedagogy," *La Voix des Femmes* 9, no. 3 (February 1947): 5.

13. See Ménard, "Occupied Novel," for more on coming-of-age stories during the US occupation.

14. Records of the U.S. Marine Corps, RG 127, "Reports on Roads and Trails," "Monthly Intelligence Reports Received Districts," NARA I. McKittrick, *Demonic Ground*, xvii. In her intervention on the landscape of enslavement, Katherine McKittrick invites us to consider "the ways in which geography, although seemingly static, is an alterable terrain." Also see Anglade, *Espace et liberté en Haïti*; Schmidt, *United States Occupation*, 214.

15. Fuentes, *Dispossessed Lives*, 16. Also see Spillers, "Mama's Baby. Papa's Maybe," 67–68 for foundational discussion about "flesh."

16. Anglade, *Espace et liberté en Haïti*, 25. "Les relations du development capitaliste au seuil du XXe siècle exigent cette nouvelle configuration de l'espace natural."

17. Charlier, interviewed by author, September 17, 2010, Montreal, Canada.

18. Vieux-Chauvet, *Love, Anger, Madness*, 20.

19. Nicholls, "Rural Protest and Peasant Revolt," 181. Jérémie is in La Grand'Anse.

20. Dominique, *Memoir of an Amnesiac*, 21–23. Also see Jonathan Demme, *The Agronomist* (2003).

21. Danticat, *Brother, I'm Dying*, 246–47.

22. "Navy Courts of Inquiry, 1909–1942," National Archives and Records Administration, Washington, D.C. (NARA I).

23. "Bullet apparently entered behind [him] in the region of the right shoulder and took a slightly downward course obliquely to the left emerging at the root of the neck . . . in front just at the left stero-clavicular joint, passing through the vena cava."

24. "Navy Courts of Inquiry, 1909–1942," NARA I. Testimony: Joseph R. Phelps, P. A. Surgeon, U.S. Navy, *U.S.S. Connecticut*, Health Officer: "The body of Ludowick Jeudi, A Haitian negro, age 17 or 19 years was found in a chair against a building on the Rue Oswald Durand, about 200 yards from the Rue du Point. Death had occurred apparently a few minutes, to half an hour previously. There was present a woman negress, who gave her name as Caroline Dagille and stated that the deceased was Ludowick Jeudi, that his parents were out in the Country, that she and Leopold Freiburg had raised the deceased from childhood and that the address of all three is Rue Oswald Durand near the Cathedral. . . . The ultimate cause of death was internal hemorrhage. Death probably occurred about 8:30 A.M. None of the natives present could state the time definitely. I authorized the transfer of the body to the residence of the deceased and gave permission for burial."

25. Lahens, *Moonbath*, 23.

26. Castor, *L'occupation americaine d'Haïti*; Renda, *Taking Haiti*; Schmidt, *United States Occupation of Haiti*; Trouillot, *Haiti, State against Nation*.

27. Dalleo, *American Imperialism's Undead*. Nadève Ménard productively asks, "What does it mean to be a citizen of the first Black Republic once US marines have invaded the territory so fiercely contested during the Haitian Revolution?" *Occupied Novel*, 30.

28. Vieux-Chauvet, *Love, Anger, Madness*, 110. Emphasis author's.

29. "Navy Courts of Inquiry, 1909–1942," NARA I.

30. Schmidt, *United States Occupation*, 102–4. See also Balch, *Occupied Haiti*.

31. "Reports on Roads Trails," August 1921, St. Marc, Haiti, NARA I.

32. "Reports on Roads Trails," NARA I.

33. In the Haitian Declaration of Independence, Dessalines states that the nation will always recall the French colonists.

34. United States Congress, *Inquiry into Occupation*, 752.

35. Quoted in Schmidt, *United States Occupation*, 100. Butler to Rooselvelt, December 28, 1917, quoted in Freidel, *Franklin D. Roosevelt*, 282n.

36. Lahens, *Moonbath*, 19.

37. Alexis, *Haiti Fights Back*.

38. "Brigade Commander, Correspondence to (3 Jan. 1918–29 Dec. 1919)," July 16, 1919 (Port-au-Prince), RG 127, NARA I.

39. In Krista Thompson's discussion of "tropicalization," she shows that the "visual economy of people as images" as "colonial representations became interwoven within the texture of colonial societies"; *An Eye for the Tropics*, 5, 11.

40. Image example in Renda, *Taking Haiti*, 235.

41. RG 127, "Political Activity," Gonaives, Haiti, May 25, 1918, NARA I. Burro is a donkey.

42. RG 127, "Political Activity," NARA I.

43. "Statement of Methius Richard. Hinche Haiti, April 18, 1920," RG 127, NARA I.

44. "District Commander to Brigade Commander," September 2, 1919, Headquarters Tenth Company Gendarmerie D'Haïti, Gonaïves, Haiti, folder "Brigade Commander, Correspondence to (3 Jan. 18–29 Dec. 19)," RG 127, NARA I.

45. Pietszak was not charged with rape. Rather, he was reprimanded for taking "the armed car [because] there is an order prohibiting marines leaving the limits of the city. Privates Pietszak and Hoppe violated this order in going as far as the iron bridge." Headquarters Tenth Company Gendarmarie d'Haiti, Gonaïves, Haiti, September 2, 1919, RG 127, NARA.

46. Naval Court of Inquiry Proceedings, folder "Brigade Commander, Correspondence to (3 Jan. 1918–29 Dec. 1919)," RG 127, NARA I. She later testified that a drunk Pietszak pulled her into the bushes that lined the street, threw her to the ground, raped her, and then "forced her to open her mouth." As evidence of the assault, a military doctor confirmed that Eleanor's dress and skin were lacerated, and that her "maindenhead" had been recently ruptured. Black women writers have attempted to capture the sentiment accompanied with the violent act of interracial rape. See Chauvet, *Love, Anger, Madness*; Danticat, *Breath, Eyes, Memory*; Dash, *Daughters of the Dust*. In *Daughters of the Dust*, for example, when Eula is raped, she has to "throw my soul into the trees; I gotta wait 'til this is over." Private Pietszak later used her survival mechanisms against her when he testified: "The girl did not resist very much." In this case and in other cases, women's perceived physical resistance was used to measure consent.

On the meaning, process, and intent for sharing narratives of trauma and injury to black women's bodies, see Young, *Haunting Capital*; Hartman, *Scenes of Subjection*.

47. Naval Court of Inquiry Proceedings, folder "Brigade Commander, Correspondence to (3 Jan. 18–29 Dec. 19)," NARA I.

48. In this forced corvée labor system, men and women were unpaid as they served jail time for petty crimes, or were commonly taken from the streets to work US government projects such as streets and railroads.

49. Women also solicited marines' in their professional capacities as sex workers. The number of sex workers during the occupation is unknown; however, McPherson, "Personal Occupations," writes, "In Port-au-Prince, a city of 100,000, there were 147 registered saloons or dance halls and prostitutes operated out of all of them" (587). The intimate access that sex workers had to marines occasionally provided them opportunities to spy on antioccupation activists and rebels. This relationship between sex work and the exchange of sensitive political and government information would later be used against Haitian women as they petitioned for the right to vote.

50. Sylvain-Bouchereau, *Haiti et ses femmes*, 156.

51. United States Congress, *Inquiry into Occupation*, 785.

52. RG 125, Navy Courts of Inquiry 1909–1942, entry 30B, NARA I.

53. According to the official, he "did not believe at the time that the impact was hard enough to knock [Jean] over," but he was in fact knocked unconscious with "a small contusion of the leg",which was according to the testifying doctor "superficial."

54. RG 125, case 7128, entry 30B, NARA I.

55. RG 94, Spot Files May 1922–July 1922, NARA II.

56. Schmidt, *United States Occupation*, 68.

57. Trouillot, "Culture, Color, and Politics in Haiti."

58. Price-Mars, *La vocation d'elite*. Haitian intellectual Jean Price-Mars attributed some of the social and economic setbacks of the nation on the Haitian elite's preoccupation with class status above the well-being of all social classes.

59. Charles, "Popular Imageries," 177.

60. In his analysis of a different Court of Inquiry case during the occupation, Alan McPherson asserts that after a sexual assault public restoration of a woman's reputation was important for her to receive future employment. See McPherson, "Personal Occupations," 596.

61. Trouillot, "Odd and the Ordinary," 5. These "unavoidable" collisions recall Michel-Rolph Trouillot's ironic critique of Haitian exceptionalism: that "the majority of Haitians . . . die quite ordinary deaths from quite ordinary accidents, quite ordinary tortures, quite ordinary diseases. Accidents so ordinary that they could have been prevented."

62. Bonilla, "Ordinary Sovereignty," 155. In her meditation on Trouillot's work, Caribbean studies scholar Yarimar Bonilla probes Trouillot's irony and asks, "What could it mean to die from 'ordinary torture'? What would make torture ordinary? How do preventable accidents become ordinary deaths?"

63. Hartman, "Venus in Two Acts," 12.

64. RG 127, folder "Bandit Activities and Descriptions," NARA I.

65. Marie Louise to Péralte, June 17, 1919, RG 127, folder "Bandit Activities and Descriptions," NARA I.

66. Verna, *Haiti and the Uses of America*.

67. RG 127, folder "Bandit Activities and Descriptions," Brigade Commander, Correspondence, "Four women, namely Louise Ismael, Marilia Lindor, Claircia Delva and Claircilia Telisma," April 19, 1919, NARA I. Trouillot, *Haiti, State against Nation*; Nicholls, *From Dessalines to Duvalier*; Schmidt, *United States Occupation*.

68. The Ministers Consellorsian Delegates of the Evolution Actually in Northern Haiti.

69. RG 127, "Political Activity," NARA I.

70. Gendarmerie d'Haiti, Quartier-General, December 9, 1921, Port-au-Prince, Haiti, RG 127, NARA I.

71. Thinking with Denise Ferreira da Silva, "To Be Announced," 114.

72. Alexis, *Haiti Fights Back*, 119–20.

73. Alexis, *Haiti Fights Back*, 122, 128.

74. Admiral H. S. Knapp, United States Navy, Report of the Secretary of the Navy, 316.

75. Some of the most highly surveilled families were the Péralte, Batraville, and Zamor families. Great military resources were spent watching and reporting on these men and the women attached to them.

76. This sentiment of surveillance and collective consequences is also echoed in Chauvet's work. Claire spends most of her life watching the street outside her home and

regularly expresses a weariness that affiliation with the wrong people could result in puni-tive treatment by the adults and the foreign and local governing forces. Chauvet, *Love, Anger, Madness*.

77. Admiral Knapp, "Admiral Knapp Answers Questions of Citizens of Oregon," Report of the Secretary of the Navy, 1920, 316.

78. Admiral Knapp, "Admiral Knapp Answers Questions of Citizens of Oregon," 316.

79. Francis, *Fictions of Feminine Citizenship*, 12.

80. "U.S. Troops Attack Haitian Girls," *Chicago Defender*, May 15, 1920.

81. "U.S. Troops Attack Haitian Girls," *Chicago Defender*, May 15, 1920.

82. RG 127 Records of the United States Marine Corps, Records of the Gendarmerie d'Haiti, 1915–1934, High Commissioner, folder "Correspondence to Bandit Activities and Descriptions," box 3, NARA I. Also see Sylvain, *Dix années de lutte*.

83. "Correspondence to Bandit Activities and Descriptions," Open letter from *caco* gen-erals, 1919, RG 127, NARA I.

84. UP membership dues were 1 gourde a month. However, the UP was flexible about payment. Sylvain, *Dix années de lutte*, 144.

85. Sylvain, *Dix années de lutte*, 11, 92.

86. Alice became the leader of the Capoise movement, which comprised women from Cap-Haitian. Correspondences between the UP and the Caproise suggest a connection be-tween Haïtien and Dominican women and their antioccupation and feminist movements.

87. Sylvain, *Dix années de Lutte*, 92–93.

88. Ten years later, on March 1, 1930, Mme. Thoby, Justinien Ricot, and Thérèse Vieux-Clesca led the largest independent protest against the US occupation during the Forbes Commission's visit to Haiti. See Manigat, *Être femme en Haïti*, 25–27; Sylvain-Bouchereau, *Haiti et ses femmes*, 81.

89. Women activists encouraged children's participation in their events. This established a precedent for multigeneration organizing that was continued throughout the twentieth century and would be essential to the women's movement's sustainability.

90. Gendarmerie d'Haiti, General Correspondence, "Bandit Activities and Descrip-tions," RG 127, NARA I.

91. See Sylvain, *Dix années de lutte*; Manigat, *Être femme en Haïti*.

92. Although the estimated 16,000 members of the Union Patriotique were asked to pay dues of 1 goude per month, many members did not pay regularly or pay at all. As a result, the organization was largely dependent on large donor contributions from affluent mem-bers of the organization and international supporters. The National Association for the Advancement of Colored People (NAACP) strongly supported the UP. During the Hard-ing administration's McCormick Commission, the leading investigator repeatedly interro-gated Georges Sylvain (UP) and James Weldon Johnson (NAACP) about their financial contributions to the UP. The interrogation suggests that the NAACP was assisting the UP financially. If this were the case, prominent women in the NAACP including Addie Hunton, NAACP treasurer, had detailed knowledge about the Haitian delegation and its grievances against the US occupation, which would strengthen the relationship between Haitian and US Black women activists. *McCormick Commission Report*, Library of Con-gress, 192.

93. Balch, *Occupied Haiti*, 126.

94. Balch, *Occupied Haiti*, 126, "the burning alive of Cazo Noel, and of Médard Belony and his wife, the summary execution of the three children of Hergénée, and of the twin sisters Athélia and Cloraine Etienne, the beating and torturing with fire of the widow of Romain Bregarde, the beating to death of the notary, M. Garnier, Jr., the burying alive of one Vixina in broad daylight in the court of the Gendarmerie at Maissade, the execution by beating of Dorléan Joseph, the execution by machine gun of the daughters of the widow Célicour Rosier in the yard of their house, when their mother, aged 84, received two bullets in her thigh" and "Madame Garnier, widow of the notary who was killed by Lieut. Williams at Maissade, told Judge Advocate Dyer privately, on November 27, 1920, of the shooting of Madame Lumenesse, mother of eight children, by Lieut. Williams"; also see H. Pauléus Sannon, Sténio Vincent, and Perceval Thoby, *Nation*, October 1920; Sylvain, *Dix années*, 183–86. Accounts were first reported in the *Courier haitien*, December 18, 1920. Listed in the open letter written by the Union Patriotique in *The Nation*, vol. 112, no. 2916, (May 25, 1921: 767–75).

95. Balch, *Occupied Haiti*, 126.

96. H. Pauléus Sannon, Sténio Vincent, and Perceval Thoby, *The Nation*, October 1920. Also see Sylvain, *Dix années de lutte pour la liberté*, 183–86; ". . . execution of Madame Eucharice Cadichon at Mamon . . . the execution of Madam Prévoit with a baby of several months at 'Savane à Lingue' . . . Hanging of Fabre Yoyo from a mango tree; [and] On Jan 30 some marines . . . killed a pregnant woman at a place called Thomans."

97. Shannon, *Jean Price-Mars*, 54. Also see Assistant Secretary to NAACP to its branches, July 28, 1920, and James Weldon Johnson to Hon. Warren G. Harding, October 27, 1920, file C 325, NAACP Papers, Manuscripts Division, LOC.

98. President Harding was not inaugurated until March 4, 1921.

99. Millery Polyné explains that some African Americans took some time to support Haiti because of their self-interests and their own concerns that Haiti's hardships as a "Black" nation would reflect poorly on US African Americans who were embattled in a fight for citizenship and civil rights in the United States. However, the violations on Haitian sovereignty were too grave to ignore. See Polyné, *From Douglass to Duvalier*.

100. Johnson and Sylvain were allies and friends since the early days of the occupation. In his book *Dix années de lutte*, Sylvain credits Johnson with supporting his (Black) nationalist vision and encouraging him to start the Union Patriotique.

101. Giddings, *When and Where I Enter*, 121.

102. Mary Church Terrell Papers, box 102–12, "Organizational Affiliations, A–N, folder 239, "International Council of Women of the Darker Races," Mooreland-Springarn (MS), Howard University, Washington, D.C. The largest and most sustained international membership were women living in Haiti. There were four women from Haiti, including founders Theodora Holly, and executive member Mme. Charles Dubé.

103. Holly, "Haytian Girl," 203–10.

104. Edwards, *Practice of Diaspora*, 122,156. Edwards calls these spaces "black communal space." See also Nicholls, *From Desselines to Duvalier*, 158.

105. Letter from to Theodora Holly to Margaret Washington, June 14, 1923, Mary Church Terrell Papers, MS.

106. Marshall Papers, "Women of Haiti," MS.

107. Jean Joseph School Brochure, Layle Lane Papers, MS. The school focused on the "special production and sale of active products and the fabrication of native materials into paper; baskets; hats; water jugs"; and "other useful materials."

108. Letter from Harriet G. Marshall to Theodore Roosevelt, June 30, 1927, Marshall Papers, box 112–2, C, folder 82: Correspondence-Haiti-R to W, MS. Rosina Jean Joseph also explained, "It is important to initiate young girls to the basic principles of housekeeping that are the foundation of the good and healthy family life. They will learn to properly do the work that is becoming of a women, suggesting to them the noble ambition of becoming a 'mama' one day. They would learn how to wash, iron, and cook without thinking. To this last point, we will never know enough how much influence one 'good broth' can have on husbands."

109. Letter from Rosina Jean Joseph to Mrs. John M. Gleen, President of the American Association for Organizing Family Social Work, Marshall Papers, MS.

110. Layle Lane Papers, MS.

111. Letter from Addie Hunton to Gibbs Marshall, Marshall Papers, folder 79, "Correspondence—Haiti D to H," June 19, 1926, MS.

112. Sylvain-Bouchereau, *Haiti et ses femmes*, 81.

113. Letter from Perceval Thoby to W. E. B. Du Bois, September 22, 1926, Special Collections and the University Archives, University of Massachusetts Amherst Libraries.

114. Gendarmerie d'Haiti 1915–1926, General Correspondences, October 18, 1924, RG 127, NARA I.

115. The Forbes commission members were Chairman W. Cameron Forbes, Henry P. Fletcher, Elie Vezina, James Kerney, and William Allen White. Hoover also commissioned a second commission that included African American representatives. See a conversation about the Moton Commission in Polyné, *From Douglass to Duvalier*.

116. Harold N. Denny, "Haitian Women Pray That We Quit Island: Lead Liberty March," *New York Times*, March 3, 1930, 1. Also see Schmidt, *United States Occupation of Haiti*, 208–9; Shannon, "U.S. Commission," 60; Sylvain-Bouchereau, *Haiti et ses femmes*, 81.

117. "La manifestation d'hier, cérémonie religieuse et procession patriotique," *Le Nouvelliste*, March 3, 1930, 1.

118. "Opposition du gouvernement la manifestation féminine d'hier intéressante interview de Mme Perceval Thoby," *Le Nouvelliste*, March 1930, 1.

119. "Opposition du gouvernement," *Le Nouvelliste*, March 1930, 1.

120. Dominique, "Mme Ghislaine Charlier, écrivaine et veuve de l'historien Étienne Charlier (1)," *Face à l'opinion*, March 14, 1997, Port-au-Prince, Haiti.

121. Ménard, "Occupied Novels."

122. Francis, *Fictions of Feminine Citizenship*, 8.

A Bridge

1. *Le Nouvelliste*, August 5, 1925, 1.

2. Sylvain, *Cric?Crac!Krik?Krak!*, 6.

3. *Le Nouvelliste*, August 6, 1935, 1.

4. Gendarmerie d'Haiti 1915–1926, General Correspondences, "Morning Intell. Reports to American High Commissioner," July–September, August 6, 1925, RG 127, NARA I.

5. *Le Nouvelliste*, August 6, 1925, 1.

6. *Le Nouvelliste*, August 5, 1925, 1

7. *La Poste*, August 6, 1925, no. 22, NARA I.

8. Gendarmerie d'Haiti 1915–1926, General Correspondences, "Morning Intell. Reports to American High Commissioner," July–September, August 6, 1925, RG 127, NARA I.

9. *Le Nouvelliste*, August 6, 1935, 2.

10. Here I am thinking about how grief and loss distort time. In a conversation with a Haitian poet about the tenth anniversary of the earthquake, we were discussing the people who died. At one moment we could not remember if a particular person died in the earthquake or several years after. In trying to figure it out, she said, "In my mind, everyone who died in the last ten years died in the earthquake."

11. Comhaire 1984, Suzanne Comhaire-Sylvain Papers, SUA.

12. Comhaire 1984, Suzanne Comhaire-Sylvain Papers, SUA.

13. Comhaire 1984, Suzanne Comhaire-Sylvain Papers, SUA. Her brother Normil Sylvain died in 1929, and her mother, Eugénie Malbranche-Sylvain, died in 1931.

14. "Exercises at the Alvernia Auditorium, Entertainment by Faculty and Students of the Immaculate Conception Academy," *Gleaner*, July 17, 1925, 6.

15. Comhaire-Sylvain, unpublished notes, 1937, SUA.

16. Comhaire-Sylvain, 1938, SUA.

17. Comhaire-Sylvain, "Mort et funérailles," 223–24.

18. These essays were four of the five essays that she wrote in LVDF over the course of its production.

19. Comhaire-Sylvain, "A propos du vocabulaire des croyances paysannes," *La Voix des Femmes* 3, no. 29 (February 1938): 6–7; Comhaire-Sylvain, "Adelmonde," *La Voix des Femmes* 3, no. 30 (March 1938); Comhaire-Sylvain, "Quelques proverbs sur la Femme," *La Voix des Femmes* 5, no. 37 (March 1939).

20. Danticat, *Art of Death*, 6. Karla F. C. Holloway's work also considers "the particular vulnerability to an untimely death in the United States intimately affects how black culture both represents itself and is represent," that is, navigated through the African American process of being "funeralized"; Holloway, *Passed On*, 2–3.

Chapter Two

1. "A Haiti, la femme n'a pas de droits," *La Presse* (Montreal), December 20, 1937.

2. "A Haiti, la femme n'a pas de droits," *La Presse* (Montreal), December 20, 1937. Madeleine Sylvain remarked, "Les femmes haïtiennes n'ont aucun droit. La loi nous traite comme si nous étions des enfants, des criminelles ou des folles."

3. Brisson, "Situation juridique et constitutionelle," 22.

4. "A Haiti, la femme n'a pas de droits," *La Presse* (Montreal), December 20, 1937.

5. "Mlle M. Sylvain parle du folklore haïtien," *La Presse*, Montreal: December 22, 1937. "L'illustration Nouvelle," December 24, 1937; "Le Canada—Montreal, Des Montrealais partent en croisiere pour Haiti," December 23, 1937; "Le Canada—Montreal, Mlle Madeleine Sylvain au dejeuner du Jeune Barreau," December 22, 1937, box 1, folder 4, SUA.

6. Sylvain-Bouchereau, "Nous revoici," *La Voix des Femmes* 9, no. 1 (January 11, 1947): 1.

7. Sylvain-Bouchereau, *Haiti et ses femmes*, 82.

8. Sylvain, "Feminist Movement in Haiti," 321.

9. Sylvain, "Feminist Movement in Haiti," 321.

10. Sylvain, "Feminist Movement in Haiti," 10.

11. Charlier, interviewed by author, September 23, 2010, Montreal, Canada.

12. George Sylvain died in 1925 and Eugénie Malbranche Sylvain died in December 1931. For more on the Sylvain legacy, see Sylvain, *Dix années de lutte*, 192.

13. Sylvain-Bouchereau, *Haiti et ses femmes*; Manigat, *Etre femme en Haiti*, 282.

14. *Premier Congres National des Femmes Haïtiennes*, Bibliothéque Nationale d'Haïti, Port-au-Prince, Haïti (1950), 1–2.

15. Candelario, Mayes, and Sanders, "Hispaniola Feminisms," Panel Presentation of Collaborative Project at Transnational Hispaniola Conference II, Rutgers University, New Brunswick, N.J., 2012; Candelario, "'When the Time Comes."

16. Mayes, "Why Dominican Feminism Moved"; Candelario, "'When the Time Comes."

17. Mayes, "Why Dominican Feminism Moved," 353; Candelario, "'When the Time Comes."

18. See García-Peña, *Borders of Dominicanidad*; Wucker, *Why the Cocks Fight*.

19. Charlier, interviewed by author, September 23, 2010, Montreal, Canada. Over the following three decades, LFAS women collaborated with women throughout the region, including Puerto Rico, Jamaica, Cuba, and the United States, but there is little evidence to suggest that any further formal collaboration between women's organizations across Hispaniola occurred until the late twentieth century.

20. Sylvain-Bouchereau, *Haiti et ses femmes*, 82.

21. Sylvain-Bouchereau, *Haiti et ses femmes*, 82–83. The exact membership numbers and demographics at this point in the organization's history are unknown.

22. Sylvain, *Haiti et ses femmes*, 82.

23. Charlier, interviewed by author, September 23, 2010, Montreal, Canada.

24. Smith, *Red and Black in Haiti*, 28. Also see Nicholls, *From Dessalines to Duvalier*, 165–66.

25. Nicholls, *From Dessalines to Duvalier*.

26. Smith, *Red and Black in Haiti*, 15, 28.

27. Smith, *Red and Black in Haiti* 15.

28. Nicholls, *From Dessalines to Duvalier*, 159; Smith, *Red and Black in Haiti*, 8.

29. Smith, *Red and Black in Haiti*, 26

30. Smith, *Red and Black in Haiti*, 18.

31. Charlier, interviewed by author, September 23, 2010, Montreal, Canada. Charlier described her grandmother's library. The books in the library were Charlier's first introduction to leftist thought.

32. Sylvain-Bouchereau, *Haiti et ses femmes*, 83.

33. Sylvain-Bouchereau, *Haiti et ses femmes*, 83.

34. Sylvain-Bouchereau, *Haiti et ses femmes*, 83.

35. Sylvain-Bouchereau, *Haiti et ses femmes*, 83.

36. See Trouillot, "Culture, Color, and Politics in Haiti." Trouillot gives particular attention to the historical shift in Haitian politics during the rise of François Duvalier that no longer exempted women from physical political repression and violence.

37. Sylvain-Bouchereau, *Haiti et ses femmes*, 82.

38. Sylvain-Bouchereau, *Haiti et ses femmes*, 82–83.

39. Interview (anonymous) by author, May 9, 2011, Pétionville, Haiti. A prominent member of both the Haitian feminist and communist movements explained that Hudicourt was extremely influential in the philosophical underpinnings and governing of the organization.

40. Sylvain-Bouchereau, *Haiti et ses femmes*, 83.

41. Sylvain-Bouchereau, *Haiti et ses femmes*, 84.

42. Sylvain-Bouchereau, *Haiti et ses femmes*, 84.

43. Sylvain-Bouchereau, *Haiti et ses femmes*, 169–81. Sylvain-Boucheareau dedicates a large section to naming the professional and scholastic achievements of Haitian women. Most of the women mentioned were also officers and members of LFAS.

44. Verna, *Haiti and the Uses of America*, 9.

45. Smith, *Red and Black in Haiti*, 20.

46. Nicholls, *From Dessalines to Duvalier*, 168. The men were known as *les Trois D.*

47. Smith, *Red and Black in Haiti*, 26.

48. Nicholls, *From Dessalines to Duvalier*, 169.

49. Smith, *Red and Black in Haiti*, 26.

50. Sylvain-Bouchereau, *Haiti et ses femmes*, 84.

51. Sylvain-Bouchereau, "La femme haïtienne lutte," 4.

52. Sylvain, "Séances d'études de la L.F.A.S.," *La Voix des Femmes* 6, no. 46 (February 1940): 2.

53. "Ligue Feminine d'Action Sociale," *Le Nouvelliste*, June 12, 1934, p. 4.

54. Price-Mars, *Ainsi parla l'oncle*, 46.

55. Price-Mars, *Vocation d'elite*. Price-Mars was particularly critical of elite women and men's material consumption and "mutual vanity."

56. Price-Mars, *Vocation d'elite*, 99.

57. Price-Mars, *Vocation d'elite*, 97

58. Price-Mars, *Vocation d'elite*, 122.

59. Price-Mars, *Vocation d'elite*, 122.

60. "Ligue Feminine d'Action Sociale," *Le Nouvelliste*, June 12, 1934, p. 4.

61. Price-Mars, *Vocation d'elite*, 122–23.

62. Price-Mars, *Vocation d'elite*, 99.

63. Esther Dartigue, "Chapter Five: Haiti, (Part 1/1931–1934)," unpublished manuscript, John Dartigue personal collection.

64. "L'education feminine en Haiti," clipping from John Dartigue Personal Archive.

65. In the years leading up to his appointment as minister of rural education under the Élie Lescot administration in 1941, Dartigue studied education throughout the region. During his tenure in the United States, he traveled to Alabama and studied the Booker T. Washington educational style and the inner workings of the Tuskegee University "Machine." For more on Dartigue and education, see Polyné, *From Douglass to Duvalier*, 78–79. Polyné points out, however, Dartigue's approach to education of the peasantry was "inherently paternalistic." He writes, "Haitian and U.S. Black elites advanced Western ideals of government—and supported mechanisms of the state, such as schools, because these fundamentals gave the appearance of an orderly, reasoned and civilized relationship between centralized authority and its citizenry." Also in the late twentieth century and early twenty-first century the idea of trade education was opposed by some Haitian feminists who saw trade education as an institutionalized

separation between classes that presumed that a class of people could only do one thing. See Charles, "Reflections on Being Machann ak Machandiz."

66. Polyné, *From Douglass to Duvalier*.

67. Dartigue, "Chapter Five."

68. Dantès Bellegarde Collection, Series A, Mooreland-Springharn Archives, Howard University, Washington, D.C.

69. Nicholls, *From Dessalines to Duvalier*, 176. Nicholls calls Bellegarde one of the "prophets of political liberalism." In particular, Bellegarde maintained that "it is to France that Haiti owes its cultural debt, not Africa." See Smith, *Red and Black in Haiti*, 27.

70. The contrasts between Bellegarde and Price-Mars were likened to the public juxtaposition of W. E. B. DuBois and Booker T. Washington.

71. Urban newspapers regularly discussed opinions on *indigénisme* versus liberalism. See *Le Nouvelliste*, June 11, 1934, p. 2.

72. Bellegarde-Smith, "Haitian Studies Association Plenary Address," 232.

73. Esther Dartigue, "Chapter Five." Also see Charles, "Popular Images," 175.

74. Du Bois, "Of Mr. Booker T. Washington and Others."

75. Meetings were regularly held in Alice Garoute's home.

76. Madeleine Sylvain, "Prononcé par la présidente de la L.F.A.S. pour l'inauguration du Congrés d'Assistance Sociale," *La Voix des Femmes* 5, no. 52 (October–November 1940): 3.

77. Fernande Bellegarde, "Rapport de la secrétaire generale," *La Voix des Femmes* 1, no. 2 (November 1935): 6.

78. Sylvain, "Notre Conception," *La Voix des Femmes* 1, no. 10 (July 1936): 4.

79. See congratulatory notes and newspaper clippings celebrating LFAS members, Suzanne Comhaire-Sylvain Papers, SUA.

80. Dartigue, "Le feminisme en Haiti 'Il était une fois quatre sœurs,'" 7.

81. Dartigue, "Le feminisme en Haiti 'Il était une fois quatre sœurs,'" 7.

82. Brochure produced by LFAS after 1946.

83. Balch, *Occupied Haiti*, 86–89. According to this report, 75 percent of the medical cases in the country were syphilis and yaws cases. This yaws epidemic is the same health crisis that Dr. François Duvalier studied during medical school in Haiti and later at the University of Michigan. Duvalier earned his nickname "Papa Doc" for his work with yaws patients in the Haitian countryside.

84. Comhaire-Sylvain Papers, scrapbook personal belongings, SUA.

85. Comhaire-Sylvain Papers, SUA.

86. Woodson, "Review." Comhaire-Sylvain wrote the first Haitian Creole–language dictionary, *Le Creole haitien* (Port-au-Prince, 1936). In an obituary, Comhaire-Sylvain was remembered as a leading scholar in "African and Afro-Caribbean scholarship." Comhaire-Sylvain Papers, "Obituary: Suzanne Comhaire," SUA.

87. Comhaire-Sylvain, *Contes du pays d'Haiti*, 1938; Comhaire-Sylvain, "A propos du vocabulaire des croyances paysannes" (1938); Comhaire-Sylvain, "Créole haïtien, morphologie et syntaxe" (1936). Book manuscripts and field notes from Sophia Smith Collection, Smith College.

88. "Autour du feminisme," *Le Nouvelliste*, no. 13652 (July 30, 1935: 1, 6), 1.

89. Print media were heavily monitored during the U.S. occupation, and many journalists and writers were imprisoned for their criticism of the intervention. See Layle Lane, "An

American Woman in Haiti," box "Layle Lane Additions," Layle Lane Papers, Moorland-Springarn Archives, Howard University, Washington, D.C. In "A Visit to Prison," Lane writes that she visited several journalists who were held for months because of their unfavorable editorials about President Louis Borno (1922–30) and the U.S. Marines.

90. From 1936 to the late 1940s, various members of LFAS conducted extended field research in rural towns and in Port-au-Prince documenting women's work routines, cultural practices, and family structure.

91. Sylvain-Bouchereau, "Nous revoici," *La Voix des Femmes* (January 1947), 1.

92. Sylvain-Bouchereau, "Nous revoici," 1.

93. Sylvain, *Haiti et ses femmes*, 85.

94. Madeleine G. Sylvain, "Message Aux Membres du Congrès de la Presse Latine," *La Voix des Femmes* 9, no. 1 (February 1936): 2.

95. The international recognition was an honor to the newspaper editors, Madeleine Sylvain, Alice Garoute, Jeanne Perez, and Cléante Desgraves Valcin.

96. Jeanne Perez, "La Semaine Littéraire du Cap et le Congrès de la Presse Haitienne," *La Voix des Femmes* 11, no. 17–18 (February–March 1937): 5.

97. Jeanne Perez, "Chronique féministe: Autour de la conférence de Mr. TH. Vilmenay," *La Voix des Femmes* 11, no. 19 (April 1937): 3.

98. Trouillot, *Silencing the Past*, 48–49.

99. Perez, "Chronique Féministe," *La Voix des Femmes* 1, no. 11 (August 1936): 3.

100. "Faits, Glanes, and Echos," *La Voix des Femmes* 1, no. 2 (November 1935): 11.

101. Joseph-Gabriel, *Reimagining Liberation*; Blain, *To Turn the World Over*.

102. Desirée Rochat, "Archiving Black Diasporic Activism," 302–3.

103. Denis and Duvalier, "La civilization haïtienne."

104. Madeleine Sylvain, "Soyons fiers d'etre Haitiens," *La Voix des Femmes* 1, no. 2 (November 1935): 2.

105. "Nos conférences—Le conflit Italo-Ethiopien," *La Voix des Femmes* 1, no. 10 (July 1936): 10.

106. Jeanne Perez, "Chronique féministe: Notre infirmière," *La Voix des Femmes* 1, no. 6 (March 1936): 3.

107. Hine, *Black Women in White*, 13.

108. Perez, "Chronique féministe," 3.

109. Perez, "Chronique féministe," 3.

110. Fernande Bellegarde, "Assemblée Générale du 7 Juin 1936, Ligue Féminine d'Action Sociale," *La Voix des Femmes* 1, no. 10 (July 1936): 6.

111. Valcin, *Cruelle destinée*; Valcin, *La blanche négresse*.

112. Madeleine Sylvain, "Notre conception du féminisme," *La Voix des Femmes* 1, no. 10 (July 1936): 5.

113. Valcin, "Compte-rendu de la séance inaugurale de notre Filiale de Saint-Marc, 15 Septembre 1935," *La Voix des Femmes* 1, no. 2 (November 1935): 8.

114. Valcin, "Compte-rendu de la séance inaugurale," 8.

115. LFAS did not have a formal headquarters until the 1940s on l'Avenue Marie Jeanne in Port-au-Prince. The LFAS met in members' homes and in public gathering locations.

116. See *Le Nouvelliste*, *Maintenant*, and *Le Matin*.

117. "Celles qui dirigent 'La Voix des Femmes,'" *La Voix des Femmes* 1, no. 1 (October 1935): 23.

118. "Bienvenue," *La Voix des Femmes* 11, no. 19 (April 1937): 4.

119. Comhaire-Sylvain, "A propos du vocabulaire des croyances paysannes, *La Voix des Femmes* 3, no. 29 (February 1938): 6–7.

120. Comhaire-Sylvain, "A propos du vocabulaire des croyances paysannes," 6–7.

121. Woodson, "Review," *Journal of Negro History*, July 1937, vol. 22, no. 3: 369–72, 369.

122. Woodson, "Review," 371.

123. Comhaire-Sylvain, "Notre paysanne: Adelsia," *La Voix des Femmes* (1938); Adelsia danced, and "what pleases her is the footwork performed alone under the tree while the drums roar and the lwas ride over the faithful."

124. Comhaire-Sylvain, "Notre paysanne," 8.

125. Comhaire-Sylvain, unpublished manuscript, Suzanne Comhaire-Sylvain Papers, SUA.

126. Trouillot, "Culture, Color, and Politics in Haiti."1996; N'Zengou-Tayo, "Fanm Poto Mitan," 118–142.

127. The marriage tax was repealed January 15, 1945 under president Élie Lescot.

128. Comhaire-Sylvain, "Notre paysanne."

129. Comhaire-Sylvain, "Adelmonde- Conte haitien," 1938, SUA.

130. Thomas, *Political Life*; Rochat, "Archiving Black Diasporic Activism."

131. Sylvain, "Séances d'études de la L.F.A.S.," 2.

132. Sylvain, "Séances d'études de la L.F.A.S.," 2.

133. Suzanne Comhaire-Sylvain, "Les loisirs des fillettes de Port-au-Prince," *La voix des femmes* 6, no. 46 (February 1940), 10.

134. Comhaire-Sylvain, "Les loisirs des fillettes de Port-au-Prince," 10.

135. Comhaire-Sylvain, "Les loisirs des fillettes de Port-au-Prince," 10.

136. Comhaire-Sylvain, "Les loisirs des fillettes de Port-au-Prince," 10.

137. Comhaire-Sylvain, "Les loisirs des fillettes de Port-au-Prince," 10.

138. Hippolyte, "Les loisirs de la jeunesse feminine," *La Voix des Femmes* 6, no. 46 (February 1940): 8.

139. Hippolyte, "Les loisirs de la jeunesse feminine," 10.

140. *La Voix des Femmes* (1940) (Port-au-Prince).

141. Sylvain-Bouchereau, *Haiti et ses femmes*, 85.

142. Letters from Madeleine Sylvain-Bouchereau to Suzanne Comhaire Sylvain, Suzanne Comhaire-Sylvain Papers, SUA.

143. Jeanne Sylvain, Letter to Suzanne Comhaire-Sylvain, January 27, 1944, SUA. *Le foyer* was also later called the *Le foyer ouvrier*.

144. Madeleine Sylvain-Bouchereau, "Une année de travail social," *La Voix des* (December 1943): 1.

145. Valcin, "Stylons nos domestiques," *La Voix des Femmes*, 2, 17–18 (February—March 1937): 10.

146. Davies, *Left of Karl Marx*, 42–43.

147. Ulysse, *Downtown Ladies*; Carby, *Reconstructing Womanhood*; Hartman, *Wayward Lives, Beautiful Experiments*.

148. Madeleine Sylvain, "Prononcé par la présidente de la L.F.A.S. pour l'inauguration du Congrés d'Assistance Sociale," *La Voix des Femmes* 5, no. 52 (October–November 1940): 3.

149. Sylvain-Bouchereau, "Une Année de Travail Social," *La Voix des Femmes* (December 1943): 2.

150. Sylvain, "Notre Conception du Féminisme," *La Voix des Femmes* 1, 10 (July 1936): 1.

A Pilgrimage

1. Madeleine Sylvain, "Notre Citadelle," *La Voix des Femmes* 1, no. 12 (September 1936): 1.

2. Jeanne Perez, "Pèlerinage," *La Voix des Femmes* 1, no. 12 (September 1936): 3.

Ainsi, quand tu voudras, me dit-elle communier avec nos aïeux par la pensée grande et l'immense vouloir, gravis un dimanche, la pente escarpée du Bonnet-à-l'Eveque. Au pied du Donjon respecté, arrête toi un moment, lève la tête et regarde le rêve héroïque d'un cœur de nègre écrit dans ces hauts mars qu'un siècle et plus ne peut détruire. Une émotion jusqu'alors inconnue te rendra ta fierté perdue. Comme la Patrie, la Citadelle a été lézardée, blessée par l'orage. Ses lessions sont apparentes peut-être, mais tout ce qu'il y a de sublime dans ces choses forgées par l'héroïsme nègre défie le temps et les vautours. Elles vivront parce qu'elles ont été les pensées les plus belles de notre vie, parce qu'elles sont notre raison d'être de dignes héritiers, parce qu'elles représentent ce qui ne meurt pas: une idée noble. Comme le papillon, amant de la lumière, revient à la flamme brûler son aile, si tu y vas un jour, tu y retourneras, inlassablement, retremper ton âme à la source vive de la foi des ancêtres. L'œuvre est titanesque. Qu'avons-nous fait depuis? Est-ce que les géants procréent des nains? L'aigle insolent s'est incliné, sidéré, devant cette prodigieuse conception. Le cerveau nègre, est-il déjà si dégénéré qu'il y soit absent toute présomption?

Que nos fils aillent en pèlerinage d'amour de la Patrie, vers ce majestueux présent qu'un Roi bronzé nous légua; qu'ils montent, sur les traces de la Reine éplorée, des Princes et des Comtes, le grand escalier vétuste qui vit passer une dernier fois le cadavre du Monarque bien-aimé, le Roi Christophe; l'escalier qui connut la vie active, les tourments, et toutes les victoires de Celui qui emporta, jusqu'au tombeau, le rêve d'une Haïti grandiose et magnifique! Que nos fils saluent les ancêtres dans les vestiges de la gloire d'hier, et qu'ils sentent monter en leurs cœurs le désir d'être de grands, de bons haïtiens!

3. Holly, "Christening of a Haytian," 348.

4. Patton, "Othermothers as Elders." Other literature about Black mothering, politics, and feminist theory include Bambara, *Black Woman*; Walker, *In Search of Our Mothers Gardens*; Griffin, "That the Mothers May Soar"; Gumbs, Martens, and Williams, *Revolutionary Mothering*.

5. Gumbs, Martens, and Williams, *Revolutionary Mothering*, 9.

6. Butterflies are usually diurnal or day-flying.

7. Kawahara, Plotkin, Hamilton, et al., "Diel Behavior in Moths and Butterflies."

8. Thompson, *Shine*.

9. Jeanne Perez, *Sanite Belair: Drame historique en trois tableaux*, Petion-Ville, Haiti: Edition de *La Semeuse*, 1942; *Le Nouvelliste*, August 11, 1942.

10. "Ils étaient légion ceux qui avaient honte de leur identité," *Le Nouvelliste*, September 26, 2008.

11. Scherpf, "Emerante de Pradines," 166.

12. Perez, *Sanité Bélair*, 1942.

13. Gumbs, Martens, and Williams, *Revolutionary Mothering*, 10.

14. "Jeanne Perez, Noted Haitian Writer Here for Lectures," *New York Amsterdam News*, November 22, 1947, 8.

15. "Jeanne Perez," 8.

16. Martelly, *L'enfant Gazelle*; Jackson, "That's the Way Love Goes."

17. Danticat. *Breath, Eyes, Memory*, 234. Danticat repeats this phrase throughout the novel. To be "free" is read as unburdened.

Chapter Three

1. Jeanne Sylvain to Suzanne Sylvain, November 30, 1943. Sylvain called the simple cold a coryza, which is inflammation, caused by a cold, of the mucous membrane in the nose.

2. Holland and Collins, "Influenza Epidemic," 1132.

3. Jeanne Sylvain to Suzanne Sylvain, January 6, 1944: "C'est devenu un fait-divers banal dans les journaux que l'annonce d'un décès par suite de misère physiologique et de sous-alimentation ou celle d'une naissance dans la rue. Et depuis ces derniers mois, on commence à y trouver des infanticides."

4. "L'Enfance Abandonnée," *Le Nouvelliste*, January 6, 1944, 4.

5. "Nouvelles Rapides," *Haïti-Journal*, January 7, 1944, 2.

6. Jeanne Sylvain to Suzanne Sylvain, January 6, 1944. Sylvain-Bouchereau, *Haiti et ses femmes*, 160.

7. Jeanne Sylvain to Suzanne Sylvain, July 24, 1943, SUA.

8. Over the course of the 1940s the Sylvain siblings lived significant amounts of time outside the country, including in the Belgian Congo, New Jersey, and Argentina (Suzanne), Philadelphia (Madeleine and Yvonne), Montreal, New York (Yvonne and Suzanne), and Ohio and Ethiopia (Pierre).

9. Jeanne Sylvain to Chers Amis, January 27, 1944, SUA.

10. Smith, *Red and Black in Haiti*, 44.

11. Jeanne Sylvain, Letter to family, August 1945, SUA.

12. Dupuy, Haiti: From Revolutionary Slaves to Powerless Citizens, 5.

13. Smith, Bernal, Schwartz, Whitt, Christman, Donnelly, Wheatley, et al. Coping with Vicarious Trauma," 4.

14. Jeanne Sylvain, Letter to Suzanne Comhaire-Sylvain, August 9, 1945, SUA.

15. Jeanne Sylvain was also editor of *La Voix des Femmes* and coordinated most of the LFAS programming.

16. Comhaire-Sylvain and Comhaire, "Urban Stratification in Haiti."

17. Comhaire-Sylvain and Comhaire, "Urban Stratification in Haiti," 182.

18. Comhaire-Sylvain and Comhaire, "Urban Stratification in Haiti," 179.

19. Jackson, *Thin Description*, 14.

20. Comhaire-Sylvain and Comhaire, "Urban Stratification in Haiti," 182.

21. Comhaire-Sylvain and Comhaire, "Urban Stratification in Haiti," 183.

22. Comhaire-Sylvain and Comhaire, "Urban Stratification in Haiti," 186.

23. Comhaire-Sylvain and Comhaire, "Urban Stratification in Haiti," 186.

24. United States Interamerican Affairs Institute, *Agricultural Progress in Haiti, Summary Report 1944–49*, 3. Estimated national population 3 to 3.5 million, one-tenth living in urban communities, and Port-au-Prince population estimated to be 125,000.

25. Comhaire-Sylvain and Comhaire, "Urban Stratification in Haiti," 185.

26. Charles, "Poor and Working-Class Haitian Women's Discourses," 177.

27. Dupuy, *Haiti: From Revolutionary Slaves to Powerless Citizens*, 56.

28. Sylvain-Bouchereau, *Lecture Haitienne, La Famille Renaud* (Livre I & II), 1944.

29. McKittrick, *Demonic Grounds*, xvi, xvii.

30. Comhaire-Sylvain and Comhaire, "Urban Stratification in Haiti," 185.

31. Comhaire-Sylvain and Comhaire, "Urban Stratification in Haiti," 181.

32. Report of the Justice Committee—The Senate of the Republic, *La Voix des Femmes* 2, no. 19 (April 1937), 4 & 6.

33. Davies, *Left of Karl Marx*, 45.

34. Correspondence between Yvonne Sylvain and Sadie Alexander, 1946, Sadie Alexander Papers, University of Pennsylvania.

35. "Report of the Justice Committee—The Senate of the Republic," *La Voix des Femmes* 2, no. 19 (April 1937), 4.

36. Suzanne Comhaire-Sylvain, unpublished manuscript, Suzanne Comhaire-Sylvain Papers, SUA.

37. Neptune-Anglade, *L'Autre moitié du développement*.

38. Lamour, "Between Intersectionality and Coloniality," 143.

39. Lamour, "Between Intersectionality and Coloniality," 143.

40. N'Zengou-Tayo, "'Fanm Se Poto Mitan,'" 123; Charles, "Reflections on Being Machann ak Machandiz," 121; Mintz, "Market Women," Suzanne Comhaire-Sylvain Papers, SUA. Many peasant women had governance over their wages, and some chose to maintain open marriages such as *viv avek* (live with) or *plasaj* in order to maintain economic independence. For more on Haitian women and peasant life, see Dartigue *L'enseignement en Haïti*, (1939); Bastien, *Le Paysan haïtien et sa famille*; Mintz, "Nana of Duverget: Market Woman of Haiti," *Haiti Sun* 7, no. 22 (February 24, 1959): 4 &13; Pascal-Trouillot, "Droit et privilèges de la femme"; Lowenthal, "Labor, Sexuality and the Conjugal Contract in Rural Haiti."

41. Comhaire-Sylvain, "Courtship, Marriage, and Plasaj in Kenscoff," 215–16.

42. Comhaire-Sylvain, "Courtship, Marriage, and Plasaj in Kenscoff," 227.

43. For example, she recounts that "at Kenscoff about seventy years ago, the girl's father would bless the plasaj before the party began. To do so he would place his daughter's hand in her lover's and would bring them before his ogatwa (the small temporary alter of a loa). He would begin by lighting a candle there, and then would pour some water and wheat flour on the ground, turning his back to the setting sun and asking his loa and his dead ancestors to protect and help the couple." In the 1950s she witnesses a "water ceremony" during a wedding, and when she asked where it came from, no one knew, or they refused to tell.

44. Comhaire-Sylvain, "Courtship, Marriage, and Plasaj in Kenscoff," 220.

45. Comhaire-Sylvain and Comhaire, "Urban Stratification," 400–401.

46. Report of the Justice Committee—The Senate of the Republic, *La Voix des Femmes* 2, no. 19 (April 1937): 4 & 6.

47. N'Zengou-Tayo, "'Fanm Se Poto Mitan,'" 123.

48. N'Zengou-Tayo, "'Fanm Se Poto Mitan,'" 122.

49. *Bulletin des lois et actes*, January 11, 1945, 204–5.

50. Élie Lescot, *Bulletin des lois et actes*, Republique d'Haiti Departement de la Justice (Port-au-Prince, 1945).

51. Élie Lescot, "Extrait du message adresse au peuple haitien par son exc. le president de la republique le 1er janvier 1945," *Statut des enfants naturels et etat civil des paysans* (Port-au-Prince: Imprimerie de l'etat, 1945), 3.

52. Allman and May, "Fertility," 513–17.

53. Dayan, *Haiti, History and the Gods*, 87.

54. Suzanne Comhaire-Sylvain, unpublished manuscript, Suzanne Comhaire-Sylvain Papers, SUA.

55. The 1944 child legitimacy law was another recall of the 1804 revolutionary period. The 1805 constitution of the nation stipulated that all children were equal under the law and citizens of the nation without distinction. But the status of child rested with the father's recognition, which was recorded on birth certificates.

56. Haitian women's rights activist Suzie Boisrond explains this sexual tiered relationship, which often left children ranked among each other. An illegitimate child could not make claims on property. In this way, class was not the only barrier to social mobility. Sex and sexual relationships could inform access to further power.

57. Élie Lescot, *Bulletin des lois et actes*, Republique d'Haiti Departement de la Justice (Port-au-Prince, 1945), 2.

58. Alexander, "Redrafting Morality," 133.

59. Republique d'Haiti Departement de la Justice, "Extrait du message adresse au peuple haitien par son exc. le president de la republique le 1er janvier 1945," *Statut des enfants naturels et etat civil des paysans* (Port-au-Prince: Imprimerie de l'etat, 1945). Lescot maintained that the law was a relic of the nation's colonial past, that the nation no longer needed a law that would make citizens born outside of marriage second-class citizens.

60. Findlay, *Imposing Decency*, 120–25. Eileen Findlay identifies a similar government strategy on the part of the United States in order to get Puerto Rican couples to legally marry at the turn of the twentieth century. There is no evidence to suggest that there was a significant decline in plasaj or other forms of noncontractual conjugal arrangements as a result of Lescot's marriage legislation. In fact, sociological studies from the 1940s through the 1970s consistently show that rural populations chose plasaj unions.

61. Charles, "Discourses," 175.

62. Charles, "Sexual Politics," 45.

63. Charles, "Discourses," 177.

64. Ghislaine Charlier, interviewed by author, September 23, 2010, Montreal, Canada.

65. Madeleine Sylvain-Bouchereau, Letter to Suzanne Comhaire-Sylvain, April 25, 1944, SUA.

66. Sylvain-Bouchereau, Letter to Suzanne Comhaire-Sylvain, June 26, 1944, SUA.

67. Sylvain-Bouchereau, *Haiti et ses femmes*, 92.

68. Sylvain-Bouchereau, *Haiti et ses femmes*, 92.

69. Sylvain-Bouchereau, *Haiti et ses femmes*, 93. *La Famille* was founded two years later on November 14, 1948.

70. They debated Article 8 of the Haitian Constitution, which maintained that "all Haitians of 18 years old had the right to politics."

71. Other members were *noiriste* sympathizers such as labor organizers and FRH vice presidents Daniel Fignolé and Juste Constant.

72. Smith, *Red and Black in Haiti*, 87.

73. Smith, *Red and Black in Haiti*, 92.

74. Sylvain-Bouchereau, *Haiti et ses femmes*, 87. Other men included Lélio Joseph, Georges O'Callagham, and Javigny Vauges.

75. Sylvain-Bouchereau, "Les droits des femmes," *La femme haitienne repond aux attaques formulées contre elle à L'Assemblée Constituante*, 5.

76. "La Séance du 9 Août de l'Assembée Constituante," *La femme haitienne repond aux attaques formulées contre elle à L'Assemblée Constituante*, 36.

77. Sylvain-Bouchereau, "Les droits des femmes," 5.

78. Sylvain-Bouchereau, "Les droits des femmes," 4.

79. "La Séance du 9 Août de l'Assembée Constituante," *La femme haitienne repond aux attaques formulées contre elle à L'Assemblée Constituante*, 29.

80. Sylvain-Bouchereau, "Les droits des femmes," 3.

81. Sylvain-Bouchereau, "Les droits des femmes," 4.

82. "La Séance du 9 Août de l'Assembée Constituante," *La femme haitienne repond aux attaques formulées contre elle à L'Assemblée Constituante*, 35. Castel Démesmin was deputé from Léogâne.

83. Madeleine Sylvain- Bouchereau, "Les droits des femmes," 3.

84. "Ladies Day," *Time*, March 27, 1950.

85. Garoute, "Lettre ouverte aux Président," *La femme haitienne repond aux attaques formulées contre elle à L'Assemblée Constituante*, 24.

86. Sylvain-Bouchereau, "Les droits des femmes," 3.

87. Smith, *Red and Black in Haiti*, 104.

88. Garoute, "Lettre ouverte aux Président," 20.

89. Sylvain-Bouchereau, "Les droits des femmes," *La femme haitienne repond aux attaques formulées contre elle à L'Assemblée Constituante*, 5. In an attempt to defend women against Démesmin and Saint-Lôt's accusations of Haitian women's hypersexuality, Hudicourt pointed at men: "In this country there are a multitude of children who do not know their father. Each Haitian is father of a string of children that he does not know. In each corner of the countryside you will meet a mother who will educate five children who do not know their father. I do not know what the statistics say, but in the education of children, the woman dominates. She can only give the education that she receives. This cannot continue. We must liberate her, educate her."

90. Sylvain-Bouchereau, "Les droits des femmes," *La femme haitienne repond aux attaques formulées contre elle à L'Assemblée Constituante*, 5.

91. Jean-Charles, "They Never Call It Rape," 5, 7. Also see Jean-Charles's discussion of "politicized-rape" in which she argues that "sexual violence as a facet of gender oppression and gender politics no matter what the situation surrounding the emergence" and that "seizure by the state also extends to the female body."

92. Alexander, "Redrafting Morality," 133.

93. Sylvain-Bouchereau, "Les droits des femmes," 7.

94. Carolle Charles's body of scholarship establishes a close relationship between women's sexual practices and citizenship. See Charles, "Popular Images"; "Reflections on Being *Machann ak Machandiz*," 122. For more the significance of sex and sexuality, rather than exclusively gender, in Caribbean studies, see Kempadoo, *Sexing the Caribbean*, 28–29.

95. Alexander, "Redrafting Morality," 137.

96. *La Voix des Femmes*, 1947.

97. Kempadoo, *Sexing the Caribbean*, 63. Trouillot also argues, "The point is that the state's importance came not from the power vested in individual regimes but from its role in the extraction and distribution of peasant surplus." Trouillot, *Haiti, State against Nation*, 83.

98. Charles, "Reflections on Being Machann ak Machandiz," 118.

99. Kempadoo, *Sexing the Caribbean*, 59.

100. N'Zengou-Tayo, "'Fanm Se Poto Mitan,'" 126.

101. Sylvain-Bouchereau, *Haiti et ses femmes*, 83.

102. "Conference au PSP," *La Voix des Femmes* 9, no. 14 (August 9, 1947). Here, the literature situates communism and the PSP together. In this contest she is referring to the PSP and not the PCH. *La Voix des Femmes* was reinstated in 1947.

103. Alice Garoute also wrote an open letter to the president, vice-president, members of the constitutional assembly, and Haitian women.

104. While the 1946 revolution was a success in overthrowing the Lescot government, the sustainability of the movement was in question almost as soon as Lescot was escorted out of the country. The members of the multipurposed and philosophically based collective of Black nationalists, *indiginists*, labor, and Marxist movements almost immediately retreated back to their own agendas and philosophical concerns. Moreover, different factions within movements were splintering off in an effort to fill the vacuum of power left empty in Lescot's departure. See Smith, *Red and Black in Haiti*, 88.

Chapter Four

1. Letter to Mes chers amis from Jeanne, April 12, 1944. Stanford University Archives (SUA).

2. Letter to Mes Chere Amis from Madeleine Sylvain, April 8, 1944, SUA.

3. Letter to Mes chers amis from Jeanne, April 12, 1944.

4. LVDF, February–March 1937, Edith Penzo, "Universal Exposition of Paris." For other examples of these kind of international displays of Black life at exhibitions, see Smith, *Photography on the Color Line*.

5. Verna, *Haiti and the Uses*, 84–85. Also see Ramsey, *Spirits and the Law*.

6. "Pan American Day," *La Voix des Femmes* 2, no. 19 (April 14, 1937).

7. Towns, "Inter-American Commission of Women," 802.

8. *Bulletin of the Pan American Union* 73, no. 6 (June 1939).

9. Manigat, *Etre femme en Haiti*, 23 and 282. This was an amendment to the Haitian Constitution of 1935.

10. The letter continued, "We organized a big rally to celebrate this event and we met up in front of the legislative palace and the national palace. The president received us and gave a big speech giving his feminist ideas. I believe that he will achieve all of our accords—that's

to say civil rights. He said that he was impacted during his last trip to see the women's effort for the war abroad and that he wanted to include the women of his country."

11. Letter to Mes Chere Amis from Madeleine Sylvain, April 25, 1944, SUA.

12. Verna, *Haiti and the Uses*, 10. Verna shows that in the 1930s Haitian intellectuals like Antoine Pierre-Paul argued, "Haiti practiced Pan-Americanism well-before the term was even created." Most histories focus on Haitian and American soldiers' battle against the British Empire in the Battle of Savannah (1779–82).

13. Verna, *Haiti and the Uses*, 80, 90.

14. The occupation revealed that the North American country perceived itself as superior to Haiti and other Latin American countries. For more on relationship between the United States and Latin American feminisms, see Marino, *Feminism for the Americas*.

15. The first issue of LVDF was an extensive coverage of the Latin American Literary Conference held in Cap-Haïtien.

16. Madeleine Sylvain-Bouchereau, "Declaration de Lima en faveur des droits de la femme," *La Voix des Femmes* 4, no. 37 (March 1939): 3.

17. Haiti was represented by LFAS member Edith Wholley.

18. Annette Joseph-Gabriel shows that Suzanne Césaire also supported French-language education in Haiti after her 1944 trip. Césaire's and Comhaire-Sylvain's support for French education had different purposes. Joseph-Gabriel, *Reimagining Liberation*, 40–41.

19. Joseph-Gabriel, *Reimagining Liberation*, 42.

20. Firmin, *Essai sur l'inégalité des races humaines*.

21. Madeleine Sylvain-Bouchereau and Yvonne Sylvain, "Let's Recover our Intellectual Capital," *La Voix des Femmes* 9, no. 3 (February 8, 1947): 1–2.

22. "Let's Fight against Illiteracy," *La Voix des Femmes* (February 8, 1947): 3.

23. Ramsey, *Spirits and the Law*, 181.

24. *Mouvement folklorique*, although derived from intellectual legacy of *indigénisme*, was not beholden to it. Different political factions participated in the *mouvement folklorique*.

25. Ramsey, *Spirits and the Law*, 182. *Indigéniste* sympathizers, Marxists, and *noiristes* all argued that the antisuperstition campaigns were an attack on the poor and working class.

26. Ramsey, *Spirits and the Law*, 217.

27. Ramsey, *Spirits and the Law*, 181.

28. Ramsey, *Spirits and the Law* 230.

29. Jeanne Sylvain, "Marassa, Eh You!," *La Voix des Femmes* 5, no. 48 (May 1940): 1.

30. Ramsey, *Spirits and the Law*. Also see Hurston, *Tell My Horse*; Dunham, *Island Possessed* (1969); Polyné, *From Douglas to Duvalier* (2011).

31. Ramsey, *Spirits and the Law*, 232.

32. Jeanne Sylvain, "Marassa, Eh You!," *La Voix des Femmes* 5, no. 48 (May 1940): 1. Based on previous dance performances produced by LFAS, the instructor was likely Mathon.

33. Verna, *Haiti and the Uses*, 2.

34. Sheller, *Citizenship from Below*, 13.

35. Comhaire-Sylvain, "Ce que font nos filletes en dehors des heures de classes," *La Voix des Femmes* 5, no. 52 (October–November 1940): 9.

36. Comhaire-Sylvain, "Ce que font nos filletes en dehors des heures de classes," *La Voix des Femmes* 5, no.52 (October–November 1940): 9. *Les veillées* are vigils often held at night, and are associated with Vodou ceremonies.

37. Jeanne Sylvain to siblings, January 27, 1944, SUA.

38. Wekker, *Politics of Passion*, 4.

39. Ulysse, *Downtown Ladies*, 6.

40. She echoes what Gloria Wekker has offered, that "but for the grace, patience, and interests of the people involved, there would be little research." Wekker, *Politics of Passion*, 4.

41. Johnson, "Black Performance Studies," 5.

42. Johnson, "Black Performance Studies," 2.

43. Dayan, *Haiti, History and the Gods*, 135. "Intentionally or not, they [bourgeois poets and other elite, urban writers] press the négresse, eulogized as the 'woman of the people' or the erotic symbol of racial recovery, into serving their myths and sanctifying their imagination."

44. Comhaire-Sylvain, Letter to Thomas Sebeok, Comhaire-Sylvain Collection, February 9, 1944, SUA.

45. Comhaire-Sylvain, *Contes du pays d'Haïti*, 1938.

46. Comhaire-Sylvain, Letter, August 7, 1945, SUA.

47. "Suzane Sylvain, notre grande amie à toutes . . ." *Courier African*, 1960.

48. Cotera, *Native Speakers*, 83.

49. Comhaire-Sylvain, Letter to Sebeok, 1944, SUA.

50. Geary, *In and Out of Focus*, 19.

51. Geary, *In and Out of Focus*, 17, 18.

52. Casimir Zagourski's full collection, *L'Afrique Qui Disparait!* Courtesy of Yale University Library and Special Collections.

53. Wexler, *Tender Violence*, 7.

54. Smith, *Photography on the Color Line*; Campt, *Listening to Images*.

55. Comhaire-Sylvain lived much of her childhood and later her adult life outside Haiti, studying and working in Paris, London, New York, Kinshasa, and Lagos. Like many Black internationalist women, she cultivated relationships and friendships with citizens from the Americas in other cities around the world.

56. *La Phalange*, August 6, 1949, SUA.

57. *La Phalange*, Port-au-Prince, 1945. After her tour of the city, she wrote that she finally arrived at the City Hotel, which was the finest hotel in the city according to First Lady Evita Perón, who picked the hotel herself as the conference site.

58. Suzanne Comhaire-Sylvain to Jean Comhaire, August 8, 1949, SUA.

59. Suzanne Comhaire-Sylvain to Jean Comhaire, August 15, 1949, SUA.

60. Roach, *Cities of the Dead*, 2.

61. Taylor, *Disappearing Acts*, 94.

62. Brooks, *Bodies in Dissent*, 7.

63. Ruth Clement-Bond to Bethune, January 21, 1947, from Port-au-Prince, NCNW Papers, box 5, folder 2, National Archives for Black Women's History, Washington, D.C (NABWH). Founder Fortuna Guery also wrote that Bethune was a "good friend of me and my country," in letter to Bethune, January 1950.

64. Lucienne was the first lady of her nation and active in philanthropic and civic work in Haiti. Bethune was known to be a close associate of Eleanor Roosevelt and other influential US officials.

65. Bethune had planned to attend the 1950 Congress. However, she was too ill to travel. Repeated illness compromised Bethune's ability to travel at a later date, and she died in 1955.

66. National Council of Negro Women Papers, letter from Bethune to Vivian Carter Mason.

67. Letter from Bethune to Fortuna Guery, July 29, 1949. National Archives for Black Women's History, Washington, D.C.

68. Francis, *Fictions of Feminine*, 13. Comhaire-Sylvain's *mannequin* status reflects Caribbean feminist scholar Donnette Francis's assertion that "transnational feminist criticism cannot become emplotments of romance, where our analyses end with the character's redemption based on some—often one—strategic agential act of overcoming"; rather, Caribbean women's political practice includes "working through constraints—with the hope that this telling will be useful for the next generation—but without guarantees."

69. Roach, *Cities of the Dead*, 5.

70. Campt and Thomas, "Gendering Diaspora: Transnational Feminism, Diaspora and Its Hegemonies," *Feminist Review* 90, Issue 1 (October 2008): 1–8.

71. W. E. B. Du Bois's time at Fisk also included studying Haiti.

72. Danticat, *Create Dangerously*, 8.

73. Danticat, *Create Dangerously*, 11. One understandings of creating dangerously is "creating as a revolt against silence, creating when both the creation and the reception, the writing and the reading, are dangerous undertakings, disobedience to a directive."

74. Danticat, *Create Dangerously*, 16. In her work, Danticat's questions about the utility of the Greek tragedy rest in "a border between Antigone's desire to bury her brother and the Haitian mother of 1964 who desperately want to take her dead son's body out of the street to give him a proper burial, knowing that if she does this she too may die?"

75. Danticat, *Create Dangerously*, 10. In the context of Chauvet's work, the character Rose has been referenced as Antigone. As explained by Régine Jean-Charles in "They Never Call It Rape," Antigone has been used, she argues, inappropriately as a familiar reference for Haitian women's "bravery," or martyrdom, 10. Here I am interested in Madeleine's use of Antigone as a site of reflexivity.

76. Danticat, *Create Dangerously*, 9.

77. Comhaire-Sylvain newspaper clippings, Suzanne Comhaire-Sylvain Papers, SUA.

78. Campt and Thomas, "Gendering Diaspora," 6. Campt and Thomas are talking about Michelle Stephens's work. Also see Michelle Ann Stephens, "The Comic Side of Gender Trouble and Bert Williams' Signature Act," *Feminist Review* 90, no. 1 (October 2008): 128–46. 143: "The space of diaspora potentially allows us to explore the possibilities and limits of these performed, intra-racial, and intercultural gestures, where blackness is created not on the body of the black performer but in his re-enactments, in the meanings that inhere in the space between the audience and the performing racial self."

79. Johnson, "Casualties," 171.

80. "Partial Diary, Trip to Haiti, Easter Vacation, April 1950," Layle Lane Papers, Mooreland-Spingarn (MS), Washington, D.C. "Partial Diary, Trip to Haiti," Layle Lane Papers, MS. Also see Estimé, *Dumarsais Estimé*, 108–10.

81. Voltaire, *Pouvoir noir en Haïti*.

82. Estimé failed to appease his Black middle-class base or his left-wing supporters who were troubled by his relationship with the bourgeoisie class. The president also struggled to maintain control over the military, which openly expressed dissent.

83. This expense would draw more criticism than praise, further spiraling the Haitian government finances into debt and making the nation more vulnerable to foreign capital and economic intervention. For more, see Smith, *Red and Black in Haiti*; Nicholls, *From Dessalines to Duvalier*.

84. Estimé, *Dumarsais Estimé*, 109–10.

85. LFAS, *Premier Congres National des Femmes Haïtiennes* (Port-au-Prince: Bibliothéque Nationale d'Haïti 1950), 6.

86. LFAS, *Premier Congres National des Femmes Haïtiennes*, 6.

87. LFAS, *Premier Congres National des Femmes Haïtiennes*, 6–7. Also see "Haiti" Countries Collection, MS 445, Sophia Smith Archives, Smith College, Northampton, Mass.

88. Women made up the majority of workforce in the urban factories.

89. Sylvain-Bouchereau, *Haiti et ses femmes*, 189. Also see Yvonne Sylvain, "La mortalité infantile," *La Voix des Femmes*, no. 53 (December 1947): 8.

90. Suzie Boisrond, interviewed by author, March 7, 2011, Montreal, Canada.

91. Regional international women's conferences included the Liga Feminista Panamericana conference (Mexico, 1923), Inter-American Commission of Women (Havana, 1930), and International Council of Women of the Darker Races (Chicago, 1933). "Ladies' Day," *Time*, March 27, 1950, advertised the congress, describing it as an "aggressive full-scale feminist crusade."

92. *Premier Congres National des Femmes Haïtiennes*, 6.

93. Letters between Alice Garoute (LFAS founder) and Mary McLeod Bethune, August 20, 1949, September 4, 1949, and October 1, 1949. Mary McLeod Bethune Papers, National Archives for Black Women's History, Mary McLeod Bethune Council House, Washington, D.C.

94. Estimé, *Dumarsais Estimé*, 109–10. Also see letters between Alice Garoute (LFAS founder) and Mary McLeod Bethune, August 20, 1949, September 4, 1949, and October 1, 1949. Mary McLeod Bethune Papers, National Archives for Black Women's History, Mary McLeod Bethune Council House, Washington, D.C.

95. In her journal from the Women's Congress, African American US Socialist Party member Layle Lane wrote that she was excited about the conference because she heard that the organizers (the LFAS) were communists. See Layle Lane, Haiti Journal, Layle Lane Papers, MS.

96. Alice Garoute, Madeleine Sylvain-Bouchereau, Lydia Jeanty, Yvonne Hakime Rimpel, "Ligue Feminine d'Action Sociale Proteste Toujours; Aux Membres de la Junte de Gouvernement," Port-au-Prince, Haiti, August 1950, Sophia Smith Archives.

97. Sylvain-Bouchereau, *Haiti et ses femmes*, 96.

98. Sylvain-Bouchereau, *Haiti et ses femmes*, 96.

99. Manigat, *Memoire de femmes*, 77.

100. Sylvain-Bouchereau, *Haiti et ses femmes*, 96.

101. Sylvain-Bouchereau, *Haiti et ses femmes*, 82.

A Feeling

1. Marie Theresa Poitevien, "La Feminisme," *La femme haitienne repond aux attaques formulées contre elle à l'Assemblée Constituante*, 1946; CIDIHCA. "Le féminisme n'est pas un

vain mot, mais une réalité. Pour être féministe, il faut avoir un idéal et être tourmenté par le besoin de secourir les autres."

2. Mrs. Rivarol Lemaire, "Woman," *La Voix des Femmes* 2, no. 17–18 (March 1937).

3. Lamour, "Between Intersectionality and Coloniality," 143.

4. Yvonne Sylvain to Suzon, January 8, 1944, SUA.

5. Madeleine Sylvain-Bouchereau to Chers amis, Suzanne Comhaire-Sylvain Papers, SUA.

6. Jeanne Sylvain to mes chers amis, May 8, 1944, SUA.

7. To Suzy from Jeanne, Suzanne Comhaire-Sylvain Papers, SUA.

8. Jeanne Sylvain to Suzanne, August 9, 1945, SUA.

9. Jeanne Sylvain to Mes cheres amies, February 9, 1944, SUA.

10. Jeanne Sylvain to Suzanne Comhaire-Sylvain, October 23, 1944, SUA.

11. Yvonne Sylvain to Suzanne Comhaire-Sylvain, June 26, 1944, SUA.

12. Jeanne Sylvain to Mes cheres amies, February 6, 1944, SUA. "Je suis encore comme l'oiseau sur la branche."

13. Jeanne Sylvain to mes chers amis, May 8, 1944.

14. "Torment," Dictionary.com: "v. to afflict or harass as by incessant repetition of vexations and annoyances." Also, "n. a state of great bodily or mental suffering; agony; misery."

15. Jeanne Sylvain to Suzanne Comhaire-Sylvain, June 5, 1944, SUA.

16. Combahee River Collective Statement (April 1977).

17. Cherríe Moraga, "Catching Fire: Preface for the Fourth Edition," in *This Bridge Called My Back*, xix.

18. Jeanne Sylvain to Suzanne Comhaire-Sylvain, May 7, 1945, SUA.

19. The 1987 Haitian Constitution made Kreyòl and French the two official languages of the country. See Freeman and Laguerre, *Haitian–English Dictionary*; Valdman, Iskrova, et al., *Haitian Creole–English Bilingual Dictionary*.

Chapter Five

1. *Le Nouvelliste*, November 21, 1956, 1, 6; *Le Nouvelliste*, November 17, 1956, 1; Madeleine Sylvain-Bouchereau, "La femme haïtienne lutte depuis vingt ans pour obtenir les droits égaux," *La Semeuse*, February 1, 1957, 3, SS; also see Verna interview with Paulette Oriol: Verna, "Ligue Feminine d'Action Sociale."

2. Madeleine Sylvain-Bouchereau, "La femme haïtienne lutte depuis vingt ans pour obtenir les droits égaux," *La Semeuse*, February 1, 1957, 3.

3. Sylvain-Bouchereau, "La femme haïtienne lutte depuis vingt ans," *La Semeuse*, (February 1957) 3.

4. *Le Nouvelliste*, November 21, 1956, 1.

5. Castor, *Théories et pratiques de la lutte des femmes*, 22.

6. *Le Nouvelliste*, November 17, 1956, 1; *Le Nouvelliste*, November 21, 1956, 1, 6; Madeleine Sylvain-Bouchereau, "La femme haïtienne lutte depuis vingt ans pour obtenir les droits égaux," *La Semeuse*, February 1, 1957, 3.

7. Signed Alice Garoute, Madeleine Sylvain-Bouchereau, Lydia Jeanty, Yvonne Hakime Rimpel, "Ligue Feminine d'Action Sociale proteste toujours; Aux Membres de la Junte de Gouvernement," Port-au-Prince, Haiti, August 1950, Sophia Smith Archives.

8. "Mme. S. Desvarieux n'est pas d'accorde avec la Ligue," *Le Nouvelliste*, November 22, 1956, 1.

9. Madeleine Sylvain-Bouchereau, "La femme haïtienne lutte depuis vingt ans pour obtenir les droits égaux," *La Semeuse*, February 1, 1957, 3.

10. "Magloire Visit, 1955," Visit Celebrities, RG 12, vol. 1679, Library and Archives Canada.

11. Trouillot, *Haiti, State against Nation*, 148.

12. Trouillot, *Haiti, State against Nation*, 144.

13. Trouillot, *Haiti, State against Nation*, 144.

14. Sylvain-Bouchereau, *La Semeuse*, 1957; Smith, *Red and Black in Haiti*, 171.

15. "La femme haïtienne a le plein et entier exercice des droits politiques," *La Semeuse* 19, no. 100 (February 1957): 10, Stanford University Archives (SUA). For more on Pierre-Louis comments on the suffrage legislation see Barnett, "Joseph Nemours Pierre-Louis interview with Claude Barnett," sound recording in Etta Moten Barnett Collection, Schomburg Center for Research in Black Culture.

16. For detailed accounts on this period, see Nicholls, *From Dessalines to Duvalier*, 1996; Trouillot, *Haiti, State against Nation*; Laguerre, *Haiti and Militarization*.

17. Smith, *Red and Black in Haiti*, 177.

18. "Woman Seeks Haitian Seat," *New York Times*, January 31, 1957, Sophia Smith Archives.

19. "Madeleine Sylvain-Bouchereau, Candidate au Sénat de la République," *La Semeuse*, SUA.

20. While all evidence points toward a genuinely enthusiastic crowd, during the 1957 election season it was common knowledge that candidates used the presence of the working and rural class to establish their authenticity as champions of the nation.

21. "Madeleine Sylvain-Bouchereau, Candidate au Sénat de la République," *La Semeuse*, SUA.

22. "Madeleine Sylvain-Bouchereau, Candidate au Sénat de la République," *La Semeuse*, SUA.

23. "Correspondence 28 January, 1957," *La Semeuse*, SUA.

24. "Letter from Sylvain to Perez," *La Semeuse*, 10, SUA.

25. Chancy, *Framing Silence*, 27.

26. Edwards explains Gilbert Gratiant's interpretation of *nègre*: "It is the lever of an anti-imperialist rallying cry that is articulated as an internationalism; a 'support for the cause of the persecuted' in a more generalized sense." Edwards, *Practice of Diaspora*, 37.

27. Sylvain-Bouchereau, "La femme haïtienne lutte depuis vingt ans pour obtenir les droits égaux," *La Semeuse* 19, no. 100, February 1, 1957.

28. Trouillot, *Haiti, State against Nation*, 147.

29. Abbott, *Haiti*, 78; Smith, *Red and Black in Haiti*, 171.

30. Abbott, *Haiti*, 73.

31. Dupuy, *Haiti: From Revolutionary Slaves*, 82.

32. Comhaire-Sylvain and Comhaire, "Urban Stratification in Haiti," 185.

33. Anonymous, interviewed by author, May 31, 2007, Montreal, Quebec, Canada.

34. Charlier, interviewed by Stéphane Martelly and author, November 2010, Montreal, Quebec, Canada.

35. Charlier, interviewed by Stéphane Martelly and author, November 2010.

36. Through oral history and limited documentation we know that some members of the leadership supported Louis Dejoie.

37. For detailed events of the 1956–57 election, see Nicholls, *From Dessalines to Duvalier*.

38. Villefranche, interviewed by author, May 8, 2010, Montreal, Canada.

39. Villefranche, interviewed by author, May 8, 2010.

40. Trouillot, *Haiti, State against Nation*, 149.

41. For more on the details of the election moment see Nicholls, *From Dessalines to Duvalier*; Smith. *Red & Black in Haiti*.

42. Zéphir, *Haitian Women between Repression*.

43. Rey, "Junta, Rape, and Religion in Haiti, 1993–1994," 84.

44. "Mme Yvonne Hakime hospitalisée," *Le Nouvelliste* 24, no. 323 (January 7, 1958). Zéphir, "Dictator Duvalier Orders the Torture of Journalist Yvonne Hakime Rimpel," *Haitian Women between Repression*, 23. Pierre, *Témoignages, 1946–1976*.

45. The letters did not name any specific assailant, but many people suspected Duvalier was involved. The risk of further retribution would have been too great to openly name the president.

46. *La Phalange*, January 11, 1958; Zéphir, *Between Democracy and Repression*, 26.

47. Zéphir, *Between Democracy and Repression*; Abbott, *Haiti*, 93.

48. Trouillot, *Haiti, State against Nation*, 149.

49. Even before he was elected president, Duvalier encouraged the military to censor the press. The women's newspapers *La Samuese* and *La Voix des Femmes* were shut down, and the institutions that remained were under constant surveillance. Zéphir, *Between Democracy and Repression*, 23; Marie Sassin, interviewed by www.teleimagetvshow.com, March 2012, Port-au-Prince, Haiti.

50. Zéphir, *Between Democracy and Repression*, 25.

51. Zéphir, *Between Democracy and Repression*, 23.

52. Sassin, interviewed by www.teleimagetvshow.com, March 2012. Rimpel's daughter, Marie Sassin, says that her mother maintained that she was not raped, despite the rumors that suggested otherwise. Sassin explains that there is the possibility that her mother was raped but did not share the details of that night because she wanted to spare her children further harm. In 1958 rape against women was considered a minor legal infraction. The charges of rape could be dropped if the attacker married their victim. See Rey, "Junta, Rape, and Religion in Haiti, 1993–1994."

53. Most people believed that Yvonne's attackers were Duvalier's secret police. Yet no one could or was willing to prove this. Zéphir, "Dictator Duvalier Orders the Torture," 27.

54. Kihss, "Tyranny in Haiti."

55. Trouillot, *Haiti, State against Nation*, 166, 168.

56. For more on women's role especially the use of the term "poto-mitan" (center pillar) in the home see Lamour, "Between Intersectionality and Coloniality."

57. Agnant, interviewed by author, May 27, 2007, Montreal, Canada.

58. Charlier, interviewed by Stéphane Martelly and author, November 5, 2010, Montreal, Canada.

59. Vieux Chauvet, *Love, Anger, Madness*, 17.

60. Trouillot, *Haiti, State against Nation*, 167.

61. Charles, "Gender and Politics in Contemporary Haiti," 139.

62. *New York Times*, July 11, 1959, in Port-au-Prince. From Stanford University Archives. A list of other members can be found in Clorinde Zéphir's "Dictator Duvalier."

63. Trouillot, *Haiti, State against Nation*, 168.

64. Agnant, interviewed by author, May 27, 2007, Montreal, Canada.

65. Trouillot, *Haiti, State against Nation*, 166.

66. Chancy, *Framing Silence*, 76.

67. Dominique and François, *Memoirs of an Amnesiac*, 66.

68. Dominique and François, *Memoirs of an Amnesiac*, 291.

69. Bellegarde-Smith, *Haiti: The Breached Citadel*, 129–31.

70. Danny Lafferiere, *Le goût des jeunes filles*, 2004.

71. Anonymous, interviewed by author, March 7, 2011, Montreal, Quebec, Canada.

72. Duvalier dressed like the Vodou *lwa* of the cemetery Baron Samedi.

73. Myriam Chancy, *Searching for Safe Space*.

74. Vieux Chauvet, *Love, Anger, Madness*.

75. For more on the military dispersal between rural and urban Haiti, see Laguerre, *Military and Society in Haiti*.

76. Villefranche, interviewed by author, May 2010, Montreal, Quebec, Canada.

77. Verna, "Haitian Migration."

78. However, several new scholars have found that the local political dynamics of the country and mountain regions did provide more flexibility of power dynamics, as Duvalier's rule was intertwined with previously existing politics. See Chochotte, "Twilight of Popular Revolutions," 277–308.

79. Anonymous, interviewed by author, March 7, 2011, Montreal, Quebec, Canada.

80. Ligue Feminine d'Action Sociale "Foyer Alice Garoute," Sophia Smith Research Archives, Smith College.

Conclusion

1. The dialogue is from Chantalle Verna's interview with Paulette Poujol Oriol. Oriol was an award-winning author of several books, including *Le creuset* (Port-au-Prince: Éditions Henri Deschamps, 1980), *La fleur rouge: Nouvelles* (Port-au-Prince: Éditions Le Natal, 1992), and *Le passage/Vale of Tears: A Novel from Haiti* (Bethesda, Md.: Ibex, 2006). Her mother was an early member of the Ligue Feminine d'Action Sociale. Oriol became president of the LFAS in 1987 and held that office until her death in 2011. I worked with Verna on her publication of the interview and conducted an interview with Oriol. See Verna, "Ligue Feminine d'Action Sociale," 246.

2. Paulette Poujol Oriol, interviewed by author, July 8–9, 2007, Bois Verna, Haiti. During this interview Oriol recounted a similar story to the one she told Verna in 2002.

3. Other archives of the LFAS and the women's movement are with ENFOFAMN and Solidarité Fanm Ayisyen (SOFA).

4. Trouillot, *Silencing the Past*, 48.

5. Trouillot, *Silencing the Past*, 48.

6. See Marisa Fuentes's "mutilated archives" in *Dispossessed Lives*.

Bibliography

Periodicals

HAITI

Haïti-Journal
l'Escale
La Famille
The Haiti Sun
La Phalange
La Semeuse
La Voix des Femmes
Le Matin
Le Nouvelliste
Maintenant

CANADA
The Gazette

JAMAICA
The Gleaner

UNITED STATES
The Chicago Defender
The New York Times
The Pittsburgh Courier
Time

Archival Sources

Bibliothèque Nationale d'Haiti, Port-au-Prince (BNH)
Bryn Mawr College Libraries, Special Collections, Bryn Mawr, Pa.
    La Voix des Femmes
Centre de Documentation Madeleine Sylvain Bouchereau ENFOFANM, Port-au-Prince
    La Voix des Femmes
    Ligue Feminine d'Action Sociale Papers
Centre International de Documentation et d'Information Haitienne, Caribéenne et
    Afro-Canadienne (CIDIHCA), Montreal, Quebec, Canada
    Duvalierism Archives
    Haitian Left Archives
    Portraits of Haitian Elite Women, Exposition

Fisk University Special Collections and Archives, Nashville, Tennessee (FUSC)
Library and Archives Canada/Bibliothèque et Archives Canada, Ottawa, Ontario,
    Canada (BACO)
  Domestic Admission to Canada
  Dorothy Wills Papers
  Movements of Domestics from Haiti
Library of Congress, Washington, D.C. (LOC)
  Mary Church Terrell Papers
  National Association for the Advancement of Colored People Papers
Moorland-Spingarn Research Library at Howard University, Washington, D.C. (MS)
  Alain Locke Collection
  Layle Lane Collection
National Archives I and II, Washington, D.C., and Maryland (NARA I and NARA II)
National Archives, Southern Regional Headquarters, Atlanta, Georgia (NARAS)
Schomburg Research Library for the Study of Black Culture, New York, N.Y. (SRL)
  Maurice Dartigue Papers
Smith College Archives, Sophia Smith Archives and Special Collections,
    New Hampshire, Mass. (SS)
  Dorothy Height Papers
Stanford University Archives, Stanford, Calif. (SUA)
  Suzanne Sylvain-Comhaire Papers
University of Ottawa Archives, Ottawa, Ontario, Canada (UOA)
  Canadian Women's Movement Archives
  Front de libération des femmes québécoises

Interviews (conducted by author and referenced in book)

Agnant, Marie-Célie. May 27, 2007. Montreal, Quebec, Canada.
Anonymous. March 7, 2011. Montreal, Quebec, Canada.
Boisrond, Suzie. March 2011. Montreal, Quebec, Canada.
Chancy, Adeline. May 2011. Port-au-Prince, Haiti.
Charlier, Ghislaine. September 23, 2010. November 5, 2010 (with Stéphane Martelly)
Montreal, Quebec, Canada.
Dauphan, Monique. May 2010. Montreal, Quebec, Canada.
Delorme, Jacqueline. June 8, 2007. Montreal, Quebec, Canada.
Étienne, Natania. September 2010. Montreal, Quebec, Canada.
Jean-Baptiste, Milose. February 2011. Montreal, Quebec, Canada.
Jeanty, Yolette. August 2008. Port-au-Prince, Haiti.
Jérôme, Mireille Pérodin. February 2011. Montreal, Quebec, Canada.
Joseph, Marlène. March 2011. Montreal, Quebec, Canada.
Longuefosse, Mozart F. May 31, 2007. Montreal, Quebec, Canada.
Oriol, Paulette Poujol. August 2007. Port-au-Prince, Haiti.
Philoctète, Alexandra. March 2011. Montreal, Quebec, Canada.
Pierre-Jacques, Fabienne. May 30, 2007. Montreal, Quebec, Canada.
Rouseau, Josette Jean-Pierre. February 2011. Montreal, Quebec, Canada.

Toussaint, M. September 2010. Montreal, Quebec, Canada.

Villefranche, Marjorie. May 2010. Montreal, Quebec, Canada.

Paulette Voltaire (pseudonym), June 7, 2008, Montreal, Canada.

Books and Articles

Abbott, Elizabeth. *Haiti: The Duvaliers and Their Legacy*. New York: Simon and Schuster, 1991.

———. *Haiti: A Shattered Nation*. New York: Overlook, 2011.

Alexander, M. Jacqui. *Pedagogies of Crossing: Meditations on Feminism, Sexual Politics, Memory, and the Sacred*. Durham, N.C.: Duke University Press, 2005.

———. "Redrafting Morality: The Postcolonial State and the Sexual Offences Bill of Trinidad and Tobago." In *Third World Women and the Politics of Feminism*, edited by Chandra Talpade Mohanty, Ann Russo, and Lourdes Torres, 133–52. Bloomington: Indiana University Press, 1991.

Alexander, M. Jacqui, and Chandra Talpade Mohanty, eds. *Feminist Genealogies, Colonial Legacies, Democratic Futures*. New York: Routledge, 1997.

Alexis, Yveline. *Haiti Fights Back: The Life and Legacy of Charlemagne Péralte*. New Brunswick: Rutgers University Press, 2021.

Allen, Jafari S. *¡Venceremos?: The Erotics of Black Self-Making in Cuba*. Durham N.C.: Duke University Press, 2011.

Allman, James, and John May. "Fertility, Mortality, Migration and Family Planning in Haiti." *Population Studies* 33, no. 3 (November 1979): 505–21.

Anglade, Georges. *Espace et liberté en Haïti*. J.-M. Tremblay, 2010.

Balch, Emily Greene, ed. *Occupied Haiti, Being the Report of a Committee of Six Disinterested Americans Representing Organizations Exclusively American, Who, Having Personally Studied Conditions in Haiti in 1926, Favor the Restoration of the Independence of the Negro Republic*. New York: The Writers Publishing Company, 1927.

Bambara, Toni Cade, ed. *The Black Woman: An Anthology*. With an introduction by Eleanor W. Traylor. New York: Washington Square, 2005.

Basch, Linda G., Nina Glick Schiller, and Cristina Szanton Blanc. *Nations Unbound: Transnational Projects, Postcolonial Predicaments and Deterritorialized Nation-States*. Langhorne, Pa.: Gordon and Breach, 1994.

Bastien, Rémy. *Le paysan haïtien et sa famille: vallée de Marbial*. Paris: Karthala, 1985.

Bay, Mia, Farah Jasmine Griffin, Martha S. Jones, and Barbara Dianne Savage. *Toward an Intellectual History of Black Women*. Chapel Hill: University of North Carolina Press, 2015.

Bellegarde, Dantès Louis. *L'occupation américaine d'Haïti: Ses conséquences morales et économiques*. Port St. Lucie, Fla.: Hope Outreach Productions, 2016.

Bellegarde-Smith, Patrick. "Haitian Studies Association Plenary Address: 22nd Annual Conference, Brown University." *Journal of Haitian Studies* 17, no. 1 (2011): 230–44.

———. *Haiti: The Breached Citadel*. Toronto: Canadian Scholar's Press, 1990.

Bello, Bayyinah. *Sheroes of the Haitian Revolution*. Thorobred Books, 2019. thorobredbooks.com.

Bentolila, Alain, Pierre Nougayrol, Pierre Vernet, Charles Alexander, and Henry Tourneux. *Ti diksyonnè Kreyòl-Franse*. Port-au-Prince: Éditions Caraïbes, 1976.

Blain, Keisha N., and Tiffany M. Gill. "Introduction: Black Women and the Complexities of Internationalism." In *To Turn the Whole World Over: Black Women and Internationalism*, edited by Keisha N. Blain and Tiffany M. Gill. Urbana: University of Illinois Press, 2019: 1–12.

Blain, Keisha N., and Tiffany M. Gill, eds. *To Turn the Whole World Over: Black Women and Internationalism*. Urbana: University of Illinois Press, 2019.

Bonilla, Yarimar. *Non-Sovereign Futures: French Caribbean Politics in the Wake of Disenchantment*. Chicago: University of Chicago Press, 2015.

———. "Ordinary Sovereignty." *Small Axe: A Caribbean Journal of Criticism* 17, no. 3 (November 1, 2013): 152–65.

Brereton, Bridget. "Gendered Testimonies: Autobiographies, Diaries and Letters by Women as Sources for Caribbean History." *Feminist Review* 59, no. 1 (June 1998): 143–63.

Brisson, Monique. "Situation juridique et constitutionelle de la femme haïtienne." In *Femme: Sociale et legislation*, edited by Suzy Castor, Monique Brisson, and Norma McLeod. Port-au-Prince: Centre des Research et de Formation Economique et Sociale pour le Développement, 1988: 21–46.

Brooks, Daphne A. *Bodies in Dissent: Spectacular Performances of Race and Freedom, 1850–1910*. Durham, N.C.: Duke University Press, 2006.

Bulletin of the Pan American Union 73, no. 6 (June 1939).

Campt, Tina Marie. *Listening to Images*. Durham, N.C.: Duke University Press, 2017.

Campt, Tina, and Deborah Thomas. "Gendering Diaspora: Transnational Feminism, Diaspora and Its Hegemonies." *Feminist Review* 90, no. 1 (October 2008): 1–8.

Candelario, Ginetta. "'When the Time Comes We Will Align Ourselves Actively': Feminist Maternalism and Anti-Haitianism in the Dominican Republic during the Trujillo Era." Women's Studies Graduate Association Annual Speaker Series, University of Michigan, March 23, 2007.

Carby, Hazel V. *Reconstructing Womanhood: The Emergence of the Afro-American Woman Novelist*. Oxford: Oxford University Press, 1987.

Castor, Suzy. *L'occupation americaine d'Haïti*. Port-au-Prince: CRESFED, 1988.

———. *Théories et pratiques de la lutte des femmes*. Port-au-Prince: Centre de recherche et de formation économique et sociale pour le dévoppement, 1987.

Césaire, Aimé. *Cahier d'un retour au pays natal*. Paris: Présence Africaine, 1983.

Chancy, Myriam J. A. "Nou Là!: Haitian Feminism as the Crossroads Politics of Theory and Action." In *Framing Silence: Revolutionary Novels by Haitian Women*. New Brunswick, N.J.: Rutgers University Press, 1997: 24–45.

Charles, Carolle. "Popular Images of Gender and Sexuality." In *The Culture of Gender and Sexuality in the Caribbean*, edited by Linden Lewis. (Gainesville: University of Florida Press, 2003): 169–89.

———. "Gender and Politics in Contemporary Haiti: The Duvalierist State, Transnationalism, and the Emergence of a New Feminism (1980–1990)." *Feminist Studies* 21, no. 1 (1995): 135–64.

———. "Sexual Politics and the Mediation of Class, Gender and Race in Former Slave Plantation Societies." In *In Social Construction of the Past: Representation as Power*, edited by George C. Bond and Angela Gilliam. London: Routledge, 1994: 44–58.

———. "A Sociological Counter-Reading of Marie Chauvet as an 'Outsider-Within': Paradoxes in the Construction of Haitian Women in Love, Anger, Madness." *Journal of Haitian Studies* 20, no. 2 (2014): 66–89.

———. "Reflections on Being Machann ak Machandiz." *Meridians: feminism, race, transnationalism* 11, no. 1 (2011): 118–23.

———. Charles, "Transnationalism in the Construct of Haitian Migrants' Racial Categories of Identity in New York City," *Annals of the New York Academy of Sciences* 645, Issue 1 (July 1992): 101–123.

Chauvet, Marie Vieux. *Love, Anger, Madness: A Haitian Trilogy*. New York: Modern Library, 2010.

Chochotte, Marvin. "The Twilight of Popular Revolutions: The Suppression of Peasant Armed Struggles and Freedom in Rural Haiti during the US Occupation, 1915–1934." *Journal of African American History* 103, no. 3 (2018): 277–308.

Claude-Narcisse, Jasmine. "Le vent du feminism en Haiti." In *Mémoire de Femmes*. Port-au-Prince: UNICEF, 1997.

Comhaire-Sylvain, Suzanne. *Contes du pays d'Haïti*. Port-au-Prince: Caravelle, 1938.

"Courtship, Marriage, and Plasaj in Kenscoff." *Social and Economic Studies, Institute of Social and Economic Research* 7, no. 4 (December 1958): 215–16.

———. "Mort et funérailles dans la region de Kenscoff (Haïti)." *Revue de l'Institut de Sociologie*, no. 2 (1959): 197–232.

———. "A propos du vocabulaire des croyances paysannes." *La Voix des Femmes* 3, no. 29 (February 1938): 6–7.

———. "Quelques autres proverbs sur la femme." *La Voix des Femmes* 4, no. 37 (March 1939): 9.

Comhaire-Sylvain, Suzanne, and Jean Comhaire. "Urban Stratification in Haiti." *Social and Economic Studies, Institute of Social and Economic Research* 8, no. 2 (June 1959): 179–89.

Corvington, Georges. *Port-au-Prince au course des ans: La capitale d'Haïti sous l'occupation, 1922–1934*. Port-au-Prince: Impr. H. Deschamps, 1972.

Cotera, María Eugenia Cotera. *Native Speakers: Ella Deloria, Zora Neale Hurston, Jovita González, and the Poetics of Culture*. Austin: University of Texas Press, 2008.

Crenshaw, Kimberle. "Mapping the Margins: Intersectionality, Identity Politics, and Violence against Women of Color." *Stanford Law Review* 43, no. 6 (July 1991): 1241–99.

da Silva, Denise Ferreira. "To Be Announced: Radical Praxis or Knowing (at) the Limits of Justice." *Social Text* 114, 31, no. 1 (Spring 2013): 43–62.

Dalleo, Raphael. *American Imperialism's Undead: The Occupation of Haiti and the Rise of Caribbean Anticolonialism*. Charlottesville: University of Virginia Press, 2016.

Danticat, Edwidge. *The Art of Death: Writing the Final Story*. Minneapolis, Minn.: Graywolf, 2017.

———. *Breath, Eyes, Memory*. New York: Vintage Books, 1998.

———. *Brother, I'm Dying*. New York: Alfred A. Knopf, 2007.

———. *Create Dangerously: The Immigrant Artist at Work*. New York: Vintage Books, 2010.

Dartigue, Esther. "Le feminisme en Haiti 'Il était une fois quatre sœurs.'" *Bulletin de l'Association France-Haiti* (May 1985): 7–8.

Dartigue, Maurice. *L' enseignement en Haiti (1804–1938)*. Port-au-Prince: Imprimerie de L'état, 1939.

Dartigue, Maurice, and Andre Liautaud. *Géographie locale*. Deschamps: Port-au-Prince, 1931.

Dash, J. Michael. "The (Un)Kindness of Strangers: Writing Haiti in the 21st Century." *Caribbean Studies* 36, no. 2 (July–December 2008): 171–78.

Dash, Julie. *Daughters of the Dust: A Novel* (based on the film). New York: Plume, 1997.

Daut, Marlene L. *Baron de Vastey and the Origins of Black Atlantic Humanism*. New York: Palgrave Macmillan, 2017.

Davies, Carole Boyce. "Beyond Unicentricity: Transcultural Black Presences." *Research in African Literatures* 30, no. 2 (June 1999): 96–109.

———. *Black Women, Writing, and Identity: Migrations of the Subject*. New York: Routledge, 1994.

———. *Left of Karl Marx: The Political Life of Black Communist Claudia Jones*. Durham, N.C.: Duke University Press, 2008.

Davis, Angela Y. *Women, Race and Class*. New York: Vintage Books, 1983.

Dayan, Colin (Joan). *Haiti, History, and the Gods*. Berkeley: University of California Press, 1998.

Demme, Jonathan. *The Agronomist*. DVD. Clinica Estetico and HBO/Cinemax Documentary, 2003.

Denis, Lorimer, and François Duvalier. "La civilization haïtienne: Notre mentalité est-elle africaine ou gallo-latine?" *Revue de la Societé d'Histoire et de Géographie d'Haïti* 7, no. 23 (1936): 353–72.

Dominique, Jan J. *Memoir of an Amnesiac*. Translated by Irline François. Coconut Creek, Fla.: Caribbean Studies Press, 2008.

Dominique, Jean L. "Mme Ghislaine Charlier, écrivaine et veuve de l'historien Étienne Charlier (1)." *Face à l'Opinion*, March 14, 1997.

Du Bois, W. E. B. "Of Mr. Booker T. Washington and Others." *The Souls of Black Folk: Essays and Sketches*. Chicago: A. C. McClurg, 1903.

Dubois, Laurent. *Avengers of the New World: The Story of the Haitian Revolution*. Cambridge, Mass.: Harvard University Press, 2005.

Dunham, Katherine. *Island Possessed*. Chicago: University of Chicago Press, 1969.

Edwards, Brent Hayes. *The Practice of Diaspora: Literature, Translation, and the Rise of Black Internationalism*. Cambridge, Mass.: Harvard University Press, 2003.

Estimé, Lucienne H. *Dumarsais Estimé: Dialogue avec mes souvenirs*. Port-au-Prince: Editions Mémoire, 2001.

Farmer, Ashley D. "In Search of the Black Women's History Archive." *Modern American History* 1, no. 2 (February 14, 2018): 289–93.

Ferrer, Ada. *Insurgent Cuba: Race, Nation, and Revolution, 1868–1898*. Chapel Hill: University of North Carolina, 1999.

Fick, Carolyn. "Emancipation in Haiti: From Plantation Labour to Peasant Proprietorship." *Slavery and Abolition* 21, no. 2 (August 2000): 11–40.

———. *The Making of Haiti: The Saint Domingue Revolution from Below*. Knoxville: University of Tennessee Press, 1990.

Findlay, Eileen. *Imposing Decency: The Politics of Sexuality and Race in Puerto Rico, 1870–1920*. Durham, N.C.: Duke University Press, 1999.

Firmin, Antenor. *Essai sur l'inégalité des races humaine.* Paris: Librarie Cotillon, 1885.

Fischer, Sibylle. *Modernity Disavowed: Haiti and the Cultures of Slavery in the Age of Revolution.* Durham, N.C.: Duke University Press, 2004.

Francis, Donette. *Fictions of Feminine Citizenship: Sexuality and the Nation in Contemporary Caribbean Literature.* New York: Palgrave Macmillan, 2010.

Freeman, Bryant C., and Jowel C. Laguerre. *Haitian–English Dictionary.* Lawrence, Kans.: Institute of Haitian Studies, University of Kansas, 1996.

Freidel, Frank. *Franklin D. Roosevelt: The Apprenticeship.* Boston: Little, Brown, 1952.

Fuentes, Marisa J. *Dispossessed Lives: Enslaved Women, Violence, and the Archive.* Philadelphia: University of Pennsylvania Press, 2016.

García-Peña, Lorgia. *The Borders of Dominicanidad: Race, Nation, and Archives of Contradiction.* Durham, N.C.: Duke University Press, 2016.

Garoute, Alice. *La femme haïtienne répond aux attaques formulées contre elle À l'Assemblée Constituante.* Port-au-Prince, Haïti: Société D'editions Et De Librairie, 1946.

Garraway, Doris Lorraine, ed. *Tree of Liberty: Cultural Legacies of the Haitian Revolution in the Atlantic World.* Charlottesville: University of Virginia Press, 2008.

Geary, Christraud M. *In and Out of Focus: Images from Central African, 1885–1960.* Washington, D.C.: Smithsonian Institute, 2002.

Geggus, David Patrick. *Haitian Revolutionary Studies.* Bloomington: Indiana University Press, 2002.

Giddings, Paula. *When and Where I Enter: The Impact of Black Women on Race and Sex in America.* New York: Bantam Books, 1984.

Glick-Schiller, Nina, L. Basch, and C. Blanc-Szanton, eds. *Towards a Transnational Perspective on Migration: Race, Class, Ethnicity and Nationalism Reconsidered.* New York: New York Academy of Sciences, 1992.

Glick-Schiller, Nina, and Georges Eugene Fouron. "'Everywhere We Go, We Are in Danger': Ti Manno and the Emergence of a Haitian Transnational Identity." *American Ethnologist* 17, no. 2 (May 1990): 329–47.

Glover, Kaiama L. "'Black' Radicalism in Haiti and the Disorderly Feminine: The Case of Marie Vieux Chauvet." *Small Axe: A Caribbean Journal of Criticism* 17, no. 1 (March 1, 2013): 7–21.

Grewal, Inderpal, and Caren Kaplan, eds. *Scattered Hegemonies: Postmodernity and Transnational Feminist Practices.* Minneapolis: University of Minnesota Press, 2006.

Griffin, Farah Jasmine. "That the Mothers May Soar and the Daughters May Know Their Names: A Retrospective of Black Feminist Literary Criticism." *Signs: Journal of Women in Culture and Society* 32, no. 2 (January 2007): 483–507.

Gumbs, Alexis Pauline, China Martens, and Mai A Williams, eds. *Revolutionary Mothering: Love on the Front Lines.* Oakland, Calif.: PM Press, 2016.

Guy-Sheftall, Beverly, ed. *Words of Fire: An Anthology of African-American Feminist Thought.* New York: New Press, 1995.

Hanchard, Michael. "Afro-Modernity: Temporality, Politics, and the African Diaspora." *Public Culture* 11, no. 1 (January 1, 1999): 245–68.

Hartman, Saidiya. *Scenes of Subjection: Terror, Slavery, and Self-Making in Nineteenth-Century America.* New York: Oxford University Press, 1997.

———. "Venus in Two Acts." *Small Axe* 26 (June 2008): 1–14.

———. *Wayward Lives, Beautiful Experiments: Intimate Histories of Social Upheaval.*
New York: W. W. Norton & Company, 2019.

Herskovits, Melville J. *Life in a Haitian Valley.* Garden City, N.Y.: Doubleday, 1971.

Higginbotham, Evelyn Brooks. "African-American Women's History and the
Metalanguage of Race." *Signs: Journal of Women in Culture and Society* 17, no. 2
(January 1992): 251–74.

Hine, Darlene Clark. *Black Women in White: Racial Conflict and Cooperation in the Nursing
Profession, 1890–1950* (Blacks in the Diaspora). Bloomington: Indiana University Press,
1989.

Holland, Dorothy F., and Selwyn D. Collins. "The Influenza Epidemic of the Winter of
1943–44 in the United States: A Preliminary Summary." *Public Health Reports* 59, no. 35
(September 1, 1944): 1131–41.

Holloway, Karla F. C. *Passed On: African American Mourning Stories.* Durham, N.C.:
Duke University Press, 2003.

Holly, Theodora. "The Christening of a Haytian." *Colored American Magazine* 4, no. 5
(April 1902), 348.

———. "The Haytian Girl, How She Is Woed and Won." *Colored American Magazine,*
January–February 1902. Grand Winter Number, 203–10.

Haynes, Tonya, "Interrogating Approaches to Caribbean Feminist Thought," *Journal of
Eastern Caribbean Studies* 42, no. 3 (December 2017): 26–58.

Hudson, Peter James. *Bankers and Empire: How Wall Street Colonized the Caribbean.*
Chicago: University of Chicago Press, 2017.

Hull, Gloria T., Patricia Bell Scott, and Barbara Smith. *All the Women Are White, All the
Men Are Men, but Some of Us are Brave: Black Women's Studies.* New York: Feminist
Press, 1982.

Hurston, Zora Neale. *Tell My Horse: Voodoo and Life in Haiti and Jamaica.* New York:
Perennial Library (original 1938), 1990.

Jackson, Janet. "That's the Way Love Goes." CD, Virgin Records Ltd., Release 1993.

Jackson, John L. *Thin Description: Ethnography and the African Hebrew Israelites of
Jerusalem.* Cambridge, Mass.: Harvard University Press, 2013.

James, C. L. R. *The Black Jacobins: Toussaint L'Ouverture and the San Domingo Revolution.*
New York: Vintage Books, (1938) 1989.

Jean-Charles, Régine Michelle. *Conflict Bodies: The Politics of Rape Representation in the
Francophone Imaginary.* Columbus: Ohio State University Press, 2014.

———. "They Never Call It Rape: Critical Reception and Representation of Sexual
Violence in Marie Vieux-Chauvet's *Amour, Colère et Folie.*" *Journal of Haitian Studies* 12.
no. 2 (2006): 4–21.

Johnson, E. Patrick. "Black Performance Studies: Genealogies, Politics, and Futures." *The
SAGE Handbook of Performance Studies.* Thousand Oaks, Calif.: SAGE, 2005: 446–63.

Johnson, Jasmine E. "Casualties." *TDR: The Drama Review* 62, no. 1 (T237) (Spring 2018):
169–71.

Johnson, Jessica Marie. *Wicked Flesh: Black Women, Intimacy, and Freedom in the Atlantic
World.* Philadelphia: University of Pennsylvania Press, 2020.

Joseph-Gabriel, Annette. *Reimagining Liberation: How Black Women Transformed
Citizenship in the French Empire.* Urbana: University of Illinois Press [2020].

Kawahara, Akito Y., David Plotkin, Chris A. Hamilton, et al. "Diel Behavior in Moths and Butterflies: A Synthesis of Data Illuminates the Evolution of Temporal Activity." *Organisms, Diversity and Evolution* 18 (2018): 13–27.

Kelley, Robin. *Freedom Dreams: The Black Radical Imagination.* Boston: Beacon, 2002.

Kempadoo, Kamala. *Sexing the Caribbean: Gender, Race and Sexual Labor.* New York: Routledge, 2004.

Kihss, Peter. "Tyranny in Haiti Is Charged Here: Terrorism and Corruption Laid to Duvalier Regime by 2 Former Backers." *New York Times,* July 27, 1959.

King Jr., Martin Luther. *Why We Can't Wait.* New York: Penguin Publishing Group, 1964.

Laferrière, Dany. *Le goût des jeunes filles.* Montreal: Grasset and Fasquelle, 2005.

Laguerre, Michel S. *The Military and Society in Haiti.* Knoxville: University of Tennessee Press, 1993.

Lahens, Yanick. *Bain de lune* (2014). Translated by Emily Gogolak, *Moonbath.* Dallas: Deep Vellum Publishing, 2017.

Lamour, Sabine, Denyse Côté, and Darline Alexis. *Déjouer le silence: Contre-discours sur les femmes haïtiennes.* Montreal: Les éditions du remue-ménage, Mémoire d'encrier, 2018.

———. "Between Intersectionality and Coloniality: Rereading the Figure of the *Poto-Mitan* Figure in Haiti," *Women, Gender, and Families of Color* 9, no. 2 (Fall 2021): 136–151.

LFAS. "La Séance du 9 Août de l'Assemblée Constituante." In *La femme haïtienne répond aux attaques formulées contre elle à L'Assemblée Constituante.* Port-au-Prince: Societé d'Editions et de Librairie, 1946: 28–36.

LFAS. *La femme haïtienne répond aux attaques formulées contre elle à L'Assemblée Constituante.* Port-au-Prince: Societé d'Editions et de Librairie, 1946: 1–36.

———. *Premier Congres National des Femmes Haïtiennes.* Port-au-Prince: Bibliothéque Nationale d'Haïti, 1950.

———. *Femmes haïtiennes.* Port-au-Prince: Henri Deschamps Press, 1953.

Lorde, Audre. *Zami: A New Spelling of My Name.* Berkeley, Calif.: Crossing, 1982.

Lowe, Lisa. *The Intimacies of Four Continents.* Durham, N.C.: Duke University Press, 2015.

Lowenthal, "Labor, Sexuality and the Conjugal Contract in Rural Haiti," in *Haiti—Today and Tomorrow: An Interdisciplinary Study.* Charles Foster and Albert Valdman, eds. Lanham, MD: University Press of America (1984): 15–33.

Lundahl, Mats. *Peasants and Poverty: A Study of Haiti.* New York: St. Martin's, 1979.

Manigat, Mirlande. *Être femme en Haïti hier et aujourd'hui: Le regard des constitutions, des lois et de la société.* Port-au-Prince: Université Quisqueya, 2002.

Marino, Katherine M. *Feminism for the Americas: The Making of an International Human Rights Movement.* Chapel Hill: University of North Carolina, 2019.

Martelly, Stéphane. *L'enfant Gazelle.* Montréal: Éditions du Remue Ménage, 2018.

Mayes, April J. "Why Dominican Feminism Moved to the Right: Class, Colour and Women's Activism in the Dominican Republic, 1880s–1940s." *Gender and History* 20, no. 2 (August 2008): 349–71.

McKittrick, Katherine. *Demonic Grounds: Black Women and the Cartographies of Struggle.* Minneapolis: University of Minnesota Press, 2006.

———. "Mathematics Black Life." *Black Scholar* 44, no. 2 (Summer 2014): 16–28.

Méltraux, Alfred. *Voodoo in Haiti.* New York: Schocken Books, (1958) 1972.

Ménard, Nadève. "The Occupied Novel: The Representation of Foreigners in Haitian Novels Written during the United States Occupation, 1915–1934." Ph.D. diss., University of Pennsylvania, 2002.

Miles, Tiya. *All That She Carried: The Journey of Ashley's Sack, a Black Family Keepsake.* New York: Random House, 2021.

Miller, Francesca. "The International Relations of Women of the Americas 1890–1928." *The Americas: A Quarterly Review of Inter-American Cultural History* 43, no. 2 (1986): 171–82.

Millward, Jessica. "Black Women's History and the Labor of Mourning." *Souls* 18, no. 1 (2016): 161–65.

Mintz, Sidney. "The Caribbean as a Socio-Cultural Area." *Cahiers d'Histoire Mondiale* 9 (1966): 912–37.

Mohanty, Chandra Talpade. "Under Western Eyes: Feminist Scholarship and Colonial Discourses." In *Third World Women and the Politics of Feminism*, edited by Chandra T. Mohanty, Chandra Talpade, Ann Russo, and Lourdes Torres. Bloomington: Indiana University Press, 1991: 51–80.

Moraga, Cherríe, and Anzaldúa, Gloria, eds. *This Bridge Called My Back: Writings by Radical Women of Color.* New York: Kitchen Table: Women of Color Press, 1983.

Morgan, Jennifer L. *Laboring Women: Reproduction and Gender in New World Slavery.* Philadelphia: University of Pennsylvania Press, 2004.

Neptune-Anglade, Mireille. L'autre moitié du développement: à propos du travail des femmes en Haïti. Port-au-Prince and Montreal: Éditions des Alizés and ERCE, 1986.

Newman, Louise Michelle. *White Women's Rights: The Racial Origins of Feminism in the United States.* New York: Oxford University Press, 1999.

Nicholls, David. *From Dessalines to Duvalier: Race, Colour and National Independence in Haiti.* New Brunswick, N.J.: Rutgers University Press, 1996.

———. "Rural Protest and Peasant Revolt, 1804–1869." In *Haitian History: New Perspectives*, edited by Alyssa Goldstein Sepinwall. New York: Routledge, 2013: 180–96.

N'Zengou-Tayo, Marie-José. "'Fanm Se Poto Mitan': Haitian Woman, the Pillar of Society." *Feminist Review* 59, no. 1: 118–42.

Oriol, Paulette Poujol. *La Fleur Rouge: Nouvelles.* Port-Au-Prince: Editions Le Natal, 1992.

———. *Le Creuset.* Port-au-Prince: Éditions Henri Deschamps, 1980.

———. *Vale of Tears: A Novel from Haiti.* Bethesda, Md.: Ibex, 2006.

Paravisini-Gerbert, Lizabeth. "Decolonizing Feminism: The Home-Grown Roots of Caribbean Women's Movements." In *Daughters of Caliban: Caribbean Women in the Twentieth Century*, edited by Consuelo Lopez Springfield. Bloomington: Indiana University Press, 1997: 3–17.

Pascal-Trouillot, Ertha. "Droit et privileges de la femme dans la legislation civile et sociale d'Haiti," Conjonction: Review Franco-Haitienne, no. 124 (August 1974): 9–22.

Patton, Venetria K. "Othermothers as Elders and Cultural Bearers in *Daughters of the Dust* and *The Salt Eaters*." In *The Grasp That Reaches beyond the Grave: The Ancestral Call in Black Women's Texts.* New York: State University of New York Press, 2013.

Perez, Jeanne, *Sanite Belair: Drame historique en trois tableaux.* Petion-Ville, Haiti: La Sameuse, 1942.

Pierre, Pressoir. *Témoignages, 1946–1976: L'espérance Déçue.* Port-au-Prince: Impr. H. Deschamps, 1987.

Plummer, Brenda Gayle. *Haiti and the Great Powers, 1902–1915.* Baton Rouge: Louisiana State University Press, 1988.

Polyné, Millery. *From Douglass to Duvalier: US African Americans, Haiti, and Pan Americanism, 1870–1964.* Gainesville: University Press of Florida, 2011.

Popkin, Jeremy David. *You Are All Free: The Haitian Revolution and the Abolition of Slavery.* New York: Cambridge University Press, 2010.

Premier Congres National des Femmes Haïtiennes. Port-au-Prince: Bibliothéque Nationale d'Haïti 1950,

Price-Mars, Jean. *Ainsi parla l'oncle: Essais d'ethnographie.* Nouvelle Édition, Présentation de Robert Cornevin, Montreal: Collection Caraïbes, (1928) 1973.

———. *Vocation d'elite,* Port-au-Prince: Imprimerie Edmond Chenet,1919.

Puri, Shalini. "Beyond Resistance: Notes toward a New Caribbean Cultural Studies." *Small Axe: A Caribbean Journal of Criticism* 7, no. 2 (January 1, 2003): 23–38.

Ramsey, Kate. *The Spirits and the Law: Vodou and Power in Haiti.* Chicago: University of Chicago Press, 2011.

Reddock, Rhoda Elizabeth. *Women, Labour and Politics in Trinidad and Tobago: A History: "Brave Danger."* London: Zed Books, 1994.

Renda, Mary A. *Taking Haiti: Military Occupation and the Culture of US Imperialism, 1915–1940.* Chapel Hill: University of North Carolina Press, 2001.

Rey, Terry. "Junta, Rape, and Religion in Haiti, 1993–1994." *Journal of Feminist Studies in Religion* 15, no. 2 (1999): 73–100. http://www.jstor.org/stable/25002366.

Roach, Joseph. *Cities of the Dead: Circum-Atlantic Performance.* New York: Columbia University Press, 1996.

Robinson, Cedric. *Black Marxism: The Making of the Black Radical Tradition.* Chapel Hill: University of North Carolina Press, 1983.

Rochat, Désirée. "Archiving Black Diasporic Activism: How the Shared Praxis of Haitian Activists at La Maison d'Haiti Built a Community." Ph.D. diss., McGill University, May 2021.

Rosen, Hannah. *Terror in the Heart of Freedom: Citizenship, Sexual Violence, and the Meaning of Race in the Postemancipation South.* Chapel Hill: University of North Carolina Press, 2009.

Roumain, Jacques. *Masters of the Dew.* Pompano Beach, Fla.: Educa Vision, 2017.

Scherpf, Stephanie. "Emerante de Pradines: The Birth of a Legend and the Making of a Tradition." *Journal of Haitian Studies* 23, no. 1 (Spring 2017): 162–68.

Schmidt, Hans. *The United States Occupation of Haiti, 1915–1934.* New Brunswick, N.J.: Rutgers University Press, 1995.

Scott, David. "The Re-Enchantment of Humanism: An Interview with Sylvia Wynter." *Small Axe* 8 (September 2000): 119–207.

Scott, Julius,. *The Common Wind: Afro-American Currents in the Age of the Haitian Revolution.* With an introduction by Marcus Rediker. New York: Verso, 2018.

Shange, Ntozake. *For Colored Girls Who Have Considered Suicide, When the Rainbow Is Enuf.* New York: Scribner Poetry, 1997.

Shannon, Magdaline W. *Jean Price-Mars, the Haitian Elite and the American Occupation, 1915–1935*. New York: St. Martin's, 1996.

———. "The U.S. Commission for the Study and Review of Conditions in Haiti and Its Relationship to President Hoover's Latin American Policy." *Caribbean Studies* 15, no. 4 (January 1975): 53–71.

Sheller, Mimi. *Citizenship from Below: Erotic Agency and Caribbean Freedom*. Durham, N.C.: Duke University Press, 2012.

———. *Democracy after Slavery: Black Publics and Peasant Radicalism in Haiti and Jamaica*. Gainesville, Fla: University Press of Florida, 2001.

Silva, Denise Ferreira da. "To Be Announced: Radical Praxis or Knowing (At) the Limits of Justice." *Social Text* 31, no. 1 (2013): 43–62.

Smith, Lauren E., Darren R. Bernal, Billie S. Schwartz, Courtney L. Whitt, Seth T. Christman, Stephanie Donnelly, Anna Wheatley, et al. "Coping with Vicarious Trauma in the Aftermath of a Natural Disaster." *Journal of Multicultural Counseling and Development* 42, no. 1 (January 2014): 2–13.

Smith, Matthew J. *Red and Black in Haiti: Radicalism, Conflict, and Political Change, 1934–1957*. Chapel Hill: University of North Carolina Press, 2009.

Smith, Shawn Michelle. *Photography on the Color Line: W. E. B. Du Bois, Race, and Visual Culture*. Durham, N.C.: Duke University Press, 2004.

Spillers, Hortense J. "Mama's Baby, Papa's Maybe: An American Grammar Book." *Diacritics* 17, no. 2 (Summer 1987): 64–81.

Springer, Kimberly. *Still Lifting, Still Climbing: Contemporary African American Women's Activism*. New York: New York University Press, 1999.

Stephens, Michelle Ann. "The Comic Side of Gender Trouble and Bert Williams' Signature Act." *Feminist Review* 90, no. 1 (October 2008): 128–46.

Stoler, Ann Laura. *Race and the Education of Desire: Foucault's History of Sexuality and the Colonial Order of Things*. Durham, N.C.: Duke University Press, 1995.

Sylvain, Georges. *Cric?Crac!Krik?Krak!* Port-au-Prince: Foundation Connaissance et Liberté, 1999.

———. *Dix années de lutte pour la liberté, 1915–1925*. Port-au-Prince: Editions Henri Deschamps, 1925.

Sylvain, Madeleine. "Séances d'études de La L.F.A.S." *La Voix Des Femmes* 6, no. 46 (February 1940): 2.

———. "The Feminist Movement in Haiti." *Bulletin of the Pan American Union* 73, no. 6 (June 1939): 315–21.

Sylvain-Bouchereau, Madeleine. *Haiti et ses femmes: Une étude d'évolution culturelle*. Port-au-Prince, Haiti: Editions Henri Deschamps, 1957.

———. "La femme haïtienne lutte depuis vingt ans pour obtenir les droits éqaux." *La Semeuse* (February 1, 1957): 3–6.

———. "Les droits des femmes et la nouvelle constitution." *La femme haïtienne répond aux attaques formulées contre elle à L'Assemblée Constituante*. Port-au-Prince: Societé d'Editions et de Librairie, 1946.

———. "Nous revoici." *La Voix Des Femmes* 9, no. 1 (January 11, 1947): 1.

———. *Lecture Haitienne, La Famille Renaud* (Livre I & II). Port-au-Prince: Editions Henri Deschamps, 1944.

Taylor, Diana. *Disappearing Acts: Spectacles of Gender and Nationalism in Argentina's "Dirty War."* Durham, N.C.: Duke University Press, 1997.

Thomas, Deborah A. "Caribbean Studies, Archive Building, and the Problem of Violence." *Small Axe: A Caribbean Journal of Criticism* 17, no. 2 (July 2013): 27–42.

———. *Modern Blackness: Nationalism, Globalization and the Politics of Culture in Jamaica.* Durham, N.C.: Duke University Press, 2004.

———. *Political Life in the Wake of the Plantation: Sovereignty, Witnessing, Repair.* Durham, N.C.: Duke University Press, 2019.

Thompson, Krista A. *Shine. The Visual Economy of Light in African Diasporic Aesthetic Practice.* Durham, N.C.: Duke University Press, 2015.

———. *An Eye for the Tropics: Tourism, Photography, and Framing the Caribbean Picturesque.* Durham: Duke University Press, 2006.

Towns, Ann. "The Inter-American Commission of Women and Women's Suffrage, 1920–1945." *Journal of Latin American Studies* 42, no. 4 (November 2010): 779–807.

Trouillot, Évelyne. *The Infamous Rosalie.* Translated by M. A. Salvodon. Lincoln: University of Nebraska, 2013.

Trouillot, Michel-Rolph. "Culture, Color, and Politics in Haiti." In *Race*, edited by Steven Gregory and Roger Sanjek. New Brunswick, N.J.: Rutgers University Press, 1996: 146–74.

———. *Silencing the Past: Power and the Production of History.* Boston: Beacon Press, 1997.

———. *Global Transformations: Anthropology and the Modern World.* New York: Palgrave Macmillan, 2003.

———. *Haiti, State against Nation: The Origins and Legacy of Duvalierism.* New York: Monthly Review Press, 1990.

———. "The Odd and the Ordinary: Haiti, the Caribbean and the World." *Cimarrón: New Perspectives on the Caribbean* 2, no. 3 (1990): 3–12.

Ulysse, Gina A. *Downtown Ladies: Informal Commercial Importers, a Haitian Anthropologist, and Self-Making in Jamaica.* Chicago: University of Chicago Press, 2007.

———. "Going Home Again, and Again and Again: Coffee Memories, Peasant Food and the Vodou That Some of Us Do." In *Geographies of the Haitian Diaspora*, edited by Regine O. Jackson, 265–80. New York: Routledge, 2011.

———. "Papa, Patriarchy, and Power: Snapshots of a Good Haitian Girl, Feminism, and Dyasporic Dreams." *Journal of Haitian Studies* 12, no 1 (2006): 24–47.

———. *Why Haiti Needs New Narratives = Sa K Fè Ayiti Bezwen Istwa Tou Nèf = Pourquoi Haïti a Besoin de Nouveaux Discours: A Post-Quake Chronicle.* Middletown, Conn.: Wesleyan University Press, 2015.

United States Interamerican Affairs Institute. *Agricultural Progress in Haiti, Summary Report, 1944–49.* Food Supply Division (1949): 1–34.

United States Senate. *Inquiry into Occupation and Administration in Haiti and Santo Domingo. Hearings before a select committee on Haiti and Santo Domingo.* 67th Congress, first and second sessions, vol 1, 1922: 1–812.

Valcin, Cléante Desgraves. *Cruelle destinée.* Port-au-Prince: Jouve et Cie, 1929.

———. *La blanche négresse.* Port-au-Prince: Presses Nationales d'Haïti, 2007 (first published in 1934).

Valdman, Albert, Iskra Iskrova, et al. *Haitian Creole–English Bilingual Dictionary.* Bloomington: Indiana University Press, 2007.

Vargas, João H. Costa. "Black Radical Becoming: The Politics of Identification in Permanent Transformation." *Critical Sociology* 32, no. 2 (2006): 475–500.

Verna, Chantalle. *Haiti and the Uses of America: Post-U.S. Occupation Promises.* New Brunswick, N.J.: Rutgers University Press, 2017.

———. "Haitian Migration and Community-Building in Southeastern Michigan, 1966–1998." In *Geographies of the Haitian Diaspora*, edited by Regine O. Jackson. New York: Routledge, 2011: 163–84.

———. "The Ligue Feminine d'Action Sociale: An Interview with Paulette Poujol Oriol." *Journal of Haitian Studies* 17, no. 1 (2011): 246–57.

Voltaire, Frantz. *Pouvoir noir en Haïti: L'explosion de 1946.* Montreal: Les Editions du Cidihca, 1988.

Walker, Alice. *In Search of Our Mother's Gardens: Womanist Prose.* London: Phoenix, 2005.

Wekker, Gloria. *The Politics of Passion: Women's Sexual Culture in the Afro-Surinamese Diaspora.* New York: Columbia University Press, 2006.

Wexler, Laura. *Tender Violence: Domestic Visions in an Age of U.S. Imperialism.* Chapel Hill: University of North Carolina Press, 2000.

Williams, Heather Andrea. *Help Me to Find My People: The African American Search for Family Lost in Slavery.* Chapel Hill: University of North Carolina Press, 2012.

Woodson, Carter G. "Review of *Le Creole Haitien* and *Les Contes Haitien* by S. Comhaire-Sylvain." *Journal of Negro History* 22, no. 3 (July 1937): 369–72.

Wucker, Michele. *Why the Cocks Fight: Dominicans, Haitians, and the Struggle for Hispaniola.* New York: Hill and Wang, 1999.

Wynter, Sylvia. "The Ceremony Must Be Found: After Humanism." *Boundary 2* 12, no. 3 (1984): 19–70.

———. "Unsettling the Coloniality of Being/Power/Truth/Freedom: Towards the Human, after Man, Its Overrepresentation—an Argument." *CR: The New Centennial Review* 3, no. 3 (Fall 2003): 257–337.

Young, Hershini Bhana. *Haunting Capital: Memory, Text and the Black Diasporic Body.* Hanover, N.H.: Dartmouth College Press, 2006.

Zéphir, Clorinde. *Between Democracy and Repression.* Port-au-Prince: ENFOFANM Editions, 1991.

Index

Note: Page numbers in italics refer to illustrations.

women's movement, Haitian: international connections, *138*; organizing practice, 11

women's movement, US, *138*

women's movements: class and, 2–4; in Dominican Republic, 88–89; doubts about efficacy, 218; international, 35–36; Latin American, *138*

women's organizations, 17; coalition of, 215; Comité Démocratique Féminin, 167; disruption of connections between, 235; ICWDR, 67–68; NACW, 67; occupation and, 69. *See also* Ligue Féminine d'Action Sociale, La

women's rights organizers, 20

women's wage law, 142

Woodson, Carter G., 116

workers' rights, 16. *See also* labor, women's

working class, 16

working women, St.-Lôt's criticism of, 171

workshops on Haitian feminism, 94–100

World War I, 41

World War II, 128–29, 141, 142, 166

Wynter, Sylvia, 21

Zagourski, Casimir, 197

Printed in the USA
CPSIA information can be obtained
at www.ICGtesting.com
CBHW030346050324
4982CB00003B/80

9 781469 673684